W9-AYZ-506

BY THE SAME AUTHOR

BOOKS

The Battles of Coxinga
The Japanese Discovery of Europe
Japanese Literature: An Introduction for the Western Reader
Living Japan
Bunraku: The Art of the Japanese Puppet Theatre
Nō: The Classical Theatre of Japan
Landscapes and Portraits
World Within Walls: Japanese Literature of the Pre-Modern Era, 1600–1867
Dawn to the West: Japanese Literature in the Modern Era
Some Japanese Portraits
The Pleasures of Japanese Literature

TRANSLATIONS

The Setting Sun (by Osamu Dazai)
No Longer Human (by Osamu Dazai)
Five Modern Nō Plays (by Yukio Mishima)
Major Plays of Chikamatsu
The Old Woman, the Wife, and the Archer (by Shichiro Fukasawa, Chiyo Uno, and Jun Ishikawa)
After the Banquet (by Yukio Mishima)
Essays in Idleness (by Yoshida Kenkō)
Chūshingura (by Takeda Izumo, Miyoshi Shōraku, and Namiki Sōsuke)
Madame de Sade (by Yukio Mishima)
Friends (by Kobo Abe)
Twenty Plays of the Nō Theatre (edited and translated)
The Man Who Turned into a Stick (by Kobo Abe)

ANTHOLOGIES

Anthology of Japanese Literature
Modern Japanese Literature

Travelers of a Hundred Ages

Donald Keene

Henry Holt and Company
New York

Henry Holt and Company, Inc.
Publishers since 1866
115 West 18th Street
New York, New York 10011

Published in Canada by Fitzhenry & Whiteside Limited,
91 Granton Drive, Richmond Hill, Ontario L4B 2N5.

Library of Congress Cataloging-in-Publication Data
Keene, Donald.
Travelers of a hundred ages.
Bibliography: p.
Includes index.
I. Japanese diaries—History and criticism. I. Title.
II. Title: Travelers of a hundred ages.
PL741.K44 1989 895.6'803 88-31585

ISBN 0-8050-0751-2
ISBN 0-8050-1655-4 (An Owl Book: pbk.)

First Edition

Designed by Susan Hood
Printed in the United States of America
All first editions are printed on acid-free paper.∞

10 9 8 7 6 5 4 3 2 1
10 9 8 7 6 5 4 3 (pbk.)

Dedicated with much affection to Jane Gunther

Contents

Contents

Preface

The essays on Japanese diaries contained in this book were first published serially in Japanese in the newspaper *Asahi Shimbun*. It was a novel and rather disorienting experience for a scholar to be obliged to produce five essays a week without the usual possibility of waiting until an additional document came to hand or until the interpretation of a difficult passage could be verified, but I somehow managed to keep up the pace. The book that later appeared was honored with two Japanese literary prizes. The present volume treats diaries written between the middle of the ninth and the middle of the nineteenth century. I have since published in Japanese a continuation, carrying my account up until about 1925.

In making the English version I have borne in mind the different level of knowledge of Japanese literature and history I could expect of non-Japanese readers. I have added explanations of passages that might present problems and have not hesitated to repeat explanations of Japanese terms that appear in the text. A glossary has also been provided. On the other hand, I have omitted a few diaries discussed in the Japanese edition, because it seemed unlikely that they would interest readers outside Japan. The English text assumes no special knowledge of Japan, but in the notes I have given references to Japanese sources and to matters of interest to specialists. Translations that are not credited to other scholars are my own.

Introduction

In every country of the world people have kept diaries. Some diaries have consisted of no more than brief notations on the weather or lists of the writers' daily engagements, but others are without question works of literary significance. This has been true in Japan for over a thousand years. In other countries a few diaries written in the past are still read for the light they shed on the authors' times or on the personalities of the authors themselves, but, as far as I know, only in Japan did the diary acquire the status of a literary genre comparable in importance to novels, essays, and other branches of literature that elsewhere are esteemed more highly than diaries.

The first question to be asked about diaries is why people bother to keep them. Scholars who have discussed diaries usually divide them into two categories—those written exclusively for the authors' own use and those written with other readers in mind. As a matter of fact, however, a great many diaries are written with at least an unconscious hope or expectation that some day other people will read them. For example, the literary sophistication of diaries of the Heian period (794–1185) surely indicates they were not intended for their authors' eyes alone, even though the writers could not have dreamed that one day their diaries would be printed and made available to countless readers. Some diarists have gone to the extreme of writing in code (or, in Ishikawa Takuboku's case, in roman letters) in order to prevent other people from reading their diaries. Other diarists leave instructions that their diaries are to be destroyed after their deaths. But it does not often happen that a diarist destroys his own diary. However many precautions he may take to keep his diary a secret, he must in his heart also hope that the secret will be penetrated. Writing a diary, like writing a poem, is often a kind of confession, and no confession can be effective unless another person hears it.

A distinction might better be made between diaries written with literary intent and those that merely record the events of a person's life. Those of literary intent are more likely to be interesting, but they are not always truthful. A writer like the mother of Michitsuna, the author of *Kagerō Nikki* (*The Gossamer Years*), may turn to writing a diary in the hopes of winning the understanding and approval of future generations who will read the diary, and she is therefore likely to omit events that do not redound to her credit. Other diarists have added events that did not actually occur, relying on their imagination to make the inadequate facts literally more satisfying. The nonliterary diary, on the other hand, is often of only marginal interest to later generations, going into unnecessary detail about the weather or about acquaintances of the diarist who have since become obscure. But the very inartistry of such diaries is the mark of their truth, and when they refer to events or people who still interest us today, they can provide human touches not found elsewhere.

In 1943, when *Sora Oku no Hosomichi Zuikō Nikki* was first published, it caused considerable consternation. This diary was kept by Kawai Sora, Bashō's companion on his journey to the north of Japan in 1689, and scholars who had revered Bashō as the "saint of haiku," a man who never told a lie, were dismayed to discover serious discrepancies between the accounts by Bashō and Sora of the same journey. It took Bashō five years to write *Oku no Hosomichi* (*The Narrow Road of Oku*). Sora's diary had obviously not entailed such manipulation of facts and is indeed so completely devoid of literary pretense that one can only suppose that it must be true.

When, for example, the two men arrived at Nikkō, Bashō was

moved by the name of the place (literally, "Sunlight") and by the association with the Tokugawa shoguns, who have their mausoleum there, to compose the haiku:

ara tōto	How awe-inspiring,
aoba wakaba no	On the green leaves, the young leaves,
hi no hikari	The light of the sun!

But Sora's diary states that it rained on the day they visited Nikkō. Bashō presumably sacrificed literal truth to poetic truth. Again, Bashō described with wonder the marvelous interior of the Konjikidō (Golden Hall) of the temple Chūson-ji, but Sora prosaically related that they could not find anyone to open the hall, so they had to leave the temple without seeing its famous sculptures.

Faced with these and other discrepancies, some scholars of 1943 were so sure that Bashō never deviated from the truth that they declared that Sora must have either lied or been forgetful. Only after some years did most scholars decide that the literary value of *The Narrow Road of Oku* was enhanced by such descriptions because they proved that Bashō was more concerned with the artistic effect of the diary than with recording facts.

Bashō's interest in writing *The Narrow Road of Oku* and the four other travel diaries describing his journeys to various parts of Japan was unquestionably literary. In *Oi no Kobumi* (*Manuscript in My Knapsack*) he considered what the content and purpose of a travel diary should be: "Nobody has succeeded in making any improvements in travel diaries since Ki no Tsurayuki and the nun Abutsu wielded their brushes to describe their emotions in full; the rest have merely imitated. How much less likely it is that anyone of my shallow knowledge and inadequate talent could attain this goal. Of course, anyone can write a diary saying, 'On that day it rained . . . it cleared in the afternoon . . . there is a pine at that place . . . the such-and-such river flows through the region,' and the like, but unless a sight is truly remarkable one shouldn't mention it at all. Nevertheless, the scenery of different places lingers in my mind, and even my unpleasant experiences at huts in the mountains and fields can become subjects of conversation or material for poetry. With this in mind, I have scribbled down, without any semblance of order, the unforgettable moments of my journey, and gathered them together in one work. Let the reader listen without paying too much attention, as to the ramblings of a drunkard or the mutterings of a man in his sleep."

Bashō recognized, first of all, the existence in Japan of a long tradition of writing travel diaries, beginning with Ki no Tsurayuki's *Tosa Nikki* (*The Tosa Diary*). He himself was participating in this tradition, but he was fully aware of the difficulty of attaining the level of excellence of his great predecessors. Their diaries were not merely accounts of sights along the way but expressed in beautiful language the authors' deepest emotions. Later diarists had been unable to create anything as distinctive. Bashō, modestly referring to his "shallow knowledge and inadequate talent," is sure that he will not equal the achievements of the past, but he is determined not to confine himself to such typical diary notations as "On that day it rained . . . it cleared in the afternoon." Anyone can write such a diary, but unless one's style has the distinctiveness of the Chinese master Wu Shan-ku or the freshness of the poetry of Su Tung-p'o, it is best not to write at all.

Bashō, though he employed the conventional expression "shallow knowledge and inadequate talent" in speaking of himself, had full confidence in his ability as a poet, as we know from other works. He must also have realized that the diaries in which he described his travels would be of the greatest interest to his many disciples and to the public, too. But his personal reason for keeping his diaries was the same as for almost all diarists, whether literary or unliterary: he wished to preserve from oblivion the experiences of his life. Even disagreeable happenings at inns along the way could offer material for conversation, providing he kept them fresh in his memory by noting them down. The diary has been used in this way by writers of many countries as the raw material from which they created works of literature; the poet's notebook or commonplace book is an example of such writing.

It seems likely that Bashō undertook his journey in the hopes of receiving fresh stimulation for his poetry, not just from the sights of nature that had inspired poets of the past, but from human experiences on the road or at inns. His success was extraordinary.

Probably no work of Japanese literature is as widely known in Japan as *The Narrow Road of Oku.* Bashō, however, disclaimed any intention of converting his diaries into works of literature. He declared in the passage I have translated from *Manuscript in My Knapsack* that he had set down his recollections without imposing any order, and he asked people to read his words as they might listen to a drunkard's raving or to a man talking in his sleep. But this request itself is proof that Bashō expected other people to read the diary. It was definitely not composed solely in order to keep himself from forgetting unforgettable events.

Bashō's diaries were also revelations of self-discovery. They were occasioned by the love of travel that runs through Japanese literature from its beginnings to our own day, but also by the desire to find in travel the source of his art and, ultimately, of his existence as a man and poet. The haiku composed after crossing the barrier of Shirakawa into Oku suggests his excitement at coming into contact with the beginning of literary creation:

fūryū no	The beginnings of
hajime ya Oku no	Artistic taste—an Oku
taue uta	Song for rice planting.

In other diaries he provides us with openly personal statements as to why he became a poet, what other professions he considered, what he believed to be the highest purposes of poetry. This is not the kind of information one usually finds in diaries written in other countries, but in Japan, from the earliest examples, literary diaries tended to become autobiography or criticism. The authors of such diaries as *The Gossamer Years* wrote most of the entries long after the events, allowing time to filter out the kind of unimportant matters that normally fill diaries. In such a case the diary became a kind of self-exploration or even a confession. The diary is the ancestor of that most typical form of modern Japanese literature, the "I novel."

Some years ago I took part, within the space of one week, in the defense of two Ph.D. theses at Columbia University. The first, in

Japanese literature, was a partial translation and study of the Heian romance *Yowa no Nezame* (*The Tale of Nezame*), the other a study of some Chinese novels of the Ming Dynasty. The contrast could not have been greater. *The Tale of Nezame* contains extremely little action, being related almost entirely from within, in terms of the thoughts of the heroine, Nezame. The Chinese novels, on the other hand, were entirely external, describing exciting or tragic events without once entering into the thoughts of the characters. These were not exceptional cases. The most typical Japanese works of literature since the Heian period have been introspective. To make a crude division, Japanese fiction tends to be autobiographical, whereas Chinese fiction is biographical. There are no Chinese autobiographies before the seventeenth century, but in Japan the diary and autobiography have blended together since the diaries of the court ladies of the Heian period. Japanese writing tends also to be personal or, to use a convenient though inexact term, emotional. This quality is most evident in such works as *The Gossamer Years*. The author is so intensely preoccupied with her own emotions that she seems incapable of putting herself in the position of another person or of seeing the world objectively. But because she writes only about human feelings that have not changed over the centuries, her writings have a universality and immediacy greater than any Chinese work of fiction with which I am familiar.

The Japanese writers of the past borrowed much from Chinese literature, but it is surprising how much they did not borrow. Postwar Japanese critics have often complained of how seldom Japanese poetry displays the social consciousness typical of many great Chinese poems. This was not because the Japanese tried and failed, but because literature served different purposes in China and Japan. In China almost every literary work was printed during the author's lifetime or immediately thereafter, but, though the Japanese had long been familiar with the art of printing, they never saw fit until the seventeenth century to print works of literature. Literature was meant to be appreciated aesthetically—in the handwriting, the paper, and the ink as well as the words. It tended to be private, or shared only by a small circle of people, rather than written for the world. One can deplore the limitations of traditional Japanese literature, but one should not forget the compensating purity of expression that Japanese poets and prose writers of the past achieved. Even when a Japanese poem borrowed imagery from a Chinese poem, it took only what could be gracefully accommodated within Japanese expression, and rarely attempted to follow the Chinese in passing from the particular experience to a generalization. The intuitive, "feminine" manner of the diarists, with their bittersweet evocations of anticipated or remembered love, was later adopted by the most resolutely "masculine" poets and writers of fiction.

The choice of intuitive, ambiguous expressions in Japanese poetry, rather than the powerful statements that were more typical of the Chinese poets, was conditioned by the expressive possibilities of the Japanese language. But why, it may be wondered, did Japanese writers turn so readily to the diary? One can imagine that for a court lady like the daughter of Takasue, who wrote *Sarashina Nikki* (*As I Crossed a Bridge of Dreams*), a journal of this kind was almost her only outlet for emotional experiences. She seems to have been inarticulate, afraid of people, readier to believe in literature than in life. On the one occasion when she met a man who attracted her, she was incapable of expressing her feelings. Her inarticulateness favored her choice of the diary as a means of expression, but probably that was not the only reason she and others preferred this form. Japanese writers have always experienced problems of structure. In the thirty-one-syllable *tanka* or the seventeen-syllable haiku the form is so short that structure is not a great problem, but only a few poets were able to combine the poetic intensity and formal architecture needed if a *chōka* (long poem) was not to fall apart. The most typically Japanese literary structure was the *renga* (linked verse). In *renga* no attempt was made to create a single, unified structure, but great care was devoted instead to making sure that each "link" fitted securely with the one it preceded and followed. The poems in the great anthologies, such as *Shin Kokinshū* (1205), have been considered by some critics to form a coherent whole, because of the carefully contrived transitions between successive poems achieved by the compilers. But nobody would claim that this element of structure was as important to the success of the *Shin Kokinshū* as structures were to *The Divine Comedy* or *Paradise Lost*.

The diary, however, is provided with a ready-made structure—

the passage of the days. The steady succession of days and months largely eliminates the need for any other kind of structure. In another sense, the passage of time itself is the subject not only of many diaries but of much of Japanese literature as a whole. The face that once was beautiful is now lined with wrinkles; the palace that once towered is now a ruin; the lover who once was assiduous is now indifferent. To keep a diary is to preserve time, to save from oblivion days that from the point of view of the historian might seem of little importance. The discovery that Proust made at the end of *A la recherche du temps perdu* that there were "fragments of existence withdrawn from Time" was made by the Heian court ladies, too. They realized also that the only way to savor impressions to which an author wishes to give permanence was, in Proust's words, "to try to get to know them more completely in the medium in which they existed, that is to say within myself, to try to make them translucent even to their very depths." This has been a fundamental strain in Japanese literature, from the early diarists to present writers of fiction.

In making my selection of diaries I have sought above all to find examples that spoke to me directly. Even if a diary as a whole was not of great literary significance, even if it was so obscure that its name failed to appear in detailed studies of Japanese literature, I did not hesitate to include it if I thought it possessed some element of unique interest. Readers may be surprised at the inclusion of works that do not conform to usual definitions of a diary. Although the Japanese word *nikki* means literally "daily record," extremely few of the diaries written in Japanese before the eighteenth century were kept day to day. Most of the classics of Japanese "diary literature" would in fact not be called "diaries" elsewhere. At times the term seems to mean little more than a factual account, as opposed to the inventions of a storyteller, though even fiction is not unknown in the diaries. Prose passages in collections of poetry were also at times called *nikki* if they gave in a detailed and chronological manner the circumstances of the composition of the poems, though this, too, is an unfamiliar use of the word "diary." My requirement for including as "diaries" even works that conspicuously violate the usual definitions was that they tell us something about the author or the Japanese people that is memorable and not easily found anywhere else. This may be too vague a justification for treating as diaries works that seem more like autobiographies or descriptions of court life, but I am in fact following a usage of the Japanese that goes back a thousand years. The special affinity of the Japanese for personal reminiscences (which they often call diaries) may account for the subjective nature of most of Japanese literature, at present as in the past.

The special interest of a particular diary is sometimes best understood in terms of other diaries. As one reads successive diaries, one soon becomes able to distinguish what is truly personal in the responses to some sight of nature or some grief and what is merely convention. The individuality of the opinions expressed by a diarist alone may make his diary seem memorable. The unknown author of *Journey Along the Seacoast Road* startled me with such statements as: "Places one has often heard about do not necessarily appeal to the eye." Virtually every other traveler went out of his way to see places that had been mentioned in poetry and was satisfied by the experience, even if a once-beautiful landscape was now desolate, but here was someone who saw with his own eyes and not with those of predecessors.

Other diaries are memorable because of the special circumstances under which they were written. *Account of Fujikawa* was written by Ichijō Kaneyoshi, the highest-ranking official in the country, at a time when he was a refugee from the warfare that wasted the capital. The great house where he and his ancestors had lived had turned to ashes, and despite his titles, he himself was forced to beg for food and lodgings. Again, *The Diary of Gen'yo*, though a minor work, presents a unique picture of the most famous poet of the day while he was living in exile.

Diaries describe aspects of Japanese life that are not touched on in other genres. For example, again and again in the novels and plays we find expressions of a character's longing to abandon the "burning house" of this world and to take refuge in some Buddhist sanctuary; but it was seldom considered what happened to the family of a man after he went to a temple in the mountains, shaved his head, and became a priest. *The Tale of the Tōnomine Captain* tells of the effects on his wife of one man's decision, *The Diary of the Priest Shunjō* of how the small children of another man were affected, and both are deeply moving.

Still other diaries have been included because of their close connections with major events of Japanese history. The invasions of Korea at the end of the sixteenth century are described in the clumsily written diaries of soldiers who took part in the campaigns. These works, though devoid of literary value, provide momentary glimpses of the savage fighting that linger in the memory because they can be found nowhere else. The last group of diaries in the book relate to the most important event of modern Japanese history, the opening of the country to the West. Of course, there are many documents describing the circumstances, written from both the Japanese and the Western points of view, but one would search long before coming across anything as humanly affecting as the moment when an American sailor took the first photograph of a Japanese. Again, we are likely to be amused by the attempts of the Japanese official to establish personal relations with the Russians with whom he was negotiating. He had been told that the best way to ingratiate oneself with foreigners was to talk about one's wife, and he accordingly boasted about the beauty of his wife, though he noted in the diary how surprised she would be to learn of this! Finally, there is the affecting moment in the same official's diary when, after having always referred to the Russians as "barbarians," in the traditional manner, he was forced to change his mind; the Russians had rescued some Japanese victims of a tidal wave. From that point on he called them not "Russian barbarians" but "Russian men."

I have included also a few diaries written not in Japanese but in classical Chinese, a learned language that fulfilled the same function for Japanese as Latin for Europeans. The diaries kept in Chinese conform much more closely to the usual definition of "diaries" than those in Japanese, showing every sign of having been kept day to day. On the whole, these diaries tend to be impersonal, though not uniformly so; *Chronicle of the Bright Moon* certainly gives us a vivid picture of the diarist, Fujiwara Teika, and the world he lived in. The massive diary *Chūyūki* is generally considered to be the finest of the diaries kept by courtiers in Chinese. Even here, despite the avowed intention of the diarist to record only official matters (so that his descendants will be better informed than other people about precedents), there are passages of great interest, when the diarist describes not only what he has observed but what he has felt. The account of the death of the Emperor Horikawa gives us a picture of this monarch that is far more appealing than descriptions in the official histories.

It will be apparent, I am sure, that the travel diaries of Bashō represent for me the summit of Japanese diary literature. They are not diaries in any usual sense. Their dating is sometimes suspect and we know that Bashō spent years revising them. He probably introduced fictitious elements, but the truth of his diaries is nonetheless incontestable: not only do they tell us much about Bashō himself, but they suggest in a way found nowhere else why the Japanese have always loved travel and what, ultimately, is the source of the love of nature that is so vital an element of Japanese literature and art.

I was first made aware of the Japanese absorption with diaries during the Second World War, when for months my chief occupation was translating diaries left on the battlefield. Some were bloodstained and had no doubt been taken from the corpses of Japanese soldiers; others had been soaked in seawater. I read these diaries not because of their possible literary interest but because they sometimes contained information of military value. A diarist might mention the sinking of a ship, the damage sustained during an American air raid, and similar matters; or, he might by his complaints or expressions of foreboding over Japanese prospects in the war provide evidence of a lowered morale among the Japanese military. The military value of the diaries was actually very limited, but every scrap of information about the Japanese armed forces was carefully stored away.

Some diaries were uninteresting from beginning to end, such as those written by model soldiers, who painstakingly related exactly what happened each day on an hourly basis along the lines of: "6:00 A.M. Got up. 6:15 A.M. Washed my face . . ." and so on. Others, of slightly more interest, parroted the clichés of official pronouncements, reporting that a unit had "with flying colors" boarded a transport, and that "morale was high." Some diaries were almost illegible, because the handwriting was so bad or because penciled notations had become blurred. In time, however, I became quite proficient at reading even the worst handwriting: the trick was to guess what the diarist was most likely to write under the circumstances and then see whether or not the handwriting could be interpreted in that way.

Obviously, the diaries would have been more interesting if the soldiers had possessed literary flair, but even if the early parts of a diary, written while the writer was in a safe area, were of small literary interest, once the man boarded a ship for the South Pacific and was in danger of American submarine attacks, or his unit was ordered to the front lines, or the man himself was stricken by malaria or some other tropical disease, the diary often became almost unbearably moving, regardless of the style. Plain, unliterary expression was actually more effective in such cases than beautiful phrases, as the simple cry of "It hurts!" moves us more than ingenious similes. The circumstances surrounding the diarists as they wrote made the contents of their little notebooks unforgettable. The sudden fear experienced when the ship next to the diarist's in the convoy was torpedoed and sunk before his eyes was fully conveyed even by nearly illiterate soldiers. I remember especially the account of a New Year's Day spent by seven Japanese, the only survivors of a company, on some island in the South Pacific. All they had in the way of New Year's food were thirteen beans that they divided among themselves.

It was impossible for me not to feel sympathy with the Japanese soldiers whose diaries were picked up in Guadalcanal, Tarawa, Peleliu, and all the other islands where the war in the Pacific was fought. Even if a diary contained absolutely no military information, I usually read it anyway. The men who wrote these diaries were the first Japanese I ever knew intimately, though we never met, and they were all dead by the time I read their thoughts.

Yet the diaries were also interesting for another reason. American military personnel were strictly prohibited from keeping diaries, for fear that they might fall into the hands of the enemy. This was not much of a hardship for the Americans, few of whom kept diaries anyway. In contrast, although the Japanese military authorities must have realized that the diaries were potentially of value to the enemy, they did not prohibit soldiers and sailors from keeping them. Quite to the contrary, Japanese military personnel were issued with diaries at New Year's and ordered to keep them, rather in the way that Japanese schools nowadays expect pupils to keep diaries during their summer vacations. Perhaps Japanese officers periodically read the diaries in order to make sure that the writers possessed the correct "spirit." Or perhaps they realized that keeping a diary was so much a part of Japanese tradition that it would be counterproductive to prohibit them. Whatever the reasons, the Japanese military produced a vast number of diaries.

Some diaries contained messages in English addressed to the American soldiers who would find them after the writer's death. They asked the finder to send the diary to the writer's family when the war ended. I put aside a number of such diaries, intending to return them when it was possible. This was illegal, since captured documents were all to be forwarded to Washington, but I took the risk. However, while I was in Okinawa someone went through my belongings left in Hawaii and confiscated the diaries. I wonder where they are now. I am sure they would be no less affecting today than they were forty or more years ago.

I had another wartime experience with Japanese diaries of a totally different nature. Before boarding the ship that was to take me to the Aleutian Islands, I bought in California a copy of the English translations of diaries by Japanese court ladies of the Heian period. Strange as it may seem, this book was what I was reading during the days immediately before the attack on Attu. I do not recall why I chose this particular book to read before my first experience of actual warfare. Certainly nothing could be further from the ugliness of war than the events at the Japanese court of the eleventh century described by three court ladies. Perhaps I supposed that these diaries might give me a better insight into what Japanese were really like than either the soldiers' diaries I had been reading or the generalizations about the Japanese character that appeared in American writings of this time. It was a peculiar choice, but not necessarily a bad one. Diaries constitute a stream of expression that runs through Japanese literature and, perhaps more than any other form, communicate how Japanese have thought and felt. Forty years later I still turn to diaries, by unknown writers as well as by the literary masters, for my most intimate glimpses of Japanese of every age.

Heian Diaries

The Record of a Pilgrimage to China in Search of the Buddhist Law

The earliest diaries kept by Japanese were written in classical Chinese (*kambun*). A few, kept by statesmen and Buddhist priests, have been preserved from the ninth century. These are diaries in the strict sense of the term: entries are given by year, month, and day, and there are reports on the weather, recent events, and sometimes the misfortunes suffered by the diarist, but very little is personal. Of course, a personal element is present when a diarist records that he was hungry that day, or that he was exasperated to be received coldly by some bureaucrat, but this is not personal in the same sense that the diaries of the court ladies were personal; the diaries written in Chinese reveal no hidden griefs, nor do they speculate on the meaning of other people's actions. These were official diaries, and the writers would not have been embarrassed to have them read by their superiors.

The most detailed of the ninth-century diaries in Chinese is *Nittō Guhō Junrei Gyoki* (*The Record of a Pilgrimage to China in Search of the Buddhist Law*), written by the priest Ennin (793–864) from the time of his departure for China in 838 until his return to Japan in 847. Much of Ennin's time in China was spent waiting for permission to travel to Mount T'ien-t'ai, the fountainhead of the Tendai Buddhist teachings. He was unsuccessful to the end in his goal, but he managed by dint of great determination (and with the help of some Koreans who had befriended him) to visit another important center of Tendai studies, Mount Wu-t'ai.

During the latter part of Ennin's stay in China the Emperor Wu-tsung initiated a persecution of Buddhism. Ennin was forced for a time to let his hair grow out and to put aside his Buddhist robes. By this time he was eager to return to Japan, but permission from the authorities was slow in coming. For a while he was faced with contradictory orders: to remain in China until authorized to leave, and to leave China as soon as possible because he was an undesirable foreign Buddhist. With the death of Wu-tsung in 846 the persecution of Buddhism stopped, and in the following year Ennin returned to Japan. He was raised in 854 to the rank of Abbot of the Enryaku-ji, the central temple of the Tendai sect. Three years after his death in 863 he was granted the posthumous title of Jikaku Daishi, or the Great Teacher Jikaku, a rare honor.

Edwin O. Reischauer, who translated this diary and also published a study of it, was of the opinion that neither the diary itself nor the various biographies written by others conveyed anything of Ennin's personality: "He was a scrupulously accurate and delightfully detailed diarist, but he was no Boswell determined to make posterity his confidant."[1] Boswell's journals owe much of their interest to his willingness to discuss his romantic involvements, and he reported his experiences with stylistic brilliance, but Ennin led a life of irreproachable virtue and was matter-of-fact in his expression. Reischauer commented, "While he was not a mind of brilliant originality and creativeness, he must have possessed extraordinary ability."[2] Unfortunately, it was his very ability at writing Chinese that has kept most contemporary Japanese from perusing Ennin's unique account of travels in China during a period of great turbulence.

Ennin went from Japan to China as a member of an official embassy. The voyage to China was dangerous, because the ships were completely at the mercy of the winds and the navigators had no compasses to guide them. It was only on the third attempt that the ships succeeded in making the crossing, and no sooner had they reached the Chinese coast than they ran aground on sand banks and had to be abandoned. Throughout their stay in China, Ennin and his companions experienced innumerable hardships, though on occasion they were also shown unusual kindness. Famine conditions prevailed in the north of China because of a plague of locusts that had devoured the crops. Almost as bad as the locusts were the officials, who seemed determined to frustrate Ennin in his desire to study at a center of Tendai Buddhism.

When Ennin finally obtained permission to visit Mount Wu-t'ai, his second choice, he was naturally overjoyed, after so many disappointments. His diary recorded in detail legends of the bodhisattva Manjusri, the object of a cult at Wu-t'ai, and the many wondrous relics and works of Buddhist art associated with the cult. He was impressed by a solemn and majestic statue of Manjusri riding on a lion, and especially so by the lion, about which he wrote, "It seems to be walking, and vapors come from its mouth. We looked at it for quite a while, and it looked just as if it were moving."[3] Ennin went on to relate the many difficulties that the sculptor had encountered while making the statue. Six times he had cast the statue, and six times it had cracked to pieces. The sculptor, realizing that his failure must be due to Manjusri's dissatisfaction with the statue, prayed to him, begging him to manifest himself so that the sculptor might know his true appearance. Hardly had he finished his prayer when he saw Manjusri before him, riding on a golden lion. When he cast the statue for the seventh time, it did not crack.[4]

Such stories are of interest, at least to the specialist in popular religion, even though few today possess Ennin's simple belief in miracles. His diary is therefore much less affecting than diaries that describe love, hate, jealousy, and other emotions that are universal and unchanging. These would be the subjects treated in the diaries written in Japanese during the century after Ennin.

Ennin's diary becomes absorbing when he writes about Chinese inns, or New Year's celebrations, or life in a monastery, but one rarely feels any personal contact with Ennin himself. He does not even voice the kind of surprise and admiration that we might expect of a Japanese traveler on visiting a great Chinese city for the first time. He was so intent on achieving his purpose, seeking the law of Buddhism, that nothing else was of more than passing interest. Only occasionally did he write about the hardships he suffered, as when he described himself in these terms in a letter sent to a Chinese official: "He makes his home anywhere and finds his hunger beyond endurance, but, because he speaks a different tongue, he is unable to beg for food himself. He humbly hopes that in your compassion you will give the surplus of your food to a poor monk from abroad."[5]

That is about as close as Ennin's diary comes to a cry from the heart. It would be against the background of this and similar diaries in Chinese that works of "diary literature" in Japanese would be created.

The Tosa Diary

Tosa Nikki (*The Tosa Diary*), the oldest surviving diary written in the Japanese language, describes a journey made in 934–35. The author, Ki no Tsurayuki (870?–945?), was appointed governor of the province of Tosa on the island of Shikoku in 930, and this diary describes his return journey to the capital after he completed his tour of duty in 934. The journey itself took fifty-five days, much of the time spent at sea. Events are related in dated entries, beginning with farewell banquets in Tosa and ending with Tsurayuki's return to his old house in Kyōto the next year.

The diary opens with the statement, "Diaries are written by men, I am told. I am writing one nevertheless, to see what a woman can do." This was, however, not the case: a man, Tsurayuki, wrote the diary, not a woman. He probably made the false claim to explain why he had written the diary in *kana*, the Japanese script, known at the time as *onna moji* (women's writing). He kept up the pretense throughout that the diary was written by a woman in the governor's entourage, though there is nothing specifically feminine about either the style or the subject matter. For example, the author declares that "she" cannot understand poetry composed in Chinese, the language of men, but there is nonetheless an unmistakable Chinese influence in the style, notably in the frequent use of parallel constructions. Tsurayuki was presumably capable of keeping a diary in Chinese if he so chose, but there were undoubtedly emotions that he could not express to his own satisfaction except in his native tongue.

As an accomplished *waka* poet, he also found it important to include the Japanese poetry composed during the journey. *The Tosa Diary* contains fifty-six poems, attributed variously to "the present governor," "a certain person," "a certain woman," and so on. Probably most, if not all, of the poems were composed by Tsurayuki himself. He obviously believed that the *waka* was a suitable poetic form for even a dignified man to use, though men of the previous century had generally chosen to write their poetry in Chinese.

A passage in *The Tosa Diary* recalls how, when Abe no Nakamaro was about to leave China and return to Japan, his Chinese friends gave him a banquet and composed Chinese poetry in honor of the occasion. Nakamaro responded, "In my country poetry of this nature has been composed even by the gods themselves, ever since the age of the gods, and people today, irrespective of their position in the world, also compose poetry when they grieve over parting—as we are now—or when they are moved by joy or sadness." So saying, he composed this *waka*:

aounabara	When I gaze over
furisake mireba	The blue fields of the sea,
Kasuga naru	I wonder if the moon
Mikasa no yama ni	Is the one that rose above
ideshi tsuki kamo[1]	Mikasa Mountain in Kasuga?

At first, the diary relates, the Chinese could not comprehend the meaning of the poem, but after Nakamaro supplied a rough approximation of the meaning in Chinese characters, and a Chinese who had learned some Japanese explained the poetic qualities, the other Chinese seemed to understand and were surprisingly appreciative. If this account is to be believed, the Chinese, normally so proud of their own poetic traditions that they were reluctant to admit there were others, were moved by the special power of the *waka*. As Tsurayuki wrote in the preface to the *Kokinshū*, the *waka* can "move without effort heaven and earth, and stir to pity even the invisible demons." It may well have been Tsurayuki's purpose when he wrote the diary to demonstrate that the *waka* was a fair match for poetry in Chinese.

The Tosa Diary is not merely a day-to-day account of occurrences in the diarist's life, in the manner of Ennin's diary, but is specifically the account of a journey. Various scholars have pointed out, however, that *The Tosa Diary* is not a good example of travel literature. Much less is said about sights along the way than about poetry; names of places passed are sometimes mistaken; and the scenery is hardly described at all. The following entry, for the 30th day of the 1st month, is typical: "Thirtieth. The wind and rain have let up. It is rumored that pirates do not operate at night, so we pushed out our boats about midnight and crossed the Strait of Awa. It was the middle of the night, and we could not tell one direction from another. Men and women alike prayed frantically to the gods and buddhas, and we safely made it across the strait."[2]

It is hard to imagine a Japanese diarist passing the whirlpool at Naruto in the Awa Strait without alluding to it. Even if it had been too dark to see anything, Bashō would surely have been able to imagine what the whirlpool was like, and might even have lied to the extent of saying that the starlight was so bright he could see the swirling waters. But Tsurayuki seems to have been uninterested in scenery. His chief concern while on the water was the danger of pirates, and his attention frequently wandered from the journey itself. But, unlike many other Heian diarists, he was at pains to maintain the pretense that an entry was made in the diary each day, even if all the entry says is, "The same place as yesterday."

One unusual aspect of *The Tosa Diary* was Tsurayuki's ascribing different personae to himself. He was not only the gentlewoman who was supposedly keeping the diary but various other people, all of whom were credited with poems that were actually by Tsurayuki. *The Tosa Diary* has even been termed an embryonic drama with different roles assigned to the characters.[3]

The distinguished scholar of Heian literature Hagitani Boku, attempting to determine Tsurayuki's motivation in writing the diary, suggested that it may have been intended primarily as a book of poetics for children of the important people of the court. He listed twenty different topics on poetic theory that are mentioned in the course of the work, including the appropriateness of vocabulary and expression, and the formal structure of the *waka*. Hagitani believed that Tsurayuki related such episodes as the near encounter with pirates in order to make the discussions of poetry more exciting for young readers, and he suggested that Tsurayuki, assuming that the parents of the children would also look over his "diary," included materials intended for adult eyes. These interpolations, mainly of a satiric nature, make fun of bribe-taking officials or mock people in the capital who expect presents from officials returning from the provinces.[4]

Intriguing as such theories are, there is a simpler explanation for why Tsurayuki wrote *The Tosa Diary*, one first suggested by Kagawa Kageki in *Tosa Nikki Sōken* (1823). The underlying theme is Tsurayuki's grief over the death of his daughter in Tosa, a theme that surfaces at critical points in the narrative and is stated most directly in the final poem and comments.

Tsurayuki was probably sixty-six years old when he left Tosa to return to the capital. References in *The Tosa Diary* to his daughter suggest that she may have been born when he was in his late fifties. A child of old age often arouses tenderer feelings than earlier ones, and that may explain the author's desire to express his grief in writing. The diary form itself could have been imitated from some monk or statesman who kept a diary in Chinese, though the contents are entirely dissimilar. Despite the precise dating of events, the highly selective nature of the contents indicates that the diary was not written day to day but after Tsurayuki's return to Kyōto, and seems to have been inspired initially by the desolation he experienced when he saw his old house. For years he had been anticipating this moment, but instead of the beautiful garden of his memories he found an untended wilderness. He was reminded in turn of the daughter who had been born in the house but whose grave was in Tosa.

The ending of the diary is poignant: "Nothing but stirred-up old memories, and the most affecting of all were those of the girl who was born in this house but has not returned with us, to our boundless grief. Other people who were on the ship all have children swarming noisily around them. Their merry shouts makes the sadness all the more unbearable. This was the poem I exchanged privately with someone who understood my feelings":

mumareshi mo	Though she was born here,
kaeranu mono wo	She has not returned with us;
wa ga yado ni	How sad it is, then,
komatsu no aru wo	To see the little pine trees
miru ga kanashisa[5]	That have grown in my garden.

The Tosa Diary is the earliest example of a Japanese literary diary. The most notable feature of the writing is its artistically conceived shape. The theme of the daughter who died gives artistic unity to the work, even when poetry is discussed or drunken parties are described. The diary literature that would later develop would be personal, like *The Tosa Diary*, and not like the diaries kept in Chinese by men of the court. Tsurayuki's decision to compose *The Tosa Diary* in the persona of a woman deprived the work of the directness and the sincerity that are so conspicuous in the diaries kept by real women during the following century, but no one who has read *The Tosa Diary* will doubt that he has come closer to Tsurayuki. The diary abounds in references to poetry, but not necessarily because Tsurayuki intended it to serve as a textbook for young people. Rather, he loved the *waka* and wanted to persuade others that it could express even the most deeply felt emotions. Writing about the death of his daughter probably assuaged his grief, and his sorrow, though indirectly presented, has the power to move us as an individual expression of a universal theme.

The Gossamer Years

The Tosa Diary was written by a man pretending to be a woman, but *Kagerō Nikki* (*The Gossamer Years*) was actually written by a woman. Not all the differences between the two diaries can be explained in terms of the authors' sex, but the most striking feature of *The Gossamer Years* is surely its intense subjectivity. It is the record of a woman's life, written passionately and without a thought to how readers might judge her actions. That other people might consider her fortunate was irrelevant to the author; she was convinced that no one had ever suffered as much as she, and she was determined that readers of her diary be fully aware of her misery.

Another contrast to *The Tosa Diary* is that events in *The Gossamer Years* were not recorded by year, month, and day. Only one year, 972, is plainly given, and other dates (from 954 to 974) are calculated from this point of reference. There is evidence that the first two of the three volumes were probably written considerably after the events described, but in the third volume the author seems to be narrating the recent past. The gap between the events and the descriptions of them make *The Gossamer Years* read more like an autobiography than a diary.

The author, the daughter of the governor of Mutsu, was the second wife of Fujiwara no Kaneie, a highborn statesman who became regent in 986 and chancellor in 989. The author's own name is not known, so she is called "the mother of Michitsuna," her son by Kaneie. She probably lived from 936 to 995. Considering the importance of her husband's position, we might expect that the diary would contain a fair amount of court gossip, but the author shows hardly a trace of interest in anyone except herself and members of her immediate family. The only political event she describes in some detail is the banishment to Kyūshū of the Minister of the Left for allegedly plotting an insurrection in 969. Moved by sympathy for this prince and his sons, all of whom were exiled to distant places, she expressed grief, adding, "These are matters that have no place in a diary that describes only things that have happened to me, but since the person who felt this grief was none other than myself, I have set down what I felt."[1]

It is clear from this passage that the mother of Michitsuna considered her diary to be a vehicle solely for describing personal experiences, and references to events of larger significance were allowable only in the exceptional circumstance that she herself was emotionally involved. At the very opening she stated her reasons for keeping this diary. She described herself as being below average in looks, a woman who had spent her life idly in this world. She had read old romances, apparently to escape the monotony of her days, and as she read such works she could not help but contrast her dreary life with the passionate affairs found in books. She decided that the romances must be untrue, and wondered if perhaps a faithful account of what the life of a wellborn lady was really like, without fictitious, romantic elements, might not interest readers. Her purpose was not to divert with fantasies but to evoke the sadness and the loneliness of the life actually led by a court lady.

We need not accept her statements at face value. We know from other sources that, far from being an undistinguished woman of mediocre looks, she was considered to be one of the three most beautiful women of her time and was admired as a poet.[2] But from the outset she chose to picture herself as a suffering wife, and not as a gifted and envied woman.

The Gossamer Years describes the author's life from the time Kaneie first sent her love notes until, twenty years later, she resigned herself to never seeing him again. She was a second wife and should not have expected him to spend more than occasional nights with her, but she thought otherwise. Her diary is filled with references to the many nights and days she waited for him in vain and to the frustration his visits caused by bringing home the realization that he could never love her as completely as she loved him. Her New Year's wish for 969 was that "he may be with me thirty days and thirty nights a month."[3] But when Kaneie attempted to please her by visiting, she was usually unresponsive and indulged her grief instead.

The whole diary is infused with her suffering, but some scholars have suggested that she was actually very fortunate. In a sense this is true. She was never deprived of Kaneie's material assistance, even when he was least attentive, and, despite his affairs with other women, he did not forget her. There is no suggestion in the work, however, that she appreciated the comforts that surrounded her. In keeping with the role she had assigned herself, she experienced extremely few moments of joy and many of desolation. Early in the diary she relates, "I concluded that my unhappiness was part of my inescapable destiny, determined from former lives, and must be accepted as such."[4] On one occasion when Kaneie visited her she noted, "Eventually he appeared, but our interview was as unpleasant as before. There seemed no relief from the gloom that had become the dominant tone in my life."[5] She bitterly resented each new affair of Kaneie's, but it never seems to have occurred to her that, when Kaneie took her as his second wife, the first wife probably felt the anguish she now suffered. She had little time to spare for other people's unhappiness. At one point, after Kaneie had been describing something that bothered him, she commented, "I was absorbed in my own grief and paid no attention to him."[6] The title of the diary itself is derived from a statement of her unhappiness at the end of the first book: "And so the months and the years have gone by, but, grieving as I am over my fate, which is to have nothing turn out as I wish it, the coming of the new year brings no joy. At the thought that this depressing life is likely to continue, it seems appropriate to call this the diary [*niki*] of a woman whose life seemed as insubstantial as the summer haze [*kagerō*]."[7]

The most striking feature of *The Gossamer Years* is its incredible honesty. Few authors have ever revealed themselves in a less attractive light. One night, when Kaneie announced his intentions of visiting the writer, "I sent back word that I was not feeling well and could not answer. I was sure that I would not see him, but presently he appeared, cool and nonchalant as ever. His playful manner I found most irritating, and before I knew it I had begun pouring out all the resentment I had stored up through the months. He said not a word, pretending to be asleep, and after I had gone on for a time he started up and exclaimed, 'What's this? Have you gone to bed already?' It may not have been entirely gracious of me, but I behaved like a stone for the rest of the night, and he left early in the morning without a word."[8]

The author could hardly have expected that such a passage would win the reader's sympathy, but she writes so vividly and exactly that we feel we have all but participated in her experience; even if we do not approve of her behavior, we understand it. She cannot refrain from pouring out her resentment, though Kaneie is trying to please her; she herself realizes that she has "behaved like a stone." It is a self-portrait devastating in its honesty.

Perhaps the most deplorable episode in the diary describes the author's exultation over the misery of a rival. Kaneie had a paramour who lived in an alley. The author was acutely aware of his visits to her rival, because Kaneie's carriage passed her house on the way. She was enraged when she learned that the other woman had given birth to his child, but soon afterward, as she relates, "it began to appear that the lady in the alley had fallen from favor since the birth of her child. I had prayed, at the height of her unhappiness, that she would live to know what I was then suffering, and it seems that my prayers were being answered. She was alone, and now her child was dead, the child that had been the cause of that unseemly racket. . . . For a moment she had been able to use a person who was unaware of her shortcomings, and now she was abandoned. The pain must be even sharper than mine. I was satisfied."[9]

The conventional reaction to the death of the child of a hated rival would have been some expression of sympathy, or perhaps contrition for her ill wishes, but the writer does not hesitate to proclaim her satisfaction. What she says is shocking, but it makes us sure we know her. Unlike the women poets depicted in such works of art as the scrolls of the thirty-six immortals of poetry, all identical in features, she is an individual.

A Japanese man of that period would not have written with such honesty; men always sought to preserve their public image. Various poems in the *Man'yōshū*, the early anthology of poetry, describe the poet's emotions on seeing a dead body by the road or on a beach. He wonders who the man is and imagines the grief of the man's wife, who has been waiting in vain for his return, when she learns that he is dead. His compassion is appropriate though conventional. But when the author of *The Gossamer Years*, on her way to Ishiyama, sees a dead body by the river, her only comment is, "I was quite beyond being frightened by that sort of thing."[10] Her pity is reserved for herself, and she cannot spare even conventional words of sympathy for a stranger. Her attitude is not endearing, but it has the ring of truth.

The diary breaks off with a description of how the author heard a knocking at the gate. Scholars conjecture that the knocking came from exorcisers who went from house to house on the last night of the year, driving away demons.[11] Even if the knocking was not caused by exorcisers, surely it was not Kaneie. The last third of the diary contains comparatively little mention of him, dealing instead with the efforts of his younger brother to marry the girl whom the diarist had adopted.

Many critics have stated that the last volume of *The Gossamer Years*, in which the author describes events that recently occurred, is from a literary standpoint superior to her recollections of the more distant past, but it is difficult to concur in this view. Like most autobiographical writings, the earlier parts are the most interesting, perhaps because the author is less constricted by facts than when relating what happened the day before. The first two books of *The Gossamer Years*, describing half-remembered events and emotions, create an unforgettable portrait of a sensitive and intelligent woman who nevertheless placed little value on what she possessed and was aware only of what she lacked.

The diary contains over three hundred poems. None is of first quality, and most, at least for modern readers, serve only to interrupt the narration. But the poems, having been written down at the time when they were composed, are probably more accurate than the author's remembrances of long-ago events. The most interesting poem is Kaneie's, a long poem he sent to the mother of Michitsuna, the only statement of his interpretation of what happened in the marriage. It opens, "True, the newly gathered red leaves will fade. Love is but love. Each autumn is the same."[12] These words indicate that, unlike his wife, he was aware of the impossibility of keeping love burning forever at the same intensity as at the beginning. But, he insists, he has never forgotten his wife or their son: "I did not forget, my purpose was as always. I sought to see the child and was turned away." His wife often refused to see him, and her women drove him to "other, kinder places. But sometimes I still came, and I slept alone. And when I awoke in the middle of the night, I found the friendly moon, quite unreserved. And not a trace of you. Thus one may find that love has lost its flavor and left one inattentive. . . ."

The Gossamer Years is the self-portrait of a woman of intense emotions, and its emotionally charged atmosphere paved the way for *The Tale of Genji*. It would be agreeable to report that Kaneie grieved as much over the death of his wife as Genji grieved over Murasaki, but his sorrow was probably tempered by relief that the demands of a woman who loved him too much had at last ended.

The Master of the Hut

The travel diary *Ionushi* (*The Master of the Hut*) was apparently written by a priest called Zōki late in the tenth century, though there is considerable uncertainty about both the author and the date.[1] The author writes about himself in the third person and gives none of the intimate details found in the diaries written by women of the time; instead, *The Master of the Hut* is closely related in spirit to the diaries of itinerant monks of the Middle Ages. Of course, there were earlier examples of travel accounts, whether Ennin's record of his journey to China or Ki no Tsurayuki's *The Tosa Diary*, but their reasons for traveling (in Ennin's case to study Tendai Buddhism at its source, in Tsurayuki's to return to the capital after finishing his service in the provinces) would not be as typical of later travelers as Zōki's account.

His diary opens: "When might it have been? There was a certain man who desired to flee the world and live as he pleased. He was also stirred by the thought of visiting all the delightful places in the country of which he had heard. At the same time it occurred to him that if he were to worship at the various holy places it might reduce his burden of sins. His name was Master of the Hut."[2]

Zōki gave three distinct reasons for making his journey. The first was his desire to escape from the mundane world and lead a life of his choosing. A similar rejection of human society was characteristic of the hermit priests of the Middle Ages, some of whom remained in lonely huts in the mountains, but others of whom constantly traveled. Zōki's second reason was to visit places whose charms were familiar to him, probably from poetry. A desire to visit "famous places" (*meisho*) or "sources of poetry" (*uta-makura*) would inspire Japanese to travel all over the country in order to see with their own eyes sites that had been described in poetry many times. The forests of monuments one still sees today, erected at places where Saigyō or Bashō wrote well-known poems, are testimony to the abiding interest of many generations of Japanese travelers in seeing places that had inspired their predecessors. Finally, Zōki expressed the hope that worshipping at holy places would reduce the burden of his sins, a hope shared by pilgrims over the centuries. Travel might give pleasure—such holy sites as Ise, Kumano, and the Ishiyama Temple were known for their scenic beauty—but that was not the main objective of the pilgrimages; the person who made his way to a holy place established direct contact with the divinity with which it was associated. One could worship the gods and buddhas anywhere, but it was most efficacious to visit the places where they had manifested themselves or that from time immemorial had been sacred to them.

Travel could be in a group, not very different from the parties of Japanese one sees today in every corner of the world, or it could be solitary. Zōki preferred to travel alone. He explained, "Various people urged me to go with them to Kumano about the 10th day of the 10th month, but this was not what I had in mind, so I left at once, secretly and by myself."[3]

Zōki's first stop after leaving the capital was Yawata. He wrote nothing about the appearance of the Iwashimizu Shrine, nor about where he stayed or what he ate, nor about pleasant or unpleasant people he met, but only about the beauty of the place: "That night the moon was lovely, and the wind was cool in the pine tops. There was a soft humming of insects, and cries of deer could be heard from afar. I felt increasingly aware as the night advanced how far I was from my usual home. Truly, I thought, this is the kind of place where a god might dwell."[4]

Both in his tone and in his choice of materials, Zōki anticipated the typical travel diaries of the medieval priests.

Zōki was sincerely moved by the beauty of Iwashimizu, but we may wonder why he invariably admired only the most familiar sights and sounds. This would be true of medieval and later travelers, too. They went to places known to them from poetry, and they admired above all cherry blossoms or reddening maple leaves, not unknown flowers blooming on nameless hills. Kawabata Yasunari would explain this phenomenon a thousand years later in these terms: "It is part of the discipline of the different arts of Japan, as well as a guidepost to the spirit, for a man to make his way in the footsteps of his predecessors, journeying a hundred times to the famous places and old sites, but not to waste time traipsing over unknown mountains and rivers."[5]

There was a contradiction involved in Zōki's pilgrimage. For a monk it was obligatory to hate the world, but how could one hate a world that was so beautiful? After expressing his conviction that the world was not for long, that it was more perishable even than foam on the water or dew on a blade of grass, he prayed, "Let me not be dazzled by the brightness, nor captivated by the colors even when I see the cherry blossoms in the spring or the crimson leaves in the autumn, but teach me the impermanence of the world even as I look at the morning dew or the evening moon."[6] Kamo no Chōmei in his retreat wondered if it was a sin to be attached to his hut, but could not renounce the pleasure of observing the changes brought by the seasons. Some monks traveled precisely in order to avoid forming such attachments.

Zōki's prayer to be left unmoved by even the most beautiful (and typical) sights did not prevent him from enjoying every stage of his journey. His diary is a tissue of clichés—or at least they seem so to us in the light of many similar works in the same vein, though his came first—and his poems are conventional. It is hard to take seriously his professions of disgust with this world. But it was never the purpose of Japanese travelers of the past to have novel experiences or to create poems unprecedented in their conception or imagery. Unlike the European who proudly claimed to be the first to set foot atop a certain mountain, the Japanese wanted to repeat the experiences of his predecessors. If he arrived at some beach that was famous for its shells, of course he gathered them. If he arrived at a place famous for certain flowers at a time when those flowers did not happen to be in bloom, he attempted to visualize them by recalling the poems that describe them. He did not waste time over flowers not celebrated in poetry.

Sometimes visits to places known from the old poetry brought sadness rather than pleasure. After Zōki crossed the Barrier of Ōsaka, he found the ruins of a once-splendid temple. "Beneath the embankment the earthen walls of the Kyōgoku Monastery were broken. Horses and oxen wandered in, and when I saw women in peasant hats striking the gong in the gallery as they walked by, I recalled how the place had looked in the past, and I reflected again on the sadness of the world." Like Hitomaro when he passed the ruins of the Ōmi Palace, Zōki was moved by the contrast between the present forlorn appearance of the temple and its glory in the past. The journeys of travelers like Zōki took them across time as well as space.

The Izumi Shikibu Diary

The first question to be asked about *Izumi Shikibu Nikki* (*The Izumi Shikibu Diary*) is whether or not it is in fact a diary. For centuries it was more commonly referred to as *Izumi Shikibu Monogatari* (*The Tale of Izumi Shikibu*), and some scholars doubt that Izumi Shikibu herself actually wrote it. It does not much resemble a diary: none of the entries is dated; it is written throughout in the third person, with Izumi Shikibu always referred to simply as *onna*, "the woman"; and the author enters into the thoughts of other people in a manner customary in a novel, not in a diary. But this is not the only Heian work that was called sometimes a diary and sometimes a tale; the subjectivity of the narration may have induced people to think of such works as "diaries." I have followed Japanese usage in treating the work as a diary.

The Izumi Shikibu Diary is a love story, related in short sections of mixed poetry (over 140 *waka*) and prose. Both the poetry and prose are of high quality, and the work as a whole suggests a fragment of a longer romance. It opens with Prince Atsumichi's first overture to Izumi Shikibu: he sends her a spray of orange blossom with a young page who had formerly served his brother, Tametaka. Tametaka and Izumi had been lovers until the year before (1002), when he suddenly died at the age of twenty-five. According to a contemporary work, Tametaka was so assiduous in his courtship that he paid no attention to a raging pestilence, but made his way through streets filled with rotting corpses to Izumi's house.[1] Perhaps he died of some disease contracted at this time.

When Izumi Shikibu received the orange blossoms from Atsumichi she was still wrapped in memories of Tametaka, and hesitated to reply. Finally, she sent a poem, and the ensuing correspondence, at first intended by Izumi Shikibu to be no more than a distraction from the "listless boredom of her existence," led to their becoming lovers. At the end of the diary Atsumichi secretly installed Izumi in his palace, to the great distress of his wife, who announced her intention of returning to her family. We are not told what happened afterward, but we know from other sources that Izumi remained in Atsumichi's palace until his death in 1007 at the age of twenty-seven.[2] She was probably twenty-nine at the time. She wrote a hundred poems after his death attesting her grief.

The tone of the diary is by no means cheerful, even though the lovers are united at the end. The poetry is filled with sad images, and Izumi Shikibu, despite her reputation as a passionate woman, seems merely to drift into her relationship with Atsumichi. We are told, "She had no fundamental desire to enter his household. What she really wanted was to live 'in a cavern deep within the crags.' But how would she cope with the melancholy that might haunt her?"[3] Izumi found in love not pleasure but a respite from the melancholy that pervaded her spirit even when she seemed most given to her pleasures.

The most prominent theme in *The Izumi Shikibu Diary* is the fear of gossip. It is easy to obtain the impression from other sources that the Heian aristocracy was so promiscuous that love affairs were genially tolerated by a broad-minded society, but Atsumichi feared not only what his wife might think but what the servants would say if he went to visit Izumi night after night. Even at the height of his passion, he reflected that "it was because of his infatuation with this woman that his brother the late Prince had been made the subject of vicious gossip until the day of his death."[4] Izumi also worried about gossip, but "she resigned herself to the thought that this was the inevitable consequence of her continued existence in society."[5]

The fear of gossip is alluded to on almost every page. When Atsumichi decided to visit Izumi, his old nurse, Jijū, tried to dissuade him, saying, "People are talking about this affair."[6] He later heard that Izumi was being unfaithful to him, and for a time he believed the rumors. She was distraught that he should listen to "contemptible gossip,"[7] but even after they were reconciled, he told her, "I have been made the object of much vexing criticism. Perhaps because my visits to you are few and far between, I have never been discovered; yet people are saying most distressing things."[8] A long list might be compiled of expressions of fear of rumors or ridicule.

It is hard to imagine why a man of Atsumichi's rank should have been worried about gossip. What difference could it have made to him if ladies-in-waiting in the palace talked about him? But one recalls the opening of *The Tale of Genji*, where we are told, "The emperor's pity and affection quite passed bounds. No longer caring what his ladies and courtiers might say, he behaved as if intent on stirring up gossip."[9] The Emperor is far from being praised for his serene indifference to court gossip; on the contrary, resentment over the Emperor's infatuation, which takes no account of people's condemnation, threatens his reign, as a similar passion had in the past shaken China. The Heian aristocrats, however exalted their rank, lived in society, and they feared what society—even their own servants—might be saying about them. Only the bravest or the most love-stricken man dared to defy society. There was only one sure way of avoiding gossip—to withdraw altogether from society, either by taking religious orders or by severing one's contacts with other people and accepting the reputation of being an eccentric. Gossip exists in every society, of course, but in Japan the dread of what people may say has often been obsessive.

Izumi Shikibu and Prince Atsumichi tried to keep their affair a secret but, realizing in the end it was impossible to keep tongues from wagging, Atsumichi boldly installed Izumi under the same roof with his wife. The *Ōkagami* records that at the Kamo festival in 1005 Atsumichi defiantly placed Izumi in the rear of his carriage and let her long sleeves and red trousers trail to the ground.[10] They attracted more attention from the spectators than the procession.

No longer constrained by the fear of gossip, the two of them flaunted their love. It is agreeable to imagine that the gossip-mongers had been silenced by more gossip than they could handle, but the diary does not tell us this. The last we hear of Izumi Shikibu is that "she decided simply to go on serving the Prince as before, but she knew that after all she was destined never to be free of sorrows."[11]

The Murasaki Shikibu Diary

Our expectations on opening the pages of *Murasaki Shikibu Nikki* (*The Murasaki Shikibu Diary*) are likely to be higher than for any other diary written by a Japanese literary figure. We hope, first of all, that it will provide clues to the mystery of how an obscure court lady, known to us only by the nickname of Murasaki Shikibu (*shikibu*, or "secretariat," was the ministry where her father had served), was able to create one of the supreme works of world literature, *The Tale of Genji*. Perhaps she was not the greatest Japanese writer. Some scholars might bestow this distinction on Hitomaro or Zeami or Bashō or a modern writer. But, viewed against the panorama of the literature of the world, no other Japanese writer is so large a presence. Arguments continue as to whether or not *The Tale of Genji* should be considered the oldest novel in the world, or whether indeed this *monogatari* (tale) was really a novel, but its importance, both within and outside Japanese culture, can scarcely be disputed. The diary of the author of this masterpiece is automatically of the greatest interest.

The diary certainly contains notable passages, and occasionally it recalls the manner of *The Tale of Genji*, but taken as a whole it is a disappointment. It consists of three main sections: a detailed description of the birth of Prince Atsuhira, the first child of the Empress Shōshi, who was the daughter of Michinaga; an account of people in the court in the form of a letter to a friend; and, finally, a collection of seemingly unrelated anecdotes about life at the court. Needless to say, every scrap of information that Murasaki Shikibu provides about herself is of unique importance to scholars of Japanese literature, whether her account of her early education, when she learned the Chinese classics so much more quickly than her brother that her father regretted she had not been born a man, or her expressions of admiration or distaste for the various ladies of the court. But how eagerly one would trade the descriptions of the costumes worn by the ladies for even one passage that revealed to us Murasaki Shikibu at work as a writer!

The Murasaki Shikibu Diary is not a diary in the normal sense. The entries are dated casually or not at all, occasioning speculation as to the years of some events, such as Murasaki Shikibu's first appearance at court. These matters are obviously worth determining, but it is of far greater importance to us to know when she began to write *The Tale of Genji*; whether she started with "Kiritsubo," the chapter that now heads the work, or elsewhere (as various traditions have it); whether the order of composition of the chapters was the same as that of the present text or if she later interleaved chapters. These and a hundred similar questions intrigue anyone who has ever studied *The Tale of Genji*, but the diary does not answer them.

The diary is in no sense a writer's notebook, and there are few mentions of *The Tale of Genji*. The best-known reference to the work is the following: "His Majesty was listening to someone reading *The Tale of Genji* aloud. 'She must have read the Chronicles of Japan!' he said. 'She seems very learned.' Saemon no Naishi heard this and apparently jumped to conclusions, spreading it abroad among the senior courtiers that I was flaunting my knowledge. She gave me the nickname Our Lady of the Chronicles."[1]

The malicious gossip of the court lady Saemon no Naishi in spreading word that Murasaki Shikibu was puffed up with her knowledge of Chinese writings again reminds us of the power of gossip in a closed society like that of the Japanese court. It is baffling all the same why *The Tale of Genji* should have reminded the Emperor of the *Chronicles of Japan* (*Nihongi* or *Nihon Shoki*), a deadly accumulation of historical (or legendary) information.

Perhaps it acquired this reputation because many incidents in the novel were based on events known to members of the court at the time.[2] Such people may have read *The Tale of Genji* in a rather different manner from ours, as a kind of veiled commentary on the times, but the clues in the diary are insufficient to enlighten us.

The Murasaki Shikibu Diary, on the other hand, is one of our best sources of knowledge concerning the realities of life at the Heian court during the period of its greatest glory. Of course, the diaries kept in Chinese by courtiers are full of information, but the lack of literary intent makes them dull reading, and the authors chose to describe only those aspects of court life that they thought posterity should know about.

Eiga Monogatari (*A Tale of Flowering Fortunes*), though ostensibly a history of the times of Michinaga, borrowed whole passages from Murasaki Shikibu's diary,[3] no doubt because the diary contains material not available elsewhere. It describes events subjectively—not merely what took place but the impression they produced on the author—and thereby establishes the individuality of the people portrayed in a manner not possible in an official account. The portrait of Michinaga in Murasaki's diary or of Kaneie in *The Gossamer Years* gives these statesmen a dimension not discernible in the histories.

It has often been suggested that Michinaga served as a model for Genji, but extremely little in *The Murasaki Shikibu Diary* substantiates this theory. We are more likely to decide that Genji was a kind of anti-Michinaga, his diametrical opposite in almost every way. The bulk of the diary is given over to a description of the celebrations attending the birth of Michinaga's grandson, the child of the Emperor Ichijō and Michinaga's daughter Shōshi. At all stages it is Michinaga, rather than the Emperor, who is in command. Murasaki Shikibu reported that before the birth, while prayers were being offered for a safe delivery, "His Excellency [Michinaga] was shouting orders to all and sundry in such a loud voice that the priests were almost drowned out and could hardly be heard."[4] His joy after the baby was born was not merely that of any grandfather but of a grandfather of a future emperor, and he was so delighted that he could not resist the impulse to visit his daughter and the baby every morning and evening, for the pleasure of taking the baby in his arms (though on one occasion the baby responded by wetting Michinaga's coat).

Genji experienced few moments of such joy. His first son, the fruit of his guilt-ridden affair with Fujitsubo, his father's consort, could not be recognized, and thoughts of this son stirred feelings of shame, not pride. Another son, Yūgiri, was born while the baby's mother, Aoi, was in a state of demonic possession, and hardly was the baby born when Aoi fell victim to the "living ghost" of Lady Rokujō. Kaoru, whom the world supposed to be Genji's son, was actually another man's, and Genji's grandchildren hardly played any role in his life.

There are, of course, even more important differences between Genji and Michinaga. The latter seems never to have heard of *mono no aware*, "the pity of things," the prevalent quality in Genji's relations with others, and his behavior on occasion is marked by a crudity unimaginable in Genji. But there is no need to belabor the point. Murasaki Shikibu attempted in writing *The Tale of Genji* to suggest what a truly civilized court might be like. Her diary, which describes what she actually experienced, rather than her dreams, may therefore at times seem disillusioning.

Life at a court, no matter where it may be, is likely to be boring. Nothing I have ever read about day-to-day activities at the courts of Europe has ever persuaded me that I would have enjoyed living there. Of all the courts about which I have read, only the imaginary one depicted in *The Tale of Genji* attracts me. Though the members of this court society had unlimited leisure and apparently unlimited funds, they never became so bored with life as to turn to mindless or perverted pleasures. The creation of beauty, whether in their surroundings, their clothes, or their handwriting, inspired their every action. No doubt there were jealousies among the different women loved by Genji, but, with the exception of the involuntary acts of the living or dead spirit of Lady Rokujō, this jealousy did not manifest itself in the spiteful form it assumed at other courts. If the world of Genji was nonetheless enveloped in sadness, this is not because malice prevails but because sadness is the human condition, because the world is colored by *mono no aware*.

In reading Murasaki Shikibu's diary, one soon becomes aware

of the great differences separating its world from that of *The Tale of Genji*, but the two worlds are not unrelated. The opening of the diary especially is filled with an awareness of beauty that proves the world of the Shining Prince (Genji) was not wholly a creation of Murasaki Shikibu's imagination: "As autumn deepens, the beauty of the Tsuchimikado mansion defies description. The trees by the lake and the grasses by the stream become a blaze of color that intensifies in the evening glow and makes the voices in ceaseless recitation sound all the more impressive. A cool breeze gently stirs, and throughout the night the endless murmur of the stream blends with the sonorous chanting."[5]

The attention Murasaki Shikibu pays in her diary not only to nature but to the beauty created by man—whether costumes or ceremonies—is also notable. There is an extraordinary indifference to food in *The Tale of Genji*, certainly when compared with Chinese works of fiction, but in her diary Murasaki found beauty even in food: "His Majesty moved to his seat and then the food was brought in. It was so beautifully arranged I cannot find words to describe it."[6]

Even though, as the many passages describing drunken courtiers and gossiping court ladies indicate, the Heian court had much in common with courts elsewhere in the world, one should not overlook its uniqueness. What a world separates the court of the Empress Shōshi from, say, that of Henry VIII, where people ate with their fingers and threw scraps from their plates to dogs! Or to the court of Louis XIV, where the Roi Soleil held audiences while seated on a *chaise percée* and where perfumes took the place of baths!

Murasaki was only intermittently happy at the court. In her diary she wrote that her loneliness was unbearable. This was not the loneliness of being totally isolated but of being surrounded by people in whom she could never confide. Perhaps it was also the loneliness of the artist who craves companionship but also rejects it, knowing that work demands solitude. Murasaki made some friends at the court, but these friendships seem not to have lasted long.

When Murasaki wrote about acquaintances at the court, it was generally in terms of displeasure and even dismay. In one famous passage that begins cheerfully enough, Fujiwara no Kintō poked his head into a gathering of ladies and asked, "Would our young Murasaki be in attendance by any chance?" Murasaki Shikibu replied, "I cannot see the likes of Genji here, so how could she be present?"[7] Perhaps this exchange gave rise to Murasaki's nickname, after the character in her book, and there is a pleasing suggestion of gallantry in the exchange. But the next sentences shake us rudely from the world of the Shining Prince:

" 'Assistant Master of the Third Rank Sanenari!' shouted His Excellency. 'Take the cup!' He stood up, and because his father, the Minister of the Center, Kinsue, was present, came up the steps from the garden. Seeing this, his father burst into tears. Provisional Middle Counsellor Takaie, who was leaning against a corner pillar, started pulling at Lady Hyōbu's robes and singing dreadful songs, but His Excellency said nothing. I realized that it was bound to be a terribly drunken affair this evening, so, once the formal celebrations were over, Lady Saishō and I decided to retire. We were just about to do so when His Excellency's sons, Yorimichi and Norimichi, Adviser of the Right Kanetaka, and some other gentlemen started creating a commotion in the eastern gallery. We hid behind the dais, but His Excellency pulled back the curtains and we were both caught."[8]

Murasaki Shikibu's diary portrays not the flawlessly decorous courtiers of *The Tale of Genji* but drunken men who make obscene jokes and paw at the women. Some modern readers may find that such proofs of the foibles of Heian courtiers make them seem more "human" and closer to us than the peerless Genji, but this was obviously not Murasaki Shikibu's point of view. Weary of such excessively "human" men, she took refuge in the world she had created.

Murasaki Shikibu's loneliness was probably intensified by her exceptional powers of discernment. The "letter" (*shōsoku*) section of her diary contains brief sketches of some fifteen or sixteen court ladies. Murasaki was not always critical; she praises a few women without qualification, and generally finds something to praise even in women whom she clearly dislikes. But her barbed criticisms are what we remember of her comments—an ability to see through seeming perfection to hidden flaws. This ability is invaluable in a novelist, but it does not promote friendships. At one point Murasaki checks herself, remarking that if she went on describing people in so unflattering a manner she would certainly acquire the reputation of being a gossip. She declares, "I shall take care to ignore those whose company I keep, and likewise refrain from mentioning anyone who has the slightest fault that might give one cause to hesitate."[9] But having written this, she immediately launches into a description of Lady Saishō which concludes with the evaluation that she is "by no means perfect"!

The most interesting of Murasaki Shikibu's comments on the court ladies of her time refer to women whom we know from their own works, such as Izumi Shikibu. She wrote about Izumi Shikibu, "She does have a rather unsavory side to her character but has a genius for tossing off letters with ease and can make the most banal statement sound special. . . . I cannot think of her as a poet of the highest quality."[10]

Such observations show how mistakenly Murasaki Shikibu was judged by people at the court. At first they supposed (because she did not take part in gossip) that she must be shy. Later they decided that, despite her literary gifts, she must be stupid. Her own self-appraisal was more astute: "Do they really look on me as such a dull thing, I wonder? But I am what I am and so act accordingly. Her Majesty too has often remarked that she had thought I was not the kind of person with whom one could ever relax, but that now I have become closer to her than any of the others. I am perversely standoffish; if only I can avoid putting off those for whom I have genuine respect."[11]

Not only is this a fair self-portrayal but it helps to explain how Murasaki Shikibu was able to keep writing her lengthy novel while serving at the court. It was by preserving her distance from the intrigues and rivalries that occupied the other court ladies; she chose not to reveal her true qualities except to those (like the Empress Shōshi herself) whom she genuinely respected.

Murasaki Shikibu's diary does not contain many references to *The Tale of Genji*. Apart from the Emperor's praise (when, as already mentioned, he conjectured that she must have read the *Chronicles of Japan*), there are only a few direct or indirect references to her work. Murasaki mentions, for example, "Her Majesty was involved in her book-binding, and so first thing every morning we had to go to her quarters to choose paper of various colors and write letters of request to people, enclosing copies of the original."[12] This statement has been interpreted as meaning that it was intended to present a beautifully written copy of *The Tale of Genji* to the Empress, and people known for their fine calligraphy were therefore asked to make copies of the manuscript on specially selected paper.[13] But does the passage mean that *The Tale of Genji* was already completed by this time?

Murasaki Shikibu soon afterward noted in her diary that one day, while she was busy serving at the court, Michinaga sneaked into her room and found a copy of *The Tale of Genji* that she had brought from home for safekeeping. He gave this manuscript to his second daughter. Murasaki expressed distress that an inferior copy (presumably not the final version) might harm her reputation as a writer. It is not clear in what way the manuscript might have been inferior, but obviously Murasaki worried about the reputation of her work.

Murasaki, much more ambitious than the writers of the old tales, included in *The Tale of Genji* not only romantic elements, in the traditional manner, but her experience of life; as time passed her outlook on life necessarily changed, and she felt compelled to revise her work. She wrote at one point in her diary, "I tried rereading the Tale, but it did not seem to be the same as before, and I was disappointed."[14] Perhaps by "the Tale" (*monogatari*) she did not mean *The Tale of Genji* but some other tale, but the meaning is similar: she has outgrown her former tastes, and what formerly pleased her no longer satisfies.

The final reference to *The Tale of Genji* describes the banter and poems exchanged by Murasaki and Michinaga after he happened to notice a copy of the work near the place where the Empress was sitting.[15] The manner of presentation of this incident (the overtones of Michinaga's poem indicate that he is not too subtly making advances to Murasaki) suggests that Murasaki Shikibu felt quietly confident in the value of her novel. The diary is of almost equal literary distinction, but it survives only in a sadly mutilated state, and of course lacks the magnitude of *The Tale of Genji*. Even in its present, unfortunately incomplete condition, it is still a high point in the Japanese tradition of "diary literature."

The Sarashina Diary

Sarashina Nikki (*The Sarashina Diary*)[1] is even less like a diary than *The Murasaki Shikibu Diary*. Hardly an entry is dated, and the "diary" covers not the events of a journey or some other limited period of the author's life but virtually her entire lifetime, suggesting an autobiography rather than a diary. But what makes it seem most unlike a diary is its implicit denial of reality. The normal diary insists on reality—whether or not it rained on a certain day, who came to visit, what was served for dinner, and so on—but in *The Sarashina Diary* the place of reality is taken by fiction or dreams. The world of fiction, especially *The Tale of Genji*, bulked larger in the writer's mind than everyday events; the people in the novel were not merely characters in a work of fiction but her most intimate friends and the objects of her emulation. Her most deeply felt hope as a child was not that she would lead a happy life as a wife, a mother, or a member of the court, but that she would be able to immerse herself to her heart's content in the old romances.

The opening paragraph of *The Sarashina Diary* sets the tone for the entire work: "I was brought up in a part of the country so remote that it lies beyond the end of the Great East Road. What an uncouth creature I must have been in those days! Yet even shut away in the provinces I somehow came to hear that the world contained things known as Tales, and from that moment my greatest desire was to read them for myself. To idle away the time, my sister, my step-mother, and others in the household would tell me stories from the Tales, including episodes about Genji, the Shining Prince; but, since they had to depend on their memories, they could not possibly tell me all I wanted to know and their stories only made me more curious than ever. In my impatience I got a statue of the Healing Buddha built in my own size. When no one was watching, I would perform my ablutions and, stealing into the altar room, would prostrate myself and pray fervently, 'Oh, please arrange things so that we may soon go to the Capital, where there are so many Tales, and please let me read them all.' "[2]

It is easy to imagine that an intelligent, well-educated girl growing up in a distant part of the country would have yearned to go to the capital, the only place in Japan where she could lead the kind of life for which her education had prepared her. She craved not the social life that actually existed at the court but the imaginary world described in works of fiction. If she could have obtained all the books she wanted without leaving the remote part of the country where she grew up, she need not have traveled all the way to the capital.

Manuscripts were scarce and expensive. If a courtier wanted a copy of a favorite book, he would have to provide the paper, itself a costly item, and then support the calligrapher for months while the manuscript was being copied. That, no doubt, is why so many works of Heian literature have disappeared, leaving only their titles, and why other works (including imperially sponsored collections of poetry in Chinese) survive only in incomplete copies. It was most unlikely that a complete set of *The Tale of Genji* would turn up in remote Kazusa, and the only way this sensitive, introverted girl could read about Genji, the Shining Prince, was to go to the capital. She remembered that she made a statue of the Healing Buddha (Yakushi-botoke) of her own size. This was an extraordinary undertaking for a girl not yet twelve years old, and shows the strength of her determination to read every last tale.

No sooner did the girl arrive in the capital than she let it be known she was desperately eager to read some tales at once. Her house, set in uncultivated grounds, in no way suggested the refinement of the capital she had imagined, and the household was in a state of turmoil trying to make the place livable, but the girl was too impatient to wait until things had settled down. She recorded that she had begged her stepmother, "Find some tales and show them to me, show them to me please!"[3] These words suggest the actual voice of the girl who was so eager, even at this early age, to escape into the world of fiction.

From the time she left Kazusa at the age of twelve until she was invited at thirty-one to serve at court, the author of *The Sarashina Diary* apparently did little else but read tales. In addition to *The Tale of Genji*, which she read again and again, she read various tales that have been lost. Even granting that there existed many more tales for her to read than now survive, this was still an astonishing way for her to have spent what were usually considered to be the most precious years of a woman's life. She was by no means unhappy to have used her time in this manner. On the contrary, she related what immense joy she felt when an aunt presented her with the fifty-odd volumes of *The Tale of Genji* and she could read the whole work for the first time. She declared, "I wouldn't have changed places with the Empress herself."[4]

Her hours were mainly spent reading, not only during the daytime but late at night by lamplight. She seems to have had no suitors who might have distracted her from her reading. Probably the young men of the court were not even aware that she existed. She recalled, "I was not a very attractive girl at the time, but I fancied that, when I grew up, I would surely become a great beauty with long flowing hair like Yūgao, who was loved by the Shining Prince, or like Ukifune, who was wooed by the Captain of Uji."[5]

It is by no means unusual for a plain girl to imagine that, like the ugly duckling of Andersen's fairy tale, she will one day turn into a swan; but the daughter of Takasue continued to entertain such hopes long after the time when the duckling should have become a swan. It is noteworthy, too, that she dreamed of becoming like Yūgao or Ukifune, both timid and extremely unhappy women, rather than like Murasaki, who enjoyed Genji's love. She obviously found it easy to identify with the most tragic characters in *The Tale of Genji*.

Her life at home was monotonous, but she had another refuge

in addition to books: the world of dreams. She recorded her dreams faithfully, many times in the diary. Often the dreams had religious significance, but, initially at least, she paid scant attention to the implications of the dreams. She wrote, "One night I dreamt that a handsome priest appeared before me in a yellow surplice and ordered me to learn the fifth volume of the Lotus Sutra as soon as possible. I told no one about the dream since I was much too busy with my Tales to spend any time learning sutras."[6]

Some years later the author's mother, worried about what would happen to a girl who lived so secluded from the world, ordered a mirror to be made for the Hase Temple, and requested a priest to remain in retreat for three days, praying for a dream about her daughter's future. The priest did what she asked, and had a dream in which a beautiful lady appeared, dressed in splendid robes. She asked if any document had been presented with the mirror. The priest replied that there was none. The lady looked surprised, but showed the priest what was reflected on both sides of the mirror. On one side a figure appeared, rolling in anguish and lamentation; on the other was reflected a springtime scene in the palace (such as Genji provided his mistresses, according to their preferred season).[7] Years later the author would decide that the unhappy figure writhing in grief was a prophetic vision of herself, but at the time she paid no attention to the dream. "So indifferent was I to such matters that when I was repeatedly told to pray to the Heavenly Goddess Amaterasu I wondered where this deity might be and whether she was in fact a goddess or a buddha. It was some time before I was interested enough to ask who she actually was."[8] She had no time to study sutras and was uninterested in the mysteries of Shintō. She lived in the world that Murasaki Shikibu had created and waited patiently for Genji to discover her.

Dreams often recur in *The Sarashina Diary*. Although the author at first was so absorbed in the tales she was reading that she did not take the dreams to heart, she accepted the assumption of her time that dreams reveal the future. But, more than the dreams that come during the hours of sleep, her mind was filled with daydreams that made her present life as uncertain and unreal as the future. This is how she described her state of mind when she was twenty-four:

"I lived forever in a dream world. Though I made occasional pilgrimages to temples, I could never bring myself to pray sincerely for what most people want. I know there are many who read the sutras and practice religious devotions from the age of about seventeen; but I had no interest in such things. The height of my aspiration was that a man of noble birth, perfect in both looks and manners, someone like Shining Genji in the Tale, would visit me just once a year in the mountain village where he would have hidden me like Lady Ukifune. There I should live my lonely existence, gazing at the blossoms and the autumn leaves and the moon and the snow, and wait for an occasional splendid letter from him. This was all I wanted; and in time I came to believe that it would actually happen."[9]

She still dreamed of herself as Ukifune, the saddest of the women characters in *The Tale of Genji*, and the only one who attempted suicide. She did not hope that Genji would install her in a wing of his palace (with a garden that reflected her preference in seasons) but only that he (or some equally gifted gentleman) would keep her in a lonely mountain village. This was a modest ambition, but she clung to the vision of a perfect man, unlike any man she had actually seen. She was sure that if such a man visited her only once a year she would be satisfied. And if in between his rare visits he favored her with a letter—of course, it would be a memorable letter—she would be happy, no matter how long she waited. Like many children, but not like most women of twenty-four, she was sure that if she wished hard enough she would obtain whatever she wanted. There is something at once childish and extremely affecting in the frankness with which she expressed her hopes.

About this time her father was appointed governor of Hitachi in the distant Eastern Region. He naturally did not consider taking his daughter with him, for fear that she might turn into a mere country woman. He recalled his previous post in Kazusa, where she had spent her childhood: "The provinces are terrible places. I could have managed if I had only had myself to think about, but it worried me to be accompanied by a large family and to know that I was hemmed in by restrictions of every kind and could not look after you as I wished."[10] He feared that he might die while in the provinces, leaving her alone and without support in the capital. He did not openly refer to the fact she was still not married, though this must have been on his mind.

After her father left for Hitachi, fewer visitors than ever came to her house. By way of distraction from her loneliness, she made a pilgrimage to Uzumasa, yet her prayers were not for salvation but for her father's return: "I prayed that somehow he might get rid of his official duties so that we could soon meet safely again. Surely Buddha must have felt sympathy for me."[11] During another pilgrimage, this one to the Kiyomizu Temple, she dreamed that a priest approached and scolded her: " 'Engaged in senseless trifling,' he said, 'you are risking your future salvation.' "[12] She added that she had told no one about this dream and left the temple without giving it further thought.

We may admire her indifference to dream warnings and may even interpret it as a sign she was a skeptic, but this is probably a misinterpretation. The diary was written in later years, after she had turned to religion, and her account of her indifference was probably intended as a warning to others who, like herself, thought only of happiness in this undependable world.

The daughter of Takasue attended court for the first time at the age of thirty-one. Her father, who had returned from Hitachi, urged her to decline the invitation, no doubt reluctant to be deprived of her company, but other people persuaded him to yield. She wrote, "My first visit to the palace was for one night."[13] This laconic statement may suggest that she spent a night in the arms of some courtier, but in fact nothing of interest occurred. The only people she knew at court were those from whom she had borrowed books, and she was accustomed to the old-fashioned ways of her parents, with whom she would gaze in the conventional manner at spring blossoms or the autumn moon. She reported, "When I arrived at court I was in a sort of daze and hardly knew what I was doing. So at dawn on the following day I returned home."[14]

She continued, "During my cloistered years I had often imagined that life in the Palace would offer all sorts of pleasures which I had never encountered in my monotonous routine at home. As it turned out, my first experience at Court suggested that I would feel extremely awkward and unhappy in these new surroundings. Yet what could I do about it?"[15]

Her youth had been spent mainly alone. She probably lacked the ability to make conversation, which enabled court ladies to pass their days amusingly, and she was so unaccustomed to the presence of strangers that when she went to court again later that year she could not sleep with strangers in the same room. When she returned home this time, her parents begged her not to go to court again, because it made them so lonely. She accordingly ceased to attend court, but she seems to have undergone a change, perhaps at the sudden realization that her childhood dreams would not be fulfilled. She wrote:

"Things now became rather hectic for me. I forgot all about my Tales and became much more conscientious. How could I have let all those years slip by, instead of practising my devotions and going on pilgrimages? I began to doubt whether any of my romantic fancies, even those that had seemed most plausible, had the slightest basis in fact. How could anyone as wonderful as Shining Genji or as beautiful as the girl whom Captain Kaoru kept hidden in Uji really exist in this world of ours? Oh, what a fool I had been to believe such nonsense!"[16]

The author says almost nothing about her marriage, which took place when she was about thirty-six, an advanced age for a Heian lady. Her husband was five or six years older than herself; perhaps he was a widower. They had several children, including a boy who is briefly described.

The one time in her life when she came close to realizing her dream of meeting Prince Genji occurred while she was at court. One night she and another lady were listening to priests intone a sutra when a gentleman approached and exchanged words with the author's companion. "He talked in a quiet, gentle way and I could tell that he was a man of perfect qualities."[17] The reader may think, "At last the gentleman for whom she has waited so long has appeared!" We hope that, in the manner of the romances she so loved, he will detect her unusual qualities even in the dark (and despite her unassertiveness), and we are pleased when he asks her companion who she is. The author comments, "There was none of the crude, lecherous tone in his voice that one would expect from most men who asked this sort of question. Then he started speaking about the sadness of the world and other such matters, and there was something so sensitive about his manner that, for all my usual shyness, I found it hard to remain stiff and aloof. I therefore joined my companion and the gentleman."[18] Nothing is directly expressed, but we sense that something has occurred between the two, and we imagine for a moment that miracles are possible.

The gentleman who addressed the daughter of Takasue and her companion described the contrasting beauties of spring and autumn, in language appropriate to this familiar theme of Japanese poetry, then related a memorable experience he had had at Ise when he went there one winter as an imperial envoy. The moonlight on the snow and the otherworldly atmosphere had so profoundly affected him that ever since, he had been moved particularly by snowy winter nights. The author commented, "After he had finished speaking and had left us, it occurred to me that he still had no idea who I was."[19]

Some ten months later the author accompanied the princess she served to the imperial palace, where a concert was being held. The gentleman with whom she had talked on the rainy night was present, but she did not learn this until afterward. Later that night he passed by her room and for several moments, until his companion joined him, they exchanged a few words. He said, "I have never forgotten that rainy night for a moment." She murmured in return the *waka*:

nani sama de	How is it possible
omoiideken	You could remember so well?
naozari no	Those were nothing more
ko no ha ni kakeshi	Than careless remarks about
shigure bakari wo[20]	Wintry rains upon the leaves.

The next day he sent the message, "If we should ever have another such rainy night, I should like to play for you all the lute pieces I know." She added, "I too waited for such an occasion, but it never came."[21]

One quiet spring evening she heard that he was visiting the palace. She made up her mind to go to the room where he was, but the place was so crowded she was intimidated and withdrew to her room. He had been equally distressed by the hubbub and left without asking for her. That was the last time they came so close. The girl who had yearned to be like Yūgao, who died the victim of Lady Rokujō's jealousy, or like Ukifune, torn between two men who loved her, achieved a pathos of her own.

From this point on there are increasing mentions in *The Sarashina Diary* of religious pilgrimages. She herself noted, "As I go along writing, without any semblance of order, about events that took place two or three, or even four or five, years apart, people may suppose that I had become a pilgrim, constantly traveling from one mountain to another, but this was not the case. There were months and sometimes years in between."[22] When she wrote these remarks she was apparently still somewhat irregular in her religious duties, but after her marriage she became stricter and went on one distant pilgrimage after another. This was especially true while her marriage was going badly; her pilgrimages were made without her husband. At the Ishiyama Temple she had a dream. In the past she probably would have ignored it, but now, she reported, "Thinking it might be an auspicious omen, I spent the rest of the night in prayer."[23]

The daughter of Takasue nowhere states why she wrote her diary. It is clear from the remark quoted above (about misconceptions that might arise in the minds of readers about the frequency of her pilgrimages) that she expected other people would read this personal memoir. Perhaps she even intended to persuade readers, particularly young women deluded by novels into hoping for worldly happiness, that real happiness is possible only through religion. After her husband died she commented, "If only I had not given myself over to Tales and poems since my young days but had spent my time in religious devotions, I should have been spared this misery."[24] Perhaps she might have avoided some of her unhappiness, but the portrait of a young woman who lived entirely in her books is curiously appealing.

The Tale of the Tōnomine Captain

A recurring theme in *The Tale of Genji* is Genji's desire to "leave the world" and become a Buddhist priest. He is unable to take this step, he tells others, because of his worries over what will happen to the many people who depend on him. After the death of Murasaki he again ponders the possibility that the time has come for him to leave the world, but decides that he does not wish to be remembered as a weakling who could not face society alone, and he postpones taking action until this immediate occasion has passed. To tell the truth, I have never really believed Genji's professed eagerness to leave the world. He is involved with too many people, and the pleasure he takes in the beauty he has created around him is so great that he surely could not seriously have considered shutting himself up in a lonely hermitage.

But some Heian noblemen did precisely that. Although they were blessed with everything their society prized—distinguished ancestry, rank, wealth, children—they took the irrevocable step of giving it all up and putting on a monk's somber robes. When we read accounts by such men as Kamo no Chōmei, who personally had witnessed the disasters that afflicted the Japanese late in the twelfth century, it is not difficult to understand why disgust and horror over the uncertainties of this world should have induced him to turn his back on human society. This was not so clear in the case of courtiers who lived during happier days and had no personal acquaintance with disaster. One cannot help wondering what were the reactions of the families of men who "left the world." Did they rejoice to learn that their son, father, or husband had entered the path of enlightenment? Or did they lament the loneliness his action had caused them?

The surviving diaries of the period make it plain that when a man took Buddhist orders this in no way altered the affection his family felt for him. Indeed, the "great step" that Kamo no Chōmei and others praised was usually the cause of bitter grief. *Tōnomine Shōshō Monogatari* (*The Tale of the Tōnomine Captain*), though not usually considered to be a diary, bears the alternative title of *Takamitsu Nikki* (*The Takamitsu Diary*), and is discussed as a diary by scholars who point out the absence of any fictional elements from the narrative. It is obviously not a *monogatari* that relates an interesting story. Instead, it consists of thirty episodes that are almost entirely devoted to descriptions of the grief of Takamitsu's family over his decision to abandon the world and live in the monastery on Mount Hiei. Soon after the "diary" was completed, about 962, he moved from Mount Hiei, not far from the capital, to remote Tōnomine, where he spent the rest of his life, occasioning the name by which he is usually known. The identity of the writer is unknown, but it has been suggested it was a woman in the service of Takamitsu's wife.

Fujiwara no Takamitsu (939–94) was not only a grandson of the Emperor Daigo but a brilliant *waka* poet. When he was barely fifteen he was acclaimed as a genius, and he was later chosen as one of the thirty-six Immortals of Poetry. But at the age of twenty-three he suddenly left his wife and daughter and became a monk. He had previously announced his intention of taking this step on a number of occasions, though perhaps only half in earnest, but once his father (who had prevented him from entering orders) died in 960, Takamitsu felt free to carry out his long-standing plan.

One day he announced to his wife, "I'm going to the mountain to become a priest." Having heard similar statements before, she refused to take him seriously: "There you go again," she said. He insisted, "This time I really mean it." But his wife, sure he would return home that night as he had before, merely laughed. Takamitsu repeated his intention, at which his wife became angry, supposing he was trying to annoy her. She composed a poem declaring that if he went off to the mountain, where human considerations are unknown, she would vanish like the dew on the grass below the mountain. He replied with another poem, in which he urged her not to grieve, because, even after he entered the monastery on the mountain, he would not forget her.[1]

The person he found hardest to leave was apparently his sister Aimiya. He visited her a final time, but refused to enter her house, saying, "I must go somewhere in a hurry." Then he proceeded to Mount Hiei and, entering the cell of his younger brother, who was already a priest, commanded him, "Shave my head!" The brother was reluctant and asked Takamitsu his reasons, but Takamitsu merely said once again, "Shave it!" Neither the brother nor the holy man Zōga, who was with them, could be persuaded to do as Takamitsu ordered, so he took the razor in his own hand and slashed his topknot, a sign that he had broken all ties with the world.[2]

The remainder of *The Tale of the Tōnomine Captain* consists mainly of descriptions of the sorrow caused by Takamitsu's decision to become a priest. His wife and his sister Aimiya at once announced their intentions of following him and taking vows as nuns, but they were unable to do as they wished, apparently because of the opposition from their families. Aimiya sent a steady stream of doleful letters to Takamitsu's wife; in one was included a poem suggestive of her never-ending grief:

nazo mo kaku	Why am I condemned
ikeru yo wo hete	To spend my life in this way
mono wo omou	In brooding endless
Suruga no Fuji no	As the smoke curling skyward
keburi taesenu[3]	From Fuji in Suruga?

Attempts made by Aimiya's sisters to cheer her had no effect. An elder sister, accepting the finality of Takamitsu's resolution to leave the world, nevertheless wished that he would visit Aimiya secretly. But, she urged Aimiya, no matter how depressed she might become, she must under no circumstances do anything so unfortunate as to take nun's vows.[4]

The expressions of grief become somewhat monotonous, but it is noteworthy that the sister was sure it would be inauspicious (*fukitsu*) for Aimiya to become a nun. Indeed, no one expresses joy over Takamitsu's having entered the path of Buddha. Not only is his action deplored all around, but people remind Takamitsu's wife and Aimiya that, even if they are so rash as to become nuns, they will not be able to be near him: men and women were severely separated at Buddhist monasteries and convents. Takamitsu also opposed any thought his wife might have of becoming a nun, as this poem suggests:

ama nite mo	Even as a nun
onaji yama ni wa	You surely could not remain
e shimo araji	On the same mountain;
nao yo no naka wo	However bitter this world,
uramite zo hen[5]	Endure it a while longer.

Takamitsu did not forget his wife, sister, or daughter, but he was inflexible in his determination to remain secluded from the world. Other people of his day (like the mother of the author of *The Sarashina Diary*) remained at home even after taking Buddhist vows, and changed their lives only to the extent of trimming their hair or wearing dark clothes, but Takamitsu was no less resolved than a Trappist monk to isolate himself from the world. His actions, as described in the diary, may seem inhuman in his disregard for the suffering he causes others, but one cannot doubt his consecration to his faith.

Perhaps the most interesting passage in the diary concerns a former suitor of Takamitsu's wife, who sends her a letter reminding her that, long ago, when she refused him, he had also considered "living in the mountains." Then, with startling unpleasantness, he declares that she should consider her present unhappiness her punishment for having made him suffer in the past.[6] He is convinced that the wife, left to spend sleepless nights alone, now suffers more than Takamitsu.

The wife for a time considers suicide, but gives up this plan out of love for her small daughter. She sends Takamitsu a long poem (*chōka*) describing the plight of their child. His reply shows that he also worries about her and wishes that he could see her again. He says that he has tried to see the girl in dreams, but he has not always been successful. When his longing becomes acute, he takes comfort even from seeing her in daytime visions.[7]

Takamitsu's late father appears in one of his dreams and demands to know what grief was so terrible that he felt he had no choice but to become a priest.[8] The father recognizes the priesthood as a holy vocation, but he is heartbroken all the same over Takamitsu's decision, even though prayers from his son may help him to attain salvation.

The Tale of the Tōnomine Captain, despite the lugubriousness of the tone, is an affecting work. More than any other work I have read, it conveys the loneliness of those left behind when a man takes the great step of becoming a priest. How wise was Genji, the Shining Prince, not to have left this world!

The Collection of the Mother of Jōjin, the Ajari

On the last day of the 1st month of 1071 an old lady, probably eighty-four at the time, began to write a diary that would have as its central theme her yearning for her son, an eminent ecclesiastic who was then over sixty years old. If I have interpreted the genealogical tables correctly, she was the granddaughter of Aimiya, Takamitsu's sister, and her great-grandfather was the Emperor Daigo. Of all the Heian court ladies who kept diaries she was of the highest rank, and doubtless had received a suitable education. However, it was not until she was in her eighties that she decided to relieve the stress of great emotional pressure by writing the work known as *Jōjin Ajari Haha no Shū* (*The Collection of the Mother of Jōjin, the Ajari*[1]). At the outset she related why she had felt impelled to set down her thoughts:

"Over the years that have fleetingly passed, so many things, both delightful and strange, have happened to me that I can no longer count them all. I have decided to write them down, not in the hopes that anyone will see them, but because, at the age of eighty,[2] I have had a most extraordinary experience. I have kept it to myself for some time, but I thought I would try setting it down on paper."[3]

The event she was about to describe was the decision of her son Jōjin to journey to China in search of Buddhist learning. His departure saddened her so greatly that she expressed the conviction (many times reiterated in the diary) that no one had ever suffered so much as she. On the surface at least, this was patently untrue. After the death of her husband she decided that the best way of providing for her two sons was to have them enter the priesthood. Both men went on to gain exceptional distinction: the elder[4] became a *risshi* (preceptor) who served in the palace, the younger was Jōjin, the *ajari*. The old lady always wrote respectfully about the *risshi*, but Jōjin was clearly her favorite. For years her fondest dream had been that when she was on her deathbed her two sons, one seated on either side of her pillow, would read the holy sutras and, with the sound of their voices in her ears, she would breathe her last.[5] She seems to have lived quite contentedly until the day when Jōjin informed her of his intention of going to China to study at Mount Wu-t'ai, the same monastery where Ennin had stayed two hundred years before. From this time on she became obsessed with her griefs, and she wrote her diary in the secret hope that some day, preferably after her death, Jōjin would read about all the suffering he had caused her.

The mother evinced not the least interest in why Jōjin should have felt impelled to make the dangerous journey to China; she was aware only of his seeming indifference to her happiness. She vacillated between the desire to die as quickly as possible and the equally strong desire to live at least until Jōjin returned from China.[6] Again and again she blamed herself for the sin of having lived too long. If only she had not been guilty of this sin, she would have been spared the agony of being separated from her beloved Jōjin.

She never doubted that special ties bound her to her son. In an amazingly outspoken passage she insisted that a mother's love differed in nature from a father's: "A mother's love for her child, regardless of whether she is noble or humble in birth, differs entirely from a father's. While the child is still in her womb she is constantly in pain, whether she is up or lying down, but she never thinks of her own comfort. She prays that the child will be superior to others in looks and in every other respect, and this hope is so strong that even the agony of giving birth to the child is as nothing to her."[7] She recalls how, when Jōjin was an infant, he would cry if anyone else picked him up, but that he stopped crying the instant she took him in her arms. And, she insisted, her love for him had not changed to this day.[8] It is hard at times to remember that she is describing not an adolescent but a man in his sixties who was revered as an outstanding cleric of his day.

Jōjin's mother was so distraught over being separated from her beloved son that she even compared herself to the sacred figures of Buddhism; she begins an account of the birth of Shakyamuni, the historical Buddha, with the words, "Lady Māyā died after giving birth to Lord Shakyamuni"[9]—implying that Lady Māyā was fortunate to have died so soon after giving birth to the Buddha, thus being spared the anguish of parting from her son.

At times the mother seems to have realized that the bitterness she felt over Jōjin's resolution to go abroad might do him harm, but she could not suppress the indignation that welled up inside her. After describing Shakyamuni Buddha's awakening to the sorrows of human life on seeing age, sickness, and death, she (as usual) applies the parable to Jōjin and herself: "He has seen that I suffer from two of these griefs, that I am old and sick. I should think that, under the circumstances, he might postpone his departure. Nothing could upset me more, but I have heard that it will be bad for him if I openly resent his coldness, so I have resolved that my only prayer will be that a quick death will relieve me of my misery. This is a worse case of disobedience than Shakyamuni Buddha's. He disregarded the wishes of his father, who yielded him the throne with the intention of enabling the Buddha to live in splendor; but my whole life depends on being able to see Jōjin every morning and every night, and he, knowing this, has deserted me. Words fail me. But I do not blame him: it is all my own fault, for having lived so long."[10]

Her writing is obviously fueled by indignation, and she hardly seems to care what weapons she uses as proof that Jōjin's behavior is unspeakably cruel. She cites the case of Shakyamuni Buddha, not (as we might expect) in his capacity as savior of mankind, but as an unfilial son who disregarded his father's wishes. And Jōjin is even worse! Although, in a sudden twist of reasoning, she admits that the cause of all her suffering is that she has lived too long, her poems, like the following, make it plain that she considers that she suffers far more than her son:

Morokoshi e	More than the person
yuku hito yori mo	Who departs for China,
todomarite	The one who remains,
karaki omoi wa	Myself, am subject to
ware zo masareru[11]	The bitterest of sorrow.

She used on occasion the verb *uramu*, meaning "to resent" or "to feel bitter," when describing her attitude toward the son who had left her. She even wrote, after recovering from an illness that she hoped would prove fatal, "I am bitter above all toward Buddha and Buddha alone. I prayed to him wholeheartedly that he would let me die quickly, and I recovered! I thought I had lived shockingly long."[12]

It is rare in the history of literature for any woman in her eighties to begin keeping a diary that is devoted almost exclusively to expressions of love for her son. Jōjin occupies not only his mother's waking hours but her dreams. Her occasional flare-ups of anger, and even of hatred toward Jōjin, stem from overpowering love. No one can comfort her in her distress, though many people (notably her other son, the *risshi*) make the attempt. She dwells on the past, recalling how she worried over the health of her sons during an epidemic,[13] but Jōjin worries her far more now than when he was ill. Her anger brings to mind the Buddhist saying, "Some children are enemies from a previous existence."[14] She regrets now that she did not scream and howl to keep Jōjin from leaving, and cannot restrain her indignation over his failure to write. Her griefs make her wonder if Buddha himself does not hate her.[15] Her only comfort apparently is to express her unparalleled griefs in this diary.

Jōjin is not an easy man to understand. After he left the capital, he got as far as Kyūshū on his way to China, but some months later he returned to the capital. He informed his mother that he had not been able to proceed farther because he had failed to secure official permission for the journey. But why, during the months while he waited in Kyūshū, could he not have sent his mother a postcard? Probably it was because he was convinced, as he often told his mother, that meetings in this world were of little importance when compared with the true joy of long, uninterrupted meetings in paradise. Gaining admission to paradise, not only for himself but for his mother and many other people, took precedence over conventional manifestations of solicitude. But even his brother, the *risshi*, could not help but express surprise that Jōjin was so unlike everyone else in the world.[16]

Jōjin eventually made his way to China, though apparently without the permission of the Japanese government. Soon afterward, a certain priest brought word to Jōjin's mother that he would be returning to Japan in the autumn of the following year, but she was not comforted, having abandoned all hope of ever seeing him again. Her premonitions proved to be correct: Jōjin was so highly esteemed by the Chinese that they refused to allow him to return to Japan. His mother died, as she had long feared, without her beloved son by her side to offer last words of comfort.

The Collection of the Mother of Jōjin, the Ajari is of intrinsic interest in its account of a mother's intense love for her son, but it also suggests that the relations of mothers and sons are of special importance in Japanese life and literature. Apart from *The Tosa Diary*, the love of a father for his daughter does not figure prominently in the Japanese diaries, perhaps because so many literary diaries were written by women who stressed their special closeness to their sons. But in other forms of Japanese literature, too, we tend to remember especially the relations between mothers and sons. This is not only true in works written by women such as *The Tale of Genji*, in which Genji's love for his lost mother, Kiritsubo, and for her substitute, Fujitsubo, is an important theme. The theme is prominent even in works of the martial tradition: the mother of the two Soga brothers is a notable example of maternal love, as is Tokiwa's love for Yoshitsune. Further examples can be found in the Nō plays, such as *Sumidagawa*.

Literature in the West has tended to place greater importance on the relationship between fathers and daughters. Shakespeare described the relations between King Lear and his daughters, between Pericles and Marina, and between Prospero and Miranda. The most moving passages in Wagner's *Ring* are devoted to Wotan's love for Brunhilde, and the duets between a father and daughter are among the most inspired parts of Verdi's operas. There are hardly any opera duets between mothers and sons.[17] In modern Western literature the relationship between mothers and sons is often described unappealingly in terms of possessive women who refuse to surrender their precious sons to daughters-in-law, but the relationships between fathers and daughters are almost always treated sympathetically. Fathers and sons, whether East or West, tend to be portrayed in terms of rivalry and reconciliation; the tensions between mothers and daughters are less often treated, though they are found in modern Japanese literature, notably in the works of Hori Tatsuo.

The relationship of mothers and sons is of paramount importance in Japan. The diary of Jōjin's mother can be viewed as an early, extreme expression of a pervasive theme, and her insistence on how much closer mothers are to their children than fathers are probably found a responsive reaction among her readers. Of course, that was not her purpose. Apart from the comfort it gave her to record her miseries, she seems to have been trying to understand the irony of her life. She recalls that she was sickly as a child and marvels at how long she has lived.[18] She remembers the early death of her mother and how brief the period of her married life was. She concludes, not unexpectedly, that hers has been a life of unparalleled suffering.[19] But the last poem in the diary ends on a note of hope:

asahi matsu	If the dew that waits
tsuyu no tsumi naku	The sunrise disappears, leaving
kiehateba	No trace of its guilt,
yūbe no tsuki wa	Surely the evening moon
sasowarazarame	Will not fail to guide me forth.
ya[20]	

For all her complaints and expressions of despair, she seems to have been confident that she would indeed meet her son again in paradise.

The Sanuki no Suke Diary

The Sanuki no Suke Diary[1] is a short account, written by the court lady Fujiwara no Nagako[2] soon after the death of the Emperor Horikawa in 1107. It consists mainly of recollections of the Emperor, whom she had served (in her own words) for eight years, though by our calculations her service was about five and a half years. The diary is a minor work, but it is given a distinctive flavor by its portrait of an emperor who, though he is hardly mentioned in histories, appears in these pages as an unusually appealing and individual figure. At times, especially when his long illness worsened, Horikawa was capricious and irritable, but he was usually so affable and so artistically gifted as to inspire love among all who served him. The author of *The Sanuki no Suke Diary* believed that it was her duty to preserve the memory of a man whose death she mourned. Probably she had no specific readers in mind when she began to write the diary, but it was definitely intended to be read by other people. It is a gesture of gratitude, rather than a formal tribute, and that no doubt accounts for its poignant charm.

Apart from this diary, Nagako hardly figures in literary history. She was not gifted as a *waka* poet, though one poem was included in an imperial collection. Unlike most Heian diaries, *The Sanuki no Suke Diary* provides little psychological insight into the author.

We do not really learn the nature of her relationship with Horikawa—whether or not they were lovers, for example—and the only emotion that is vividly presented is her grief.

Nagako wrote near the beginning of the diary that she was never far from Horikawa's side during the eight years she served him. We know exactly when Nagako first waited on the Emperor: on New Year's Day of 1102 Nagako, who the previous night had been appointed *naishi no suke* (lady-in-waiting), offered the emperor the traditional spiced wine.[3]

Horikawa was sickly through much of his reign and died in 1107 at the age of twenty-eight. *Gukanshō* (*The Future and the Past*[4]), a history of the time written by the priest Jien in 1219, related how the Emperor Shirakawa, Horikawa's father, was desperately eager to have a son by his consort Kenshi. He asked Raigō (1001–84), a famous priest of the Miidera, the great Tendai Buddhist temple, to pray for an imperial son, promising him in return anything he desired. Raigō's prayers were effective, and the overjoyed Shirakawa asked Raigō what he might give him. The latter asked that an ordination hall for priests be established at the Miidera. Shirakawa was afraid, however, that if he granted this request it would lead to fighting between the monks of the Miidera and those of Mount Hiei, hitherto the only place a monk of the Tendai sect could be ordained. He offered Raigō whatever else he desired. Incensed by Shirakawa's failure to live up to his promise, Raigō left, predicting that he would soon die of disappointment and that the prince who was born in response to his prayers would also die. Raigō refused all nourishment and presently did die, and the prince, as Raigō had predicted, died at the age of three.

Shirakawa turned now to the abbot Ryōshin of the Enryaku-ji on Mount Hiei, and asked him to pray for an imperial prince. Ryōshin was also successful, and the prince born in response to his prayers eventually became the Emperor Horikawa. But Raigō's malice was not exhausted: when Horikawa lay on his deathbed, a malevolent spirit tormenting him identified itself as Raigō.[5]

Modern readers are likely to have trouble in accepting such stories at face value, picturesque as they are. Presumably priests or other learned men of the time, searching for some reason why

Horikawa's brother should have died as an infant and Horikawa while still a young man, hit upon the wrath of Raigō as the cause. In the world depicted in *The Sanuki no Suke Diary* the supernatural was never far from the surface. A famous grafitto discovered on a palace wall in 1102 predicted, "The Buddhist Law will perish in fire, and the Throne will end with a war."[6] These words were discovered in the autumn of the same year that Nagako first began to serve Horikawa, and it was against this ominous background that she related her reminiscences of an emperor whom she remembered not with awe but with affection.

Most of Nagako's anecdotes concerning Horikawa are trivial. One gesture of his lingered so vividly in her memory that she would describe it twice in this short work. During the Emperor's final illness she was obliged to lie beside him, lest he should suddenly need her. She recalled, "On one occasion the Regent approached from behind. I rose, and was about to withdraw, as I felt that it would be ill-mannered and unseemly to remain lying where I was, when the Emperor, realizing that I must be feeling that I should not be seen, said 'Stay where you are. I shall make a screen.' He bent up his knees and hid me behind them. I recalled this considerate action as if it had just happened."[7]

There is something psychologically true about the importance Nagako gave to so minor an incident. We are apt to remember dead friends in terms of similar small gestures that may have been instantly forgotten by the persons who performed them; and when one attempts to convey to someone who never knew the friend what he was like, these gestures are often more effective than abstract descriptions of his character.

The diary has been dismissed by many scholars as being inferior to others of the Heian period, but it is peculiarly affecting to be present and so close when an emperor dies. Small details make a passage like the following memorable: "Nobody slept a wink, but kept watch over the Emperor. He seemed to be in great pain, and rested his foot on me. 'Could anything ever equal this total lack of concern over the probable death, tomorrow or the next day, of somebody of my position? What do you think?' he asked."[8]

During this stage of his illness the Emperor had begun to feel sorry for himself. The people serving him, even the woman who gladly served as his footstool, seemed to be indifferent to his imminent death. He turned his gaze to another lady-in-waiting and rebuked her. "You're slacking, aren't you? Don't you realize that I'm probably going to die today or tomorrow?'"[9] When dawn came and Nagako thought that she might rest for a few moments, the Emperor noticed her pulling an unlined robe over her head and pulled it back. She took this as meaning that she was on no account to sleep, and she got up.[10]

If the Emperor had been portrayed as a tyrant, this gesture would not seem admirable, but we sense that his fear of approaching death, and especially of being left alone, is so extreme that he behaves for a moment not like an emperor but like an ordinary, frightened man.

Nagako recorded details of each day of Horikawa's final illness. At the very end, after a violent spasm of coughing, the Emperor declared, "I am going to die now. May the Ise Shrine help me. I put my faith in the *Lotus Sutra* which tells of the Buddha of impartial benevolence and great wisdom." But these words were followed by his cry, "It's agonizing. I can't bear it. Hold me up."[11]

When Nagako took his hands they were cold to her touch. Soon afterward the lips of the emperor, which with all his remaining strength had been pronouncing the Invocation to Amida Buddha, finally stopped moving.

Nagako was inconsolable after the death of Horikawa. She wrote in her diary, "I must find some way of becoming a nun. But then, I seem to remember that even in old romances, people who capriciously have their heads shaved are criticized by the world in general as being 'superficial.' "[12] In the meantime, messages arrived from the court asking her to be present at the accession ceremony of the new Emperor. This order no doubt originated with the Retired Emperor Shirakawa, who soon afterward directed her to put aside the mourning robes she was still wearing for Horikawa.

Much against her inclinations, she finally agreed and visited the palace once again. The experience of seeing the new Emperor, a boy of four, was almost too much for her. She recorded, "The Emperor was decked out very prettily, but the sight of him seated upon the Imperial Throne was a severe shock to me. A haze swam before my eyes, and, I am ashamed to admit, I felt so distressed that I could not look at him directly."[13]

She could not force herself to feel the appropriate awe and respect for the new Emperor. Some time later she was once again summoned to the palace by Shirakawa. She wrote of this experience:

"When I arose next morning, I found that there had been a heavy snowfall overnight. It was still snowing hard. When I looked over at the Emperor's quarters, I felt that nothing particular had changed. Then just when I felt that everything was conspiring to convince me that the late Emperor was still here, I heard a childish voice singing, 'Fall, fall, powder-snow!'

" 'Who can that be? Whose child is it?' I was wondering. Then it hit me—it must be the Emperor! How absurd! If this is the master whom I am to regard as my lord and protector, I am certainly not filled with a sense of security, I thought desolately."[14]

Eventually the boy Emperor won her affection, not as her lord and protector but as a lovable child. Nagako decided to stay with him, touched to see how eagerly the child ate when she served his meal. She came to realize that the best way of cherishing Horikawa's memory was to watch over his child.

Sometimes she and the Regent reminisced about the past. The Regent recalled how on one occasion Horikawa had asked who was to serve his meal that day. On being informed that it was the Regent himself, the disappointed Emperor had stuck out his tongue, girded up his trousers, and fled. Such memories, trivial in themselves, add movingly human touches to the portrait of Horikawa. Nagako recalled also his love of poetry and especially of music. One day, when the boy Emperor asked her to lift him up so that he could see the pictures on the sliding doors of the imperial dining room, she happened to notice on the wall the tattered remains of musical scores which Horikawa had copied out and pasted there, hoping that if he saw them all the time he would naturally memorize them.[15] Regardless of what festivals she now attended, or how devotedly she served Horikawa's son, the Emperor Toba, her thoughts always reverted to the past. She realized that readers might be baffled by her insistence on old memories, but felt sure that they would understand her attitude if only they had known the man.

Nagako constantly thought about future readers of this diary. She defended herself against possible criticisms of the minute attention she gave to seemingly unimportant memories of the man she worshipped: "This will all seem of no consequence to those who do not cherish the memory of the late Emperor. However, I felt so unworthy of, and so lost without, the tenderness of my late master the Emperor—one might have expected such attentions from a mistress—that I just had to record it so that it would live on in people's minds and never be forgotten."[16]

The death of Horikawa seems to have affected everyone who knew him just as profoundly. *Taiki*, the diary of Fujiwara no Yorinaga (1120–56), records that a member of Horikawa's bodyguard named Sadakuni, distraught over the Emperor's death, decided that he had become a dragon king living in the northern sea. Sadakuni, hoping to rejoin his late master, built a "dragon-head boat" and set sail for the north. He was never seen again.[17] Yearning for Horikawa inspired even such preposterous actions.

Horikawa is remembered today mainly for his interest in poetry. During his reign, on at least twenty-four occasions there were officially sponsored poetry gatherings, notably the one preserved in *Horikawa-in Ontoki Hyakushu Waka* (*One Hundred Waka of the Time of the Cloistered Emperor Horikawa*). This sequence not only set the pattern for future sequences of this length but tested the mettle of court poets by assigning them set, rather than general, topics for poetic composition. Another well-known poetic composition of his reign was *Horikawa-in Ensho Awase* (*Competition of Love Poems of the Time of the Cloistered Emperor Horikawa*), compiled in 1102. This consisted of exchanges of love poems between men and women, many taking the form of poems of courtship by the men and the women's responses, or else poems of resentment by the women followed by the men's responses.

Nagako could not endure the thought that so extraordinary a monarch might be forgotten. Of course, his name and the principal events of his reign would be preserved in official documents, but Nagako believed that it was essential to preserve not only bare facts but the humanity of Horikawa. In the epilogue to her diary she asked, "I pondered on how I would like to show this record to someone who shared my feelings. But is there anyone who does not yearn for the late emperor?"[18] She decided in the end to show the manuscript to a court lady named Hitachi. The last sentence of the diary states, "We talked together until it grew quite dark." No doubt their reading of the diary together was interrupted many times by recollections of the man whom they recalled with such yearning and love.

Chūyūki

Chūyūki,[1] the massive diary kept by Fujiwara no Munetada from 1087 to 1138, covers the reigns of three emperors—Horikawa, Toba, and Sutoku. It is perhaps the most valuable source material for the political and social life of the latter part of the Heian period. This is the kind of diary that is usually described as being "public" rather than "private," in the manner of the diaries kept by the Heian court ladies, but it was by no means public in the modern sense. The diary was in fact a closely guarded secret which Munetada intended to transmit only to his eldest son. In 1120, after he had been keeping the diary for thirty-four years, he made a classification of the contents of the diary for the benefit of this son, Muneyoshi. At the time he gave an explanation of why he had made the classification and also, indirectly, why he had kept the diary: "I have made these extracts so that the Captain of the Fourth Rank [Muneyoshi], if he is to carry out his ambition of serving at the court, will be able to perform his public duties. Perhaps outsiders will express dismay, but how could it fail to be of service to our family in providing against forgetfulness? That is why I have exhausted my old bones in making a classification. This must definitely not be shown to others. In general, no one else should see it. Absolutely not. If one of your sons should be on palace duty he may borrow it from you."[2]

Munetada's purpose in keeping the diary was elsewhere stated in terms of "preserving the succession of the family."[3] A knowledge of what had occurred in the past was of absolute importance in determining whether or not precedents existed for actions contemplated by the court, a matter of the highest significance for a society bound by tradition. Most of the annual rituals and religious observances described by Munetada are of interest today only to specialists, and even specialists surely have trouble keeping their attention focused on minor events recorded with patient exactitude. But Munetada believed that keeping this diary was the most important work of his life.

Such consecration to the keeping of records for the sake of men of future times reminds me of the monk Pimen in the opera *Boris Godunov*, who, after a long life spent as a chronicler of events in Russia, recalls, "One more tale and my chronicle will be ended. I, sinful though I am, will have completed the work commanded to me by the Lord. It has not been in vain that my Master has shown me many things over the long years. Some day, a diligent monk, lighting a lamp as I have, will brush away the dust of centuries that has accumulated on these records and will copy these true tales."

Munetada's devotion to his diary increased with the years. One quiet, rainy day in the 8th month of 1133, Munetada, then seventy-two years old, spent the day making additions to incomplete records. He wrote, "Quiet day at home. Fine rain and misty. Alone, I spread out the table of contents of the family record, and wrote in missing public functions. This is both to disperse uncertainties at the present time and to provide against their being forgotten and abandoned in the future."[4] In the following year he had a dream in which his ancestor Fujiwara no Morosuke showed Munetada his diary. Munetada commented, "Surely it must have been an auspicious dream to have seen the records kept by my ancestor."[5]

The most affecting parts of *Chūyūki* describe the Emperor Horikawa, whom Munetada served for over twenty years. Horikawa selected him to be a chamberlain in 1094, passing over the heads of senior men. This promotion naturally aroused jealousy among other officials, but Horikawa never wavered in his support of

Munetada. After one particularly spectacular promotion Munetada at first refused out of modesty, but Horikawa insisted, calling Munetada "someone who is dear to me."[6] Munetada's gratitude was immense, and it carries over into his descriptions of Horikawa's life and death.

Munetada's account of the death of Horikawa, unlike most other entries in *Chūyūki*, is filled with emotion. The entry for the 19th day of the 7th month of 1107 opens with the statement that the illness of the Emperor had taken a sudden turn for the worse. Yin-yang diviners were summoned, but they declared after performing their divination that the imperial destiny had reached its limits and nothing could now save the Emperor. A thousand Buddhist monks intoned sutras and recited spells in unison, there being a suspicion that evil spirits were at work. Later the Chancellor emerged from the sickroom and whispered to Munetada that the Emperor had lapsed into a profound sleep after invoking by name the Lotus Sutra, and the divinities Fudō, Shakyamuni, and Amida. He was lying facing west, in the direction of Amida's paradise. The Chancellor ordered those in attendance not to attempt to waken him, for fear of evil spirits. Munetada was dazed by the sad news.

At the hour of the sheep (between two and four in the afternoon) it was finally announced that the Emperor had passed away. As the report spread through the palace, people wept and sobbed uncontrollably, all but shocked out of their senses. Members of the court were allowed one last look at the Emperor. Munetada reported that his features were unaltered, and he looked as if he were asleep. Overwhelmed by grief as he was, Munetada could not forget his official responsibilities, and he described how he arranged for the transference of the imperial regalia to the new Emperor. He then gave a short but moving account of Horikawa's life and character.

Munetada related how Horikawa from the age of nine could read such Chinese classics as *The Book of Songs* and *The Book of History*. He was not only an accomplished Confucian scholar; the Buddhist Law was also deeply engraved on his heart. During his reign of twenty-one years he showed himself slow to punish but quick to reward, and everyone in the land, from the princes and ministers of state down to the humblest classes of men and women, was struck by his kindness. The death of the Emperor was for one and all like losing a father or mother. He was well versed in the arts of government, but his skill in wind and stringed instruments was such that not even the masters of antiquity could have put him to shame.[7]

Munetada's language was conventional, and his account of the death of Horikawa is less vivid than Nagako's, perhaps because he was not actually present during the Emperor's last hours, but there can be no doubting the sincerity of his grief. He recorded in *Chūyūki* several dreams about Horikawa. In these dreams the Emperor looked as he had in life, dressed as when he played music at a banquet.[8] One strange dream about Horikawa that Munetada had in 1137, when he was seventy-five, puzzled him so much that he debated its meaning in his diary.[9]

Even seen through the medium of Munetada's sometimes opaque classical Chinese, it is apparent that Munetada, no less than Nagako, was haunted by the memory of the sovereign he had served. *Chūyūki* is seldom discussed as a work of literature. Indeed, Munetada would have been much surprised to think that he had written one. But here and there in this long work, so full of boring information about court functions, we find touches of the qualities that move us in literature. *Chūyūki* and *The Sanuki no Suke Diary* are totally dissimilar in manner and content, but there runs through both a nostalgia for the most memorable person each of their authors had ever known.

Poetry Collections and Poem Tales

The last entries of *Chūyūki* describe events of 1138. During the next half-century many other diaries composed in classical Chinese by members of the court would record their activities. These works are normally not treated in histories of literature, because they are so largely devoted to accounts of day-to-day activities at the court. Even if one can read classical Chinese with confidence, it is difficult to keep one's attention focused on the many arid stretches. But every now and then one encounters passages that are remarkable, either for their content or for the light they shed on the backgrounds of works of literature. An anthology of such excerpts from the "official" diaries would make a welcome addition to existing studies of the Heian diary.

However, not a single diary by a woman survives from the period of over a century between the writing of *The Sanuki no Suke Diary*, about 1109, and the completion of *The Poetic Memoirs of Lady Daibu*, about 1224. This may be merely an accident of what was preserved; it is possible that some, perhaps even many, diaries by women were written only to be lost, but we have no clues to either the authors or the contents. The typical literary products of the court society during this period were the *uta-awase*, or poem competitions on set topics composed by two "teams." They sometimes included prose passages, either in classical Chinese or in Japanese, which are designated as *nikki*, but these "diaries" generally relate the circumstances of the poem competitions in a factual manner reminiscent of the official diaries of the period and are not at all like the famous diaries kept by women of the previous century.

The collected poems (*kashū*) of poets were more likely to resemble real diaries. Extended prose introductions to the poems of the collection (called *kotobagaki*) sometimes contained enough autobiographical information to suggest a diary. *Murasaki Shikibu Shū*, a collection of the poems of Murasaki Shikibu, includes some introductions that go far beyond merely stating the circumstances of composition, and are splendid examples of her prose: "Day was just dawning as I went out on the bridge and leaned on the balustrade, watching the water flow from under the rooms in the back corridor. The sky was no less beautiful than when filled with spring haze or autumn mist. I knocked at the corner shutters of Lady Koshōshō's room. She opened both halves, top and bottom, and came out onto the veranda. As we both sat there looking out over the garden, I wrote . . ."[1]

The Shijōnomiya no Shimotsuke Collection, a selection of poems by a lady with a rather overpowering name, does not compare in the quality of either the poetry or the prose to Murasaki Shikibu's collection, but the *kotobagaki* are unusually long, and the work as a whole provides many charming vignettes of life at the court. Shimotsuke was a lady-in-waiting to the Empress Kanshi from about 1050 to 1068, when Kanshi took Buddhist vows following the death of the Emperor Goreizei. Shimotsuke also "turned her back on the world," and some of the last poems in the collection were written after she became a nun. The work as a whole, both in content and mood, is typified by the first *kotobagaki* and poem, apparently written in 1053: "One spring when the blossoms were even more beautiful than usual, branches of splendidly flowering cherry blossoms were planted along both sides of the staircase of the palace, just at the height of the trees. As some of us were gazing at them from the entrance to Her Majesty's rooms, His Majesty approached. The moon was still bright, and His Majesty proposed that we have a blossom-viewing. Kochūjō, Koshōshō, and others joined his party under the blossoms, along with his regular lady attendants, Shōshō no naiji, Shikibu no myōbu, and the rest. His Majesty asked someone to break off a branch of flowers, then presented it to me with the words, 'How slow you are!' I had no time to put my thoughts in order properly, but hid my embarrassment by the speed with which I composed this poem:

nagaki yo no	Were it not for
tsuki no hikari no	The light of the moon
nakariseba	Through the long night,
kumoi no hana wo	How could we see to pick
ikade aramashi	Blossoms here above the clouds?

"His Majesty, evidently surprised by the quickness of my response, graciously said, 'Most extraordinarily interesting.' He murmured the poem to himself, then said, "I am sure that if I attempted a response it would be so ordinary that people would only laugh at it.' He looked really splendid as he walked about, singing the poem, a delightful sight I shall not soon forget."[2]

The point of Shimotsuke's poem is the play on the word *kumoi*, which means both "above the clouds" and the "imperial palace," the latter because the Emperor and the high nobles were considered to be "above the clouds." There is surely no emotion behind such a poem, which would not have been out of place if it had been composed at the court of Versailles, though mention of the "long night" and the moon is likely to suggest a reference to Buddhist belief.

Even when circumstances would seem to favor more serious poetry, opportunities to make a clever play on words were not often missed. The following excerpt relates an event that occurred after the death of the Emperor, which Shimotsuke chooses not to discuss, and her own retirement into a Buddhist retreat. Tsunenaga asks to borrow a *shū*, or collection of poetry, but her response refers to a different kind of *shū*, a Buddhist term meaning "attachment to the world": "With the change of reign many sad and profoundly moving things occurred, and various people, including myself, considered writing about them, but somehow it seemed it would be better not to write. After I had turned my back on the world, the Major Counselor Tsunenaga asked if he might borrow my copy of *Kingyoku Shū*,[3] and sent this poem:

ima wa to te	I have heard that you
soru to kikishi wo	Have shaved your head; I wonder
hashitaka no	If, like the falcon,
koishiki koto ni	You now flee from the world
shū ya nokoreru	Or have you kept the books you love?

"My reply was:

yo no naka wo	I did indeed plan
soru to suredomo	To renounce the world, but still
hashitaka no	Bait for the falcon
koishiki koto zo	—The things I have loved—
ogie narikeru[4]	Keeps me prisoner yet."

Although *The Shijōnomiya no Shimotsuke Collection* contains autobiographical material, and diligent scholars have managed to assign dates for the poems from the scanty clues within the *kotobagaki*, the collection lacks almost totally the introspective quality of the diaries written by earlier women, and seems less like a diary than a poem-tale (*uta monogatari*) such as *The Tales of Ise*. But it is difficult to draw clear distinctions among *nikki* (diaries), *kashū* (poem collections), and *uta monogatari* (poem-tales); as I have mentioned, the same work may be known by various titles—diary, tale, poetry collection. Whatever name was chosen for a particular mixture of poetry and prose, the mixture itself was typical of Japanese literary expression. A collection of poetry (like Dante's *Vita nuova*) could be rich in autobiographical materials.

The outbreaks of warfare toward the end of the Heian period, especially the war between the Minamoto and the Taira in the 1180s, would bring a new, dramatic element to diaries. It is hard to imagine the men who figure in the diaries of Izumi Shikibu or Murasaki Shikibu going off to die in battle, but in this later period it would be by no means unusual. The few surviving diaries by women written during the years when the authority of the Heian court gave way to the feudal regime of the shoguns in Kamakura were conspicuously colored by the extraordinary changes that occurred in the world around them but, unlike the collection of Shimotsuke's poetry, these later diaries were in the traditions of the women who created this unique genre.

The Poetic Memoirs of Lady Daibu

Kenreimon'in Ukyō Daibu no Shū (*The Poetic Memoirs of Lady Daibu*)[1] is a collection of *waka*, many of them preceded by a *kotobagaki* that explains the circumstances of composition. It is nevertheless properly treated as a diary, if only because the *kotobagaki* are often as long as diary entries and contain much autobiographical material. The work in any case is not a random collection of poems by one poet, arranged in the usual manner by season or topic, but an aesthetically pleasing whole in which the poems are used as a framework for an account of the life of a court lady. The author served at the court from about 1170 until the Heike fled the capital thirteen years later. Her lover, Taira no Sukemori, was the grandson of Kiyomori. Although he was a gentleman of courtly accomplishments, he was also a soldier, and he left the author not for another woman but to fight in a war.

When Sukemori left the capital he declared, "I have renounced all attachments to this world."[2] In the past this probably would have meant that he had decided to become a monk, but the new meaning was that he was sure he would be killed in battle and had prepared himself spiritually. Sukemori in fact leapt into the sea and drowned at Dannoura, along with many other celebrated Taira warriors, as we know from *The Tale of the Heike*.

A new kind of tragic parting that caused women to grieve, not over a man's indifference, but over the likelihood of his death, imparts special intensity to Lady Daibu's diary. The poems that form the core of the work acquire special coloring from the unquestionably tragic character of her grief. Earlier women poets had often expressed their desire to vanish like the dew, and they brooded over falling cherry blossoms as if they signified the end of happiness; Lady Daibu's grief was too intense for such metaphors. When she learned of Sukemori's death she cried out,

kanashi to mo	If only, oh, if only
mata aware to mo	We could use some
yo no tsune ni	Common, ordinary words,
iubeki koto ni	And call this
araba koso arame	Pitiable or sad![3]

This poem, in which Daibu expressed the desire, most unusual for a Japanese poet, to express her grief in the plainest, most ordinary words, is followed by her prose: "In this state I let the days and the nights go by, shutting myself off from the normal life of the world, even while I was still living in it. . . . I was not the only one to have endured such a short-lived and heartbreaking love affair. There were many people, both known and unknown to me, who had lived through the same nightmare in their relationships with the Taira family, but at the time I felt that my experience was utterly without parallel. Natural deaths at their natural hour had brought about many separations in the past and even in my own day, I reflected, but such a bitter parting as mine could never have happened to anyone else."[4]

The shadow of death lies over the second half of the diary. During the first half Lady Daibu had recorded more cheerful experiences. She explained in the brief introduction, "A personal poetry collection is something written by the poet for posterity. This, however, is far from being that sort of thing. I have merely recorded, just as I happened to remember them, my immediate feelings at those times when something moving, sad, or somehow unforgettable occurred; and I intend these memoirs for my eyes alone."[5]

Perhaps Lady Daibu meant these words literally when she wrote them, but surely she hoped, at least unconsciously, that someone else would read about her experiences. She suggests this in the poem that follows:

ware narade	If not myself,
tare ka aware to	Who, then, will be moved by pity
mizuguki no	As they gaze upon my words,
ato moshi sue no	Should they be handed down
yo ni tsutawaraba	To later days?[6]

The poem indicates that Lady Daibu was aware, perhaps even desired, that future readers would share her expressions of poignancy over the crumbling of a dynasty.

The Poetic Memoirs, however, opens in quite a different mood: "While His Majesty the Retired Emperor Takakura was still on the throne—it would perhaps have been the fourth year of Jōan [1174]—he visited the apartments of the Empress on the first day of the new year. The two of them were, of course, always imposing, but on that day he in his normal attire and she in full court dress seemed to me quite dazzling, and as I watched from a passageway I felt in my heart":

kumo no ue ni	Here above the clouds,
kakaru tsukihi no	I gaze upon the brilliance
hikari miru	Of such a sun and such a moon,
mi no chigiri sae	And I can only feel
ureshi to zo omou	How blissful is this fate of mine.[7]

One seldom finds in the diaries kept by the Heian court ladies such an unalloyed expression of joy. But behind these words, despite their celebratory mood, one senses tragic overtones. The passage recalls to me a scene in the Danish film *Day of Wrath*. A young man and a young woman are running in a wood. Sunlight filters through the leaves, and the radiant joy on their faces presents a convincing impression of untroubled young love. But the woman is the second wife of the young man's father, and their relationship, even as they run in the sunlight, is doomed. The background music, in contrast to the woodland scene, is the ominous hymn *Dies Irae* ("The Day of Wrath"). Our eyes and ears are presented with contradictory impressions, but we know instinctively that only our ears are to be trusted. In Lady Daibu's diary, despite her description of the dazzling beauty of the Emperor and Empress, we know something that renders the evidence before our eyes untrustworthy. The Empress is Kenreimon'in, who would throw herself into the sea at Dannoura when the Taira family, to which she belonged, was destroyed, and who, after being rescued from the sea against her will, ended her days as a nun in the lonely convent of Jakkō-in.

The author, of course, knew these facts when she wrote her diary, long after the events described. She herself served Kenreimon'in, and the name by which she is known was derived from her office in the Empress's service. The opening of the diary describes Kenreimon'in while she was still happy, but by the time Lady Daibu wrote this passage she had already seen Kenreimon'in in her nun's hermitage.

Lady Daibu did not allow this foreknowledge to affect the words preceding the happy poem at the head of the work. The tone is festive, and the emphasis is on the beauty of the court—the costumes, the music, the solemnity of the rituals. The poetry of the diary is conventional, the kind of poems a young woman might write before she had been touched by poignant emotions:

nodoka naru	The joyfulness
haru ni au yo no	Of this illustrious reign,
ureshisa wa	Which welcomes such a tranquil spring,
take no naka naru	Echoes even in the warbler's song
koe no iro ni mo	Within the bamboo groves.[8]

A little later Lady Daibu writes: "I used to be amused by the various love affairs I saw around me or heard about, though I myself had no thought of following everybody else in such behavior. But among the many men who used to mingle with us at all times of the day and night, just like other ladies-in-waiting, there was one in particular who made approaches to me, though after seeing and hearing of other people's unhappy love affairs I felt I ought not to let anything of the sort happen to me. Destiny, however, is not to be avoided, and in spite of my resolve, I also came to know love's miseries."[9] From this point on, the diary acquires both sadness and beauty.

Lady Daibu's first affair was with Taira no Sukemori (1161?–1185), a married man who was probably a few years younger than she. Her poems change in character immediately after her first mention of the affair, as this poem will suggest:

yūhi utsuru	Caught in the last rays
kozue no iro no	Of the setting sun, the treetops
shigururu ni	Darken in the chilling rain:
kokoro mo yagate	So too my heart is dimmed
kakikurasu kana	And clouded over in its misery.[10]

She later recalled, "Now, when I look back on it, the affair was not totally unhappy, but right at the time, when I was in the middle of it, I felt mortified and resentful, and was frequently depressed."[11]

Lady Daibu nowhere named her lover, but undoubtedly she assumed that people at the court would have no trouble in identifying him. She supplied some unmistakable clues: "While the man who was causing so much heartache was still a courtier of middle rank, he went with his father, the Grand Minister, on a pilgrimage to Sumiyoshi Shrine."[12] She obviously fell deeply in love with Sukemori. She recalled: "One morning at my own home, as the snow lay thick, I was looking out at the unkempt garden and distractedly murmuring the lines 'The person who will come today,' when [Sukemori] appeared, unannounced, through the garden gate. . . . He looked so much smarter than I did, so splendid, that I can never forget it. Though the years and months have gone by, it seems so recent in my heart that the pain still haunts me."[13] The words "The person who will come today" were an allusion to the poem in the collection *Shūishū* by Taira no Kanemori:

yamazato wa	In this mountain village
yuki furitsumite	Snow lies thickly piled,
michi mo nashi	And the path is covered:

kyō kon hito wo How lovingly I shall look
aware to wa min On the person who will come
today.[14]

Lady Daibu, like many other women diarists, worried lest the affair become known to the court ladies with whom she associated or, worse, to men of the court. But, even while she was worrying, she was approached by another man and seems to have yielded to him. The man was Fujiwara no Takanobu (1142–1205), a poet and painter who is known today mainly for his remarkable portraits of statesmen of the time. It was only in 1934, when some of Lady Daibu's poems were discovered in the collected edition of Takanobu's poetry, that it first became apparent that the unidentified lover must be Takanobu. She wrote, "Though it began as a lighthearted affair, his attentions became very serious. My only thought, however, was that it should never develop into the usual kind of relationship, and I remained firm."[15] But apparently she accepted him in the end. At first she seems to have been happy with this new lover, but eventually the affair lost its charm, and she wrote, "I felt our relationship was no longer at all what it had been."[16]

Lady Daibu left service in the palace for unstated reasons, much against her own inclinations. Toward the end of the first half of her diary she wrote, "When I heard that the Retired Emperor Takakura had passed away, I remembered countless things from the time when I had been so used to seeing him; and though his death was a matter in which I could not be directly involved, I was immeasurably affected by it."[17] Takakura had been like the sun, his consort Kenreimon'in like the moon; but the world was about to be plunged into the darkness of civil war.

The second half of *The Poetic Memoirs* opens in a totally dissimilar mood to the first: "Such was the upheaval in our world at the time of Juei and Genryaku [1182–85] that whatever I may call it—dream, illusion, tragedy—no words can possibly describe it. It was so confused that I cannot even say exactly what occurred, and in fact right up till now I have repressed all thought of it. What can I say, what am I to feel about that autumn when I heard that those whom I knew were soon to be leaving the capital? No words, no emotions can do it justice. None of us had known when it might happen, and faced with the actual event, we were all stunned, those of us who saw it with our own eyes and those who heard about it from afar. We could only feel that it was just some indescribable dream."[18]

Most of the court ladies who kept diaries maintained an almost ostentatious indifference to political events or, if they included any, felt obliged to apologize for having allowed such materials to intrude into a personal record. But the shock of the events just when Lady Daibu was writing these words was too great for her to pass over it in silence, and too harsh for her to communicate in a poem about the scattering of the cherry blossoms. She had served the Taira family without question, and her devotion to Kiyomori's daughter Kenreimon'in was so profound that (as she records in an epilogue to her diary), when the great scholar of literature Fujiwara Teika asked her what name she would like to have signed to those poems of hers he had chosen for an anthology he was compiling, she replied, "Just as in the old days," meaning the name Kenreimon'in Ukyō no Daibu, rather than the title she had been granted under the new regime.

The abandonment of the capital by the Taira adherents brought Lady Daibu acute personal grief. Her lover, Sukemori, had to leave with the others for the west. He was sure that he would not return alive, and he told her, "In all that concerns this world I have come to think of myself as one already dead."[19] She herself considered taking a nun's vows, or even committing suicide, but she decided against such precipitate actions: "Our lives, however, must go on for their allotted span; we cannot end them as we wish; and even my desire to enter holy orders was frustrated, since I could not flee the house myself."[20]

The next spring she heard terrible reports after the battle of Ichinotani that "great numbers of my friends had been killed, and that their heads were being paraded through the streets of the capital."[21] Taira no Shigemori, the son of Kiyomori, earlier figured in the diary as an amusing man who entertained the ladies of the palace with funny or frightening stories;[22] but now he was taken prisoner at Ichinotani and brought back to the capital. After being paraded through the streets, he was turned over to the Nara monks for execution, his punishment for having led the forces that burned the Tōdai-ji. But it was not in such terms that Lady Daibu remembered him; she wrote that "among all those I had known he had been especially close to me. He would say such amusing things, and even in the most trivial matters he used to be so considerate towards other people."[23]

When she learned that Taira no Koremori had drowned himself at Kumano she wrote, "Whenever I meet anyone these days, I can only think what truly superior figures the Taira were."[24] She remembered that when Koremori danced "The Blue Waves of the Sea," his beauty had reminded people of the Shining Prince Genji himself. Finally, in the spring of 1185, she learned that Sukemori was dead. Her mind turned to religion, but she could find no comfort. Instead, she wondered, "What had I done to deserve this? I began to resent even the gods and buddhas."[25]

Lady Daibu was persuaded by a friend to return to the court, though it was now dominated by the Minamoto family, who had defeated and killed the Taira men she loved. No doubt the routine of daily activities helped to divert her mind from thoughts of Sukemori, but he continued to appear in her dreams. She could not keep from contrasting unfavorably the Minamoto nobles who now lorded it over the court and the Taira nobles she had known: "Those whom I had known in the old days as courtiers of no great eminence were now in the highest ranks, and I could not help imagining how things might have been if Sukemori had only lived. I now felt even more heartbroken and miserable than before I had come to court."[26]

In the brief conclusion to the diary Lady Daibu insists, as in the introduction, that what she wrote was intended for her eyes alone. But she revealed, "Once in a while people would ask me whether I had any such writings, but what I had written was so much my own personal thoughts that I felt embarrassed, and I would copy out just a little to show them."[27] No doubt that is how the diary came to attract the attention of Teika, who preserved it for readers of the future.

Even the minor figures in the diary share the added dimension of what we know about them from history or from literary works based on the warfare of the late twelfth century. The reader familiar with the Nō play *Tsunemasa*, and knowing how the character met his tragic end, will surely feel a pang as he reads the charming description of how Tsunemasa played his lute one bright moonlit night when the cherry trees were in full bloom. Characters who appear in the Nō plays as ghosts reenacting their last moments are here living presences.

In much the same way, the mention that the Empress had safely given birth to a child is far more than the mere chronicling of an imperial birth; readers are likely to know from their readings in other books that this baby was the future Emperor Antoku, who would perish in the sea after the battle at Dannoura.

The Poetic Memoirs of Lady Daibu does not enjoy the popularity of the earlier diaries by court ladies, but it is an unforgettable document. Although its poetry is unremarkable, there are prose passages of a beauty second to none in the diaries, as in this description of how the author woke up one night: "I pushed the quilt off and looked up into the sky. It was unusually clear and had turned a lighter blue, against which large stars appeared with unusual brilliance in one unbroken expanse. The sight was extraordinarily beautiful. It looked just as if pieces of gold and silver leaf had been scattered on paper of pale indigo. I felt as though I were seeing such a sky for the first time that night. I had often before looked at starlit skies so bright that the moon might almost have been shining. But perhaps because of the time and place, that night made a particularly vivid impression on me, and I could only remain there sunk in thought":

tsuki wo koso	The moon
nagamenareshika	I have often gazed upon,
hoshi no yo no	But the stirring beauty
fukaki aware wo	Of a night of stars
koyoi shirinuru	I have understood this night.[28]

Diaries of the Kamakura Period

Chronicle of the Bright Moon

Meigetsuki (*Chronicle of the Bright Moon*) is the diary of Fujiwara Teika (1162–1241), a man equally celebrated as poet, critic, and editor. His diary is written in classical Chinese, and is therefore much more difficult for most Japanese to understand than his poetry. However, even if it had been written in Japanese, the contents would still be largely of historical rather than literary interest, and the work is known today mainly for a few often quoted passages.

The most celebrated passage in *Chronicle of the Bright Moon* is dated the 9th month of the 4th year of the Jishō era (1180), when Teika was eighteen: "Reports of disturbances and punitive expeditions fill one's ears, but I pay them no attention. The red banners and the expeditions against the traitors are no concern of mine."[1] This is generally taken as a statement of Teika's attitude with respect to the world around him: he is so immersed in his poetry that he has no time or inclination to pay attention to the fracas of war. The "red banners" are usually interpreted as standing for the Taira clan, whose color was red, or else as bloodstained emblems of war. But the word Teika used, *kōki*, denoted not a battle flag but an imperial standard, and, far from being bloodstained, it was embroidered with felicitous designs of phoenixes and dragons. The words "red banners" and "expeditions against the traitors" probably referred to two different factions—that of the Emperor and that of the Shogun, who was known as *seii taishōgun*, or "great general subduing the barbarians," a title similar to Teika's phrase "expeditions against the traitors." Teika was declaring that he sided with neither faction.

Professor Tsuji Hikosaburō, the author of an important study of *Chronicle of the Bright Moon*, demonstrated that Teika wrote this passage (and the rest of the entries for 1180 and 1181) many years later, when he was about seventy. The feelings expressed in this passage were therefore not those of a young man who disdained to become involved with the vulgar passions of the world but of an old man who reached this conclusion in looking back on his life.

There is another complication. The line "The red banners and the expeditions against the traitors are no concern of mine" was undoubtedly derived from a line of a poem by Po Chü-i, "The red banners and the crushing of the bandits are no concern of mine." The poem, after relating how the poet has been neglected by the court and how remote he is from the seat of power, ends with an account of how he spent the night playing Go, betting with cups of saké as the penalty for the loser, until the dawn. Po Chü-i was not so much rejecting involvement in worldly concerns as expressing resignation over having been neglected; he makes the best of the neglect by indulging in quiet pleasures. Perhaps Teika also found consolation for the long years while court promotion was denied him by borrowing from Po Chü-i's poem an attitude that was essentially foreign to his nature—detachment from worldly ambitions.

This rather extreme example may suggest the difficulty of reading *Chronicle of the Bright Moon* but also its richness. It covers a long and—for a courtier—unusually eventful life, a period of fifty-six years if we accept Teika's dating. Even if we disregard the entries for 1180 and 1181, the diary extends over a period of forty-seven years, from 1188 to 1235. Sections of the diary have been lost, but what remains is a priceless record of the life of the leading literary figure of the age. The diary is not, however, poetic in its expression. The following, dated 1188, is about as poetic as this diary ever becomes:

"A cloudy day. As it grew dark it began to rain. A lucky day was ending pointlessly. It seemed a pity to waste the day, so at dusk I went to the Impumon'in and had a pleasant chat with Daibu.[2] Before long it was ten o'clock. There was no one around, and the place was utterly still. Just when I was thinking of leaving, there was a sudden flash of torches before the gate. Somebody was arriving, much to the surprise of people inside and outside the house. The Acting Middle Captain[3] appeared. He explained, 'I was already about to go to bed when some leaves suddenly fell from a tree in my garden, and I heard the storm wind. I couldn't manage to get to sleep, so I rushed outside, got on a horse and came here. I didn't expect anyone else to be here. When I saw your carriage I was moved to tears.' The lady was delighted by his words. Lanterns were lit, and *renga*, *waka*, and other poetry composed. The Shin Chūnagon Owari[4] and others joined in, and there were all kinds of humorous poems, too. After the cocks had crowed a couple of times, the rain gradually grew more intense. I thought that it would be awkward if I were to travel a great distance in broad daylight, so I hurried outside. But still I lingered, and composed a few lines on the theme of 'drops of water on the empty stairs.' I borrowed a hat and left. While I was on my way back home, the dawn gradually broke."[5]

If this passage had been written in flowing Japanese instead of the clipped phrases of classical Chinese, it surely would be as memorable as most descriptive passages in Heian diaries, but although Teika wrote Chinese skillfully, he never achieved the ease of expression that he commanded when writing his own language.

As one might expect of the diary of a great poet, Teika's contains innumerable references to the composition of poetry. His first recognition as a poet came in 1200. He had encountered almost insuperable obstacles in gaining admittance to the circle of poets who were privileged to appear before the Cloistered Emperor Gotoba, himself a distinguished *waka* poet. Minamoto Michichika, the father-in-law of Gotoba, seemed absolutely determined to keep Teika from participating in an announced poetry competition. When Gotoba, moved by a plea from Teika's father, Shunzei, agreed to include Teika among the poets who were invited to submit a hundred poems of their composition, Michichika succeeded in changing the invitation by restricting participation to "senior poets" (*rōsha*). Teika was furious. He was only thirty-eight years old, by no means a senior poet. He wrote on the 18th day of the 7th month, "I have never heard, in all the history of poetry, of making old age a factor when determining skill in *waka*. This was surely arranged by somebody who had been bribed by Suetsune[6] to drop me."[7]

Teika's bitterness increased day by day. On the 26th day of the 7th month he wrote, as if no longer caring about whether or not he participated, "I gather that it was probably not the Emperor who decided on the rules for the hundred-poem competition. It was due entirely to the machinations of Michichika. One feels like flicking him away in disgust."[8] But, as the result of a personal letter from Shunzei, Gotoba once more overruled Michichika, and commanded that Teika be included among the participants. Teika expressed his joy in these terms: "I was delighted to learn this time that I am to be included. Now there is nothing to hesitate about, but it was all the doing of that evil man. In any case, the situation is different now. I have already had the wish of two lifetimes granted."[9]

Teika set about preparing his hundred poems. Ten days later he noted in *Chronicle of the Bright Moon*, "Having great trouble with the poems. I haven't left the house."[10] On the 25th he finally completed the hundred poems and submitted them. On the following day Gotoba sent word that Teika would henceforth be allowed to enter his presence, a privilege he had been denied ever since Gotoba abdicated. Teika was overjoyed, though he professed in his diary that the honor had not been of his seeking. "This development was quite unexpected. I had never sought it. I was astonished. . . . It was not even my aspiration. To be commanded to compose and present a hundred poems on this occasion was an act of deep insight that redounds to the glory of the art of poetry. It will become a source of inspiration for future generations. It inspires me with boundless self-confidence. The revival of the art of poetry is already apparent from this gesture."[11]

The hundred poems submitted by Teika contain some of his

finest work. He does not quote these poems in *Chronicle of the Bright Moon*, but they include such splendid *waka* as:

koma tomete	I stop my horse
sode uchiharau	And brush off my sleeves;
kage mo nashi	No shelter here
Sano no watari no	This evening of snow
yuki no yūgure	At the crossing of Sano.

Many commentators have pointed out that the great collection of *waka* compiled in response to an order issued by the Emperor Gotoba in 1201, *Shin Kokinshū*, had its genesis in the sets of a hundred poems composed by Teika and others. It is curious that so much of our knowledge of the background of this quintessentially Japanese collection of poetry is derived from a diary written in classical Chinese.

Teika considerably enhanced his position at the court by winning the respect of Gotoba with his poetry, but relations between the two men eventually deteriorated as Teika became increasingly aware of his own importance in the world of poetry. In the 6th month of 1207 he was commanded by Gotoba to compose *waka* that were to be inscribed on screens (*tsuitate*) at the Saishō Shitennō Temple. Forty-six of these screens, decorated with paintings of various celebrated landscapes of Japan, were to be graced with *waka* composed by the leading poets, including Teika. Teika seems to have been annoyed at having been given very short notice. The entry in *Chronicle of the Bright Moon* continues, "I was so troubled mentally and spiritually that I collapsed. I pondered over the art of the *waka*. . . . Kengozen came to see me. I told her about the poems for the screens. Now that, in my old age, I have been deprived of parental guidance and have lost my father, there is no one else to whom I can show my poems."[12] Teika was expressing his loneliness at being deprived of the guidance of his father, the great poet Shunzei, who was the only person with whom he could really discuss *waka* composition. Obviously, he did not consider the other poets of the day (including Gotoba) to be worthy partners in a discussion of poetry. His sister Kengozen, though not an important poet, seems to have been the best substitute for Shunzei he could find.

Two days later Teika presented the required poems. The Emperor Gotoba praised them, but later rejected one:

aki to dani	Its color has changed
fukiaenu kaze ni	Though the winds of autumn
iro kawaru	Have yet to blow:
Ikuta no mori no	The dew-laden undergrowth
tsuyu no shitagusa[13]	Of the Wood of Ikuta.

Years later, while in exile, Gotoba explained why he had rejected this poem. He admired the diction and Teika's unique charm in the form, but insisted that this *waka* would make a poor model for inexperienced poets to imitate because it lacked a firm structure.[14] Gotoba admitted that Teika's poem was superior to the one by the priest Jien that was selected to be inscribed on the painting of the Wood of Ikuta, a place celebrated for its autumn colors, but he recalled with evident distaste that when Teika learned his poem had been rejected he had gone about mocking the Cloistered Emperor and speaking ill of him. "He did not realize that he was exposing his own willfulness."[15]

On the 13th day of the 2nd month of 1220 there was a poem competition (*uta-awase*) held in the palace, and Teika was asked to participate. He declined, because it was the anniversary of his mother's death. He was repeatedly asked to report to the palace, regardless of his mourning, and he finally yielded, bringing with him two *waka* on the assigned topics, including the following, "Willows in the Fields":

michinobe no	Under the willows
nohara no yanagi	In the fields by the roadside
shitamoenu	The young sprouts burgeon
aware nageki no	In competition as to which,
keburikurabe[16]	Alas, has most to bewail.

The point of the poem lies in the double meanings: usually, *keburikurabe*, literally "a comparison of smoke," was used in reference to "the flames of love," and meant which of two lovers had the deeper affection; but here the "flames" are the fresh sprouts of willow rising from the ground. This should have been auspicious, but *aware nageki* ("alas, the griefs") imparts a tragic tone. Gotoba was enraged by the last two lines, interpreting them as meaning that Teika was not only angry at having been called away from a service for his mother but resentful at having been denied an expected promotion. (These were the two "griefs" competing within Teika's breast.) Gotoba accordingly forbade Teika to appear at court in the future.

Teika's *waka* was the last straw in his deteriorating relationship with Gotoba. This rebuff would surely have ended his career as a court poet but for an unexpected event, the Jōkyū Rebellion of 1221, in which Gotoba participated. After the defeat of Gotoba's forces and his exile to the lonely Oki islands, Teika's position—social and economic as well as artistic—markedly improved. When the extant text of *Chronicle of the Bright Moon* resumes in 1225, after a break of six years, Teika was again in the imperial favor, but under a different emperor. He wrote on New Year's Day, "This year, from the very beginning, we will change the rule of the ignorant monarchs and return to the court of the Sage Kings."[17]

Teika's expectation that 1225 would mark a return to the glorious days of the legendary Chinese emperors Yao and Shun was not fulfilled by what actually happened. An epidemic broke out, and by the end of that year the streets were filled with corpses. The next year was marked by a severe drought and by a plague of locusts that occurred at the end of the year rather than in the summer. In 1227 typhoons, the flooding of the Kamo River, and various other disasters brought starvation and death. But these misfortunes were dwarfed by the events of 1230. That summer snow fell in the provinces of Mino, Musashi, and Shinano. By the 7th month, normally the hottest month of the year, most of the country was suffering from the cold. Teika learned in the 9th month that there would be no harvest at all in provinces along the Sea of Japan coast because of the cold.[18] Every day brought reports of new disasters. Even in areas that had escaped the cold and where plentiful harvests had been anticipated, endless rain kept the crops from ripening. The sufferings of the people were extreme. Teika heard reports of disorders even in the great monasteries.[19]

During this period Teika was unwell most of the time, and his diary contains numerous references to his illnesses. Referring to himself, perhaps ironically, as a "poor man" (*hinsha*), he wrote, "The poor man has no way to buy another life, and his own life is nothing he has any reason to regret losing."[20] He survived his illnesses, but even he experienced hunger. On the 13th day of the 10th month Teika recorded in his diary, "Today I had my servants dig up the garden (the north one), and plant wheat there. Even if we only grow a little, it will sustain our hunger in a bad year. Don't make fun of me! What other stratagem does a poor old man have?"[21] Teika must have been terribly pained to destroy his beloved garden in the hopes of raising a small amount of wheat, but at least he was spared the worst of the famine that afflicted the country.

The famine continued into the next year with even more deadly effects. Accounts written at the time describe the streets of the capital as being filled with corpses, and the bodies of people who had starved floated in the Kamo River. The diary entry for the 2nd day of the 7th month of 1231 states, "Starving people collapse, and their dead bodies fill the streets. Every day the numbers increase. . . . The stench has gradually reached my house. Day and night alike, people go by carrying the dead in their arms, too numerous to count."[22] Even persons in Teika's employ, including his aged carriage attendant, died of exhaustion induced by the famine.

Such passages reveal how much more can be found in *Chronicle of the Bright Moon* than accounts of rivalries among court poets. Unlike the diaries kept by women of the time, however, it contains long, arid stretches. It takes some determination to read more than a few pages at a time, but the effort will be amply rewarded by the unique insights it provides into the life of the court in a time of unusual difficulties.

The Diary of Minamoto Ienaga

The Diary of Minamoto Ienaga is a literary curiosity. Unlike most diaries by Heian courtiers, it was written in Japanese, rather than in Chinese, and unlike the diaries in Japanese by other men of the period, the diary does not describe the author's travels. As I read this diary I recalled the passage in *The Tosa Diary* in which the author, Ki no Tsurayuki, stated that he was a woman. *The Diary of Minamoto Ienaga* at times suggests that it might have been written by a woman rather than a man. It is true that the descriptions of scenes in and around the palace give the impression that the author was familiar with court routine, but otherwise the writing is poetic rather than factual, though occasionally some event is reported in a manner that reveals an interest in the intrigues of contending factions at the court.

The diary covers the decade from 1197 to 1207, from shortly before the abdication of the Emperor Gotoba to about the time when he built the magnificent Saishō Shitennō Temple. The same period is covered by *Chronicle of the Bright Moon*, and it is therefore possible to supplement Ienaga's diary with Teika's fuller account. Sometimes the two diaries are so similar that one is tempted to think, unlikely as it is, that the men read each other's diaries; in any case, Ienaga's diary makes more pleasurable reading than Teika's. Ienaga obviously wrote with literary intent, giving his work unity by focusing his attention on Gotoba's life after his abdication. Ienaga derived immense satisfaction from his close association with the Retired Emperor. Although he was of relatively humble rank, he had been chosen to accompany with his flute Gotoba's *biwa* (a kind of lute). He noted that Gotoba invariably chose to play unusual and difficult pieces but never made a mistake. He modestly avowed that his accompaniment was "stumbling," but Gotoba overlooked his lapses. Gotoba's amiable condescension inspired Ienaga to write a diary in the form of a panegyric of this not uniformly admired emperor.

Ienaga nowhere stated why he wrote the diary. It is not a record of daily happenings in the manner of *Chronicle of the Bright Moon*, probably because it was written years after the events described. It contains little of a personal nature, such as mentions of illness, family matters, or private opinions. The main subject is the compilation of the *Shin Kokinshū*, the great anthology of *waka* poetry assembled at Gotoba's command, but Ienaga was really interested only in Gotoba's part in the editing. He paid tribute to Gotoba's high standards and to his insistence on including poems without regard to the ranks of the authors.[1] Moreover, he informs us, Gotoba did not reject poems simply because they were marred by petty faults, as was true of the compilers of earlier imperially sponsored collections, but he overlooked technical flaws if the poems were otherwise of surpassing quality.[2] After the two thousand poems had been chosen, Gotoba read them again and again until he had memorized them all. So absorbed was he with the anthology that he begrudged time for unimportant matters of state.[3]

Ienaga emphasized that not only was Gotoba a superb poet in his own right but he encouraged other poets, especially young ones, out of eagerness to maintain the art of poetry.[4] He was upset by the scarcity of women poets in this anthology, recalling the traditions of the past, when women had played an important part in the composition of *waka* poetry.[5] Ienaga claimed that the *waka*, under Gotoba's guidance, reached heights it had never attained before. He did not hesitate to rank Gotoba higher even than the emperors of the "golden age" of the Heian court in the tenth century, though it was normal in Japan to consider the present to be inferior to the past.

If this diary had been written after the death of the Emperor it celebrated, there would be no reason to question the author's motives, but it is quite possible that Ienaga showed the diary to Gotoba for his approbation. His attitude verges on the sycophantic. He praised Gotoba's extraordinary gifts in every art, especially that of *waka* poetry: "Some people may think I exaggerate, but many of his poems are in circulation, and their quality can be verified."[6] Gotoba was praised also as an incomparable musician, a master of stringed instruments and woodwinds alike. He delighted in the pleasures of the seasons, including hunting, though he never killed a single animal.[7] Twelve priests had been in constant attendance ever since he was a child, and they delivered Buddhist sermons to him regularly. If Gotoba had any faults (such as those *Chronicle of the Bright Moon* indicates), Ienaga chose not to mention them.

Despite the flattery directed at Gotoba, an unattractive feature of the diary, there are many passages of charm. The description of the daily routine at the palace with which the diary opens is particularly striking, because the details are more vivid than in other diaries of the period. Ienaga noticed the crooked cap of the man who did the morning sweeping, the aimless wandering of a flunky in a courtyard, the pompous airs of a minor official.[8] He related how impressed he was with the dignified manner in which the Emperor's meals were served, though he failed to mention the nature of the food, as if this were a subject unworthy of attention. (How greatly the Japanese differ in this respect from Chinese or Europeans!)

The section describing the abdication of Gotoba is also affecting because of the details. Gotoba had been planning to take this step for some time, as Ienaga had surmised from the lavishness with which the palace dances were staged in the previous year, seemingly a final gesture of magnificence. But when the moment came for Gotoba to surrender the sacred sword and mirror, two of the three imperial regalia, "he unexpectedly burst into uncontrollable tears."[9] The sword and mirror were to be delivered to the new Emperor in the palace, but on the way the party bearing these treasures encountered an unruly group of men and a quarrel broke out. The imperial carriage was smashed, and blood spilled over the imperial seal. The incident is also reported in *Chronicle of the*

Bright Moon, but that diary fails to give the more "human" details. Ienaga is at his best as he tells how Gotoba looked after the abdication, when he put on ordinary clothes—in place of the imperial robes—for the first time. He made an awkward figure in this unfamiliar attire: "This evening was also the first time that he wore an *ebōshi* [a ceremonial cap]. He got it to stay somehow on his head, but he laughed when he saw how unsteady it looked."[10] Such moments come alive in a way that does credit to Ienaga's skill as a writer.

Ienaga devoted considerable attention in the diary to poets of his day. After Gotoba, he admired most Fujiwara Shunzei, the father of Teika. His account of the celebration of Shunzei's ninetieth birthday is more effective than those found in other diaries, no doubt because of the personal note in his description of the old man: "The lay priest [Shunzei] entered the imperial presence after a short wait. He was supported by the newly appointed Councilor of the Third Rank[11] and by Teika. He was indescribably stooped with age and so frail he was painful to look at. I felt both moved and awed that he had prolonged his life for such a long time in anticipation of this day. He was unable to mount the dais, but prostrated himself instead. His two sons helped him to his feet."[12] This is a moment of truth.

Ienaga's description of the famous priest and poet Kamo no Chōmei is also affecting. Chōmei was so thin and debilitated that Ienaga at first did not even recognize him. Obviously he had suffered much, especially because of his frustration at having failed to become the Chief Priest at the Kamo Shrine. To the end Chōmei was unable to give up poetry, though he had come to believe that it was an impediment to salvation.[13] Such passages give life to Ienaga's diary and are its claim on the attention of readers today.

The Visit of the Emperor Takakura to Itsukushima

In the spring of 1180 the Emperor Takakura abdicated in favor of his small son, Antoku. Shortly before he made this painful decision, he resolved to make a pilgrimage to Itsukushima. This shrine, on the island of Miyajima in the Inland Sea, was sacred to the Taira family especially, and it may have been under pressure from Kiyomori, the head of the Taira clan until his death in 1181, that Takakura undertook the journey, but the fact that his mother was a Taira may also have influenced him. He was accompanied by various courtiers, including Minamoto Michichika, the enemy of Fujiwara Teika, and an adviser of Gotoba who consistently gave him bad advice. Michichika wrote the official account of Takakura's journey, *Takakura-in Itsukushima Gokō Ki* (*The Visit of the Emperor Takakura to Itsukushima*), at the very end of the Heian period, but it is often treated as the first of the many travel accounts of the Japanese medieval period.

Although a retired emperor customarily visited the Kamo or Iwashimizu shrines, both near the capital, after his abdication, it was unprecedented for a pilgrimage to be made to so distant a place. However, the diary comments enigmatically, "None spoke his mind, since the way ahead was rough as the waves and as unabating as the wind."[1] Reference is apparently being made (in this poetic manner) to the events leading up to the enforced seclusion of the Cloistered Emperor Goshirakawa, and to the fear of Kiyomori, which kept people from voicing opposition to his plan for an imperial visit to Itsukushima.

At the time Kiyomori was residing in Fukuhara, the new capital he had built on the coast, near the modern city of Kōbe. We know about Fukuhara from the description of Kamo no Chōmei in *An Account of My Hut*, written in 1212. Chōmei was appalled, first of all, by Kiyomori's decision to move the capital from Kyōto, its site for almost four hundred years. The sight of the houses of Kyōto being dismantled and sent down the river to the coast was heartrending, and the desolate appearance of the new capital, with its hastily erected houses and rustic-looking "palace," convinced Chōmei that this was one more sign of the undependability of the world. Michichika painted quite a different picture. He related how Takakura was brought to Fukuhara aboard a "Chinese boat" sent by Kiyomori. He commented, "It was truly an astonishing ship, exactly like those one sees in Chinese paintings, and there were even a few Chinese sailors to go with it. It did seem improper that they should have been allowed to approach the Retired Emperor indiscriminately, this in spite of a previous emperor's exhortation against foreigners coming into the imperial presence except on special occasions."[2] When Takakura reached the temporary palace in Fukuhara that Kiyomori had built for him, he could scarcely believe his eyes. "Words cannot adequately describe the magnificence of the construction on which Kiyomori had lavished every attention. Imagine how one who commands the resources of the entire world can have a palace decorated! . . . The garden and trees were so beautifully arranged that one would have wished to capture the scene in a painting."[3]

The reader is likely to suspect the worst of Michichika and to doubt the truthfulness of his description of the palace in Fukuhara. He may well have been writing in these terms in order to flatter Kiyomori. But even Michichika could not completely conceal the tension of the journey. The night of the arrival in Fukuhara, when the former Emperor retired to his quarters, "he confided in me that he felt no attraction to such luxuries."[4] Even after Takakura had seen the island of Miyajima, which impressed Michichika as being like "an abode of the immortals,"[5] he still "had good reason not to be able to enjoy himself. Nothing could distract him. We felt this was understandable."[6] The final sentence of the diary, written after Takakura had returned to the capital, stated, "The news spread that the Retired Emperor had suffered an alarming loss of weight, and that doctors had prescribed moxa treatment."[7]

The account of the journey to Takakura seems to have set a pattern for the travel diaries of the Middle Ages. Few of these diaries are of major literary importance, and even when the descriptions of famous places have charm, the charm is apt to be conventional. Cherry blossoms and crimson autumn leaves invariably excited exclamations of delight, but few travelers saw fit to comment, say, on the first shoots of green along willow boughs. Observations of nature tended to be variations on what predecessors had written, much as the *waka* poetry of the time consisted of variations on earlier themes. Herbert Plutschow pointed out, however, that few European travelers of the time even mentioned nature in their diaries. He wrote, "For a human being to be captivated by the beauty of nature, the direct relations between the human being and God must first be cut, for it is a profanation toward God and even a sin."[8] Nature, at least until the rise of romanticism, was almost always ignored in European diaries.

Viewed in this light, even the most conventional descriptions of nature in a Japanese diary have a charm missing from European diaries of approximately the same period. But the medieval Japanese diaries suffer from the lack of individuality that enhanced not only the best European diaries but the diaries of the Heian court ladies. It is often hard to distinguish the diary of an ambitious courtier like Michichika from the diary of a blameless Buddhist priest, though the latter was more likely to intersperse his account with reflections on the meaninglessness of human life.

The most interesting sections of travel diaries are apt to be the accounts of people met along the way. Michichika, for example, reported that after the Retired Emperor Takakura had bathed at the Muro anchorage, "a number of pleasure girls, who looked like foxes who live in old grave mounds and assume human form after dark, approached the temporary palace[9] in their boats, vying to see who could come the closest. Nobody paid any attention to them, so they went away."[10] At the Kojima anchorage, however, no pleasure girls appeared, and this upset Michichika. "Why have they stayed away from us, considering that they go up to every traveler? But even if they put in an appearance, I wonder if these beach girls would be worth looking at."[11] Such observations, though not exactly personal, tell us more about Michichika than the dreary poems he scattered through the diary.

The Visit of the Emperor Takakura to Itsukushima inspired several chapters in *The Tale of the Heike*, but even when its phrases were directly borrowed, the effect is strikingly different. Although the diary is in places affecting, it is only when the incidents are set against the tragedy of Takakura's whole life, as related in *The Tale of the Heike*, that they acquire their full significance. The melancholy from which he suffered during this journey developed into a wasting illness, and he died at the age of twenty.

The Ascension to Heaven of the Late Emperor Takakura

Early one morning in the spring of 1181 the Cloistered Emperor Takakura, who had developed a mysterious illness after his journey to Itsukushima in the previous year, made up his mind that death was imminent. He prepared for the end by moving his pillow to the north and directing his gaze to the west.[1] So Minamoto Michichika recorded in *Takakura-in Shōka Ki* (*The Ascension to Heaven of the Late Emperor Takakura*), a diary in the form of a dirge that describes Takakura's last illness and the religious rites performed after his death. The word *shōka* (literally, "ascension into the mist") in the title refers to the cremation of the Emperor after his death. The image recurs many times in the diary, notably in this *waka* by Michichika:

nani wo ka wa	What shall I take as
katami to mo min	A memento when the last trace
noborinishi	Has disappeared
haru no kasumi no	Into the mists of spring
ato mo kienaba[2]	Where he has ascended?

Michichika's grief over the death of Takakura is the sole subject of the diary. No mention is made of the death of Kiyomori in the same year, or of the defeat inflicted by the Minamoto general Kiso no Yoshinaka on the Taira forces. Michichika expressed his grief in extraordinarily long sentences that are full of stereotyped phrases borrowed from Japanese poetry and Chinese history. The work is so lugubrious it is painful to read, but gradually Michichika's grief becomes an incontestable reality, thanks mainly to small but telling details.

For example, shortly after the traditional observances on the forty-ninth day after the Emperor's death, Michichika went to Kan'in Pavilion, a place Takakura had often favored with a visit. Michichika noted that a little pine planted in a courtyard, which hitherto had been flourishing, was now withered, and he was touched that the pine, instead of living out the thousand years that pines were traditionally said to live, had died out of grief for its master. He noticed, however, that a plum tree, originally transplanted from his own garden, had burst into flower, as it always had in the past. He broke off a bough, to take to the Hokke-dō, where Takakura's ashes were enshrined, and murmured to the blossoms, "Don't change your scent, even if you have no master." He also composed the *waka*:

haru ya aranu	Is this not the spring?
ume mo mukashi no	The plum blossoms are still
hana nagara	The blossoms of old;
ueshi niwa nomi	How sad that only in the garden
chiru zo hakanaki[3]	He planted, flowers should fall.

This *waka* is so close to the celebrated one by Ariwara no Narihira[4] as to suggest parody, but Michichika was unquestionably sincere.

On the hundredth day after Takakura's death Michichika called on the child emperor Antoku. Everything in the familiar place seemed changed: "I went to the palace and had an audience with the Emperor, but everything had changed from what it was. Looking at the sky, I murmured to myself, 'It's still the same dwelling in the clouds. . . .' "[5] Michichika often recalled the journey to Itsukushima when he had accompanied Takakura. His memories of Takakura were all of a nature that made him feel boundlessly grateful: "I kept thinking that never during all the fourteen years when I served him day and night did I see the least trace of harshness in his face."[6] This was not flattery but an expression of the genuine love and admiration he felt for his late master.

Fujiwara Teika kept a diary of the journey he took with the Cloistered Emperor Gotoba to Kumano in 1201. This work, called *Gotoba-in Kumano Gokō Ki* (*The Visit of the Cloistered Emperor Gotoba to Kumano*), is written in classical Chinese, though the *waka* composed on the journey are quoted in Japanese. It is difficult to detect any indication of friendship between the two men. Both were superb poets and were soon to collaborate in compiling the *Shin Kokinshū*, but the diary is curiously unconcerned with poetry. Teika worried about the proper costume to wear on various occasions, complained about the state of his health, and emphasized the religious intent of the journey by repeatedly mentioning precisely where they worshipped. As for the scenery along the way, Teika's comments were no more enthusiastic than "When I looked out over the distant sea, the view was not without interest."

Teika obviously did not enjoy the journey. He seems to have been an unwilling companion to Gotoba, who was so devout a believer in the Kumano shrines that he made the journey over thirty times. A fundamental lack of rapport between these two difficult men keeps the diary from attaining even the level of interest of *The Visit of the Emperor Takakura to Itsukushima*. In this test between the enemies Michichika and Teika, the former was clearly the victor.

Journey Along the Seacoast Road

The travel diaries of the Japanese medieval period most often had their origins in the writers' visits to places that were either of a sacred character or familiar because of frequent mentions in poetry. A special reason for travel during the Kamakura period was the presence of the Shogun's government in the city of Kamakura, a long distance from Kyōto, the site of the Emperor's court. The inhabitants of Kyōto, accustomed to thinking of their city as the focal center of all aspects of Japanese life, were dismayed that this was no longer true. On the other hand, they were intrigued by reports they heard about the splendid new city in the east. Some journeyed there out of curiosity, to see the Shogun's capital for themselves. Others made the journey in order to place petitions before the law courts in Kamakura.

Naturally, the famous places along the way were not ignored, even by people who were in a hurry to reach Kamakura. None of the diarists failed to mention Yatsuhashi, the Eight Bridges poetically described in *The Tales of Ise*. Mount Fuji and Mount Hakone rarely failed to inspire travelers to compose poetry and prose in emulation of their predecessors.

The journey itself, which had taken ninety-one days when the author of *The Sarashina Diary* traveled in 1020 (mainly because of lengthy stops at various places), by 1223, the year when *Kaidōki*

(*Journey Along the Seacoast Road*) was written, normally required twelve to fifteen days. There were inns (and houses of prostitution) along the way to cater to the needs of travelers, though in the past it had sometimes been necessary for them to build their own shelters. It was also possible to travel more lightly, confident that food, which earlier travelers had always carried with them, would be available at inns.

Of the many diaries that describe the journey between Kyōto and Kamakura, the most absorbing is *Journey Along the Seacoast Road*, though others are better known or more gracefully written. When one takes up this diary after having read those by the Heian court ladies, one is immediately made aware of the great change that had occurred in Japanese prose style. The typical Heian diary contained few words of Chinese origin, but *Journey Along the Seacoast Road* not only has many such words but is crammed with allusions to Chinese poetry and history. The most conspicuous stylistic feature is the parallelism, so characteristic of Chinese compositions. A typical example of this parallelism is found in the description of Hashimoto, a post-station on the shore of Lake Hamana: "The light of the fishing torches sinks to the bottom of the waves and startles the fish; the oarsman's song on the nocturnal boat rises upward to waken the traveler from sleep."[1]

A similar use of parallelism is found in the celebrated essay *Hōjōki* (*An Account of My Hut*), written in 1212 by Kamo no Chōmei, where it is much less ponderous. Stylistic and other similarities between *Journey Along the Seacoast Road* and *An Account of My Hut* probably occasioned the long-standing attribution of the former to Kamo no Chōmei. Bashō, writing in 1687, included Chōmei among the great diarists for this reason. Nobody accepts this theory of authorship any longer, if only because Chōmei died in 1216 and the journey described in the diary took place seven years later. But *Journey Along the Seacoast Road*, regardless of who wrote it, is a masterpiece of its kind, quite worthy of being attributed to the great Chōmei.

Although the unknown author provided extremely few clues to his identity, his diary is intensely personal. He discussed at the outset his reasons for making the journey to Kamakura, and gave a glowing account of the city that was based on what he had heard from people who had actually been there. This description is also typical of his Sinicized style: "The county of Kamakura in the province of Sagami is the armory of Sakra transported to the world of men, the Yen-chou of the Chinese erected in our country.[2] Soldiers are numerous as trees in a forest; their splendor flourishes like a myriad of blossoms. Brave warriors are in full glory along the roads; unerring archers shoot willow leaves at a hundred paces. . . ."[3] Although he had yet to see Kamakura with his own eyes, the reports he had heard induced him to compare the city to strongly fortified places mentioned in the Buddhist and Confucian classics. The author, who had never traveled far from the capital, was impressed not only by what he had heard of the imposing appearance of Kamakura and the military discipline prevailing there but by testimony that the Shogun's government honored the rituals and etiquette prescribed in Confucian texts. For a long time, he says, he had supposed that Kamakura had nothing to do with him, and he had never even considered making the long journey to see its glories, but a good opportunity for visiting Kamakura had come up, and he decided on the spur of the moment to go.

The author, who was about fifty years old, apparently became a Buddhist priest shortly before he set out on his journey, but it was not religious devotion (as in the case of many other travelers of the age) that spurred him to leave Kyōto. He declared that his life had been a failure, that he had been unable to accumulate wisdom or a knowledge of the arts. This may sound like Oriental modesty, but his despair was real enough for him seriously to have considered suicide. Though he would have had no regrets over giving up his life, he lacked the courage to drown himself by leaping into a pond. Travel seems to have been an escape.

He does not reveal what personal factors caused this desperation, or why he became a priest so late in life, but there is perhaps a clue in the statement that before he left the capital he promised his aged mother he would see her again, though he realized that this promise was necessarily uncertain. Leaving behind his mother, who had lapsed into second childhood, gave a somber tone to his departure. Later, he had hardly reached Kamakura when he felt obliged to rush back to Kyōto to rejoin his mother, who was waiting for his return. "I have an old mother in the capital. She has returned to infancy and longs for her foolish son."[4] His Buddhist faith was insufficiently strong to provide the certainty of rebirth in paradise, together with his mother. If he had possessed this faith, it could have sustained even a long separation. He was afraid she might suppose he had abandoned her and hate him for it.

His relations with his mother constantly preyed on his mind. He asked rhetorically what effect his prayers to the buddhas and gods could have if he failed to serve his parents day and night. He wondered if his neglect of his mother was the result of some sin committed in a previous existence. "Long ago, in my prime, I trusted in the future and prayed to heaven, but now, in my declining years, I think of the retribution from former lives and I hate myself."[5] He hoped that at least his having taken Buddhist vows would help his mother to gain paradise.

The emphasis on his relations with his mother makes one wonder if the author did not take the journey to Kamakura in order to escape for a while the heartrending spectacle of her being reduced to senescence. When he reached Kamakura, however, he recalled his action with shame and could not linger. This is only a guess, but the manner of narration, so unlike that of other travel diaries, suggests a powerful grief that the writer can neither fully describe nor totally suppress.

Despite the troubles weighing on the author's mind when he set out for Kamakura, *Journey Along the Seacoast Road* is filled with a vivid appreciation of everything he saw. He disclaimed any intent of creating a work of literature: "This was not primarily intended as a literary composition, nor was it inspired by poetry. All I have done is to record the moving qualities of things that have aroused my interest."[6] All the same, he took such great pains with the expression that he created the most complex style of any diarist of the period. The crabbed expression suggests the author was trying to create a new kind of Japanese, one more effective in conveying his emotions than the more mellifluous Heian Japanese. He failed, in the sense that he was not imitated by later writers, but his attempt compels admiration.

One of the author's typical stylistic devices is personification. He addressed a bridge, some shrimps, an old horse as if they could answer him. The words he spoke to the horse are particularly touching: "Old horse, old horse. You are wise, so you surely are aware not only of what lies beneath the snows on the mountain roads but even the essence of the water at the bottom of the river."[7] The passage contains a pedantic allusion to the Chinese classic *Meng Ch'iu*, but the personification—the attribution of great wisdom to an old horse—originated in this diary.

This and other stylistic features, such as a Chinese-influenced violation of normal Japanese word order, make *Journey Along the Seacoast Road* harder to understand than other travel accounts of the period, and the many references to Buddhism and to the Chinese classics give the pages a curiously crowded look, but this diary is far more ambitious than any other of its time. It is the account of a man's attempt to discover who he is and why he exists in a world in which he seems to have no place. At the end of the diary he stated his reason for writing it: "I have written this because, ever since I 'left my house' and entered the True Path, people have felt sorry for me. I have written this account, ignoring the possibility that people may mock it, in order to convey my feelings. I have not written for the amusement of other people."[8]

The rather embittered tone of these last remarks should not suggest that the diary is uniformly gloomy from beginning to end. At times the author is so carried away with delight in his experiences that he forgets the grief that inspired the journey. Here, for example, is what he wrote about crossing the Bay of Narumi: "Although I did not see the blessed isles of paradise, nor did I obtain the elixir of immortality, I thought that the pleasure of floating over this sea was the joy of a lifetime, and wondered if this were not the true art of prolonging life."[9]

The most striking feature of the diary is the author's unconventionality, mirrored in his style. Most travelers indiscriminately praised every "famous place" they visited, but this author declared, "Famous places are not necessarily enjoyable. Places one has often heard about do not necessarily appeal to the eye."[10] He remarked, with a touch of cynicism, that the pleasures to be enjoyed in a curtained bed inside the palace do not differ from those available at a cheap whorehouse in the country. He demonstrated his skepticism by questioning the possibility of immortality: "The medicine bestowed by the Buddha in heaven is of no use to people down in the world below."[11] He even had a bad word for Kaguya-hime, the heroine of *The Tale of the Bamboo Cutter*, whom he described as a "poisonous, transformed woman."[12]

The most affecting parts of *Journey Along the Seacoast Road* refer to the ill-fated Jōkyū Rebellion. This disturbance of 1221, staged by the Cloistered Emperor Gotoba and his adherents against the Hōjō regents, was unsuccessful, and most of the people on the losing side were either killed or sent into exile. The author of this diary, despite his professed admiration for the shogunate (and thus sympathy for the Hōjō family), did not hesitate to express commiseration with those who had died in the attempt to destroy it. He described how he stopped at the post-station of Kikugawa because his horse was tired, and found on a pillar in the house some lines of poetry written by the Middle Counselor Muneyuki contrasting the *kikusui* (chrysanthemum water) of China, which was said to prolong life, with Kikugawa (Chrysanthemum River) in Japan, where he was likely to lose his life. The author, moved by these words, recounted Muneyuki's tragic life. Born in an illustrious family, he had risen to high position, and had been the cynosure of the Cloistered Emperor Gotoba's court, surpassing everyone else in the magnificence of his appearance. People from far and near had craved to bask in his glory. Could anyone have imagined that he would meet with such a fate?

Here is the description of the outbreak of the Jōkyū Rebellion: "In the middle of the 6th month of the 3rd year of Jōkyū the winds blew fiercely over the entire country, and within the seas the waves broke in reverse. The soldiers who started the rebellion rushed pell-mell from the capital, and their antagonists emerged from the uncivilized provinces to do battle. Wild lightning flashes tore through the clouds; the sun and moon hid their light; common soldiers overran the land; bows and swords displayed their might."[13] The writing is poetic, rather than historical, but one cannot miss the contrast between *kajō* ("flower city," used to indicate the capital in Kyōto) and *ikoku* ("barbarian provinces," used for Kamakura). A similarly decorous style is used to indicate the billeting of rough warriors in the houses of aristocrats: "The brocade curtains and jade-decorated beds had lost their masters and turned into hostelries for soldiers."[14]

After Muneyuki was captured, not even his most trusted retainers could help him. Everyone, noble and baseborn alike, who had participated in the ill-fated rebellion was now in the same "pit of hell." The author imagined Muneyuki, surrounded by hostile guards, writing his message on a pillar, expressing his grief over impending death. The author composed this *waka*:

kokoro araba	Travelers at this inn
sazo na aware to	Who search for traces of the past,
mizukuki no	If you have hearts
ato kakiwakaru	Surely you will look with pity
yado no tabibito[15]	At the words his brush has left.

Muneyuki was not in fact executed at Kikugawa. The author, farther along on the journey, discovered another poem by Muneyuki, this one expressing the realization that he had at last reached the place where he was to die. The author, imagining what had passed through Muneyuki's head, composed this *waka*:

miyako woba	The flower of men
ika ni hanabito	Have fled from the capital,
haru taete	The spring is no more;
azuma no aki no	Must they fall, then, like the leaves
ko no ha to wa chiru[16]	Of autumn trees in the East?

For the aristocrats who had abandoned the capital to join in the rebellion there would be no more springs. They would fall in the east, like autumn leaves.

Much of *Journey Along the Seacoast Road* is eminently quotable. It is a profoundly moving diary, marred only by a pedantic style that tends to keep the reader at arm's length. But this style, so irritating at first, contributes to the total effect of a work that is the account not merely of a journey but of a troubled man's attempt to understand an uncongenial world.

The Diary of the Priest Shunjō

The priest Shunjō, known as Utsunomiya Asanari before he took the tonsure in 1220, traveled from Kyōto to Kamakura in 1225, just two years after the author of *Journey Along the Seacoast Road*. The strongly religious nature of this journey is suggested by his decision to continue his travels beyond Kamakura to the great temple of Zenkō-ji before he returned home. It was probably also because his journey was a pilgrimage, rather than an excursion, that Shunjō (as was rare among Japanese travelers) paid virtually no attention to the scenery along the way but instead devoted his pages largely to Buddhist reflections.

Shunjō had originally been a liegeman of the Kamakura shogunate, and he had personally served the third Shogun, Sanetomo, until the moment when Sanetomo was assassinated before his eyes. Soon after Sanetomo's death in 1219 over one hundred persons who had been close to him, from his wife on down, took Buddhist vows. Shunjō returned home to put his affairs in order before "leaving the world." His wife had died, leaving two small children. Shunjō realized that becoming a priest would in effect make orphans of his children. It was a painful decision, as we know from a preface given in his collected poems:

"When, after the death of His Excellency, I was considering

becoming a priest, it was difficult for me to abandon motherless little children. I went to the shrine of our clan and offered up this poem:

aware mi yo	Take pity on them!
ware mo arashi ni	I, too, am fated to vanish
narinubeshi	In the same tempest
ha wa chirihateshi	That has left the leaves lying
mori no ki no moto[1]	Beneath the trees in the wood.

"At length, when I made my decision, it must have shown on my face. I heard the servants whispering together, 'What are we to do now?' and my children—the girl of eight and the boy of seven—said, 'It has been so lonely just without Mother, but what will we do if Father also abandons us and goes away?' The children went into our private chapel and prayed to the Buddha that he would keep their father with them. Their nurse told me that she was wondering where they were when she became aware somebody was inside the chapel. She listened and heard their young voices saying sadly, 'Buddha, you grant the prayers of people who come before you. Don't let Father leave us this way. Please keep him here.' Everything I heard made me feel sorrier for them."[2]

But Shunjō, as a retainer of Sanetomo, had no choice but to show his loyalty to his late master by "leaving the world" and becoming a priest. At daybreak on the morning when his head was shaved he composed this poem:

mayoikoshi	After long turmoil
kokoro no yami mo	The darkness in my heart, too,
harenubeshi	Will surely be cleared:
ukiyo hanaruru	In the sky a bank of clouds
yokokumo no sora[3]	Draws away from the floating world.

The differences in manner between Shunjō and the author of *Journey Along the Seacoast Road* are apparent even from these brief extracts from Shunjō's writings. Shunjō, though compelled by his close relationship to the assassinated Sanetomo to turn his back on the world and become a priest, could not forget his worldly ties, especially to his children, and he described his emotions far more openly than the earlier diarist. His journey was an act of religious devotion, and each experience along the way was recorded because of the moral lesson it taught. At the post-station of Ono, for example, he observed the prostitutes and was moved to comment, "Every way of making a living in this world is painful, but to rely on empty words spoken at night, to have no choice but to wait for men who promise nothing, and in the process to be constantly piling up sins—this is to be pitied. It is impossible to doubt the truth of the words, 'Because of greedy craving and attachment, one will be afflicted with pains of every description in this world and with hell, famished demons, and beasts in the world to come.' "[4]

There was nothing exceptional in this Buddhist warning against the sins of the world, but Shunjō, even after he took vows, remained acutely aware of his worldly past. At the post-station of Ikeda there was a prostitute named Jijū whom he had frequented in the past. He was refused lodgings at the place, and the woman acted as if she had never seen him before. Perhaps she did not recognize him in Buddhist robes and with his head shaved. He sent her the poem:

mukashi mishi	I no longer look
sugata ni mo arazu	As I did when you knew me;
narinureba	That, no doubt, is why
Ikeda no mizu mo	The water at Ikeda
kage wo yadosazu[5]	Refuses to reflect my form.

Shunjō, like the author of *Journey Along the Seacoast Road*, was moved to tears when he saw at Kikugawa the pillar on which the condemned Muneyuki had inscribed his farewell poem. He composed a *waka* describing his emotion, but his tears were certainly not of sympathy for the rebel cause. Shunjō was an unwavering adherent of the shogunate, and the longest passages in his diary are devoted to his reminiscences of Sanetomo. After he arrived in Kamakura, he spent a night in prayer at Sanetomo's grave. He remembered everything that had happened from the time he took up service under Sanetomo until the terrible moment when the Shogun's corpse turned to smoke rising in the dawn sky.

Seven years had elapsed since Sanetomo's death, and although Shunjō of course knew that all who are born must die, he could not help shedding tears of longing for his late master.

From Kamakura he traveled to the Zenkō-ji, the temple in the province of Shinano. He had intended to visit Hōjō Masako, the widow of the shogunate's founder, Minamoto Yoritomo. But it was not until he reached Zenkō-ji that he learned she was ill, and before he was able to get to her she had died. He wrote in his diary, "There was no reason why her death should have startled me into recognizing afresh the truth that all things that exist are impermanent, but I remembered that she had said to me, 'This autumn, without fail, I will do penance,' and tears of frustration that I could not transcend life and death wetted the sleeve of my habit, too many to dry."[6]

The most affecting parts of Shunjō's diary, however, describe experiences closer to him than the death of an exalted personage like Masako. On his way to Zenkō-ji, Shunjō stopped to visit an old friend, Mitsumune, who was living in exile near Obasuteyama[7] because of his involvement in a political dispute. Mitsumune, confined now to a wretched little thatched hut, described the hardships he had endured, but his small son, unable to comprehend what the grown-ups were discussing, tugged at them, begging them to play with him. Mitsumune continued, "I wish I could renounce the world as you have. I envy you, but as an exile I do not dare to take such a step. Besides, I have these ties that are hard to break." The "ties" referred to his two young sons. Shunjō commented, "I could see why the 'darkness in his heart' should have led him into delusion,[8] and I felt sorry for him." The two men parted, promising to meet again if they remained alive.

Shunjō's reactions to Mitsumune's story may seem a trifle smug. He seems to be congratulating himself on having successfully broken his ties to the world even though he, too, had children. But when, at the end of the diary, Shunjō returned to his old home, he could not remain complacent as he looked on his daughter and son. They reminded him that it was the thirteenth anniversary of their mother's death. He wondered why he had lived and his wife had died, then related, "There was no sign that the children, whom I had not seen in such a long time, had achieved peace of mind.

All they could say, in tears, was, 'We want to shave our heads, too, and go to the capital, where we can look after you.' I could not help feeling sorry for them."[9] The children's devotion moved Shunjō, and he wavered in his resolution for a moment at the thought that this was likely to be the last time he would see them in this world. But he reminded himself of the mutability of all existence and of the fact that no bonds last forever. The thought aroused his courage, and the diary concludes with his poem:

ima sara ni	Why should I bewail
kono nagori wo ya	This separation after
nagekamashi	All that has happened?
tsui no wakare wo	If I did not consider
omowazariseba[10]	The ultimate parting . . .

In this poem Shunjō is saying that, having broken his ties with his children when he became a Buddhist priest, he has no reason to bewail leaving them now. If he did not think of the final parting—that is, death—he might be more moved by parting in this life. There is something rather chilling about Shunjō's self-possession. Mitsumune's sons live in a hovel, but at least they have their father. Shunjō's children can only hope that some day they will be able to take Buddhist vows and serve their father. Shunjō rejects this thought. In this lifetime his path will be solitary, and he is resolved to journey without hindrances.

A Journey East of the Barrier

Tōkan Kikō (*A Journey East of the Barrier*) is often paired with *Journey Along the Seacoast Road*. Both describe travels between the capital and Kamakura, and they share such stylistic features as the use of parallelism and allusions to Chinese literature, but otherwise the resemblances are slight. Unlike *Journey Along the Seacoast Road*, this diary is not an attempt to present a self-examination within the conventions of a travel diary, but the uncomplicated account of an actual journey. Again, despite some similarities of style, it is vastly easier to read; the graceful prose is in fact its most memorable feature. The sentences, unencumbered by the tortured phraseology of *Journey Along the Seacoast Road*, flow naturally and effortlessly. It is easy to see why *A Journey East of the Barrier* was read devotedly for centuries and why (far more than the earlier diary) it influenced later writers of travel diaries, notably Bashō.

The author was apparently a gentleman of leisure who lived in the capital. The diary opens with this self-portrait: "Now that I am approaching half a hundred years, the frost on my sidelocks has at length become chilly, but, not being the kind of person who spends his days idly doing nothing and, moreover, not having settled on any particular place to live the rest of my days, I could not help comparing myself sadly to Po Chü-i, who wrote of himself that his body was like a drifting cloud and his head was like the frost."[1] These words and those that follow, apart from the usual modest disclaimers, inform us that the unknown author did not seek rank or fame, but lived in a quiet retreat. The "mountain" where he chose to live was not, however, some distant peak but Higashiyama in Kyōto, and his chosen way of life was not to practice Buddhist austerities but to "follow a path of life like most other people." But even though he mingled with other people, in his heart at least he tried to maintain an elegant detachment from the world.

For unexplained reasons, the author set out on a journey to the east in the autumn of 1242. He informs us that he kept this diary because "I thought that if I set down the various sights that had struck my eyes and the experiences that lingered in my memory, if anybody in the future still remembered such things with nostalgia, my account would of itself provide them with a memento."[2]

Wherever he went, the author recalled the appropriate poetic allusions. When he reached Ōtsu, for example, he remembered that the Emperor Tenchi had moved his capital there many years before, and he composed a poem with the correct *makurakotoba* (fixed epithet) for Ōtsu:

sazanami ya	Lake of little waves!
Ōtsu no miya no	Ever since the Ōtsu Palace
areshi yori	Went to rack and ruin
na no mi nokoreru	The old capital of Shiga
Shiga no furusato[3]	Survives only as a name.

The journey continued pleasantly and uneventfully. The style is limpid, and there are some lovely passages: "We traveled until it grew dark, then stopped near a mountain temple called the Musadera. As the night advanced, the autumn wind blowing over our crudely made pallets penetrated our flesh, and we felt that without realizing it we had passed into a world utterly unlike that of the capital. The voice of a bell, near our pillows, reverberated in the dawn sky. It was moving to think that Po Chü-i's awakening in the grass-thatched hut by the I-ai Temple must have been very much like this."[4]

Only occasionally is the reader struck by an especially vivid or original observation, as in this passage: "Today, we were told, was market day. Everybody along the streets was carrying heavy-looking parcels, gifts for people at home. I thought that these gifts were quite unlike the cherry blossoms mentioned in the poem 'Is seeing them enough? One wants to tell others about them.' "[5] These words effectively suggest people in the market buying souvenirs, no doubt as common a sight in those days as at present.

Perhaps the most interesting passage of all describes the temple erected by a man from Tsukushi who had traveled all the way to Kamakura in the hopes of winning a suit. He prayed before the Kannon of Kamakura, promising that if he won his suit he would erect a new building at the temple. He was successful and carried out his vow. Ever since then countless other people have visited the same temple to pray for Kannon's help.[6]

The author of *A Journey East of the Barrier* apparently had no lawsuit or other favor to ask of Kannon, but the next traveler to Kamakura who left a diary, the nun Abutsu, would initiate one of the best-known lawsuits of Japanese history.

Fitful Slumbers

Utatane (*Fitful Slumbers*), the diary written about 1240 by the nun Abutsu when she was seventeen or eighteen, is one of the finest examples of the introspective diary. It opens with a long sentence (divided in the translation) that establishes the mood: "It brings no comfort, I know, to brood over things, but I have become accustomed on sleepless nights to leave my door ajar and wait for the moon to rise, hoping to make it my companion. As I gaze outside, alone as always, I notice the autumn dew on the withered garden, and I hear the plaintive cries of insects, and each sight or sound becomes something to wound me. Checking the tears that well confusedly in my heart, I reflect for a time on what has happened and what is to come, and I reproach myself again and again, wondering why I should be obsessed in this way with so demeaning and so hopeless an affair."[1]

The writer is a young woman who had her first affair with a man in the spring of that year. She fell desperately in love, but now it is autumn and his visits have become infrequent. Realizing the hopelessness of ever recapturing his love, she lies awake at night, brooding over her unhappiness, though she knows that brooding can do her no good. Even things that normally give her pleasure—the moonlight, the garden dew, the singing of insects—now cause her pain. The author is young and vulnerable, and she is writing this diary in the vain hope that describing her suffering may bring relief.

Abutsu's lover was a married man, a member of a social class so much superior to her own that, even after his wife died, she could not hope he would ever marry her. She was in fact keenly aware of their difference in social status and did not dare to offer condolences on the death of his wife. She nonetheless continued to wait for a secret visit at the time the man customarily appeared. She was ashamed of this yearning and wondered what would become of anyone as helpless as herself.

To her great joy, a letter came from him, and one night, so long past his usual hour that she had gone to bed, despairing of a visit, she heard his soft knocking on the gate. She went outside to meet him. The moonlight in the garden was bright and she felt embarrassed, lest she be seen. She hid behind the fence, but he caught sight of her, and teased her with an allusion to the passage in *The Tale of Genji* where Genji glimpses another man who has come to court the same lady as himself, only to recognize the man as his closest friend. As Abutsu's lover approached in the moonlight, she was stunned by his beauty, which she thought comparable to that of the Shining Prince himself.

Like the author of *The Sarashina Diary*, the young Abutsu lived in two worlds, that of reality and that of *The Tale of Genji*. Her intensely romantic feelings for a man who considered her to be of only passing interest probably reflected the unconscious hope that he would prove to be like Genji, who never forgot or deserted any woman he had once loved. However, at the end of the year (1240?) Abutsu's lover ceased to visit her altogether. She recalled on the 7th day of the 12th month that it was exactly one month since his last visit. But although her memories were vivid, she discovered that she had trouble recalling his features. A recent commentator has opined that in those days, when there were no photographs, it was difficult to remember the faces of people one had met only at night,[2] but surely that is not what makes Abutsu's remark so affecting. The more one loves a person, the more difficult it is to remember that person's face with clarity, if only because love prevents us from seeing the other's face as objectively as we might see a stranger's. *Fitful Slumbers* owes its moving quality to its psychological truth and its universal intelligibility.

Abutsu related that even as she tried to recall her lover's face tears came into her eyes, blotting out the moonlight, and at that moment she had a vision of Buddha. The vision induced her to consider the desirability of taking vows and becoming a nun. One calm spring evening, a month or so later, as she was tearing up and throwing away drafts of her poetry, she found letters from her lover mixed among the manuscripts, arousing feelings of desolation at the thought they might never meet again. She recalled the course of their love—from early spring, when plum buds first colored the boughs, to the desiccation of winter, when their love died. That night, when others in the room had all fallen asleep, Abutsu crept out silently. She had already made preparations for the step she was about to take. Scissors and a box were ready for the symbolic gesture of cutting her hair and becoming a nun. Naturally, she did not shave her head but, in the manner of Heian court ladies, she cut her hair to shoulder length. She wrapped the hair in paper, put the packet in the box, and wrote this farewell poem:

nagekitsutsu	In my grieving,
mi wo hayaki se no	Though I sink to the bottom
soko to dani	Of the river rapids,
shirazu mayowan	How sad I shall still wander
ato zo kanashiki[3]	Even then not knowing my fate.

This was a strange poem to have written under the circumstances. One might have expected that a girl of seventeen, driven by despair to renounce the world, would have written a simpler, more obvious expression of her grief and her trust in the Buddha, but this poem contains complicated puns and allusions to *The Tale of Genji* and *The Tale of Sagoromo*. Probably an involved stylistic manner had become so much a part of Abutsu that she did not realize that the poem might seem artificial. It is curious, all the same, that, instead of voicing hopes for salvation, she expressed fear that even after her death her soul would wander aimlessly as she had in life. The poem suggests not so much entering a religious life as an anticipated suicide, and this impression is reinforced by her appended comment, "Did I intend to drown myself, I wonder?"

Once Abutsu had cut her hair and composed her farewell poem to the world, she set out for a convent in a distant part of the capital. She probably had never walked so far before. It was dark, and she had only a general idea of the location of the convent. She could not ask directions, because she was afraid of being brought back to the palace and reprimanded. It started to rain, and soon her clothes were soaking wet, but she persisted, a sign of the indomitable determination we associate with the mature Abutsu.

She trudged on in the rain until dawn. She had lost her way, was exhausted, and so soaked that she compared herself ironically to the fishergirls who dive into the sea at Ise.[4] While taking shelter for a while under a pine, she heard the voices of young women—country girls, as she could tell from their rustic accents. They noticed her, and one cried out, "Who do you suppose *that* is? Oh, you poor thing! Have you run away from somebody, dear? Or have you had a fight with somebody? What brings you into the mountains in the pouring rain? Where have you come from? And where are you going? I've never seen the likes."[5]

This passage, with its suggestion of the actual speech of the village women who took pity on Abutsu, is particularly striking. Abutsu grew up at the court and had probably never before been addressed by such humble people. Perhaps she did not consider them to be fully human beings. But at this most desperate moment of her life, when she felt close to death from exhaustion and exposure, kindness from this unexpected quarter saved her. The women brought her to the convent.

People in the convent were startled by Abutsu's bedraggled appearance, but they took her in, and she was soon accepted as a nun. The silence of the place suited her, and the regular activities of the nuns at their daily chores—the offerings at dawn and dusk of holy water, the tinkling of prayer bells—had so soothing an effect that she shuddered to think she might have died without finding this sanctuary. The impetuous girl who had braved the danger of leaving the palace alone seemed to have found surcease from her griefs.

This tranquillity did not last. It was not long before she started to think of her lover again, and once her thoughts turned in that direction, religion had no power to calm her "extraordinary bitterness and grief."[6] She had taken refuge in a convent not to find Buddha but to forget her lover, and in this she failed. Even in the convent so many things recalled him: the sound of a stream brought back memories of a night when he had secretly crossed such a stream to meet her. She wrote him, but his reply, alluding to his fear of what people might think, was cold. She composed a poem:

kie haten	When I have vanished
keburi no uchi no	I doubt he will even glance
kumo wo dani	At the cloud within
yomo nagamejina	The smoke from my remains
hitome moru tote[7]	For fear that people might see.

Her love for the man was now tinged with contempt.

Not long afterward Abutsu left the convent. She explained that she was feeling unwell and did not wish to cause the convent any trouble. This may have been true, but one can also imagine that she had come to realize that the convent could not alleviate her grief. She did not inform her lover of the decision to leave the convent, but by an extraordinary coincidence his carriage passed hers at precisely the moment when she was leaving. She recognized his outriders, but made no sign, and the two carriages passed without stopping. She turned back for a final glimpse. She never saw him again.

When she reached the house where she would now live, she composed the poem:

hakanashi ya	How futile they are!
mijikaki yowa no	Dreams of a night so short
kusamakura	They hardly begin
musubu mo naki	Before they are over
utatane no yume[8]	On a traveler's pillow.

This poem probably occasioned the title of the diary.

After Abutsu recovered from her illness, she did not return to the convent but went back home instead. Although she gave no reasons for this decision, we can infer that she regretted her impetuosity in having "left the world." The silence of the convent, at first so congenial, provided her with too much time to brood over her lost love. But even at home there was nothing to occupy her mind. She wrote, "I was so desperate that I thought I would go anywhere to obtain relief, 'if only there were water to invite me.' "[9] The last words are a quotation from the poem by the ninth-century court lady Ono no Komachi:

wabinureba	So lonely am I
mi wo ukikusa no	My body is a floating weed
ne wo taete	Severed at the roots.
sasou mizu araba	Were there water to entice me,
inan to zo omou	I would follow it, I think.

The "water" took the form of an invitation from her foster father to visit his house in the province of Tōtōmi. He said that he thought the quiet life in the country would cheer her. Abutsu was reluctant to leave the capital, supposing that her foster father's house was in a cultural desert, but she went anyway, hoping that life in a new place would help her to forget her sorrow.

The journey began toward the end of the 10th month, about a year after the first entry in the diary. Abutsu passed many places mentioned in the old poetry, and she responded to each, though not in the mechanical manner of her later *Diary of the Waning Moon.* The most interesting moment of the journey occurred at the ford of Sunomata, where Abutsu witnessed a quarrel among "mean, lower-class men."[10] She was startled by the display of brute force, something she had never before experienced, and the sight brought home the reality of how far behind she had left the civilized ways of the capital. When she reached Yatsuhashi, the Eight Bridges mentioned in Narihira's poem, she was saddened that only one was still standing, and that the irises for which the bridges were famous had all withered. The journey brought no pleasure.

When she reached her foster father's house, it was hard to imagine living there. The place was big but crudely appointed, and it was so close to the sea that the thundering of the waves reverberated throughout the house. She recognized that these rustic surroundings had charm; all the same, each passing day brought greater longing to return to the capital. When, about a month after her arrival, she learned that her old nurse was ill, this provided a perfect excuse for returning home. She was by now frantically eager to leave, and though aware that people in her foster father's household might criticize her haste, she was unwilling to allow such considerations to delay her departure.

The return journey, unlike the outward one, was filled with anticipation. As soon as she arrived in the capital, she rushed to the bedside of the nurse, who was visibly comforted by Abutsu's presence.

The diary concludes with the confession that, although the author has tried to examine herself and the world around her calmly and analytically, her heart by nature is governed not by reason but by her emotions. The last words of the diary are the poem:

ware yori wa	Though these words are sure
hisashikarubeki	To last longer than myself,
ato naredo	Even if he sees them,
shinobanu hito wa	The man who has no love for me
aware to mo	Is not likely to be moved.
miji[11]	

It was somewhat unusual for her to have predicted that her diary would outlast her. She was correct in this belief, and probably correct, too, in assuming that even if her lover happened to read the diary it would not reawaken his love. But if the lover felt no sympathy, we, living seven hundred years later, can feel spiritual kinship with a woman who wrote with such honesty and passion.

The Diary of the Waning Moon

Although Abutsu took vows as a nun when she was seventeen or eighteen and is known today by her name as a nun, her life was certainly not spent in devotions within convent walls. Many details of her life are unclear, but we can gather from *Izayoi Nikki* (*The Diary of the Waning Moon*) that she had a son and a daughter while in her twenties. When she was about thirty, she met Fujiwara Tameie, the son of the great Teika. He was impressed by her knowledge of the art of *waka* poetry and of *The Tale of Genji*, and seems to have employed her at first as a secretary. They were married about 1250, and she bore Tameie three sons.

As the wife of Tameie, the heir to the traditions of his father, she commanded considerable respect in the world of the *waka*, as we can gather from *Yoru no Tsuru* (*The Crane at Night*), a work enunciating her opinions on *waka* composition, written in response to the request of some exalted person who had asked for guidance. Her tone is modest, but her opinions are expressed with authority.

Abutsu is best known for *The Diary of the Waning Moon*, the account of her journey from the capital to Kamakura in order to win title in the Kamakura law courts to the manor of Hosokawa for her son Tamesuke. When her husband Tameie died in 1275, there was uncertainty about which of his sons would inherit this estate—Tameuji, his eldest son by a previous marriage, or Tamesuke, Abutsu's second son. Abutsu probably exerted considerable influence over her husband in his declining years, and she was especially at pains to obtain for Tamesuke various secret documents explaining *waka* traditions. Perhaps she induced Tameie to change his will in favor of Tamesuke, but Tameuji, refusing to admit the validity of the new will, took possession of the estate. Abutsu decided, with characteristic determination and impetuosity, to seek justice in Kamakura.

A reader's opinion of the literary worth of *The Diary of the Waning Moon* is likely to depend on how highly he or she rates the eighty-eight *waka* and one *chōka* (long poem) contained in the text. Each sight along the way inspired a poem, but the displays of poetic virtuosity in her poems create an impression of technical proficiency rather than of deeply felt reactions to experience. Some poems have allegorical overtones, alluding to her grief over separation from her children or to her hopes for a successful conclusion to her suit, even though on the surface they seem to refer only to the scenery. The following *waka* is typical:

tazune kite	Searching, I have come
wa ga koekakaru	To Mount Hakone, which now
Hakoneji wo	I begin to cross;
yama no kai aru	I have found in a valley
shirube to zo omou[1]	A guide I think I can trust.

This *waka* displays a mastery of technique—there is a *kakekotoba* (pivot word) on *yama no kai* (mountain valley), and *kai aru* (there is value), *shirube* (guide), and *ji* (path) are *engo* (related words)—but there is none of the immediacy that makes *Fitful Slumbers* so memorable. The poem seems to be saying that Abutsu has discovered in a remote valley someone (or something) that will guide her in her future poetry. Read in conjunction with other poems composed when she visited the Mishima Shrine, it is clear that she is referring to the shrine itself as her guide. But without this context all one could tell was that some allegorical meaning was involved.

The prose parts of *The Diary of the Waning Moon* suffer from a similar excess of technical skill. Here are the opening words:

"Children today never dream that the title of the book discovered long ago in a wall has anything to do with them. Although what was written down by his brush, 'from the hillside fields of arrowroot,' is absolutely definite, the admonitions of a parent have been to no avail."[2] Abutsu is saying (but not very clearly!) that Tameuji pays no attention to the *Classic of Filial Piety* (the book found in the wall), acting as if the principles of filial piety were no concern of his. He has defied his father's will, though it was most explicit, and unlawfully appropriated the estate that his father meant Tamesuke to inherit. The "hillside fields of arrowroot" (*oka no kuzuhara*) add nothing to the meaning, but they decorate the expression with traditional pillow words.

This kind of writing appealed to Japanese who had greater familiarity with old works of literature than most modern readers possess, but unless one knows in advance the subject matter of *The Diary of the Waning Moon* one might read the entire text and still not be aware of the central theme. Near the opening of the diary, after Abutsu has established the importance of her position in the world of poetry by virtue of having borne three sons to Tameie, the son of Teika, she alludes to the disputed manor of Hosokawa in terms of her husband's dying instructions: "Because of some connection, whatever it was, between us, he entrusted me with hundreds and thousands of old sheets of scrap paper,[3] and said, 'Foster the Way of poetry, rear our children, pray for my repose in the next world.' But even the flow of the narrow stream that he left me with, an exchange of solemn promises, has been dammed for no reason. . . ."[4] It would be easy to miss the special significance of the words "narrow stream" (*hosokawa*, the name of the disputed manor) in so poetic a context.

Similarly, Abutsu's decision to do battle in Kamakura for her son's rights is stated in a most oblique manner: "I care nothing for myself, and if it were only for me I would gladly abandon all thought of it, but the darkness in a parent's heart when he thinks of his children[5] is difficult to repress, and when I think of the art of poetry my bitterness is not easily assuaged. So, then, I could not keep from thinking that if I were to let the matter be reflected in the tortoise mirror of the east[6] the truth would stand revealed, cloudlessly clear. I forgot all manner of hesitation and, resigning myself to being dismissed as a person of no worth, I reached the unexpected decision that I would set forth on the journey, enticed by the waning moon."[7]

Such elaborate expression, though much esteemed by readers who revere *The Diary of the Waning Moon* as a classic of its genre, is likely to disappoint anyone who admires *Fitful Slumbers*, a far less popular work. The intense directness of a young woman has been replaced by the involuted phrases of a professional poet. But behind the fancy language we may discern a familiar theme of Japanese diary literature, a mother's love for her son. In *The Diary of the Waning Moon* Abutsu quoted one poem by each of her five children, written before she left for Kamakura. She mentions this apologetically, but her tones are those of a mother who is proud of her children: "For me to have written down poems by all five children may suggest I dote on them, but they touched a mother's heart, and so I put them down together."[8] She followed this with a more characteristic remark: "Thinking it would not do to continue in so fainthearted a way, I brushed them off with no show of emotion." Perhaps Abutsu's heart was breaking when she pushed away her children, knowing it would be months or years before she saw them again, but (in the manner of a samurai wife rather than of a court lady or a nun) she showed no outward sign of tenderness toward her children. On the other hand, she displayed the ferocity of a tiger when fighting for her young, especially for Tamesuke.

Perhaps the most affecting section of this diary is the description of her visit to Hamamatsu, where, as she related in *Fitful Slumbers*, she had spent an unhappy month at the home of her foster father. When she visited the place the second time, she seems to have forgotten how desperately eager she had been to get away while she lived there; she remembered it now with a nostalgia unusual in so unsentimental a woman. For a moment she lets us see, through a crack in her armor, the sensitive and impetuous girl who had lived in Hamamatsu forty years before.

The Diary of the Waning Moon concludes with the long poem in which Abutsu summed up her grievances, notably her failure to obtain satisfaction from the authorities in Kamakura with respect to her petition to have the Hosokawa estate granted to

Tamesuke. Abutsu spent four years in Kamakura fruitlessly waiting for a favorable verdict. She failed to win her case during her lifetime, but thirty years after her death Tamesuke was at last awarded the estate. Abutsu in heaven no doubt composed a *waka*, with the proper number of *kakekotoba* and *engo*, to celebrate this victory.

The Diary of Asukai Masaari

Asukai Masaari was a fifth-generation descendant of a family that had continuously served the court as masters of *kemari*, the ritual Japanese football. There was also a strong tradition in his family of composing *waka*. Both his father and grandfather had had *waka* included in an imperially sponsored anthology. His elder sister was the wife of Tameuji, the son of Tameie by his first marriage, who was so bitterly attacked by Abutsu for failing to observe the provisions of his father's will. Masaari rose to high rank at court, mainly because of his proficiency at football, but he was also a scholar of poetry and prose. His own collection of *waka*, however, has been termed "a dreary compilation of the dregs of poetry."[1]

Masaari's surviving diaries are all written in *kana*. Probably he also kept a diary in classical Chinese, in the manner expected of gentlemen of the court. A diary entry for 1269, written while Masaari was in Saga, to the northwest of the capital, recovering from an illness, related that he had made the acquaintance there of Tameie. He wrote:

"I was spending my time in useless brooding, with nothing better to do, when I learned that the lay priest and Major Counselor Lord Tameie had been living for years in the vicinity. His family and mine had known each other for generations, so we came to meet from time to time in a friendly way. He lent me *The Tosa*

Diary, *The Murasaki Shikibu Diary*, *The Sarashina Diary*, *The Gossamer Years*, and other books. The authors being women, they wrote in *kana*.[2] . . . Though I am a man, I intend to use *kana*, because there are precedents in this country. Even *The Tales of Ise* was written in Japanese script. Of course, when one is writing about formal matters, Chinese is to be preferred, and for this reason, I myself have used Chinese when writing in that vein. But when writing about poetry and suchlike matters, I have thought it preferable to use *kana*, and I shall continue to do so, adding to my account events of the past as I remember them."[3]

Even in translation it should be apparent how much simpler Masaari's style was than Abutsu's. The sentences are relatively short, and there are no complicated allusions. The passage reveals Masaari's special interest in diaries, indicated by his choice of books to borrow from Tameie. It also reveals his conviction that it was appropriate not only for women but for men to write in Japanese. Classical Chinese was preferable when relating "formal matters" (*uruwashiki koto*), but for thoughts and emotions that spring from the heart, like the *waka*, it was more natural to use *kana*. Masaari's statements are too vague for us to obtain any specific definition of the occasions when he thought it proper to write in *kana* rather than Chinese characters, but it is clear that his insistence that the nature of the text to be written should determine the language employed was at the same time a defense of the propriety of men's writing prose in Japanese.

Masaari's exceptional familiarity with the diaries of the past was recognized by people at the court. In his last surviving diary, *Haru no Miyamaji* (*Mountain Path in the Spring*), which describes events of 1280, he related how, when he paid a visit to the Cloistered Emperor Gofukakusa, the latter, "unlocking his storeroom, took out a number of old diaries written in *kana* and, since he knew I had long wanted to see them, he urged me to do so."[4]

Masaari's exceptional interest in the diaries of Heian court ladies did not lead him to write with the subjectivity and sensitivity I associate with the women diarists. Indeed, it is hard to imagine a more resolutely masculine diary, in both style and content. In his younger days at least, Masaari was a playboy who enjoyed nothing more than spending a night drinking with friends or amusing himself with prostitutes, and page after page of his diaries is devoted to accounts of his pleasures.

It is refreshing, after reading the melancholy reflections of so many diarists, to come across a diarist who obviously derived much pleasure from his daily life. Masaari traveled frequently between Kyōto and Kamakura, no doubt because of the close connections his family enjoyed with the shogunate; but his accounts of his travels are by no means confined to references to places mentioned in poetry, in the usual manner. He related, for example: "When I dismounted at a place called Echi River a nun, a girl of eleven or twelve years, came out to beg. She was what they call an albino, absolutely devoid of coloring, from her hair to the pupils of her eyes. I had long heard of such people, but I had never seen one before. I could not bear to look at her. She was pitiful. I continued on my way, thinking how unusual it was, when I came across another curiosity, a child of six or seven. This one had hair growing down, leaving only a circle from the middle of his forehead to underneath his nose.[5] I have never seen such a sight anywhere. I thought how unlikely it was one could see such things except on a journey. These are matters of no consequence, but they are such rarities that I have written them down."[6]

A report that the daughter of a nobleman had become a prostitute excited his curiosity, and he sent for her, but bad weather kept them from meeting.

Although a pleasure-seeker and a lover of curiosities, Masaari also had a serious side to his personality, which revealed itself in his study of the Japanese classics. He wrote that he began reading *The Tale of Genji* with Abutsu on the 17th day of the 9th month of 1269, and completed reading the whole work, after twenty-six sessions, on the 27th day of the 11th month. The following day he turned his attention to the study of the *Kokinshū*.[7]

Masaari was no mere dilettante, but really loved Heian literature. Tameie, impressed by Masaari's devotion to these studies, offered to instruct him in the secret traditions of the *Kokinshū*. After they had gone over the most difficult passages together, Tameie, drinking with Masaari, remarked that his own son, Tameuji, had not yet gone through the whole of the *Kokinshū*. He had never given Tameuji instruction in *The Tale of Genji*. In fact, he doubted that *anyone* had ever been given such detailed instruction in the classics before.[8]

Masaari's descriptions of Abutsu as a teacher are of particular interest. He related, "On the 17th, about noon, I paid a visit. It was arranged that I was to begin *The Tale of Genji*, and the mistress of the house was summoned. She read inside her curtains. It was really interesting. It was not like the way ordinary people read. There must be some family tradition. She read as far as 'Young Murasaki.' When it grew dark we drank saké."[9] Abutsu's husband, Tameie, sent for two ladies to pour the liquor, and Abutsu, calling Masaari close to her curtained enclosure, described the illustrious ancestry in poetry shared by both her husband's family and Masaari's, concluding, "Poets, ever since long ago, have resided here by Ogura Mountain—it has always been highly reputed as a place to live—and it was wonderful how they used to enjoy themselves by indulging this way in conversations about the charm of the old novels. People nowadays are not like that any more, but you make me feel you are a person of long ago."[10] Masaari also gave this brief description of Tameie at their drinking party: "The master of the house is a mild-tempered, elderly man, and the saké therefore had an especially strong effect, inducing tears. I left when it was growing light."

Masaari's last diary, written in in 1280, is conspicuously less frivolous than the earlier ones. Perhaps the death of his eldest son turned him away from worldly pleasures. This is the only one of Masaari's diaries not to contain mention of *shirabyōshi*, the dancers with whom he was long accustomed to divert himself. His own life, and perhaps the times as a whole, had grown darker.

The Diary of Lady Ben

The diaries of the two court ladies Ben no Naishi and Nakatsukasa no Naishi[1] are often described as "sister diaries." On the surface, this appellation seems plausible: both diaries were kept by women who served at the court in the thirteenth century, one about twenty years after the other. But even scholars who link the diaries in this manner have felt it necessary to contrast the "cheerful, innocent nature" of *The Diary of Lady Ben* with the darker, more personal *Diary of Lady Nakatsukasa.* The scholar of Japanese literature Tamai Kōsuke, to whose pioneering studies of diaries of the tenth to fourteenth centuries I am much indebted, contrasted the two diaries in this manner: "The former sings the joy of life; the latter tells of the sadness of death."[2] Other scholars, some of whom have actually counted the number of times that such words as *okashi* (amusing) or *aware* (pitiful) appear in the two diaries, have reached similar conclusions.

The evaluation of the literary importance of the two diaries has not been uniform. One scholar who approvingly referred to *The Diary of Lady Ben* as "smiling literature," said of Lady Nakatsukasa's diary that it "reveals to us a woman who, though she writhes and gasps, is unable to do anything about the terrible bitterness of her life, victim as she is to the pitiful anguish and desperation of a split personality."[3]

I confess that I find *The Diary of Lady Ben* an entertaining but superficial work, whereas *The Diary of Lady Nakatsukasa* impresses me as a work of haunting beauty. The two diaries share one basic assumption that is quite at variance with what modern scholars have told us about the faded prestige of the Kyōto aristocracy during the thirteenth century: both women were sure that the court they knew was a place of unrivaled splendor. There is not so much as a hint that they were aware that any falling off had occurred since the height of the glory of the Heian court.

Lady Ben is a most engaging woman, and she quite won my heart early in her diary. On the 17th day of the 11th month of 1246 (her dating is much more precise than that in other diaries by women) she served as an emissary of the court to the festival of the Yoshida Shrine. On her way back to the palace, she suddenly felt an urge to visit her younger sister at the Women's Ceremonial Office (*nyokudokoro*), and asked that her carriage proceed there. However, the official who was accompanying her refused, saying that it was too late to take such a roundabout route. Lady Ben, determined to have her own way, insisted that it had always been the custom for the emissary to call at that place on the way back from the festival. Obviously, she had invented this "custom" on the spur of the moment, but her escort yielded, muttering in resignation, "Well, if there really is such a precedent . . ." When the carriage reached the office, it was so late that the doorkeeper was reluctant to open the gate. This time Lady Ben's escort, by now persuaded that there really was such a practice, scolded the gatekeeper, demanding to know why the gate was not open to receive the emissary, in accordance with long-established usage. Lady Ben records that she was much amused to discover how easily a tradition could be created.[4] The Japanese fondness for precedents has seldom been made fun of with such charm.

Unfortunately, not many passages reveal the author's personality so clearly. Much of the work resembles a diary less than a collection of poetry, with prose sections serving mainly as background material for the poems. The last part of the diary has suffered much from the depredations of bookworms, but enough remains elsewhere to attract the reader to the diary of this long-forgotten lady.

Lady Ben's most attractive feature is her love of fun. This quality is definitely not characteristic of most diaries kept by court ladies, who seem to have turned to their diaries mainly in times of loneliness or depression. Even the pleasures described in such diaries are usually tinged with sadness, if only because of the realization that these pleasures cannot last. In Lady Ben's diary, however, a carefree mood prevails. If the diary were translated into an appropriate modern Japanese idiom, the reader would have little trouble in identifying her with the contemporary Tokyo smart set, abreast of the latest fashions and eager to see for herself whatever people were talking about.

Her diary describes not only such traditional diversions of the aristocracy as admiring the moon or watching *kemari*, but distinctly new amusements such as cockfights. Here is how she described one cock after a bout: "One eye had been gouged out, blood dripped from his comb, and he had lost his tail. In short, he was unrecognizable when he left."[5] Her reaction to this spectacle was certainly not of joy over the carnage, but she nevertheless stayed long enough to witness a cock belonging to Kintada, the Middle Captain from Iyo, jump high into the air in order to escape the cock belonging to Tō no Chūjō Kinyasu, a sight that made the courtiers present laugh and inspired Lady Ben to write a sarcastic poem.

Lady Ben also described dances and popular songs, one with the catchy refrain, "*Saemon no jin yori mairan ya, Emon no jin yori mairan ya*" (roughly, "I've come from the camp of Saemon; I've come from the camp of Emon").[6] She attended a drunken party at New Year's in 1250. Promotions, which were to be officially announced on the 13th of the month, had privately been agreed on, and the party was a celebration. The Major Counselor who presided over the affair insisted that two men who would soon be promoted must do something to make the occasion lively, and they complied, performing one dance ten times.

People at the court considered Lady Ben to be the life of the party. One day when there were not many people at court because of a religious ceremony taking place, the bored Emperor commanded her, "Put on a mask and frighten people!" Lady Ben put on a devil's mask, raised her divided skirts up to her chest, pulled a dark robe over her head, and, attired in this strange fashion, stood by the entrance to the retiring room of the ladies-in-waiting. The soldiers of the palace guards raised a great commotion, aiming their bows at her and running around. She writes, "I was supposed to frighten them, but in fact I was so frightened that I fell into a stream in the garden. People laughed at me, saying that I was a cowardly devil."[7] The next day her parents, who had heard of this prank, sent her a taboo tag (*monoimi*), meaning that she should remain confined in her room to avoid disaster. She expressed gratitude for their solicitude.

Perhaps the best-known episode of the diary occurred in the 1st month of 1251, on the day of the Full Moon rice gruel (*mochigayu*). One element in the festivities consisted in hitting people on the behind with rice-gruel sticks. The Emperor commanded the ladies of the court to watch for a chance to hit the distinguished courtier Tameuji, but Tameuji got in the first blow, whacking Lady Shōshō when she moved her curtains a bit. Two days later Shōshō got her revenge with the assistance of the Retired Emperor, who kept the stick hidden inside his cloak. Shōshō sprang on the unsuspecting Tameuji as he was paying his respects to the Retired Emperor, and she hit him until the stick all but broke. Everybody, from the Retired Emperor on down, joined in the laughter.[8]

Lady Ben's diary may be lightweight, but it adds welcome variety to Japanese diary literature, evidencing the spirit of fun and love of practical jokes characteristic of both modern Japanese and those of the Kamakura period.

The Diary of Lady Nakatsukasa

The Diary of Lady Nakatsukasa, despite the general opinion of Japanese critics, is in no sense gloomy. It is filled, on the contrary, with descriptions of the pleasures of life at the court during the thirteen years (1280–92) covered by the diary. Various disasters struck Japan during these years, notably the abortive invasions of the Mongols, but, with one exception, Nakatsukasa omits all mention of such unhappy events. The exception was the incursion into the palace in 1290 by Asahara Tameyori and the consternation this caused. Nevertheless, the diary account does not conclude with expressions of fear as to what this inauspicious act might portend. Instead, Lady Nakatsukasa gives a lengthy description of the costume the Emperor wore when he moved to his mother's palace in order to escape the defilement the rebellious Asahara was wreaking on his own palace.

Lady Nakatsukasa served the Emperor Fushimi both while he was crown prince and after he succeeded his father, the Emperor Gouda. An early entry in the diary, for the 8th month of 1281, suggests its characteristic tone: "The rain, which had fallen since dusk, cleared up as it grew late, and the moonlight, shining so brightly that the sky itself seemed different, was lovely. People came from the crown prince's palace to enjoy the moon. The enchanting mist in the air, the dew still sparkling unclouded, and the cries of the insects, singing in their different voices, all combined to produce an unforgettable impression. Drops of dew, shivering heartbreakingly as the wind caught them, gave a special light to the pine branches. They looked like precious jewels of the Buddha, and I thought that not even the jewel of the Buddha at Sagano could be more beautiful."

onozukara	It did not take long
shibashi mo kienu	For them to vanish of themselves.
tanomi ka wa	Can one depend on them?
nokibe no matsu ni	The drops of white dew hanging
kakaru shiratsuyu[1]	On the pine trees by the eaves.

There is perhaps nothing remarkable about this passage, but it perfectly conveys the atmosphere of an autumn evening. The poem tells us Lady Nakatsukasa is poignantly aware that such beauty cannot last, that the joy beauty brings is apt to evaporate like the dew. But this is far from a rejection of beauty, in the manner of Buddhist writers who spurned the ephemeral beauty of this world because their hearts were set on the eternal beauty of the world to come. Nakatsukasa deeply loved the beauty of this world, as she revealed in many similar passages in her diary, but its perishability induced tears. Yet perishability was itself a necessary condition of beauty. This perception would be elevated by the priest Kenkō in the fourteenth century into a philosophy of beauty: "If man were never to fade away like the dews of Adashino, never to vanish like the smoke over Toribeyama, but lingered forever in the world, how things would lose their power to move us! The most precious thing in life is its uncertainty."[2] The importance of perishability as an essential part of beauty had long been tacitly recognized by the Japanese, who prized the cherry blossoms that fall after their brief flowering more than the hardier plum blossoms or chrysanthemums that fade slowly. In the West men built marble temples for their gods in the hopes that their beauty would last forever, but the most striking feature of the Great Shrine of Ise, renewed every twenty years, is its perishability.

Nakatsukasa probably wrote her diary after she completed service at the court, and she remembered with mingled joy and nostalgia the days she had known. Even sad occasions were too precious to forget, and she described them in her diary: "Living in the world, one naturally has many unforgettable experiences, and some of them are the cause of tears, but those are the ones I want most to preserve. . . ."[3] This clearly was not an expression of disenchantment with life. Surely no one has savored more deeply the pleasures traditionally evoked in the *waka* than Nakatsukasa, and her diary preserves her perceptions with rare skill.

The prevailing impression one receives from Nakatsukasa's diary is of an exquisitely refined court whose members delighted in playing and listening to music, especially music heard while in a boat in the moonlight. Many passages describe such entertainments, which sometimes continued until dawn, as on this occasion in 1294: "On the 5th day of the 7th month His Highness the crown prince visited the Kitayama Mansion.[4] The Retired Emperor[5] also came, and this made the imperial outing especially brilliant. During the day His Highness visited various places, including the mountain waterfall, and when it got dark he boarded his boat. From the time of the month that the evening moon appeared in the sky until the time that the moon appeared at daybreak, he did not miss a single night.

"On the 9th, when the moon first showed itself, he boarded his boat as usual. His host, the *daibu*,[6] said, 'The boat is late this evening,' adding, 'We are exhausted with our pleasures!' His Highness rested for a while at the Angling Pavilion, but presently his boat was pushed out. Music was played. No words can describe the delightfulness of the sounds exchanged by the courtiers playing in antiphony from small boats on either side of the island in the pond. The faint beating of a drum could be heard from one boat that had been rowed far from shore. This took everyone by surprise and people asked each other where the sounds could be coming from. 'It must be the *daibu*,' someone said. A boat was rowed out to meet his, and those aboard played music and chanted poetry. The *daibu*, as his boat drew near, had flares lit, a sight that much delighted His Highness."[7]

It is tempting to quote page after page of Nakatsukasa's diary. Her descriptions of evenings spent making music are without exception lovely. It is baffling how anyone could have derived the impression that she was a tormented woman. Indeed, the problem in this diary is not that it is likely to depress readers by its pervading gloom but that it presents so enchanting a picture of court life that the reader is likely to wonder: was there no rivalry among the courtiers? no harsh exchanges of words? no women seduced against their will? We know, as a matter of fact, from the almost exactly contemporaneous diary *The Confessions of Lady Nijō* that all these ugly elements were in fact present at the court, and the author of that diary described them vividly. But Nakatsukasa evidently did not wish to write about such matters. She was not making a confession and had no desire to expose the seamier side of court life. It must be admitted that there is some monotony in the many pages of the diary devoted to descriptions of music-making, but it is the monotony of the *waka* composed on prescribed topics, where the intent is not to impress with novelty but to come even slightly closer with each attempt to the heart of the subject treated.

Nakatsukasa's descriptions are not confined to the court. She occasionally traveled, especially to places she knew from literature. This is what she wrote when she visited the Pond of Sarusawa in Nara: "When I looked at the Pond of Sarusawa, the water was perfectly clear, and I felt as though I could see the maid of honor float up to the surface, just as she appeared long ago when she threw herself into the pond. How sad she must have felt when she looked at her reflection, clear as in a mirror, for the last time." It is much harder today to imagine the maid of honor (*uneme*) throwing herself into the pond after looking at her reflection, if only because the surface is likely to be littered with debris, but the Byōdō-in (Phoenix Hall) at Uji fortunately is still much as it was in Nakatsukasa's day: "When I saw the Byōdō-in, I realized why people said it is possible here to visualize the splendor of paradise. Even the colors of the autumn leaves are different, perhaps because the autumn rains dye them in particularly lovely colors here and only here. I wanted to pick some as souvenirs for people in the capital, but put it off until my return. As I was passing the pond of Nieno, many birds had come down on the water and were frolicking there."[8]

Nakatsukasa excelled at pictorial descriptions. She wrote about a festival at Iwashimizu, "The cherry blossoms were in their full glory, and when a wind blew a little, the dancers under the cascading petals looked as if they had been drawn in a picture."[9] I was moved also by her account of *kagura* dances in the palace on a winter night: "The snow that had fallen on the black of the dancers' robes, caught in the light of the garden flares, looked extraordinarily pure and holy even when it was brushed away, especially because of the occasion."[10] Her diary is a poetic evocation of *temps perdu*, written not out of depression but nostalgia.

Nakatsukasa traveled even beyond the immediate region of the capital. Her journey (for unspecified reasons) to Amagasaki was recorded with particular felicity, as this passage may suggest: "I left the capital late at night. By the time I reached the Toba Palace, the night was gradually giving way to the dawn, and since it was just the time of year when the leaves were beginning to turn, the tops of the trees against the sky were lovely and quite delightful. I went to board my boat, but there were so many boats I could hardly pick my way among them, and there were men with frightening voices talking in a way I had never heard before. But even as I listened to their jabbering, I felt moved to be in these unfamiliar surroundings. I recalled the Kitayama Mansion,[11] but there was nobody with whom even to exchange comments on my impressions. As we were rowed far out from shore the river fog rose, and soon it was impossible to see where we had come from or where we were going. When we passed Katano, the old imperial hunting preserve, I gazed at it for some time, thinking that this was a place I had known only by repute and never seen before. It was too far away to get a good look, but somebody said that the birds we could see flying up from the low bushes in the fields were pheasants."[12]

The place was intriguingly unfamiliar, and even the noisy boatmen seem to have charmed Nakatsukasa, enjoying a rare glimpse of the world outside the capital. The name Katano recalls the beautiful poem by Fujiwara Shunzei, written about a century earlier:

mata ya min	Shall I see it again?
Katano no mino no	The hunt in the Katano fields

sakuragari	For cherry blossoms
hana no yuki chiru	One early morning in spring
haru no akebono[13]	When a snow of flowers fell.

The mood of this *waka* is the prevailing mood of Nakatsukasa's diary. Each landscape she saw stirred in her the uncertainty Shunzei felt—would she ever see such loveliness again? Nakatsukasa must have known that she would not, for she was writing this part of her diary at a time when age and illness had forced her to withdraw from the court. She now had only memories, but these were by no means unhappy memories. On the contrary, she felt compelled to describe their beauty. We can imagine that, even as she wrote, she reenacted her experiences with the same mixture of joy and regret found in Shunzei's poem.

Again and again in Nakatsukasa's diary there are echoes of the poetry of *Shin Kokinshū*, the great anthology of *waka* compiled at the beginning of the thirteenth century. The overall tone is suggested by another *waka* by Shunzei:

tare ka mata	Who in the future
hana tachibana ni	Will recall me in the scent
omoiiden	Of orange blossoms
ware mo mukashi no	When I, too, shall have become
hito to narinaba	A person of long ago?

Nakatsukasa probably did not much care whether or not she would be remembered by people of future times, but she could not bear to think that the beauty she had witnessed might some day be forgotten.

Even critics who dislike this diary concede that the descriptions of the abdication of the Emperor Gouda and the accession of the Emperor Fushimi have historical importance, but in literary terms these are not the most important parts of the work. Nakatsukasa was not interested in politics. She paid no attention to court gossip. She sensed that the world she had known would not last much longer, and in her diary she preserved its beauty for all time.

The Confessions of Lady Nijō

One is likely to obtain the impression from *The Diary of Lady Nakatsukasa* that the court in Kyōto of her day was a place of incomparable refinement. *Towazugatari*[1] (*The Confessions of Lady Nijō*), which portrays the same court, creates (without in any way contradicting Nakatsukasa's diary) an impression of a den of rampant promiscuity and moral corruption. Of the many diaries written by court ladies, none is as startling or shocking as *The Confessions of Lady Nijō*.

The diary opens on New Year's Day of 1271. That day Koga Masatada, a distinguished official and poet and the son of Fujiwara Teika's enemy Minamoto Michichika, served the traditional spiced wine to the Retired Emperor Gofukakusa. When the latter (and everyone else) had become completely inebriated, the Retired Emperor murmured to Masatada, "Let the wild goose of the fields come to me this spring."[2] The words contained an allusion to a passage in *The Tales of Ise*[3] and meant in this context that the Retired Emperor wanted Masatada to send him his daughter, Nijō, in the spring. Masatada was far from resenting the proposal; in fact, he was absolutely delighted by this mark of imperial favor.

Nijō was then fourteen (thirteen by Western reckoning). From her early childhood, Gofukakusa had guided her in artistic pursuits, but he had been impatiently waiting all the while for her to reach an age when he could make love to her. The time had now arrived. When Nijō returned to her room after the New Year's ceremony, she found a present of elaborate robes, together with a poem that hinted at the desirability of greater intimacy. Bewildered, she returned the gift, only to have it sent back with another poem. This time she accepted, not knowing what else to do, but she still did not understand the significance of the gift. Her father, seeing her wear the robes, asked knowingly, "Did you receive them from the Palace?" Nijō, realizing that there was a hidden meaning in the question, lied, saying the robes were a gift from her great-aunt.[4]

Ten days later Nijō returned home from the palace at her father's command. She was surprised to see how lavishly the house had been decorated, and asked the reason. She was informed that the Retired Emperor would be stopping here, in order to avoid traveling in a prohibited direction. Her father, warning her not to fall asleep that night until His Majesty appeared, reminded her, "A lady-in-waiting should not be stubborn, but should do exactly as she's told."[5] She fell asleep anyway, and when she opened her eyes the Retired Emperor was lying beside her. He declared that he had loved her since she was a small child, but all she could do by way of response to his words was to weep. He made no attempt that night to force her, but the following night he came to her room again, and this time treated her so mercilessly that her thin gowns were ripped. She wrote, "By the time I had nothing more to lose I despised my own existence."[6] Then, imagining that she was already the subject of gossip, she wrote the poem:

kokoro yori	Not of my choosing,
hoka ni tokenuru	My undersash was untied
shitaobi no	In surrender, now
ika naru fushi ni	I wonder in what manner
uki na nagasan[7]	Gossip will spread about me.

She had been raped by a man she trusted, with the connivance of her own father. But afterward, when the Retired Emperor insisted that she see him off, she discovered that her feelings of indignation had dissipated. She wrote, "I felt more attracted to him than I ever had before, and I wondered uneasily where these new feelings had come from."[8]

One may admire the honesty with which Nijō recorded her induction into the world of adults, her revulsion and subsequent abrupt, inexplicable change of feelings. Nevertheless, the modern reader is apt to be shocked. The rape itself was probably less upsetting to people of Nijō's day. Had not the peerless Genji done precisely the same to his young ward, Murasaki? "Murasaki was at first horrified and bitterly disillusioned: She had not dreamt he had anything of the sort in mind. What a fool she had been to repose her trust in so gross and unscrupulous a man."[9] But the resentment that Murasaki felt over this betrayal soon gave way to love for Genji, and Genji's behavior has ever since seemed to most readers not only forgivable but inevitable.

The acquiescence of Japanese women to being seduced by men of superior social status was probably not much different from what actually occurred in the West, but any father who actively promoted the seduction of his daughter would have been harshly dealt with in European fiction, if not in reality. In Richardson's *Pamela* (1740) the father, though a manual laborer, warns his beautiful daughter to beware of the kindness of the man in whose household she is employed, lest her gratitude to him induce her to yield her virtue. He declares, "Arm yourself, my dear child, for the worst; and resolve to lose your life rather than your virtue." *Pamela* is a long novel devoted to one theme—how the heroine maintained her chastity in the face of the repeated onslaughts of her master. Nijō, for all her initial shock over being violated, would probably have found Pamela's resistance exaggerated, or even comic, and so would most people of her time. The rape of the girl Nijō, occurring early in her diary, sets the tone of the entire work in its combination of brutality and elegance and its pervasive odor of moral decay.

The Retired Emperor, having taken Nijō, insisted that she accompany him to his palace. She recorded, "I suppose our ride might be considered amusing, for all the way to the palace Go Fukakusa pledged his affection to me as if he were a storied lover making off with his mistress, but for me the road we travelled seemed so dreary I could do nothing but weep."[10] But gradually the Retired Emperor's demonstrations of affection melted her resistance, and soon she was reading his letters with eagerness.

Later in the same year, 1272, Nijō's father died, to her great sorrow. Among his deathbed injunctions was the command that she be faithful to her master—that is, the Retired Emperor Gofukakusa. If she should by some chance incur his ill will, she was to enter a convent immediately and pray that she, her family, and her lover would all be joined in paradise. "But if, finding yourself forsaken and alone, you decide to serve another master or try to make your way by entering any other household whatsoever, consider yourself disowned even though I am already dead."[11] Nijō does not seem to have taken these injunctions to heart. Her passionate nature was not to be constrained by conventional morality, and the ripe corruption of the court fostered her wayward inclinations.

A certain man who had inquired about Nijō every day since her father's death visited her one night by moonlight, and they spent the night talking. Both wore mourning dress, and that may be why they did not get into bed together. When he left he said, "I suppose people will gossip about my staying here all night even though things aren't what they seem."[12] Not long afterward he visited her again. Nijō at first refused to admit him, but he promised not to do anything rash. However, Nijō continues, "His eloquence throughout the long night would have softened the heart of a Chinese tiger, not to mention my own, which is far from adamantine, so although I had not the slightest intention of giving myself, I did. I wondered if perhaps His Majesty would learn of my unexpected new love in a dream, and I was afraid."[13]

Nijō referred to this lover as Yuki no Akebono (Snowy Daybreak, from the night they met) in passages dealing with their intimate relations, but elsewhere by his real name, Saionji Sanekane.[14] He remained her lover for some years and was the father of one of her four children. The acquisition of this lover did not cause any crisis in her relations with the Retired Emperor Gofukakusa; in fact, they became more intimate than ever, even though each was aware of the infidelities of the other. When the Retired Emperor learned about Nijō's relations with Sanekane, he sent her a letter written in exceptionally tender language:

mubatama no	In the darkness of
yume ni zo mitsuru	A dream I thought that I saw
sayogoromo	Another man's sleeve
aranu tamoto wo	Lying upon the garment
kasanekeri to wa[15]	You wear in bed at night.

Nijō commented, "Only too aware of my shamelessness, I attempted to mislead him."[16]

On other occasions the Retired Emperor even arranged for Nijō to give herself to men. We are told, in the most shocking incident of the diary, how one night in the dark a man (probably the Chancellor) suddenly grabbed Nijō's sleeve and professed his love.[17] She managed to escape, but the next night, while she was massaging the Retired Emperor's back, the same man called to her, asking to meet her when the Retired Emperor was asleep. She writes, "The Retired Emperor then whispered to me, 'Hurry up, go. You have nothing to worry about.' I was so embarrassed I wanted to die. Then His Majesty reached out, and seizing my hand, he pulled me up. Without intending it, I was compelled to go."[18]

Nijō and the man made love in the next room, separated from the Retired Emperor only by a paper partition. "Though he feigned sleep I was wretchedly aware that he was listening. I wept, but my accoster was very drunk." The next night the same man returned, and once again the Retired Emperor urged Nijō to go to him. His action suggests not so much generosity as contempt for Nijō as a woman, but Nijō, with her incredible candor, concludes this chapter of her diary with a description of the departure of the previous nights in these terms: "For some reason I gazed after my visitor's carriage as though I regretted our parting. When, I wondered, did such feelings arise in my own heart?"[19] The reader might be tempted to ask the same question if he had not already been alerted to Nijō's capacity for loving more than one man at the same time.

Nijō's deepest emotions were aroused by the priest she calls Ariake no Tsuki (The Moon at Dawn). He was a half-brother of Gofukakusa, and was otherwise known as the Cloistered Prince Shōjo. He resided at the Ninna-ji, one of the great Shingon temples in Kyōto. Nijō relates how in 1275 a visitor (whom she does not identify) came to the palace while the Retired Emperor was attending a lecture given in memory of the late Emperor Goshirakawa. She writes, "Because he was not the kind of person who normally would have aroused my suspicions, I remained and listened to him talk about the past." Suddenly he blurted out, "I wonder if the Buddha knows with what a tainted heart I perform my services."[20] He seized her sleeve and insisted, "At least promise that we can meet!" Nijō comments, "To make matters more complicated, tears of sincerity glistened in his eyes. I pulled free and escaped only because His Majesty's return was announced."[21]

Ariake continued during the following months to seize every chance to declare his love. One evening, after he had been praying at the palace for Gofukakusa's recovery from illness, he followed Nijō into a small room, where he told her, "Even when we walk in paths of darkness we are guided by the Lord Buddha."[22] He embraced her, and insisted that she come to him after the final service that night. She recalls, "My heart was not entirely possessed by love, and yet late that night, seen by no one, I slipped out and went to him." From then on they met almost every night. "This meant that Ariake was offering prayers with an impure heart. I was ashamed of what Buddha must think."[23]

Nijō at one point decided to break with Ariake. She made excuses not to meet him, but her uncle, a major counselor, sent a letter urging her to be kinder to Ariake, "for surely an inescapable fate is causing him to love you so fervently."[24] He enclosed a letter from Ariake describing his love: "Night after night I wept out of longing for you; every time I faced the holy image to read a sutra your words came to mind; I placed your letters on the altar of sacred fires and made them my private sutra; I opened them by the light of holy candles and let them soothe my heart."[25] Ariake foresaw that the punishment for his sin in having violated his vow of chastity would be consignment to the lower realms of existence in future reincarnations, but he was powerless to control his love.

One day when Gofukakusa summoned Ariake, he took advantage of the opportunity to meet Nijō and declare his love for her openly. She writes, "At a loss for a reply, I simply listened—unaware that His Majesty had returned soon after he had left us and was standing on the other side of the *shōji*, where he could surely hear Ariake's oft-repeated laments."[26] The Retired Emperor, far from being upset to have heard Ariake's declarations of love, urged Nijō to be kinder to Ariake and in this way help to free him of his attachment. She remarks, "I wonder why he was not feeling aggrieved."[27] The modern reader is likely to share her bewilderment. In any case, Nijō complied with the Retired Emperor's request, and eventually she bore Ariake two children.

Nijō's promiscuity was not entirely of her own choosing. At the end of one drunken party, for example, she was made to lie in bed between Gofukakusa and his brother Kameyama, the "new Retired Emperor," and soon the latter led her behind a screen and they became lovers. The next night Nijō again slept between the two brothers, with the same results. She comments, "Once more I was made painfully aware of this world's trying ways."[28]

The fourth book of *The Confessions of Lady Nijō* opens with the abrupt disclosure that Nijō, who had become a nun at some time between 1285 (when the third book ends) and 1289, was about to leave the capital on the first of her pilgrimages. She gave no explanation of her reasons for taking vows. She had certainly considered it before, but had hitherto refused to take the step because of worldly ties. Presumably she was sincere when she at last became a nun, but she did not change much even after putting on somber robes. Her mind continued to dwell on the past, especially her life in the palace and the love she had been shown by Gofukakusa. Unable to keep such memories shut up within herself, she decided to write what she called *itazuragoto*, "a piece of mischief." She apparently hoped that describing the events of her life in this way would enable her to escape feeling that her life had been meaningless. She wrote that she did not expect her "confession" to survive her very long, a prophecy that almost proved to be accurate: the sole manuscript, long lost, was not rediscovered until 1940.

The immediate impetus for writing her confessions may have been the need she felt to record the pilgrimages she made as a nun to various holy sites, but the account of her life as a nun occupies only the last two of the five books of the diary. The first three books may have been intended as a public confession, though Nijō does not seem to repent of any of her sins. Perhaps she was affected by a dream in which her father recited a poem urging her to continue the family traditions of poetry.[29] Nijō's intent was obviously literary, and she was no doubt influenced by her readings in "the old tales."[30] She would not have been satisfied with writing merely a factual account of her distant and recent past. But, regardless of the degree to which she allowed her imagination to interpret the facts or the amount of wholly fictitious material in the diary, most of the work has the unmistakable ring of truth.

A revealing anecdote is related toward the end of the diary. Learning that Gofukakusa was seriously ill, Nijō prayed at the Kitano and Hirano shrines: " 'Take my life instead of His Majesty's!' Then I realized that if my supplication were to be granted and I disappeared like dew I would have died for His Majesty without him even knowing of it. That too made me sad."[31] Her generosity in offering to die in place of a man who did not always treat her well is vitiated by her desire to be given credit for her generosity. This sentiment is easily intelligible, but most writers—even of confessions—would have suppressed mention of a thought that brought them so little credit.

Nijō seems to hide nothing, and we are therefore apt to accept without question her account of life at court, especially the amorous intrigues in which former emperors, chancellors, high-ranking courtiers, and priests all participated. It would be an oversimplification to attribute this moral laxity to the age. Similar accounts of European courts could easily be written. The most distinctive features of the Japanese court of the thirteenth century are also described in Nijō's diary, but in parts that the reader is likely to forget—descriptions of gatherings at which members of the court assumed the roles of characters in *The Tale of Genji*, the frequent exchanges of poetry, the music-making, the cult of beauty that extended to the most trivial aspects of life. This was the side of court life that Lady Nakatsukasa chose to describe. Neither she nor Nijō can be trusted fully as a chronicler of her times, but each, in the manner of every diarist worthy of the name, provides us with an unforgettable portrait of the author herself.

Account of the Takemuki Palace

Takemuki ga Ki (*Account of the Takemuki Palace*) is the diary kept by the court lady Hino Nako.[1] Apart from its intrinsic interest, this diary has the melancholy importance of being the last written by a court lady, at least for many hundreds of years; with it the tradition begun with *The Gossamer Years* comes to an end. The title of the diary refers to the place where Nako lived at the time when she wrote the latter half of the work. It opens in 1329 with a description of the *gembuku* (coming-of-age) ceremony of the crown prince and continues until 1349 with a description of a visit to a temple to the north of Kyōto when the cherry blossoms were at their height. Nako died in 1358, probably about fifty years old.

Account of the Takemuki Palace is not as artistically satisfying as the diaries of earlier court ladies but, read in conjunction with what we can discover about the author from other sources, it is at times almost unbearably moving. The diary consists of two books, the first centered on the love shared by Nako and Saionji Kinmune before they were torn apart by the warfare waged by adherents of the Southern Court and the Northern Court; the second is devoted mainly to Nako's efforts to have her son succeed as the head of the Saionji family and to restore the family's glory. Ever since the diary was first printed in 1911, there has been speculation about the likelihood that there was originally a middle volume. The gap of over three years between the end of the first book and the beginning of the second suggests that an in-between account once existed. This middle volume would have related the death of Kinmune, the birth of their son, the years when Nako and the son were in hiding, and, finally, the return to power of the Northern Court—in other words, the most dramatic years of Nako's life. Most specialists today, however, tend to doubt that Nako ever wrote the middle volume, if only because she would not have wished to treat materials that so conspicuously violate the expectations of what a diary kept by a court lady should contain.

The opening sections of the diary are written in a rather stiff, formal style, somewhat resembling that of the official diaries kept by the men of the court. Nako listed the people who played musical instruments, recited poetry, performed dances, and so on during the entertainments that accompanied the *gembuku* ceremony of 1329 at the Jimyōin-den, the residence of the two retired emperors Gofushimi and Hanazono. The impression of an official document is underlined by Nako's mention of a diagram of the ceremony that was to be attached to *go-nikki*, presumably the diary kept by the crown prince himself.[2]

The description of these entertainments is reminiscent of court life in more tranquil days, but it is followed immediately by mention of an event that would alter Japanese history: "The report that His Majesty had disappeared on the night of the 24th day of the 8th month of 1331 reached our ears at dawn on the following day, causing immense confusion."[3] The Emperor Godaigo had secretly left the imperial palace, taking with him the imperial regalia. This action presaged the bitter conflict that would soon develop between the Southern Court (Godaigo's adherents) and the Northern Court (the shogunate). Nako lived through this conflict and was deeply involved. Her uncle Hino Suketomo[4] colluded with Godaigo and was later captured by the shogunate and exiled to the island of Sado, where he was executed. But Nako's husband and most of her family, including her father and brothers, were supporters of the Northern Court and suffered during the years 1333–36, when Godaigo returned to power.

Initially Nako could have had no idea of the magnitude of the coming conflict. Godaigo was captured and the regalia were handed over to a new emperor, who had been chosen by the shogunate. Nako herself was entrusted with rewrapping the box containing the Sacred Mirror, and was overwhelmed to think that she held in her hands a treasure that dated back to the age of the gods.

The next episode in *Account of the Takemuki Palace* opens, "On the 1st day of the 11th month there was a solar eclipse. A heavy snow had been falling since the previous night, and the Emperor was unhappy to be shut up indoors. The Saionji Major Counselor,[5] in attendance on His Majesty during his seclusion, opened the sliding door in the Upper Chamber a crack, and informed His Majesty that he might look outside. The Emperor did so."[6] Solar eclipses were dreaded by the court, and not only did everyone stay indoors but people feared to look outside; however, the new Emperor, Kōgon, was so disappointed not to be able to gaze on the newly fallen snow that Saionji Kinmune opened the door just wide enough for a glimpse. This disregard of custom may have accounted for the misfortunes that afflicted both men. Kōgon was soon forced to flee the capital by Southern Court troops, and Kinmune would be put to death at the age of twenty-five.

Perhaps Nako had some instinctive belief that the prohibition on exposing oneself to the baleful light of a solar eclipse was more than mere superstition. In one of the rare characterizations she gave of herself in the diary, she wrote that, although others crowded to the open door to look at the snow, "I, in my usual timid way, did not get up at once." Kinmune, seeing her hesitate, teased her. "What's this? You must be afraid of the snow!"[7] The diary was written after Kinmune's death, so this lighthearted jest, recalled after the painful events that ensued, must have had especially poignant overtones for Nako.

The first book of the diary contains various accounts of festivals and entertainments in the palace. Nako had an extraordinary memory for precisely what each person had worn on such occasions. She enumerates, for example, the colors of the costumes of almost every dignitary who attended the coronation of Kōgon in 1332. One can gather from the diary with what mixed emotions she recalled in later years the splendor of that occasion: "The sight of His Majesty in his formal robes and jeweled headdress, his scepter[8] held precisely at the right angle, added an extraordinary dignity to his Chinese-looking attire. . . . This Chinese dress was so unusual that it did not look like anything belonging to our world. . . . The smoke rising from the incense burners seemed to be the same color as the clouds, and I thought I heard someone say that even in China they would be able to tell that a new reign had begun in Japan."[9] She added the *waka*:

kyō ya sa wa	Today, in that case,
karakunibito mo	Even the men of China
kimi ga yo wo	Will know from the clouds
ama tsu sora yuku	Traveling across the sky
kumo ni shiruran	That a new reign has begun.

The unfamiliar splendor of a coronation, with its many exotic "Chinese" decorations, persuaded Nako that even in China people would learn of so auspicious an event. But by the time she wrote these words, some years later, she knew just how turbulent the new reign would actually be.

The most notable development in Nako's personal life is described at first in deliberately vague terms: "I happened, quite unexpectedly, to spend a night in travelers' lodgings. This was at the beginning of the 2nd month, and I was staying at the usual place. I was awakened by bird cries and the sound of bells. The dawn sky was covered with haze when I had my carriage drawn out, and a band of clouds over the peak was barely turning white. In the wind, strongly blowing, the fragrance of plum blossoms from somewhere unseen was wonderfully romantic, but, as I now recall, I was too preoccupied even to notice."[10]

This passage is taken by commentators to refer to the beginning of her love affair with Saionji Kinmune. They met "at the usual place," somewhere away from the court. From this time on, the diary includes poems exchanged by the lovers, starting with:

aratama no	At the beginning
toshi machiete mo	Of the year, long awaited,
itsu shika to	I still wonder when

kimi ni zo chigiru	You and I will be wedded
yuku sue no haru[11]	In the spring of our future.

Some scholars believe that Nako and Kinmune were already married, but others insist that the time of their marriage is not known. Regardless of when the marriage occurred, however, it is clear that Nako was accepted as Kinmune's wife by the Saionji family, making it possible for their child to be recognized one day as the head of the family.

The happiness of Nako and Kinmune was rudely interrupted in the 1st month of 1333 by the news that Godaigo had escaped from his place of exile in the Oki islands and was on his way to the capital. People flocked to the court to hear the latest rumors, and the streets were so jammed that the lovers were unable to meet. She wrote, "It was by no means easy for the carriages of ladies of the court to reach the palace, and it was all the more difficult for anyone attempting to make a secret meeting to get through."[12]

On the 16th day of the 3rd month of 1333 the Emperor and the two retired emperors moved to the headquarters of the shogunate agent at Rokuhara, no doubt so as to be under the protection of the military. Nako wrote, "He and I were so bewildered that we were completely at a loss what to do, but there is a danger that my words may be misconstrued, so I shall not record what I then thought." She realized that there was little place for women at Rokuhara, but she was reluctant to leave the Emperor without any ladies-in-waiting to serve him. She finally decided to go there, though some people tried to dissuade her by insisting that this would be a "very unbecoming thing."[13] Perhaps this is a reference to a first pregnancy (a pregnant woman would not have appeared before the Emperor), but her son, Sanetoshi, would not be born until two years later.

Nako was appalled by what she saw at Rokuhara. The place was full of people, and there was almost no privacy for the emperors. Worst of all, "to see savages so close at hand made me think I was in a different world." The word "savages" (*ebisu*) referred not to foreign barbarians but to armed warriors from Kamakura, who constituted the presence of the shogunate in the capital; it suggests how uncouth and frightening she found their military attire. Nako had intended to begin serving the three emperors the night of her arrival, but a report reached Rokuhara that the enemy—the forces of the Southern Court backing Godaigo—would attack at dawn. The military ordered all women to leave, and Nako was obliged to comply.

The next day it was discovered that the rumor had been false, but Nako had no way to return to Rokuhara. She moved to Kiyomizu, to be as near to Rokuhara as possible. Her days there were spent in anxious waiting. "Even as we all wondered, 'Will it be today? Will today be our last?' we passed the 20th of the 4th month."[14] That day she had a message from Kinmune that he had managed to arrange a meeting.

"He arrived when it was still evening. Soon we could hear the crowing of cocks and the voices of bells from here and there. He said, rather in a daze, 'Those are only imitations.' But after I had reminded him again and again how unbecoming it would be if they found him here when it grew light, he slid open the door. The dawn moon was very bright, and the *hagi* leaves near the eaves, much higher than usual at this time of year, grew so thickly not a crevice was visible through them. Even the lower leaves sparkled with the moonlight on the dew, too bright to hide. The sight of the dawn brightening the autumn sky surely would have been moving even if today had not had any special significance, but at the thought that this was our last time, as we confusedly sensed the terrible pathos of our love, we knew that whether we left or stayed there we could only be all the more forlorn."[15]

Dawn was now at hand. Kinmune, after first running a comb through his hair, left. Nako, too weak even to stand up and see him go, lay where she was, staring helplessly in his direction.

On the 7th day of the 5th month the Southern Court army surrounded Rokuhara, and that night set the place afire. Nako's house was near, and she could all but see her lover trying to escape in the smoke. She learned the next morning that he had succeeded in making his way to the east, but that his place of refuge was not secure. Nako herself with difficulty managed to reach the Saionji residence, where she learned that the flight of the Emperor, the two retired emperors, and their followers had been intercepted in the province of Ōmi, and that they were all being sent back to the capital. One elder brother had been wounded by a stray arrow. Her *waka*, in which she expressed astonishment that she still went on living, is probably the best in the diary:

kakute dani	How wretched our way
sutenu narai no	Of not giving up the world
mi no usa wa	Even after this—
omoishi yori mo	I have lived much longer
ararekeru kana[16]	Than I could have expected.

On the 21st day of the 5th month the Emperor Kōgon and the others of the Northern Court were brought back to Kyōto. Nako was shocked to discover that her father and eldest brother were now wearing priests' robes, having "given up the world." She does not write when or under what circumstances she again saw Kinmune, only that he forbade her to return to her parents' house as she wished. Perhaps he wanted to make the ties between Nako and his family as close as possible. He spoke of becoming a priest, but the retired emperors ordered him to abandon this thought. The first book concludes with Nako and Kinmune at a loss as to what they should do. She wrote, "I wonder if there is still anything left for me to relate in this pointless account that nobody has asked to hear."[17]

The second book of the diary, though not without interest, is far less dramatic than the first. It opens with a description of the ceremony during which her son, Sanetoshi, ate fish for the first time. He was two years old, and the diary takes him up to the age of fourteen, when he had already received the title of Middle Captain and Middle Counselor of the Third Rank. The restoration of the Northern Court in 1336 had brought the Saionji family back into favor again. Nako was determined that Sanetoshi, rather than his uncle Kinshige, should be recognized as the head of the family, and did what she could to promote his candidacy. She frequently expressed nostalgia for the past, but in general terms, rather than in memories of her husband. She took comfort from the sights of nature, and seemed to enjoy such palace festivities as the *Tale of Genji* party, an echo of a similar one described in *The Confessions of Lady Nijō*. The last entry in the diary, describing an excursion to view the cherry blossoms in the rain, contained an appropriate combination of happy and sad imagery.

In between the two books of the diary, in the middle book that was probably never written, there should have been an infinitely more exciting story than the one Nako chose to relate. Kinmune conspired to restore the shogunate. He was betrayed by his younger brother Kinshige and arrested in the 6th month of 1335. The Southern Court decided to exile him to the province of Izumo. The night before Kinmune's departure the Major Counselor Sadahira informed Nako of this decision, and she secretly went to Kinmune's place of confinement. She found him trussed in a tiny cell, unable even to move. He had been weeping, and seeing her induced a fresh flood of tears, but at length he checked his tears and said, "I am sinking in the depths of my sins like an abandoned boat that nobody is willing to row. But now that I have learned that your physical condition is not usual,[18] I can imagine how much you must be suffering on account of me, and I feel sure that this, too, will be a source of delusion in the darkness of the path ahead of me. If the child is a boy, please do not give up hopes for him in the future, but cherish him in your bosom and make him into a man."[19] He gave her for their unborn child, as a memento of the father whom the child would never see, some secret pieces for the *biwa* and an amulet, possessions of his family.

Kinmune was turned over to Nawa Nagatoshi, the governor of Hōki, in preparation for his departure the next morning at dawn. Nako hid behind a fence and watched as Kinmune was dragged to the central gate. He was about to be put into a palanquin when Sadahira, turning to Nagatoshi, said, "Quickly [*haya*]!" Nagatoshi, supposing this meant that he should dispose of Kinmune quickly, grabbed him by the hair and forced him to the ground. Then, unsheathing his sword, he cut off Kinmune's head. The *Taiheiki* (*Chronicle of Great Peace*), which records this incident, states, "His wife, seeing this, uttered a shriek without realizing it, and collapsed inside the fence."[20]

Nako fulfilled Kinmune's last request. Hardly had their son Sanetoshi been born when Southern Court soldiers came looking for him, but she gave out word that the infant had died, and this was believed. The child was kept in hiding until the warlord Ashikaga Takauji seized the capital in 1336 and restored the Northern Court. Saionji Sanetoshi (1335–89) rose to be Minister of the Left, a worthy successor to his father.

It cannot be pretended that *Account of the Takemuki Palace* possesses the literary value of the great diaries kept by the Heian court ladies. The second book is only intermittently interesting, and even the first book contains dull passages. Nako's fascination with what people wore interrupts the narrative with unnecessarily detailed descriptions. Her language is also so vague that at times it is not clear to whom she is referring. This is definitely not polished writing.

But, no matter how many qualifications are made concerning the literary value of this diary, it is an unforgettable document. Unlike the court ladies of the Heian period, whose chief concern was their poetic vision of the world, Nako was faced with disasters. It is true that Lady Daibu also lost a lover in the wars, but she did not actually see him die, nor did she smell the smoke of burning buildings. Nako, having experienced two violent changes of regime in a short period of time, had reason to dread that her son might not survive to manhood. Even during the relatively quiet years described in the second book, warfare still continued outside the capital.

We are likely to regret that Nako did not describe the death of her husband before her eyes and the other tragedies she witnessed, but perhaps the vocabulary she had inherited from the Heian diarists did not permit expression of such heartrending violence. Some scholars have suggested that she might have feared the consequences if a diary that described political events was discovered. Perhaps so, but since there is no record of anyone having even noticed the existing diary before the twentieth century, she might just as well have written an absolutely frank account. Perhaps, too, she assumed that the most likely reader of her "unasked-for tale," her son, would have known about his father's fate, though not about less dramatic events.

It seems likely that Nako wrote the diary not for distant posterity but for her son, Sanetoshi. She wished to tell him, in the only way an unliterary woman could, what her life was like before he was born, and afterward. She was unfamiliar with politics as such, and never even expressed an opinion of Godaigo's revolt, which precipitated the civil war. All military men were for her "savages," regardless of the side to which they belonged.

Japanese works of history and literature tend to induce contemporary readers to admire the Southern Court and its adherents. It comes therefore as a shock to read the diary of a woman who dreaded the return to the capital of Godaigo, the exiled Emperor. It is startling also to discover that many aristocrats welcomed the warlord Ashikaga Takauji when he entered Kyōto. This discovery recalled a childhood experience of mine. When I was growing up in New York, I lived next door to an English family, and read their son's books when he had finished them. How surprised I was to read an account of the American Revolution so unlike the one in my history textbook! Years later, when reading the wartime diaries of Japanese soldiers, I felt similar doubts concerning the truth of the American characterization of the war. Reading *Account of the Takemuki Palace* brought back these experiences, and I may as a result have overvalued its importance. But, regardless of its literary value, it suggests what life was like during a particular turbulent era, and it is hard not to admire the unassertive Nako for the strength of her love.

Diaries of the Muromachi Period

As far as I am aware, not a single diary written by a woman has been preserved from the period of over two centuries after *Account of the Takemuki Palace*. The men who kept diaries during the Muromachi period (1336–1573) consisted mainly of officials who wrote in classical Chinese, and Buddhist priests who described their travels (and other worldly experiences) in Japanese. The diaries in Chinese contain valuable information, especially for scholars of Muromachi history, but their intent was seldom literary, even when the writer was, like Sanjōnishi Sanetaka (1455–1537), an established poet. The diaries in Japanese are unquestionably of greater literary interest than the ponderous court records kept in Chinese, but even so, their relative lack of appeal for contemporary readers is suggested by the fact that not one has been included in any of the standard collections of classical Japanese literature that have appeared since 1945. Many are available only in *Gunsho Ruijū*, a massive compendium originally published in 1819.

The lack of appeal of these diaries is surely related to the loss of subjectivity. The male diarists of the Heian and Kamakura periods who wrote in Japanese were following introspective traditions established by the court ladies, and their diaries, consciously or unconsciously, revealed the different personalities of the diarists. This feminine influence on the diary was similar to the feminine influence on the *waka*. A sensitivity to beauty and an awareness of its perishability, together with a preoccupation with the passage of time, were typical of both the *waka* and the diaries in Japanese, whether written by women or men.

The Muromachi-period diarists were not insensitive to beauty. They also had many occasions to reflect on the devastation wrought by time—and by warfare—but they rarely chose to reveal their feelings openly. Their deepest emotions were hidden under bare statements whose full import is not always clear. Their sensitivity was reticent rather than poignant in its expression.

When reading Bashō's *The Narrow Road of Oku*, the culmination of the medieval traditions of the diary, we are apt to be overwhelmed by the beauty of the language, the aptness of the evocations of famous places, the moving content of the author's reflections on such eternal themes as the sadness of the passage of time. But Bashō reveals little concerning his private emotions. When the gods of the road beckoned, he could not resist their invitation to make a journey, but he does not mention, for example, if his decision to travel in that particular year was influenced by the fact it was the five hundredth anniversary of the death of Saigyō, nor does he give any clues into private motives he might have had, such as increasing the number of his disciples in the northern provinces. There is naturally no suggestion of emotional involvement with the people he met along the way, or mention of ties in Edo that might have made him want to return home quickly. He allows us to see only what he wishes us to see of himself, whereas the Heian court ladies not infrequently seem willing to tell us everything.

The Narrow Road of Oku is one of the classics of Japanese literature. The diaries of the wandering monks and officials of the Muromachi period are by no means of comparable literary distinction, but they are in the same tradition, and some undoubtedly contributed to the formation of Bashō's masterpiece. Unlike the diaries of the court ladies, they at least pretend to have been kept day by day. They also insist on the truth of the events they record, while the court ladies had not hesitated to describe their imaginings. In the hands of ungifted diarists the preoccupation with facts often cramps the style and diminishes the universality of the themes; but at times, too, such diaries, by virtue of their truth if not their beauty, make us forget how much was lost with the disappearance of the feminine tradition.

Account of a Pilgrimage to the Great Shrine of Ise

Ise Daijingū Sankeiki (*Account of a Pilgrimage to the Great Shrine of Ise*), the diary in which the priest Saka Jūbutsu described his journey to Ise, is interesting less because of what it reveals of the author than because of the special insights it provides into the strange relationship that existed at the time between Buddhism and Shintō, the native religion. The Buddhist priests of the Heian period had explained the Shintō gods as manifestations in Japan of eternal Buddhist divinities; in accordance with such explanations, the Shintō god Hachiman had been accorded the Buddhist title of "great bodhisattva." The union of the two religions, despite their contradictory tenets—Buddhism being essentially otherworldly and Shintō this-worldly—eventually came to be accepted by most Japanese, who turned to Shintō for help in this world, but to Buddhism for the promise of happiness in the next. As early as 768 a Buddhist temple had been erected in the vicinity of the Great Shrine of Ise, and from that time on many priests officiated at both Shintō and Buddhist places of worship.

The union of Buddhism with another religion had existed long before Buddhism reached Japan. Shakyamuni Buddha himself had recognized the existence of popular gods called devas who, though far less powerful than himself, were superior to ordinary men. There are many references to the conversion of the devas to

Buddhism after they heard the Buddha preach. In China, too, the Buddhists had at times claimed that Confucius, Lao Tzu, and other great philosophers had been sent to this world by the Buddha in order to help mankind.

Kūkai (or Kōbō Daishi, 774–835), usually considered to have been the greatest Japanese Buddhist theorist, was often mentioned as the originator of the doctrine of *honji suijaku* ("original substance manifests its traces"), according to which various buddhas had manifested their "traces" in the form of the Shintō gods in Japan. Although many forged works on the subject are attributed to Kūkai, there is no proof that the doctrine was known in his time. However, it is quite true that Kūkai offered special reverence to the Japanese gods: when he built the temples on Mount Kōya that became the headquarters of Shingon Buddhism, he called on the help of the local divinities, and he also ordered evil gods, who might hinder or even destroy Buddhism, to flee the place. In time a special relationship developed between Shingon Buddhism and Shintō. The Shintō priests adopted the incantations, gestures, ritual fire, rites, and other features of Shingon, and an equation was made between the two mandalas, or Shingon representations of the cosmos, and the Inner and Outer Shrines at Ise.

The two unsuccessful Mongol invasions of Japan in the thirteenth century led to strong sentiments of national consciousness among the Japanese, and by the beginning of the Muromachi period forged documents, which purported to have been written in remote antiquity, set forth a Shintō philosophy and ethics. Before long it was claimed that the Japanese gods were in fact the "original substance" and the Buddha and bodhisattvas were only "manifested traces" in foreign lands. The writings of Yoshida Kanetomo (1435–1511) contain the claim that Shintō was the "roots and trunk" of civilization, the Chinese religions only the "branches and the leaves," and the Indian religions the "flowers and the fruit."[1]

Saka Jūbutsu's pilgrimage to Ise in 1342 took place against this religious background. The bulk of his diary is devoted to his conversations with Watarai Ieyuki, the Chief Priest of the Outer Shrine at Ise. Jūbutsu was deeply impressed by Ieyuki, one of the leading Shintō theorists of the day. It is hard to imagine that under normal circumstances a priest of one religion would find himself in complete agreement with a priest of a totally different religion, but Jūbutsu may have felt that the Buddhism he had learned was inadequate to deal with the chaos he observed in the world around him. He seems to have turned to the wisdom of Shintō, as communicated by Ieyuki, without reservations and with an intensity of feeling close to desperation.

Jūbutsu gave no reason why he, a Buddhist priest, should have chosen to make a pilgrimage to Ise. He apparently considered that it was quite natural even for a Buddhist to pay his respects at the most sacred of Shintō shrines. The tone of the diary is set at the very beginning by his description of Anonotsu, his first stop on the way to Ise: "This port is situated at some distance from the coast on a twisting river, and at dawn, as I lay on my traveler's pillow, I could hear the voices of boatmen as they passed back and forth, rowing in the moonlight. The rough waves and the sound of the wind made it difficult to sleep, and I wrote":

kaze samuki	Awaking from dreams
iso ya no makura	On a pillow by the shore
yume samete	Where the wind is cold,
yoso naru nami ni	See how my sleeve has been soaked
nururu sode kana[2]	By waves not of my making.

Not only is the writing poetic, but Jūbutsu, in the manner of earlier diarists, epitomized each experience with a *waka*. However, he departed from this particular convention elsewhere in the diary by including also poems in Chinese and several *chōka* (long poems).[3] He was obviously a learned man, well acquainted not only with the Buddhist texts a monk was expected to know but with the secular Japanese literature of the past.

The most affecting parts of the diary are Jūbutsu's descriptions of the desolation of the landscapes he passed on his travels: "After I passed the purification hall on the Kushida River, it became apparent how terribly the southern part of this province has been devastated ever since the country fell into disorder. Even in places where bamboo groves or stands of shady trees grew thickly, one could see on approaching that there were no houses. At breaks in the *susuki* grass and lemongrass, a newly cut path was visible, with many withered stumps along the way. When I asked a man I chanced to meet about the place, he answered that this was what had happened to neglected rice fields. His words made me feel all the sadder that the world should have changed so much.

"I arrived at the residence of the High Priestess. There were what looked like the remains of old earthen walls, and here and there were tall bushes and trees. The torii had fallen over and the pillars lying across the road were so completely rotted that, if a person did not actually know what they were, he would pass them by without a second glance, supposing they were merely fallen trees."[4]

Jūbutsu, alluding to *The Tales of Ise*, contrasted the romantic atmosphere in the description of Ise in that work with the desolation that met his eyes: "The dreams of that night, about which he [Narihira] wrote in his line 'Did I sleep or was I awake?'[5] have turned into clouds, have turned into rain, and are now no more. The past had old dreams, the present has new dreams. If one does not discover reality in a dream, who knows but that what one supposes to be reality may prove to be a dream?"[6]

Jūbutsu's dejection at the sight of the devastation caused by the years of warfare was alleviated by his conversations with the Chief Priest of the Outer Shrine. Jūbutsu's description of this man suggests the painting of a Taoist immortal: "His frost-touched eyebrows, his snowy beard, the whole aspect of his face was in accord with the season;[7] and the clarity of his mind, the wellspring of his words, the eloquence of his tongue made the past live again. He seemed to be truly and inspiringly a priest of the Great Shrine, and I am writing down our nightlong conversation before I forget it, giving my brush free rein and not bothering to make a first draft."[8]

The discussion between Jūbutsu and the eloquent Watarai Ieyuki constitutes the bulk of the diary. Because he recorded the conversation immediately afterward, it has an appealing immediacy, even if the details of Ieyuki's arguments are no longer of much interest. Jūbutsu was so moved by the conversation that he felt somehow impure, and wished that he could visit the Great Shrine often, to renew himself; but, already over sixty years of age, he thought it unlikely he would ever be able to visit Ise again. In any case, it was hard to control his profound emotion at being in so holy a place, and it was with the utmost difficulty that he finally succeeded in tearing himself away.

There were, however, ample reasons to lament the present state of the Great Shrine. No *saiō* (imperial princess resident at the Great Shrine as the High Priestess) had been sent to Ise since the reign of the Emperor Godaigo a decade earlier, and this ancient practice would never be resumed. The year of Jūbutsu's visit was the twentieth since the last rebuilding of the Great Shrine, but he saw no sign that a rebuilding was even contemplated.[9] The long years of warfare between the Northern Court and the Southern Court had no doubt interrupted the flow of funds needed for the restoration. This is how Jūbutsu described the scene: "The time for the rebuilding having passed, the roof tiles were broken, and the rains dripped to the base of the oak pillars. The eaves sagged, and storm winds swept the pines that in summer gave shade. I had lamented that the warfare in the land had caused a decline in the good government of the country, but at the thought that disturbances in the world had brought about even the ruin of this holy shrine, the tears flowed, too many for my sleeves to absorb."[10]

His tears did not blind Jūbutsu to the special holiness of the place as he walked under the trees to the shrine buildings. He noted that the waters of the Isuzu River were always clear, even in the rainy season or after an evening shower. He watched with admiration as pilgrims to the shrine poured water over themselves in ceremonial ablutions, not seeming to feel the cold. "Even humble peasant women dressed in hempen clothes seem to be happy at the thought that they are purifying their bodies. And even people whose brightly colored sleeves are heavy with perfume seem not to be embarrassed to expose their naked flesh. The water of Mild Light does not choose whether it cleanses dust from the good or the bad, and the pool of Beneficial Things reflects without distinction the shadows of high and low alike."[11]

Jūbutsu seems to envy those who perform their ablutions so cheerfully. He confesses that he has never cleansed himself in the "pure waters" (*shinsui*) of Amida Buddha. Instead, "I have of my own free will sunk in the mud of impurity, refused to allow my mind to enter the sea of his holy Vow;[12] and it has only been by chance that I have formed this connection with the stream of purity. Thinking over such matters, I was weeping as I left the precincts of the shrine."[13]

He went then to a nearby temple that was sacred to Kannon. Until recently many priests had lived here, but conditions in the world were now so unsettled that it had become impossible to sit in quiet meditation. Now there were only four or five fishermen's huts. Jūbutsu described the place: "No torches were lit this cold night; all one saw were the reflections burning in the waves of fishing-boat lights. The frost-coated temple bell did not stir; all one heard was the meaningless echoes borne by the wind of the woodman's ax. Not one flower, not one stick of incense was offered; it seemed as though the vow of deliverance made by the Buddha of a thousand hands and the thousand eyes had ceased to exist. I thought that the neglect of the images of Buddha was a result of the falling off of human beings, and, mingled with tears for the sadness of the world, tears for my journey spilled over copiously."[14]

The style of this and many other passages of the diary is the parallel prose found in works influenced by Chinese, notably such diaries as *Journey Along the Seacoast Road*, and the language is colored by the author's grief over the times. The words "the falling off of human beings" (*ningen no otorouru*) were probably an expression of Jūbutsu's belief in *mappō*, the doctrine that the world had entered its last, degenerate phase, but they remind me of words written on a wall of a church in England after the plague of the Black Death, when a third of the population died in 1349: "The dregs of the population live to tell the tale."[15] The desolation that Jūbutsu witnessed, as well as the many reminders of how much better life had been in the past, may have inspired similar thoughts—the good people had perished, and only the dregs were left. But even though the world was crumbling around him, Jūbutsu had been able to find comfort in the words of Ieyuki and in the majestic silence of Ise.

Gifts from the Capital

Miyako no Tsuto (*Gifts from the Capital*) describes a journey made in about 1350 from the capital to Matsushima in the northeast. The author, the priest Sōkyū, seems to have had an incurable urge to roam, not only to places of religious importance but to *utamakura*, the sites mentioned in the poetry of the past. He states early in the diary that the High Priest of a temple on Mount Hiei had dismissed the *waka* as being nothing more than a frivolous amusement, but had changed his mind one day when, as he watched boats moving out into the distance over Lake Biwa, he heard someone recite the celebrated poem by the acolyte Mansei:

yo no naka wo	To what shall I compare
nani ni tatoen	This world of ours?
asabiraki	It is like the wake
koginishi fune no	Disappearing behind a boat
ato naki gotoshi[1]	That is rowed away at dawn.

The effectiveness for the High Priest of this *waka* was that it both portrayed a landscape he knew well and suggested the implications of this scene for all of human life; it persuaded him that poetry could help people to attain a state of enlightenment. Sōkyū was of the same opinion, and he followed the traditions of earlier diarists in composing a poem at each famous place he passed on his journey.

Sōkyū was not a distinguished poet, and his diary is of only moderate intrinsic interest. It is hard to share the enthusiasm for the diary expressed by Nijō Yoshimoto in a postscript written in 1367: "I was so overcome by admiration that I could not refrain from adding a few inept words of my own."[2] *Gifts from the Capital*, however, possesses a special interest in that again and again it seems to anticipate Bashō's masterpiece *The Narrow Road of Oku*. Comparing the two diaries is unkind to Sōkyū, but parallel passages will suggest the closeness of the resemblances. The following excerpts occur near the beginning of *Gifts from the Capital*: "It was still dark when I left the capital. The light of the daybreak moon was reflected in the waves of the eastern river, and lingering cockcrows could be heard even after I had passed some distant villages. The sky, completely misted over, looked extremely beautiful. . . . I had left the capital before I knew it, but I felt as if I were already three thousand *ri* away, and I felt greater reluctance to leave than when I first went from my old home."

Here is the similar passage by Bashō: "On the 27th of the 3rd month the dawn sky was misty. Though the pale morning moon had lost its light, the peak of Fuji could be seen faintly, and the blossoms at the tops of the cherry trees at Ueno and Yanaka stirred sad thoughts, as I wondered when again I should see them. . . . The thought of the three thousand *ri* ahead of us on the journey filled my heart with apprehension, and I shed tears of farewell at the crossroads of this realm of unreality."

Obviously, Bashō is a far better writer, and the similarities between the two passages—the departure at dawn, the early moon, the author's forlorn feelings as he contemplates a journey of three thousand *ri*—may be no more than coincidence or a reflection of the conventions of the travel diary; but it is clear that the two men belonged to the same tradition. They both remembered the poet-travelers of the past, especially Saigyō, and they sought out the places mentioned in his poetry. Often their poetic imagination was stronger than the reality before their eyes. When Sōkyū passed Utsunoyama, he noted, "The path, buried under ivy, was still green with the leaves, but I could imagine what it would look like in autumn, when the leaves turned crimson." When Bashō visited Miyagino he wrote, "The *hagi* bushes grew thickly, and I could imagine what they would look like in autumn."

Passing the Barrier of Shirakawa had special significance for both men. Sōkyū wrote, "One should really decorate oneself a bit when one passes this place, even if one does not go so far as Takeda Tayū Kuniyuki, who plastered down his sidelocks in honor of the occasion. I didn't do anything, which was rather insensitive of me." Bashō remembered that the men of former times had "adjusted their headgear and straightened their clothes" before passing through this famous barrier.

For anyone familiar with *The Narrow Road of Oku* the inadequacy of Sōkyū's descriptions of the same scenery is all too apparent. In one passage, for example, he mentions three place names that are prominent in Bashō's diary: "We reached the village of Taga in the province of Michinoku. From there we took the Narrow Road of Oku southward to Sue no Matsuyama, which we visited; when we looked far out over the pine grove, it really did seem as if the waves might cross over the mountain." The names Taga, the Narrow Road of Oku, and Sue no Matsuyama are like the first notes of three great symphonies by Bashō, but Sōkyū does not supply any further music. Even Matsushima failed to excite Sōkyū, though Bashō's evocation of the pine-covered islands rising from the sea will never be forgotten even if an earthquake should some day submerge them. But we must be grateful to Sōkyū for having kept one of the first poetic diaries that describe the region. Perhaps his diary even helped to arouse Bashō's interest in the Narrow Road of Oku.

Reciting Poetry to Myself at Ojima

Travel diaries of the Muromachi period, even those written by learned men, were usually in Japanese. This did not mean that such men were incapable of composing in classical Chinese in the manner of the Heian courtiers, but that Japanese seemed a more appropriate medium for what they wanted to express. The tradition of including *waka* in the diaries kept by the court ladies of the past may account for the decision of Nijō Yoshimoto (1320–88), a *waka* poet and an outstanding writer of linked verse, but also (at various times) the Chancellor, Prime Minister, and Regent, to keep a diary in Japanese, rather than follow the many statesmen of the past who had found classical Chinese more in keeping with their great offices. *Ojima no Kuchizusami* (*Reciting Poetry to Myself at Ojima*), Yoshimoto's account of a journey he made in 1353, is one of the most affecting of Muromachi diaries.

The diary opens with an account of Yoshimoto's illness. He writes in the manner of an old man, though he was only thirty-five at the time. Despairing of a physician's cure, he resorted to magic (*majinai*), though this only aggravated his illness, which was a kind of malaria. At the time, the capital was in the hands of the Southern Court, and the Northern Court Emperor had fled to the province of Mino. Yoshimoto, though an adherent of the Northern Court, had been left behind in the capital because of his illness, but when word reached him from "east of the barrier" that he was wanted in Mino, he decided to make the journey despite his poor health. He writes: "Some days past the 20th of the 7th month, in the depths of the night, when the dawn moon still lingered in the sky, I set out from my thatched cottage, my thoughts running ahead to the east, along the distant road. I felt somehow sad. It was quite without example for a person in my condition to travel all the way east of the barrier, but I took comfort from the thought that, since my journey was occasioned by a desire to serve my country, how could it be that the gods and buddhas would fail to protect me?"[1]

The journey was painful. Even the boat ride across Lake Biwa, which generally was pleasant, was marred by rough waves that made Yoshimoto seasick. He was in such a bad mood when he reached Moruyama that he sourly commented, "The place has quite an imposing reputation, but there is nothing special to see." But then he recalled that it was here that Ki no Tsurayuki had composed the *waka*:

shiratsuyu mo	At Moruyama
shigure mo itaku	Both the white dew and the rains
Moruyama wa	Fall terribly thick;
shitaba nokorazu	That must be why the under leaves
irozukinikeri	Have all put on fall colors.

Yoshimoto composed a dejected rejoinder to Tsurayuki's *waka*:

Moruyama no	The under leaves at
shitaba wa imada	Moruyama have still not
irozukade	Changed color; instead,
ukiyo ni shigururu	My sleeves are soaked with the dew
sode zo tsuyukeki[2]	That falls in this floating world.

Yoshimoto's destination was Ojima, in the province of Mino, where Gokōgon, the Northern Court Emperor, had his temporary residence. The journey took him past various *uta-makura*, sites mentioned in old poetry, including the Gatehouse of Fuwa. Yoshimoto wrote, "Even in the old days the Barrier of Fuwa had fallen into ruin."[3] Now it was a derelict structure, hardly more than a name. He struggled on, fighting his illness and the hardships of the journey, until he at last reached Ojima. His description of the place, like all the descriptions in this diary, is at once faithful to the actual scene and evocative of the literature of the past: "I was unfamiliar with scenery of this kind. There was not a break in the clouds that hung heavily over the mountains to left and right. Truly, nothing is so heartrending as such a place as this. No words can convey the look of these remote mountains, especially in autumn, and the indescribable pathos of the landscape squashed in between the hills."[4] The language recalls another famous place of exile, Suma in *The Tale of Genji*.[5]

The first house in Ojima where Yoshimoto stayed was so wretched that it was unbearable even for one night. The next day he went to the temporary palace. This, too, was a depressing sight: "The palace had a shingled roof, a rarity in this part of the country. The mountains virtually touched the edges of the eaves. There was no clearing in the clouds and fog. Presently I was summoned before His Majesty and reported on recent happenings in the world." The Emperor in turn had "all kinds of sad tidings" to pass on to Yoshimoto.

Fortunately, Yoshimoto was able to find agreeable lodgings at a nearby temple, but his illness persisted: "One more day went by, another day spent in sickness. And then, in this wretched state, I passed the night. There is no way at all to dispel the forlorn loneliness of sleeping away from home."[6]

The only hope for the Emperor Gokōgon and the Northern Court was Ashikaga Takauji (1305–58), the most powerful military leader of the time. Again and again the exiles heard rumors of Takauji's imminent arrival, but each time they were disappointed. It rained day after day, and the "temporary capital" was shut in by constant clouds and fog. On the night of the mid-autumn moon (i.e., full moon) of the 8th month there was no break in the clouds, but toward dawn the wind that had been howling all night abated, and the skies cleared. It was decided to celebrate the harvest moon the next night. The moon might be a trifle smaller than when it was full, but at least it was likely to be visible. Members of the court set about composing *waka*, just as if they had been back in the capital, but somehow the atmosphere did not seem right. Yoshimoto noted that everyone was in "barbarian clothes" (*ebisu koromo*, meaning military costume), rather than in proper court attire, and the nobles looked more like soldiers than poets. All the same, the moon shining in a cloudless sky that night seemed a harbinger of improving fortunes.

While waiting for Takauji's army to arrive, the court moved to the nearby village of Tarui, where a more comfortable temporary palace had been built by the provincial constable (*shugo*) of the region. Word now reached the exiles that bandits in the province of Ōmi were blocking the road to the capital. The word "forlorn" (*kokorobososhi*), which frequently appears in Yoshimoto's account, seems to convey the feelings of all that was left of the Northern Court.

On the 3rd day of the 9th month Takauji at last arrived. With him came many soldiers and the needed equipment. Yoshimoto's tone changed from despair to jubilation: "Takauji wore brocaded armor over an informal robe, gauntlets, and greaves, and rode on a chestnut horse. . . . Armor of every kind and brilliant helmets with hoe-shaped crests glittered to the fore and sparkled in the evening sun."[7] Yoshimoto praised the horses as the finest in the eastern provinces. Takauji later presented the Emperor with some of these horses, a gift unthinkable in more peaceful times.

On the night of the 15th, the full moon of the 9th month, the courtiers composed *waka* in their accustomed manner. Yoshimoto reluctantly agreed to grade the poems, knowing how much they meant to poets who had no other diversion. He refused, however, to evaluate linked verse (*renga*), which he haughtily dismissed as a rustic entertainment: "Country people enjoy composing something called linked verse."[8] A week or so earlier, on the 9th day of the 9th month, the courtiers had held a chrysanthemum festival at which they composed poetry in Chinese.

Eventually the Northern Court armies under Takauji's son, Yoshiakira, took the capital, and the way was open for the Emperor Gokōgon and his court to return in state. The nobles wore formal court costume for the return procession, attracting gaping sightseers all along the way.

The nobles discovered that everything in the capital was much as they had remembered. Yoshimoto exclaimed, "The terrible nightmare that had been afflicting us disappeared without a trace, and now everything was indescribably joyous."[9] Finally, Yoshimoto explained how he happened to write this diary: "Thinking that it might provide material for future stories, I decided to employ my hours of boredom by writing down everything that had happened, just as it had occurred, so that I would not forget. I wrote on scraps of writing paper I tore up for the purpose, a most unattractive-looking manuscript. It is commonly the case that the past is hard to forget. Why, then, should not these few words, scribbled down by my brush, become a source of nostalgic remembrance?"[10] The title of the diary was supplied by the Emperor Gokōgon himself.

In the following year Gokōgon and the rest of the Northern Court, together with Takauji's forces, were driven from the capital, but in the year after that they recovered it. In the meantime almost every building in the city had been destroyed in the fighting. At our distance from the events, it really does not matter much which side held the capital in a given year. The Northern Court has generally been treated unfavorably by Japanese historians, and its champion, Takauji, has never been a popular favorite. But readers today can sympathize even with people "on the wrong side" when their sufferings are related as poignantly as by Yoshimoto.

Pilgrimage to Sumiyoshi

Nothing I know about Ashikaga Yoshiakira (1330–67) suggests that he had a poetic disposition. He spent most of his life actively engaged in warfare—capturing, losing, and recapturing Kyōto several times—and died at the age of thirty-seven while still fighting the Southern Court forces. It is hard to imagine when he could have acquired a knowledge of traditional Japanese culture. A European general of the same period who was so involved in warfare throughout his life would probably not have been able to write much more than his name, but if we can accept the usual attribution, Yoshiakira wrote *Sumiyoshi Mōde* (*Pilgrimage to Sumiyoshi*), describing, in language identical to that of the most polished courtiers and with a suitable admixture of *waka*, his journey to the Shrine of Sumiyoshi. He stated his purpose in these terms: "It has been said since ancient times that this god vouchsafes his protection to all those who are deeply involved with the Way of poetry. In particular, those who aspire to write poetry of intricate expression will assuredly succeed in their aim if they pray to this god."[1] He appended the following *waka*:

kamiyo yori	Is it possible
tsutaetsutauru	Anyone would neglect the Way
Shikishima no	Of Shikishima,

michi ni kokoro mo	Transmitted by word of mouth
utoku mo aru kana[2]	Since the Age of the Gods?

Some scholars question the attribution of the diary to Yoshiakira, if only because the motivation for the journey—to ask the god of Sumiyoshi for assistance in the art of poetry—is so atypical of the fierce Yoshiakira of history. But it is at least possible that he wrote this short diary, and that says much about the dissemination of the court culture among the warriors. Kawabata Yasunari, writing about a later period of Muromachi history, declared, "It has been said that unless one reads *The Tale of Genji* it is almost impossible to understand the culture of the Muromachi period. Shōtetsu delivered lectures to Yoshimasa on *Genji*, and the Shogun Yoshihisa commanded Sanetaka to lecture him on *Genji*. In short, one might attribute the decline of the Ashikaga shogunate to *The Tale of Genji*."[3]

The close association of military leaders with poetry is typical of Japanese culture. The feminine ideal of *taoyameburi* has had the power to temper and often to overcome the masculine ideal of *masuraoburi*.[4] A contemporary of Yoshiakira, General Kō no Moronao, a man noted for his brutality, took lessons in poetry from the poet-priest Kenkō. When Oda Nobunaga entered Kyōto in 1568, he was preceded by his reputation for cruelty and violence, and the citizens of Kyōto dreaded this monster "more terrifying than any demon." To their astonishment, his first act on entering the city was to display his skill at composing linked verse. "Old and young, learning of this, were speechless with amazement. They had supposed that, given the fierceness of this warrior, things would go as badly for them as when Kiso no Yoshinaka burst into the capital many years ago, but Nobunaga seemed gentle and refined."[5]

Pilgrimage to Sumiyoshi is a slight work, but it demonstrates that even in the midst of a civil war the old culture did not die. Yoshiakira—or whoever wrote the diary—made no attempt to reveal by his expression that he was a Muromachi warrior and not a Heian courtier. His language is so refined it is almost a parody of the old literature: *"Koroshimo uzuki no hajime nareba, chirinokoritaru kishi no yamabuki wo mireba"* ("The time was the beginning of the 4th month, and just to look at the kerria roses on the bank that had not yet fallen was enough to make one regret the passing of the spring. The mountain cuckoo came to visit the verbena, which was like snow on the garden fence.")[6]

The diary provides only one indication of the troubled nature of the times. The diarist, looking westward, saw Suma, the island of Awaji, and the Bay of Akashi, all places well known from classical literature. "I thought I would like to cross there by boat, but I could imagine how anxious people would be, given the unsettled nature of the times; so, after spending one night, I returned to the capital." His staff was no doubt worried lest he expose himself unnecessarily to danger. The diary concludes with Yoshiakira's explanation of why he wrote it: "I have written down in this manuscript the appearance of different places, allowing my brush free rein. I thought that perhaps it might become the entertainment of a moment."[7] We seem to hear in these words not the fierce soldier but a dilettante in the Heian manner.

The Visit to Itsukushima of the Lord of the Deer Park

Considering that even the warlike Ashikaga Yoshiakira kept a poetic diary, it might have been expected that his son, the third Ashikaga Shogun, Yoshimitsu (1358–1408), a man famous for his patronage of the arts, would keep a conspicuously more poetic diary. Unfortunately, however, no such diary was written, and the only extant diary in Japanese that directly relates to Yoshimitsu was the work of another man, the general and poet Imagawa Ryōshun (1326–1414?). *Rokuon'in-dono Itsukushima Mōde no Ki* (*The Visit to Itsukushima of the Lord of the Deer Park*),[1] the account of Yoshimitsu's visit to Itsukushima in 1389, is a disappointing work, especially when compared with the diary written two hundred years earlier describing the Retired Emperor Takakura's visit to the same shrine. Yoshimitsu remains a remote figure throughout the diary and does not even compose a *waka*.

By this time Yoshimitsu had established himself as one of the most powerful rulers in Japanese history; that may be why he appears in this diary as a Sun King surrounded by constellations of lesser luminaries. Over one hundred ships accompanied Yoshimitsu's barge as it made its way through the Inland Sea to Itsukushima.

Perhaps the most memorable part of the diary is the description of how Yoshimitsu and the members of his suite were dressed.

Unlike earlier visitors to Itsukushima, who had worn formal court attire, "on this occasion everyone was dressed most unusually." The account continues: "They all wore narrow-sleeved, wide-hemmed outer robes tie-dyed with dotted pale-blue patterns, red sashes, green leggings, and short red trousers. The members of the escort carried three-foot-long golden swords. Some observers criticized their appearance, but in such matters regulations or rituals are not necessarily to be observed; the essential thing is to follow the times. There are many instances, even from antiquity, of people who broke precedent by adopting and using inventions that were at first condemned as mere novelties. Such criticism in fact has always revealed a parochial outlook."[2]

Apart from the bold colors of the costumes, this account sounds a new note in the phrase "follow the times" (*jidai ni shitagau*). It was normally considered far more important to follow precedents than to keep up with current tastes. About fifty years earlier the priest Kenkō had written, "In all things I yearn for the past. Modern fashions keep on growing more and more debased."[3] But Yoshimitsu preferred to be up to date, rather than look back to some golden age for precedents. His protégé Zeami expressed similar views: "In response to each different age, they changed the words a little and also changed the melodies, in this way keeping the flower of the art blooming year after year. In the future, too, the same should be observed."[4]

The journey itself was plagued by bad weather. Yoshimitsu had originally intended to travel as far as Kyūshū in order to examine "the remains of the ancient capital,"[5] but after encountering repeated storms turned back, much to the disappointment of the author of the account, Imagawa Ryōshun, who was then the governor-general (*tandai*) of Kyūshū. All the same, Yoshimitsu managed to visit not only Itsukushima but two celebrated places on the island of Shikoku, Yashima and Shiramine, though his pleasure in the journey was no doubt marred by the rough winds and waves.

Imagawa Ryōshun was a poet and critic of considerable accomplishment, and excelled especially at linked verse. After losing his position as commanding general of Kyūshū in 1395, he devoted himself entirely to literature, and became the mentor of the outstanding poets of the next generation, including Shōtetsu and Sōgi, whose diaries are discussed in subsequent chapters. *The Visit to Itsukushima of the Lord of the Deer Park* is not one of his major works, but it is noteworthy that a military man, then on active duty, should have written such an account at all. Not many generals have been involved in so elegant a sightseeing excursion.

A Source of Consolation

Nagusamegusa (*A Source of Consolation*) opens with the account of the journey made in 1418 by the priest Shōtetsu (1381–1459) from the capital to Kuroda, in the province of Owari. The journey itself lasted only three days and involved no special hardships, but the diary is worth reading for the endearing self-portrait Shōtetsu paints. Shōtetsu was the leading *waka* poet of the time, and although he was thirty-seven, he says that he had never left the capital before. This experience was far more important than the facts of the journey.

Shōtetsu did not state why he felt impelled to travel. Some scholars have suggested it was because of his grief over the deaths of two *waka* poets under whom he had studied: Imagawa Ryōshun had died about 1414 and Reizei Tametada in 1417. But this does not explain why Shōtetsu went to Kuroda or why he stayed there (and in nearby Kiyosu) for three months. Perhaps, as has also been suggested, he felt a need for a break from the busy and restricting life he had led at the Tōfuku-ji, the great monastery in the capital.

The writing, as one might expect of a man of Shōtetsu's reputation, is highly poetic from the start. He left Kyōto at the end of the 3rd month, when there were fallen cherry blossoms floating on the waves of Lake Biwa, just as in the old poems. Inevitably, he recalled the famous *waka* by the acolyte Mansei on the subject.

On the other side of Lake Biwa, Shōtetsu passed Moruyama, a town that he, like Nijō Yoshimoto before him, found highly distasteful, despite its associations with Ki no Tsurayuki. "The place called Moruyama is most uncongenial. It is a village in the shade of a forest, and its only distinction is the noise of the village women and merchants hawking their wares."[1]

Not until he reached Ono, where the late Tametada had lived, does the diary acquire special literary interest. Shōtetsu's account of Tametada begins, "Lord Tametada was a master of the art of the *waka*, but with the passage of time and the degeneration of the world, this art has been completely abandoned. . . ."[2] Tametada had been present when Shōtetsu, then a boy of thirteen, made his debut in the world of *waka*. This is how he described the occasion in *Shōtetsu Monogatari* (*The Tales of Shōtetsu*): "On the twenty-fifth I went to attend the meeting. Inside the house, Reizei no Tametada and Reizei no Tamekuni sat in one place of honor, and the former governor-general of Kyūshū in the other. Between them were their close retainers and my host's family, over twenty persons in all, seated impressively in rows. I had arrived late, so I was shown to the central place of honor."[3]

At the time the very existence of *waka* was threatened by the enormous popularity of linked verse. Shōtetsu would eventually emerge as the last important *waka* poet of the Muromachi period. Not for many years—or, it might be argued, never again—would the *waka* serve as the vehicle for the finest poetic expression of the age.

Shōtetsu revered his teacher Tametada, who in turn must have seen in the boy of thirteen the last "hope" of the *waka*. Shōtetsu attributed the temporary decline that had occurred in the popularity of Tametada's "school" to his having been deprived by the shogunate of his estates at Ono in Ōmi and Hosokawa in Harima.[4] The latter was the estate for which Tametada's ancestress, the nun Abutsu, had fought so determinedly 130 years earlier. Later, Tametada was unexpectedly asked by the Shogun Yoshimochi for a sequence of a thousand poems. The poems Tametada wrote conveyed his grief over the loss of his estates, and so impressed the Shogun that he returned both of them. Other favors were subsequently bestowed on Tametada, and "it seemed as though he would restore the art of the *waka* to its former glory when in the next year, before the dream of the cherry blossoms of the spring, he disappeared into the clouds, was separated from us by the mists. . . ."[5] It was left to Shōtetsu to preserve the art of the *waka*. Perhaps the real reason for making the journey was that he wished to immerse himself completely in *waka* composition at a place where he knew no one, and no one could interfere.

On his journey to the province of Mino, Shōtetsu naturally stopped at the various *uta-makura* (places mentioned in poetry) and composed an appropriate *waka*, or at least referred to the particular feature of the place that had been celebrated by earlier poets. He mentioned, for example, "I crossed the Fuji River at Seki and arrived at Fuwa.

mukashi dani	Although I had heard
arenu to kikishi	It had gone to rack and ruin
yado nagara	Even long ago,
ikade sumuran	How can the keeper live here
Fuwa no sekimori	At the Barrier of Fuwa?

Hardly anything is left of Nogami and there are no prostitutes."[6]

This passage contains literary references to the Barrier of Fuwa, traditionally known for its dilapidated state, and to the village of Nogami, where, according to the Nō play *Hanjo*, there was a house of prostitution. More interesting than these allusions are the descriptions of sights that caught Shōtetsu's eye. While on a boat crossing the Sunomata River, the boundary between the provinces of Mino and Owari, he saw "three or four village boys carrying baskets filled with something that looked like watercress, and an old man bent with age who had come on board with us. The boys had difficulty getting ashore from the boat, but the old man helped his children (or were they grandchildren?) ashore. I had a great deal of trouble myself, but somehow I was touched by the sight."[7]

The most important parts of *A Source of Consolation* are those devoted to Shōtetsu's experiences after he reached his destination. One evening he visited a temple in Kuroda. He relates: "Not many people had come to worship. There was no one to light the holy candles, and the perpetual incense was depressingly faint. I had heard about the Buddha here while I was in the capital. I was told that in the past many people used to visit, and the decorations of the temple were brilliant. But people also told me that, ever since the area became the scene of fighting during the Meitoku era [1391], it had lost its former appearance. It moved me to think that prosperity or decline in this world affects even the person of the Buddha."[8]

As Shōtetsu sat quietly meditating on the sad changes that had been brought about by the wars, an old man with white hair and a white beard approached. His unearthly appearance at first made Shōtetsu wonder if he might be a Chinese: "He looked extremely Chinese, but he was wearing a white Korean robe and a yellow hat. Leaning on a stick that was forked at the end, he stood below the garden lantern and bowed in worship."[9] When Shōtetsu got a better look at the man, he recognized him as a lay priest (*ubasoku*) he had known in the capital, a man who for years had traveled around the country practicing Zen. The two men renewed their acquaintance with great pleasure, and soon Shōtetsu was invited to join the old man and various others who engaged in Zen meditation and study at a mountain temple. The place was remote, but it was fortified against soldiers and bandits. Shōtetsu was told, "It has a defense tower and is strongly enclosed. It can hold out for quite a while in fighting against soldiers, and there is no danger of bandits."

Shōtetsu accepted the invitation and was happy in the temple, though, by his own admission, he indulged in worldly pleasures instead of studying Buddhism: "I piled up books of poetry composition on the desk that was meant for the study of Zen sayings, and on the floor, where I should have sat on a mat in meditation, I would sprawl out with a pillow book.[10] Unable to endure the heat, I would forget my surplice and robe. Day after day I did exactly what I pleased, and indulged myself with saké and meat. That was not all. Twenty-four hours a day I never stopped my shameless self-indulgence. Nevertheless, he [the old priest] was so full of compassion that he neither chose the good nor rejected the bad, and he paid no attention to my sins."[11] It is not clear to what degree this confession should be taken at face value, but obviously Shōtetsu was not spending his days in Zen meditation and study.

One day Shōtetsu, having nothing better to do, went to the

covered passageway that ran alongside the priests' quarters. "I peeped through a crack in the south wall, and I saw four or five laymen, of a kind I had not been accustomed to see of late, including two boys with clean figures and hair done up in unusual triple loops. Remembering the capital, I felt drawn to them." He learned that they were a party of travelers on their way from Azuma to Koshi[12] who would be stopping here for a time. The boys[13] made excellent companions for Shōtetsu. He wrote: "Sometimes we rode horseback, side by side, up steep mountain roads; sometimes we shared a boat going up a distant stream. Or again, standing in the dew of a boundless meadow, we would regret the shortness of the moonlit night, or at dawnings, when the wind was cool, we would go together to gaze wistfully at the fireflies in the darkness under the trees. We spent the 5th and 6th months growing more familiar each morning, more intimate each evening."[14] The interest of one or both boys in literature was the immediate occasion for Shōtetsu's writing this diary.

The literary opinions expressed by Shōtetsu in *A Source of Consolation* are not systematically presented, and sometimes they are vague, but taken together they afford proof that the diary could be used to convey not only the writer's experiences and emotional reactions but also his opinions on art. One day the old priest whom Shōtetsu had met in Kuroda asked him what made *The Tale of Genji* so uniquely distinguished. He told Shōtetsu that for years he had devoted himself to linked verse, but of late he had given it up, finding that there were "little color in the language and insufficient wellsprings of feeling."[15] Only *The Tale of Genji* still held his interest.

Shōtetsu replied that, although the craze for linked verse had swept the country, the masters of the art were all dead, and linked verse itself had become corrupt. No doubt he was thinking of the competitions and even the gambling that had come to be associated with linked-verse composition. He declared that there was no longer any straightforward artistic interchange in linked-verse sessions, but only noisy arguments. He himself had in his youth attempted to learn linked verse, but his teacher's pessimism with respect to the future of the art had induced him to give it up. He was nevertheless saving linked verse as a diversion for his old age.

Shōtetsu then turned his attention to *The Tale of Genji*. He briefly described the traditions of *Genji* scholarship and the generally accepted belief that Chancellor Fujiwara no Michinaga had "added his brush" to the text written by Murasaki Shikibu. But Shōtetsu himself could not accept this explanation of why *The Tale of Genji* is so much harder to understand than the *waka* composed about the same period. He gave as his interpretation: "Perhaps it is because the wording of the tales recorded the actual language of the time, just as it was spoken; but as the times have entered their final phase, people's speech has changed accordingly. The old language has become unintelligible to most people. In the art of the *waka*, on the other hand, there is nothing striking about the language, and it was the advice of our predecessors to write in such a way that the meaning could be grasped even by ignorant rustics. It is particularly true, because of the profound meaning implied in this tale, that when this meaning floats up in one's unconscious, it naturally conveys the real shape of the work, and an intent, quite apart from the words, can be detected. At least such is my opinion."[16]

These last words were one expression of Shōtetsu's belief that in true works of art something is always implied that goes beyond overt language. He called this quality *yūgen*, and he believed that the presence of *yūgen* was the secret of the greatness of *The Tale of Genji*. Elsewhere, he defined *yūgen* in these terms: "What we call *yūgen* is something within the mind that cannot be expressed in words. The quality of *yūgen* may be suggested by the sight of a thin cloud veiling the moon or by autumn mist swathing the scarlet leaves on a mountainside. If one is asked where the *yūgen* in these sights lies, one cannot answer, and it is not surprising that a man who fails to understand this truth is likely to prefer the sight of the moon shining brightly in a cloudless sky. It is quite impossible to explain wherein lies the interest or wonder of *yūgen*."[17]

Shōtetsu explained toward the end of the diary that he had been led to write the diary by the request of a youth that he write something explaining the inner meaning of *The Tale of Genji*, and he had taken the opportunity not only to express his views on the work but to relate the circumstances of his journey and the other events described in the diary. He evidently fell in love with one of the boys, as we know from the exchanges of poems recorded in the diary.[18] The title is explained by his statement that he wrote the work to console himself when he awoke at night and could not sleep ("*nezame no nagusamegusa*"). The diary combines a travel account, random jottings, and literary theory, but, like other diaries that linger in the reader's memory, it is above all a portrait of the author himself.

Journey to Fuji

In the 9th month of the 4th year of Eikō (1432) the Shogun Ashikaga Yoshinori (1394–1441) set out from the capital with a large entourage on a sightseeing journey to Mount Fuji. Three diaries—one by Asukai Masayo (1390–1452), a nobleman and poet; the second by the Buddhist priest and poet Gyōkō (1391–1455); and the third anonymous—commemorated this excursion, which was on an unprecedentedly large scale. Yoshinori's purpose in making the journey was not purely aesthetic. He intended to affirm his authority with respect to Ashikaga Mochiuji (1398–1439), the chief shogunate officer (*kubō*) in Kamakura, who was suspected of harboring seditious ambitions.

Yoshinori's advisers urged him not to make the journey, lest it provoke the alarmed Mochiuji into open rebellion, but Yoshinori dismissed their counsels with a *waka*:

nakazora ni	Do not leave dangling
nasu na yo Fuji no	In mid-air my resolution
yūkemuri	That rises like smoke
tatsu na ni kaete	At evening over Fuji
omou kokoro wo[1]	All for the sake of a name.

This ingenious poem combines the intended destination, Fuji, with Yoshinori's resolution to put Mochiuji in his place, and is unified by the imagery of smoke rising into the sky. The advisers, even those who had attempted to dissuade Yoshinori from making the journey, were so impressed by his display of literary skill that there was no further opposition to the journey.

The three diaries consist mainly of poems composed at *uta-makura* and other places of interest. Asukai Masayo, the author of *Fuji Kikō* (*Journey to Fuji*), recorded only his own poetry, but the other two diarists included many *waka* composed by Yoshinori. None of the poetry, regardless of the author, is of much literary value, but the reader may be surprised by the unusually sycophantic tone of the poems addressed to Yoshinori. The following poems by Masayo refer not to the Emperor, as one might suppose, but to the Shogun:

tare mo mina	Everyone who bathes
hikari ni ataru	In the glorious sunlight
hinomoto no	Will surely recognize
kami to kimi wo to	You, my lord, as the god of
sazo terasuran[2]	The land of the rising sun.

kimi ga yo wa	The reign of my lord
nagare mo tōshi	Will flow on long years to come;
Samegai no	Though one dips the water
mizu wo kumu tomo	Of Samegai Well, I am sure
tsukiji to zo omou[3]	It will not be exhausted.

Gyōkō's diary, *Ran Fuji Ki* (*Account of Viewing Fuji*), opens in much the same vein of celebration of the blessings everyone enjoys because of Yoshinori's enlightened reign: "The winds have abated in the Seven Circuits,[4] the waves of the Eight Islands[5] are calm. The guardians of the barriers in the four directions have forgotten to lock their gates, leaving no hindrances to travel; and because the whole people shares a deep-seated resolution to offer their humble abodes to whatever traveler wishes to spend the night, one's heart melts with affection; this is truly an age of many joys."[6]

Were these men sincere or merely flatterers? We know that both Asukai Masayo and Gyōkō enjoyed Yoshinori's favor as his tutors of *waka*. However, Yoshinori's fondness for *waka* did nothing to soften his inborn violent disposition. The peace he had brought the country, celebrated by the diarists, was achieved by brute force, not by good government, and before long Yoshinori would be murdered by one of his officers under circumstances of revolting barbarity.

Masayo and Gyōkō could not have been unaware of Yoshinori's disposition, or of the grim nature of the peace he had brought to the country. They knew from the wanton killings he had ordered of persons at the court that they were living under a reign of terror. Their diaries were intended to ingratiate themselves with a hateful despot. This use of the diary, never dreamed of by the court ladies of the past, is easily comprehended, but it was nevertheless a lamentable perversion of tradition.

Journey to Zenkō-ji

In the 6th year of Kanshō (1465) Gyōe, a Buddhist priest and disciple of Gyōkō (one of the chroniclers of Yoshinori's visit to Fuji), traveled to the Zenkō-ji, the great temple in the province of Shinano which still attracts pilgrims from all over Japan. He started out from the Shrine of Kanetsurugi in the present Ishikawa Prefecture, and he made his way to the Zenkō-ji, in the central mountainous region, along a route that took him through other remote provinces. These place names should suggest how dissimilar the area covered by his journey was from the areas described in earlier diaries, generally confined to travel to or from the capital. Gyōe lived in the province of Kaga, and his is the oldest extant diary devoted to travels in the provinces facing the Sea of Japan. The names of the places he visited and of the mountains he gazed at from afar strongly suggest that his journey was connected with the austerities of the *yamabushi*, mountain priests who served as faith healers and workers of magic.

The Zenkō-ji was a center of popular Buddhism at the time. It was believed that anyone who made a pilgrimage there would enjoy the blessing of Amida "in this flesh," and would without fail be reborn in paradise. Among the earlier diarists, only Lady Nijō and Shunjō had made their way as far as the Zenkō-ji, but its fame extended throughout the country.

As soon as Gyōe arrived, he went to the central hall to offer prayers, then spent the night inside the building before the sanctum (*naijin*). The next day he performed the traditional circumambulation of the sanctum in the utter darkness of an underground passage. This experience profoundly moved him: "It truly seemed that my bond with eternity was no casual one, and I could not check the tears of joy. My thoughts went back to the ancient past, when the Nyorai[1] first manifested himself in this country, and the lines came to me":

terase nao	Illumine us yet,
nigori ni shimanu	Still untouched by muddiness,
Naniwae no	O moon at dawning
ashima ni mieshi	That first showed itself among
ariake no tsuki[2]	The reeds of Naniwa Bay.

The central divinity (*honzon*) of the Zenkō-ji was believed to have been the first statue of Buddha brought to Japan, a gift from the Korean kingdom of Kudara (Paekche). It had reached Japan at the port of Naniwa.

The parts of Japan where Gyōe traveled had not often been commemorated in the old poetry. It is true that places mentioned in poems composed by Ōtomo no Yakamochi while he was the governor of Etchū were familiar to *waka* poets, but Gyōe noted, "I asked people about the whereabouts of the Bay of Tago, which Yakamochi visited and described with delight, but no one could answer for sure."[3]

It was precisely because Gyōe was not looking for the usual *utamakura* that his accounts of the landscapes he visited have a freshness not found in the diaries of travelers who visited more familiar places. Here, for example, is his description of Oyashirazu (Not Knowing One's Parent), a particularly frightening stretch of coast where people, able to think only of saving their own lives, forget everyone else in their mad dash to safety on the other side: "Immense cliffs rose precipitously, a thousand fathoms above us. Looking up was enough to make one lose one's equilibrium. Layer on layer of waves crashed to shore over an expanse of ten thousand miles, and innumerable cascades tumbled down. One has no friend on whom to depend save for isolated, lone figures, and one can only trust in the eternal power of prayer. . . . "

nami wakete	As one passes through,
sugiyuku hodo wa	Making one's way through the waves,
tarachine no	How likely one is
oya no isame mo	To forget the admonitions
wasururu mi yo	Of one's nurturing parent.[4]

This account of Oyashirazu is far more elaborate than the one given by Bashō in *The Narrow Road of Oku*, but it nevertheless typifies the concision and dignity of Gyōe's style, a combination of pure Japanese and classical-Chinese elements.[5] The markedly Buddhist tone, revealed especially in the allegorical interpretation of the landscape, marks this diary as belonging to a different world from Bashō's, but the distance between the two men is conspicuously less great than between Bashō and earlier diarists.

Twenty years later (in 1485) Gyōe wrote another travel diary, *Hokkoku Kikō* (*Journey to the North*), describing his extensive wanderings from Mino to Musashino by way of Hokuriku. In between the writing of these two diaries the Ōnin War had devastated the capital, and fighting still continued sporadically. *Journey to the North* is disappointing because it touches on the warfare so indirectly that one might almost miss the references, and this is precisely what we would most like to hear from an eyewitness. For more convincing evocations of the disaster one must turn to other diarists.

Account of Fujikawa

The most distinguished of the diarists who described the Ōnin War (1467–77) was Ichijō Kaneyoshi (1402–81).[1] Not only was he of impeccable lineage (he was a grandson of Nijō Yoshimoto), but at the time that fighting broke out in the capital he was the Regent. He was a scholar of Chinese and Japanese learning, an authority on precedents and usages, a poet of *waka* and linked verse, a literary critic, and a scholar well versed in both Buddhism and Shintō. Fifty of his works are known by title, though some were lost during the fighting. At the outbreak of the war he was living in a manner befitting a person of his exalted status, blessed with twenty-six children, and the possessor of a library that was a great repository of the history and literature of the past. He seemed, even to himself, to be invulnerable to the vagaries of fate, and boasted that in his learning he excelled even the great scholar Sugawara no Michizane.

All this soon changed once the fighting began. His house was destroyed and his library wantonly ransacked. His grandson, though dressed so splendidly that "no barbarian, no matter how savage, should have failed to recognize that he was a person of the highest station,"[2] was brutally slaughtered. He himself was forced to take refuge in Nara at the Ichijō-in, a part of the Kōfuku-ji monastery where his son Jinson was in residence as a prince-priest (*monzeki*), and he depended on the charity of others even for his food. Sometimes he was forced to humble himself to the extent of sending letters reminding people that their gifts of food were late. The celebrated priest Ikkyū wrote a poem in Chinese with the title "Lamenting the Starvation of His Excellency Ichijō."[3] Others suffered at least as much as Kaneyoshi during the Ōnin War, but he is an emblematic figure who seems to symbolize the aristocratic culture that was destroyed in the war. His various writings, including the diary *Fujikawa no Ki* (*Account of Fujikawa*), present a unique picture of the most senseless war of Japanese history.

Kaneyoshi's book of *renga* criticism, *Fude no Susabi* (*Consolations of the Brush*, 1469), opens with an account of the many wars that had ravaged the capital since the Hōgen Disturbance of 1156. His conclusion was that none of the earlier wars could bear comparison to the present one in its scale and destruction. He described how the fires set during the fighting of the Ōnin War had swept through the capital: "Not one of the official buildings, from the Department of Shintō and the Grand Council of State on down, survived. . . . The temple buildings and pagodas that had honeycombed the eastern and western mountains, so proudly rearing roof against roof, were also totally destroyed in the flames, and now not so much as an inch of green grass is left. Only layers of clouds cover the remains."[4]

Kaneyoshi went on to relate his personal experiences. His residence in the capital was situated on the borderline between the two opposing camps, and people warned him to flee. For a time he found lodgings in the south of the city. He recalled: "Before I knew it a column of smoke went up, and the whole area was devastated. My library escaped the remaining flames, perhaps because it was roofed with tiles and had earthen walls, but bandits of the neighborhood swarmed around the building, supposing that it contained money and other valuables, and in no time they smashed their way in, scattering the dwellings of hundreds of bookworms. Not one of the Japanese and Chinese books that had been passed down for over ten generations was saved."[5]

Not long before, Kaneyoshi had prepared a collection of linked verse in twenty volumes, which he intended to be a sequel to the collection *Tsukuba Shū*, which his grandfather Nijō Yoshimoto had compiled over a hundred years earlier, but this, too, was scattered and lost forever.

It was while he was living in Nara at the Kōfuku-ji that he wrote *Consolations of the Brush*. The diary *Account of Fujikawa*, written in 1473, described his journey to the province of Mino, where he had gone to express his gratitude to the provincial constable (*shugo*) for having kept him supplied with food during his exile. It opens with the words "butterfly dream" ("*kochō no yume*"), a reference to the familiar parable of Chuang Tzu, who dreamed of a butterfly and then was uncertain whether he, Chuang Tzu, had dreamed he was a butterfly or whether he was a butterfly who had dreamed he was Chuang Tzu.[6] Perhaps this allusion was no more than a literary flourish intended to display his familiarity with the Chinese classics (otherwise revealed by the poems in Chinese scattered throughout the diary), but it more probably expressed his feelings of uncertainty about his life at an age (he was then seventy-one) when all uncertainties should have been resolved.

Another allusion to Chuang Tzu occurs immediately afterward. It is to the parable of the snail: "On top of its left horn is a kingdom called Buffet, and on top of its right horn is a kingdom called Maul."[7] The quarrel over territory between the kingdoms on the horns of a snail seems to have been Kaneyoshi's sardonic way of characterizing the meaningless war that was tearing Japan apart.

Kaneyoshi's language is elaborate and filled with hackneyed references to the old poetry. Modern readers are likely to find such expression irritating, serving only to impede understanding, but Kaneyoshi evidently associated this language with the traditions of the Japanese diary. Indeed, it has been suggested that one reason Kaneyoshi made the journey was to emulate his revered grandfather Yoshimoto, who had adopted a similar style when writing *Reciting Poetry to Myself at Ojima*. However, when one reads *Account of Fujikawa* after *Journey to Zenkō-ji*, one has the impression of traveling backward from the simple style that had evolved in the Muromachi period to the more flowery expression of an earlier day.

From the outset of his journey, Kaneyoshi referred repeatedly to the changes brought about by the war. Hardly had he left Nara when he encountered a new barrier that had been established on the road under pretext of military necessity. The local manor lord interceded in his behalf, but Kaneyoshi wrote, "Everything that happened was disagreeable." To this comment he added a *waka* that, unlike the usual "poetic" travel poem, referred specifically to the difficulties he was encountering:

sa mo koso wa	In just such a way
ukiyo no tabi ni	One wanders on a journey
sasuraete	Through this uncertain world:
michi samatage no	Do not set up barriers
seki na todome so[8]	To block the road before us!

Not only were the roads blocked, but there were no longer any decent inns along the way. Kaneyoshi more than once spent the night in a hovel by the road. It is surprising that, although he certainly complained, he never seems to have felt self-pity. In fact, the diary is astonishingly cheerful, considering that he was an old man traveling through dangerous country under the worst possible conditions. He crossed Lake Biwa by boat, though the journey by water was considered to be even more perilous than going by land. The area was infested with men who had fled the war-torn capital and turned to banditry or piracy to support themselves.[9] A little farther along the way Kaneyoshi noted, "On seeing that the pilings of the bridge over the Fuji River had collapsed, I wrote,"

tazunebaya	I should like to ask
ikutoshi nami wo	How many years have men been
watarebaya	Crossing over the waves
nakaba taenuru	That it has broken in two,
Fujikawa no hashi[10]	The bridge on the Fuji River?

Like every other traveling poet, Kaneyoshi was fascinated by *uta-makura*, the places mentioned in poetry. When he reached the Barrier of Fuwa, its ruined state, commented on by every visitor, elicited the comment, "When I thought of the past, I sensed the pity of things."[11] This was a surprising avowal by Kaneyoshi, who claimed (unlike most poets) not to feel *aware* (pathos). A *waka* given later in the diary expressed this conviction:

Echigawa no	With spray from the water
sade sasu seze ni	Flowing through the rapids of
yuku mizu no	The Echi River
aware mo shiranu	Dripping from my net, my sleeves
sode mo nurekeri[12]	Are soaked, but not with sadness.

This is the only *waka* I know in which the poet declares that his sleeves are wetted not by tears but by water. It made me feel special affection for this unconventional old man.

When Kaneyoshi reached his destination—Kawade, in the province of Mino—he was royally received by his benefactor, Saitō Myōchin (1410–80). After the austerities of his life in Nara and the fatigue of the journey, the reception was undoubtedly most welcome. Kaneyoshi was lodged at a recently built addition to the Shōhō-ji, the oldest Zen temple in Mino. The meals he was served were so elaborate that he decided not to describe them in his diary, contenting himself with the ironic comment that the only items missing from the menu were roast phoenix and dried giraffe.[13] The following day there was a poetry reading, and on the day after that a *renga* sequence in one hundred links was composed. Myōchin seems to have expected Kaneyoshi to sing for his supper.

Although Kawade seemed like an island of tranquillity in a country that was largely ravaged by fighting, the castle commanded by Saitō Toshikuni, Myōchin's adopted son, was stripped for action. Kaneyoshi reported, "When I went to his castle I saw that the whole place had been swept clean. Weapons were stacked, and preparations completed for immediate action in case anything arose. But," Kaneyoshi hastened to add, "they seem not to have abandoned the arts of poetry, music, and dance."[14] At a party held in the castle, the nine-year-old son of the governor of Mino danced so beautifully as to bring to Kaneyoshi's mind a party of almost five hundred years earlier, when the sons of the Midō Chancellor Fujiwara no Michinaga had danced *bugaku* together.[15] He commented, "The dances of antiquity undoubtedly were unlike modern ones in the use of the hands and the stamping of the feet, but when boys have acquired such skill in the dance as to arouse the admiration of spectators, this is a case of 'the same skill applied to different pieces.' "[16] The emotions produced in the spectators may well have been similar, but the circumstances under which the dances were performed differed immensely.

A few night later there was a performance of *sarugaku.* Kaneyoshi knew a good deal about this art, more commonly known as Nō, and apparently even wrote a Nō play, though it was lost in the flames of the Ōnin War.[17] While living in Kawade, he also composed poetry in Chinese at the request of his host, though Kaneyoshi felt compelled to confess that it had been so long since he last composed a poem in Chinese that he had almost forgotten the rules.

Kaneyoshi planted two pine trees before the priest's quarters of the Shōhō-ji. Later in the diary he would describe his visit to a temple where Gokōgon, the Northern Court Emperor, had stopped on his flight from the Southern Court armies in 1353. The Emperor, on his way to refuge at Ojima, had paused long enough to plant a pine, which was now 120 years old, an ancient tree. Kaneyoshi knew the story of the pine from his grandfather's diary, *Reciting Poetry to Myself at Ojima*, and this made the pine doubly affecting.

After spending about two weeks at the Shōhō-ji, Kaneyoshi set out on his return journey to Nara. Shortly before he arrived, he composed this *waka*:

kumo no ue ni	High above the clouds,
sono akatsuki wo	While we have been awaiting
matsu hodo ya	The coming of dawn,
Kasagi no mine ni	Behold the moon of daybreak
ariake no tsuki[18]	Over the Kasagi peak.

A commentator has interpreted the poem as meaning that, even while members of the court (those "high above the clouds") have been awaiting the end of the long night, the rain has ended, and the dawn moon, presaging a revival in the fortunes of the court, is now in the sky.[19] Certainly, no one desired peace more than Kaneyoshi. He bitterly resented the destruction of the civilized way of life that had been the tradition of his family, and in *Shōdan Chiyō* (*A Woodcutter's Chats on the Essentials of Government*), written in 1480, the year before his death, he singled out for special condemnation the *ashigaru* (foot soldiers) who had burned and plundered all that had survived in the capital of the ancient culture:

"From the distant past the country has at times been disturbed by warfare, but there is no mention in the old records of anything called *ashigaru*. . . . These *ashigaru*, who have appeared for the first time, are rogues of the worst sort. The destruction both within and without the capital of the shrines, temples, great monasteries, palaces of the nobles and prince-priests has been their doing. . . . The way they have broken into places, set them afire, and plundered their treasures earns them the name of daytime robbers. Such instances were unknown in former generations. These events have occurred because of the decline in the martial arts. It is because, at times when distinguished samurai themselves should have fought, they let these ruffians do their work. That is why so many people have lost their lives to the arrows of the *ashigaru*. This is not merely the disgrace of a moment, but something of a nature to besmirch the reputations even of future generations. . . . Ours indeed is a world where those below conquer those above [*gekokujō*]. If word of this got abroad, it would be something of which we should feel ashamed."[20]

The prevalence of "those below conquer[ing] those above" now enjoys a kind of vogue among scholars, who contrast the vigor of the culture of those below with the stale, etiolated writings of those who maintained the old culture. A change was probably inevitable, but it is hard not to sympathize with Ichijō Kaneyoshi, the last to uphold the culture into which he was born, as he contemplated a world that seemed to have been turned upside down.

Journey to Shirakawa

The journeys described by Sōgi in his two travel diaries represented only a small fraction of his travels. He went, for example, no fewer than seven times to the province of Echigo on the Sea of Japan coast, but these travels were not recorded in any diary or similar account. On reading Sōgi's two surviving diaries, or even simply examining the chronology of Sōgi's incessant wanderings around Japan, we are likely to be struck first of all by the ease with which he seems to have moved around a country that was torn by bitter warfare. Sōgi probably assumed that the fighting was no concern of his; apart from minor irritations occasioned by skirmishes of soldiers along the roads he traveled, he remained as serenely indifferent to warfare as he was to politics. Travelers in wartime countries today, even if they are poets, cannot hope to escape becoming involved if they pass through places where battles are being waged, but for Sōgi this was possible. It was possible, too, in Europe during the eighteenth century: in 1762 Laurence Sterne traveled on the continent, in the manner he described in *A Sentimental Journey Through France and Italy*, at a time when England and France were at war. Sterne experienced no inconvenience, and even made the pleasant discovery that he was just as famous and esteemed in France as in his own country. Fujiwara Teika's "The red banners and the expeditions against the traitors are no concern of mine" seems to have been as acceptable an attitude in the Europe of the past as it was in Teika's Japan, though it is hardly true any longer.

The first diary recorded Sōgi's experiences during the relatively short journey from Mount Tsukuba to the Barrier of Shirakawa. In 1468 he was able to satisfy his long-standing desire to climb Mount Tsukuba. This mountain, though not especially tall or beautiful, was revered by poets of linked verse because the origins of their art were usually traced back to a dialogue poem composed partly by Prince Yamato Takeru and partly by an old charcoal-maker, as recorded in the *Kojiki*, the most ancient of Japanese texts. Yamato Takeru asked the old man:

Niihari	How many nights
Tsukuba wo sugite	Have I slept since passing
iku yo ka netsuru	Niihari and Tsukuba?

The old man gave his answer in verse:

kaganabete	The days put together
yo ni wa kokonoyo	Make of nights nine
hi ni wa tōka wo	And of daytimes ten.

Because of the prominence of the place name Tsukuba in this joint effort, the words "Tsukuba no michi" ("The Way of Tsukuba") came to be used as an elegant way of referring to the art of *renga*. When Nijō Yoshimoto compiled the first important anthology of *renga* in 1356, he gave it the name *Tsukuba Shū*, and his most complete statement of his theories of linked-verse composition were presented in *Tsukuba Mondō* (*Questions and Answers About Tsukuba*, 1372). Climbing Mount Tsukuba was for Sōgi not so much a test of his prowess as a mountain climber as a return to the source of his art.

In any case, Sōgi never questioned the importance of visiting the various *uta-makura*. Any landscape, no matter how ordinary or even unattractive, was redeemed in his eyes, providing someone had composed a poem about it. Even a frightening place could be made bearable by having been mentioned in poetry. When, on this journey, Sōgi crossed the Nasu Plain with only a single samurai for a bodyguard, he felt apprehensive. Tall *kaya* grass grew on both sides of the path, so high that Sōgi could not see the tip of his escort's bow. He was sure that if he had been alone he would have perished in the wintry wasteland, and was cheered only by recalling the *waka* by the Shogun Sanetomo that describes the region:

mononofu no	As the warrior
yanami tsukurou	Straightens the arrows in his quiver,
kote no ue ni	The hail pelts down
arare tabashiru	Upon the wrist guard of his lifted hand
Nasu no shino-hara	And beats before him in the bamboo plain of Nasu.[1]

The journey to Shirakawa was gloomy, but Sōgi attempted to restore his spirits with this *waka*:

nagakeji yo	I shall not complain:
kono yo wa tare mo	In this world everybody
uki tabi to	Makes a sad journey;
omoinasu no no	At the thought, in Nasu Plain,
tsuyu ni makasete[2]	I leave my fate to the dew.

It may be wondered what was the magic of the *uta-makura* that induced Sōgi and other poets to make long and sometimes painful journeys just to see places known to them from poetry. It is understandable that they should have wished to see Miyajima, Matsushima, and other places of exceptional scenic beauty, or that they should have traveled to Nara and other ancient sites for the pleasure of musing on the past, but many *uta-makura* are in themselves quite unremarkable spots that merely happened to have been mentioned in an old poem. One might suppose word would get around that there was nothing left of the Barrier of Fuwa, and that the irises at Yatsuhashi had long since withered and disappeared, but each poet seems to have wanted to verify the changes with his own eyes. Sometimes there was uncertainty concerning the exact location of a particular place that was known from the old poems. Several different places, none of them impressive, had been identified as the site of the vanished Barrier of Shirakawa, but this did not bother Sōgi when he set out. He was not an archaeologist but a poet, and he desired to familiarize himself with the particular qualities of places that had inspired earlier poets; as long as he supposed that he was at an original site, that was quite sufficient.

Bashō, paraphrasing the religious teacher Kūkai, once advised a disciple, "Do not seek to follow in the footsteps of the men of old; seek what they sought."[3] This superb piece of advice on the true significance of artistic traditions explains what inspired Bashō's own travels. Following tradition did not mean a slavish adherence to the imagery or language of one's great predecessors; the reason for traveling to the places where Saigyō or Sōgi had composed poetry was to steep oneself in their atmosphere, savoring both what remained from the past and what had changed, and then to join the long line of poets who had made these particular spots immortal. Travel was a means of revivifying one's art by discovering fresh inspiration in sights that had inspired other men's poetry; they would never lose this power, even if earthquakes changed the face of the landscape.

In effect, Bashō's journeys (and Sōgi's, too) were a way to follow in the footsteps of all the poets of the past who had ever visited remote parts of the country. Places that had not been mentioned in poetry were of slight interest. When Bashō traveled along one section of the Sea of Japan coast, he wrote in his diary *The Narrow Road of Oku*, "We spent nine days on this section of the journey. Exhausted by the heat and the rain, I fell ill and did not write anything."[4] But his companion, Sora, who faithfully recorded every event of note, made no mention of Bashō's illness, suggesting that this may have been an example of Bashō's departure from literal truth. Finding nothing to admire in places that had not been mentioned in poetry, he pretended to have been too unwell to describe the journey.

Sōgi made no such pretense, but it is clear that, no less than Bashō, he was uninterested in places without poetic significance.

He wrote of one place, "Not being a 'famous place,' it did not attract me."[5] There was one exception to the general rule that unless a place had been mentioned in poetry it was not worth noticing: if a place resembled some site in the capital and stirred nostalgic thoughts, it was also worth a visit. A certain river made Sōgi think of the Ōi River in the capital, and he asked its name. He was told that it was called the Nakagawa (Naka River), the name of another river in the capital. He wrote, "I could visualize the capital all the more clearly, and I thought this was surely a consolation."[6] When he crossed the river on horseback, the splashing of the water recalled to him a ford mentioned in a *Man'yōshū* poem.

When Sōgi reached the Barrier of Shirakawa, he was deeply moved by the solemn atmosphere that pervaded the place. This is his description of the dilapidated shrine at the barrier: "Moss served for its eaves, and maples made its fence, and in place of sacred streamers, ivy hung before the altar. At the thought that now only cold winds came to make offerings here, I could not check the tears of emotion. I imagined how deeply Kanemori and Nōin[7] must have been moved and, although I hesitated to compose a poem that would be so much rubble when compared with their masterpieces, my thoughts were too many to keep to myself."

miyako ideshi	There was mist and wind
kasumi mo kaze mo	When I left the capital
kyō mireba	But today I looked:
ato naki sora no	They had vanished from the sky,
yume ni shigurete	Dreamlike, and wintry rain fell.

yuku sue no	I do not expect
na woba tanomazu	The future to bring me fame,
kokoro wo ya	But I hope to keep
yoyo ni todomen	Future poets from forgetting
Shirakawa no seki[8]	Shirakawa Barrier.

It is perhaps no exaggeration to say that it was in order to write these two *waka* that Sōgi had made such a dangerous journey. He says that his own poem on the Barrier of Shirakawa is not comparable to the great ones of the past and will not bring him fame, but he hopes that it will help to keep poets of ages to come from forgetting the *uta-makura* that had inspired so many poems. His wish would be granted: a little over two hundred years later Bashō would be inspired by Sōgi's example to travel to the Barrier of Shirakawa and beyond and to create his masterpiece, *The Narrow Road of Oku.*

Journey Along the Tsukushi Road

Sōgi's journey to the northern part of the island of Kyūshū in 1480 was made possible by the patronage of the Ōuchi family, who had invited him to Yamaguchi, a town not far from the narrow Shimonoseki Strait that separates Honshū and Kyūshū. His gratitude for the entertainment he received in Yamaguchi and his reasons for going on to Kyūshū were succinctly expressed in these terms: "My decision to depend on a single, lofty tree proved to be efficacious: from its shade the dew of generosity was shed abundantly on the grasses below. The months and days passed quickly and, to my heart's delight, in numerous sessions of poetry on many different occasions, and soon it was the 9th month. Many invitations came to visit the cedars of Kashii and the pines of Iki,[1] and, moved by gratitude, I made up my mind to undertake the journey."[2] The "lofty tree" upon whom Sōgi depended was Ōuchi Masahiro (d. 1495), one of the most powerful warlords in the country; his generosity ("dew") enabled Sōgi and various other refugee poets from the capital to live comfortably in Yamaguchi, and he thereby succeeded in transforming a cultural desert into a center of literary and artistic creation. At the time, Masahiro controlled the Shimonoseki Strait, and one of his vassals made detailed arrangements with suitable people in Kyūshū (called Tsukushi, its old name, by Sōgi) for Sōgi's travels to places of interest in the area. Sōgi was provided with so considerable an escort that his journey this time suggested not the wandering of a lonely traveler but something close to a state visit.

Sōgi's account describes in poetic language the sights along the way. The writing is so beautiful that it is impossible to suppose that he jotted down his observations carelessly; he was consciously creating a work of literature. Almost any passage will suggest the quality of Sōgi's prose: "Then we continued on again until we came to a simple rustic shrine. On one side, where the trees grew thick, the evening sun was going down and the hoarse shrilling of the pine-crickets was deeply moving. The day was the sixth of the Long Month,[3] but for all that famous dawn at the Shrine in the Fields with 'add not your dismal voices' and the rest, I myself had nothing to regret."[4] The allusion in the closing words is to a *waka* recited by Lady Rokujō in the *Sakaki* ("Sacred Tree") chapter of *The Tale of Genji*. She and Genji were about to part at dawn. The place was Nonomiya, the Shrine in the Fields, and the season was autumn. Sōgi is reminded of this poem because the shrine before him resembles the description of Nonomiya, and because it is just the day mentioned in the novel. In the poem Rokujō asks the pine crickets not to make a sad occasion even sadder with their doleful piping but, Sōgi tells us, he himself is not unhappy.

After travels by land and sea, Sōgi and his escort reached a town (the present Shimonoseki) where they stayed at a temple that overlooked the waters of Dannoura, the bay where the Taira family had met their end. Sōgi's description of the scenery—the towering crags, the waterfall, the rocks—is extremely accomplished writing: "Our lodging in this district was the Amida Temple. Behind it is a steep hill of great, towering crags. Water comes cascading down to form a stream below, and the rocks beneath the falls make an interesting view in themselves. Even the stout roots of the pines that spread among the boulders have an ancient and venerable aura about them. Branches stretch out across the stream and press upon the eaves of the temple. Time has left its mark on the great hall; here and there the cypress-shingled roof is broken, lending a most melancholy charm."[5]

Sōgi visited a hall where a statue of the boy emperor Antoku, who drowned at Dannoura, was enshrined. He wrote, "He had a most pleasing countenance and appeared to be smiling. He looked just as he must have been in life; you forgot that this was the image of one long dead."[6] There were statues of other Taira nobles and court ladies who had also drowned at Dannoura. Sōgi was moved to compose the *waka*:

azusa yumi	Their fame, undying,
yae no shioai ni	Will not ebb, an unstrung bow,
kienu na mo	With the tide waters;
aware hakanaki	But how quick to disappear
ato no shiranami[7]	Is the wake behind a boat!

The last line of this *waka* was borrowed from the well-known poem by the acolyte Mansei,[8] which contradicts the claim made here that the fame of the warriors will not disappear: everything in this life is doomed sooner or later to disappear like the wake behind a boat. The mood anticipates Bashō's most moving haiku, written two centuries later:

natsukusa ya	The summer grasses—
tsuwamonodomo ga	For many brave warriors
yume no ato	The aftermath of dreams.

Many other passages in *Journey Along the Tsukushi Road* are likely to remind a reader of *The Narrow Road of Oku*. Sōgi wrote at the Barrier of Karukaya, "And when I looked upon these ancient ruins, I saw that all that remained unchanged from olden times were the mountains and rivers, the earth and the rocks."[9] Bashō, however, insisted that the written word lasted even longer than mountains and rivers: "Mountains crumble, rivers flow away, roads are changed, stones are buried and hide in the earth, trees grow old and give way to saplings, time passes and the world changes. Everything is uncertain, but coming here and seeing an inscription that without doubt was a thousand years old, I felt I was now seeing before me the minds of the men of old."[10] Sōgi's words have by now lasted five hundred years, and no doubt will still remain when every mountain he saw has been leveled to build a housing project and every river has been dammed.

Everywhere Sōgi went he saw the ravages of time. Famous temples were crumbling, their tiles fallen and their eaves broken, and weeds grew forlornly among them. After he and his party had crossed over to Kyūshū and reached Hakata, he visited the Shrine of Sumiyoshi: "A row of venerable pines ranged all around the extensive wattled fence. The roofed gate was half-broken and even the shrine itself was no longer whole. When I asked the reason for this, I was told that it was because of the more than ten years of strife and trouble we have passed through. It saddened me greatly. My prayer before the shrine was solely for the Way of poetry."[11] The destruction of the Ōnin War had extended even to this place, so far from the capital.

Sōgi's impressions, however, were not confined to scenes of destruction. When he visited the famous pine grove at Hakozaki, he was first saddened, then cheered by what he saw: "Tall trees were few; rather, there were trees of about a hundred years or less. The ancient trees were decaying and such one day would be the end of all the trees. When we observed the trunks, we saw that some were five or six feet tall, some only one or two, and some the merest seedlings, like young grass of the fields in spring. Any of them may live through ten thousand generations, but this depends on the grace of the gods."[12] At this shrine Sōgi prayed for the security of the nation (*kokka anzen*). The shrine had been rebuilt not long before, and there were new trees and new buildings.

The general tone of *Journey Along the Tsukushi Road* is not as dark as that of *Journey to Shirakawa*, but it nevertheless leaves the impression that Sōgi found the world, despite its consolations, a place of sadness. The most affecting passage in the diary describes his reactions as he looked out over the beach at Kashii: "The winds were rough and the waves billowed high. Disconsolately I watched the little fishes gaily leaping out of the water. I realized that even they must live in great fear of the bigger fishes that inhabit the ocean depths, and so I did not envy them. Again, when I saw a shell being carried to and fro by the waves, I observed that when it approached the shore and was far from the great ocean it did not grieve, nor did it rejoice when it was drawn back into the sea again. All living species are of a sadness beyond compare. The world we live in, whether in pleasure or in pain, is ultimately a place of lamentation. Since I knew this lesson all too well, I reflected that the only thing I envied was this empty shell."[13]

This was the closest Sōgi came to describing his own feelings. Though he was revered as a master of *renga*, treated with deference by people who normally would not have dreamed of associating with anyone of his humble origins, and offered hospitality by the local potentates wherever he went, the one thing in the world he envied was a shell tossed meaninglessly by the waves, a shell that knows neither the pleasure nor the pain of human life. This was his terrible judgment on the value of existence. Perhaps these words came from nothing more than momentary depression. Perhaps the words were only an allusion to some forgotten work and had no real emotion behind them, but this statement accords exactly with the total impression produced by the diary. It is true that Sōgi spent pleasant hours composing *renga* with old acquaintances, and he was glad to have seen the various *uta-makura* on his path, but the gloom is present all the time, and it surfaces in such remarks as, "It will prove of no avail if you enter on the Way of Yamato poetry unless you come from one of the great families or you are of noble lineage."[14] His conclusion, after a life spent at making poetry, was that, unless one belongs to the Nijō, Kyōgoku, or other "families" of poets, or else was of noble birth, it was impossible ever to become a full-fledged *waka* poet, even though the preface to the *Kokinshū* had asked rhetorically, "Which among living creatures does not compose poetry?" Regardless of the high honors that had been heaped on him, Sōgi was resentful that his birth had denied him the possibility of becoming recognized as a master of the *waka*. He had, it is true, established himself as a master of linked verse, but the *waka* was the only Japanese poetic art blessed by the gods.

Journey Along the Tsukushi Road is beautifully written, but its pervasive gloom and lack of human warmth have denied it the popularity enjoyed by Bashō's diaries. Sōgi's poetry commands our respect; Bashō's, without asking for it, has our love.

Account of Sōgi's Last Hours

In the spring of 1499 Sōgi, then seventy-eight years old, decided to leave the capital and take what he expected would be his last journey. *Sōgi Shūen no Ki* (*Account of Sōgi's Last Hours*), written by his disciple Sōchō (1448–1532), opens, "The old man Sōgi, having wearied perhaps even of the thatched cottage where he had lived for many years, wrote at the beginning of spring of the year, when he decided to depart from the capital, this *hokku*:[1]

mi ya kotoshi	This year I intend
miyako wo yoso no	To depart the capital
harugasumi[2]	Swathed in the spring mist."

Sōgi gave no particular reason why he might have felt "weary" of his cottage, but he was such an inveterate traveler that perhaps he was restless over having remained too long in one place. That year, as it turned out, he managed to travel only as far as nearby Ōmi Province, but early in the spring of 1500 he set out for distant Echigo. He had no expectation of ever returning to the capital, and was resolved to die on a journey, like Saigyō in Japan or Tu Fu in China before him. When Bashō wrote, near the opening of *The Narrow Road of Oku*, "Many of the men of old died on their travels," he was probably thinking of all three men, but of Sōgi especially. Most Japanese have desired nothing more than to die at home, surrounded by their family; it is rare for anyone to display Sōgi's determination to die among strangers.

Sōchō, the author of *Account of Sōgi's Last Hours*, apparently first met Sōgi in 1466, when Sōgi was forty-five and Sōchō was seventeen. Sōgi, then visiting Sōchō's native province of Suruga, invited the young man to participate in a *renga* session held at the famous temple Seiken-ji. Ten years later, in 1476, when Sōgi was at the height of his fame, they met again, and this time Sōchō was accepted as a disciple. When Sōgi traveled to Echigo in 1478, he took Sōchō with him. They were again traveling companions when Sōgi made the journey to Kyūshū that he described in *Journey Along the Tsukushi Road*. During the next thirty years Sōchō often accompanied Sōgi, both on his travels and at *renga* sessions. Sōchō participated in Sōgi's two most famous *renga* sequences, *Minase Sangin* (*Three Poets at Minase*) and *Yunoyama Sangin* (*Three Poets at Yunoyama*).

It was particularly appropriate for Sōchō, of all Sōgi's many disciples, to be present when the end came; but Sōchō was initially reluctant to accompany him on this journey, and once they reached Echigo he planned to leave Sōgi there with the Uesugi family (the local potentates) and return to the capital. However, he related, "perhaps because of accumulated fatigue from the days of travel through the hinterland, I fell ill, and the illness lasted many days. It was already past the 20th of the 10th month when I at last recovered, and just when I had made up my mind to leave it began to snow and the wind blew fiercely."[3] Sōchō had no choice but to wait for the spring to carry out his travel plans. That winter the snow was the heaviest anyone could remember, and in the 12th month there was an earthquake in which many people perished.

By the end of the 2nd month Sōchō had fully regained his health, and he informed Sōgi of his plans. He intended to go first to the hot springs at Kusatsu for the waters, then return to his home in Suruga; Sōchō, unlike Sōgi, was much attached to the place where he was born. When Sōgi learned Sōchō's plans, he replied that he had been expecting to die in Echigo but, contrary to his hopes, there was no sign of the imminent approach of death. He felt embarrassed at having to depend on the kindness of the Uesugi family, whose fortunes were on the decline; at the same time, however, he was reluctant to return to the capital. He decided therefore to accompany Sōchō to Suruga, and then go on by himself to Mino. He said that acquaintances in Mino had often urged him to spend his declining years with them. He also wanted to see Mount Fuji once again before he died.

Sōgi evidently was loath to let Sōchō go, and Sōchō feared it would be a sin if he refused Sōgi's request, though obviously he would have preferred to make the journey alone. The two men traveled first to Kusatsu, then to the hot springs of Ikaho, in the same province. Sōgi had heard that the waters were good for palsy and other complaints, and decided to stop there. Ironically, his final, serious illness started while he was taking a cure at Ikaho. His robust health had enabled him to travel extensively even in his old age, but now he had received the first warning of approaching death.

Sōgi's illness understandably depressed a man who was quite unaccustomed to being ill. He complained of being unable to sleep at night, and although he and Sōchō continued their journey beyond Ikaho, the stops at each place on their route became longer. Sōgi continued to participate in *renga* sessions wherever they went, in response to the importunate requests of local poets. At the beginning of the 7th month, when they at length reached Edo, it seemed as if his last hour had come,[4] but he once again recovered; his energies were restored when he was engaged in composing *renga*.

At a place near Kamakura he joined in a *renga* sequence one thousand links long, including this verse by another man:

kyō nomi to sumu	How long it has been since first
yo koso tōkere	I thought, "Today may be my last!"

Sōgi responded:

yasoji made	When did I ever ask
itsu ka tanomishi	That I might prolong my days
kurenaran[5]	Until I was eighty?

Most of his friends were dead, and he was about to journey into the darkness alone. A later pair of links in the same thousand-verse sequence emphasizes the same point, that he had lived too long. Another man provided the previous link:

toshi no watari wa	No one but myself will cross
yuku hito mo nashi	From the old to the new year.

Sōgi's rejoinder was:

oi no nami	How many times must
iku kaeriseba	The waves of old age return
hatenaran[6]	Before they are spent?

Sōchō, after recording these verses by his master, added, "It startles me to realize that these were the last poems he ever wrote."[7]

On the 27th day of the 7th month the two men set out for the province of Suruga. On that day, about noon, Sōgi suffered a rheumatic seizure. The alarmed Sōchō fed Sōgi medicines and arranged for a palanquin to carry him to the next inn. The following morning Sojun, the son of his patron Tō no Tsuneyori and one of Sōgi's disciples in *renga*, came rushing to his bedside. This seems to have cheered him, and the next day he continued his journey to Yumoto, at the foot of the Hakone mountains. Seemingly in somewhat better spirits than while on the road, he ate some rice gruel and, after recounting some stories, dozed off.

That night Sōgi seemed to be suffering in his sleep, and Sōchō awakened him. Sōgi said, "In my dream just now I met Lord Teika." He repeated the words pronounced by Teika: "Jeweled thread of life, if you are going to break, break now." But, as Sōchō and the others present immediately recognized, these lines were not by Teika but from a celebrated poem by Princess Shikishi. Sōgi then murmured a verse from the thousand-link sequence composed not long before:

nagamuru tsuki ni	Along with the moon I gaze on,
tachi zo ukaruru[8]	I rise and float in the sky.

Sōgi then said, "I have trouble adding a link. All of you, try to supply one." Sōchō continued, "Even as he spoke in these jesting tones, his breathing ceased, like a lamp that goes out."

Sōchō, summoning up the life of this perpetual traveler, quoted the *waka* by the priest Jien:

tabi no yo ni	To sleep on a journey
mata tabine shite	In a world itself a journey
kusamakura	On a pillow of grass
yume no uchi ni zo	Is to see within a dream
yume wo miru kana	Still another dream.

Sōchō had Sōgi's remains buried at the Jōrin-ji, a temple at the foot of Mount Fuji. Sōgi's last wish, to see Fuji again, was not granted, but he would rest forever in its shadow. Sōchō described the burial and the site of the grave in these terms: "It was on the 3rd of the 8th month, still in the dawn's light, at a place a little inside the temple gate where a clear stream flowed. There are cryptomerias. There are plum and cherry trees. I buried him here and, remembering the look he always wore, I planted a pine by way of a marker, erected a gravestone, then put a fence around the grave. I remained there for some seven days, then set out for the capital of the same province. On the way every single person I encountered had a sad expression, and amid the gloom of the old mountain paths we talked with tears and laughter. On the 11th I arrived at the Barrier of Seiken."[9] The diary concludes with the *chōka* (long poem) composed in mourning for Sōgi by the *renga* master Inawashiro Kensai (1452–1510).

Account of Sōgi's Last Hours is related without any display of overt emotion. Needless to say, the death of Sōgi profoundly affected Sōchō, but, rather than express his own grief, he quoted Kensai. Perhaps, though he nowhere suggests this, the strain of watching over an old man who was so obsessively eager to travel had in the end exhausted Sōchō, and Sōgi's death may have been a release as well as a source of sorrow. Sōchō was an entirely different kind of man. His devotion to *renga*, unlike Sōgi's, was not a religious consecration but the professional competence of a man who was otherwise much concerned with this world. The eccentric priest Ikkyū, more than Sōgi, provided the model that Sōchō consciously followed.

Account of Utsunoyama

Although Sōchō was Sōgi's chief disciple and his companion for forty years, the two men were of entirely dissimilar temperaments. The austere Sōgi seldom overtly expressed an emotion or revealed details of his private life in his works, but Sōchō's are dotted with autobiographical material that reveals a conspicuously down-to-earth, open personality. Perhaps his most memorable account of himself is found in *Utsunoyama no Ki* (*Account of Utsunoyama*), a mixture of diary and autobiography written in 1517, when he was sixty-seven.

Toward the close of that year, "in the boredom of the snow," he wrote this work for the information of friends in the capital and elsewhere. Thoughts of old age had come to obsess him, probably because he had led an unusually active social life and feared that his days of drinking, singing, and other amusements might be approaching an end. He wrote, "Has there ever been anyone, in ancient or modern times, who has not bemoaned the coming of old age? There is a *dengaku*[1] song that goes, 'How I long for the past! The waves of old age never turn back. . . .' "[2] It occurred to him, too, that more than a hundred of the verses he had composed during the past ten or more years were on the theme of old age. This thought induced him to recall events of his life:

"I was born the son of a humble artisan, but in my eighteenth year I became a priest and underwent the rituals of ordination, preparatory discipline, and baptism. The country broke out in disorder while I was in my twenties, and this lasted for six or seven years. There was fighting also in the province of Tōtōmi for three years running. I mingled with the dust of the encampments, but in my diet alone I remained a priest, eating thistles and suchlike vegetarian food."[3]

Although Sōchō referred to his father as a "humble artisan," he was a swordsmith, the fourth to bear the name Gisuke, and descendants who took the same name continued to make swords until the 1740s.[4] Sōchō himself became a priest at the age of eighteen, as mentioned. He apparently was inducted into the priesthood at a Shingon temple, but his later writings reveal a much closer identification with Zen. He often visited the Daitoku-ji, the great Zen monastery in the capital, and the Shūon-an, the hermitage outside the city where Ikkyū, the onetime abbot of the Daitoku-ji, lived and died.

Sōchō does not mention when he first heard about Ikkyū, but it may have been while he was serving Imagawa Yoshitada (1442–76), the daimyo of Suruga, during the period of fighting in Tōtōmi when Sōchō "mingled with the dust of the encampments." Though he maintained religious discipline, at least to the extent of eating vegetarian food, his life in the field probably differed little from that of a soldier. Sōchō, living under such conditions, probably realized that being a priest did not shield him from worldly desires, and this discovery may have drawn him to Ikkyū, who was widely known for his disregard of monastic rules. Soon after Yoshitada's death in battle in 1476, Sōchō went to Kyōto, mainly because he wanted to meet Ikkyū. The relationship they formed continued until Ikkyū's death five years later.

Sōchō's narration of his life in *Account of Utsunoyama* goes on to describe his visits to "the holy shrines of the capital, the Seven Great Temples of Nara, and to Kōya."[5] Sōchō's devotion to his native province of Suruga made him feel embarrassed, in retrospect, that he had spent so much time in pilgrimages elsewhere and had neglected the holy sites of Suruga. While in Kyōto he was accepted by Sōgi as his disciple in *renga*, and thanks to Sōgi he was able (despite his humble origins) to attend formal gatherings at which noblemen composed *renga*. He commented, "How strong the bond must have been between us from a former existence!

On my recent visits to the capital I often was reminded of him."[6]

At this point in his recollections Sōchō shifts abruptly to his personal life. While in Suruga he became acquainted with a woman who washed his clothes, and eventually she bore him two children. The son, now an acolyte, had been left with a high-ranking official of the province, in anticipation of his one day becoming a full-fledged priest. Sōchō wrote about his daughter, "My daughter is now thirteen. I had planned also to have her become a nun, but a certain man was fond of her, and at the close of the year I learned that they were engaged. It is a relief for a man in his seventies to have both children disposed of. Even when my last hour comes, I shall probably have nothing whatsoever to regret."[7]

It is hard to imagine Sōgi openly admitting that he was the father of two illegitimate children, but Sōchō does not seem embarrassed. Perhaps his attitude should be interpreted as revealing the influence of Ikkyū.

Account of Utsunoyama opens with a brief description of Sōchō's reasons for building his hermitage (which he called Saiokuken) in the province of Suruga. When he returned to the capital from Kyūshū, where he had traveled with Sōgi, he discovered that his house had been burned during the warfare. This decided him to return to his native province, and, having found a site near Utsunoyama that pleased him, he obtained permission to erect his hermitage there.

At first Sōchō led an idyllic life, enjoying, in the manner of the hermits of the past, the changes in the foliage brought by the seasons: "I praised the song thrushes in my odes to a spring that was uninterrupted by visitors. Later, people from the ends of Tsukushi and the depths of Azuma[8] came on occasion to visit me."[9] On the thirteenth anniversary of Sōgi's death, conditions in the capital were still too disordered for poetry gatherings. Sōchō therefore held services in Saiokuken and, by way of offering to the dead, presented a *renga* sequence in a thousand links.

Eventually, however, Sōchō seems to have tired of his quiet life in the country, and he began to dream of following in the footsteps of the poets of old who journeyed to the Barrier of Shirakawa. *Azumaji no Tsuto* (*Gifts from the Azuma Road*), the diary in which Sōchō described these travels, was written in 1509. Sōchō visited various famous places along the way to the north, but he did not manage to reach the Barrier of Shirakawa; when only two days away from his destination he learned that new fighting had broken out in the area, and that it was impossible for travelers to get through.

The most interesting parts of *Gifts from the Azuma Road* are Sōchō's descriptions of people he met on the way. Wherever he went there were naturally exchanges of *renga* with local poets, and once the *renga* was over, saké appeared, and Sōchō and the others drank until late in the night. At a temple near Nikkō there was an especially enjoyable session. Sōchō recalled, "The scribe was a boy who looked as if he might be sixteen or seventeen. The party lasted all day and was highly enjoyable. Miyamasu Genzō[10] and other *sarugaku* [Nō] performers fell in with us on their way to the capital, and drank with us until late at night. Their singing and dancing made for an evening that was so delightful we were all convinced it would not be forgotten for a thousand years."[11]

On the return journey, after visiting Edo, Sōchō witnessed a festival where there was a performance of an old form of Nō known as *ennen no sarugaku*. A couple of days later, after a *renga* session that had gone so smoothly that the whole sequence was completed in a single day, "At night twenty or more young *ennen* performers with good voices played music, sang, and danced. It was quite amusing, and what with all the saké we consumed and all the many antics, the party did not break up until it was close to dawn."[12]

These extracts will suggest how much more cheerful a diarist Sōchō was than his master Sōgi. It is hard to imagine Sōgi merrily drinking until dawn with actors. The only point in the diary where the reader's attention is drawn to the warfare that was then tearing the country apart is Sōchō's mention of the difficulty of getting to the Barrier of Shirakawa.

Account of Utsunoyama is in a less engaging mood. The journey of 1515 that forms the core of the work took Sōchō across the mountains into Shinshō, then on to Tsuruga on the Sea of Japan coast, and from there to the capital. Whole areas of the capital had been devastated by warfare, and the section around Nijō in particular had become a den of robbers. He heard people say, "What a world to live in!" But there were *renga* parties as usual, and Sōchō confirmed with his own eyes that men and women sightseers were "as numerous as clouds." Life went on in the ruins of the capital, and there was even time for gaiety.

Sōchō's Notebook

If we knew Sōchō only from his *renga*, we should probably suppose him to be little more than a faithful imitator of his master, Sōgi. His early *renga* cannot match his master's, though his later ones are rather more skillful, but we miss a distinctive tone that would reveal (as his prose works do) his individuality. He does not seem to have put either his heart or his quirkiness into his poetry, following instead Sōgi's tradition of impersonality; but in his prose, notably *Sōchō Shuki* (*Sōchō's Notebook*), written between 1522 and 1527, we find unmistakable proof that he was not merely a competent poet but also an unforgettably original one.

Sōchō's Notebook is not an artistically finished work, and it contains many dull pages, but it reveals more of the author than most of the artistically superior diaries kept during the Muromachi period. In the opening Sōchō described his mood as he was about to set out on his most ambitious journey: "In the 5th month of the 2nd year of Daiei [1522] I set out on a journey to the northern lands, in the suite of an acquaintance from Echizen.[1] I did not know whether I would return alive from Mount Kaeru,[2] but I crossed Utsunoyama and reached Sayo no Nakayama.[3]

kono tabi wa	On this occasion
mata koyubeshi to	I feel sure that I shall cross

omou tomo	Once again, and yet
oi no saka nari	The slope of old age is steep:
Sayo no Nakayama[4]	Nakayama of the Night."

The uncertainty expressed about his chances of ever crossing the mountain again were occasioned by Sōchō's age—he was seventy-four at the time. The *waka* given above is all but a plagiarism of Saigyō's celebrated:

toshi takete	Did I ever dream
mata koyubeshi to	I should pass this way again
omoiki ya	As an old man?
inochi narikeri	I have lived such a long time—
Sayo no Nakayama	Nakayama of the Night.

However, the mood of the two poems is dissimilar: Saigyō expresses surprise that he is still alive, but Sōchō, though he hopes to see Nakayama of the Night again, fears that he is going down the slope of old age too rapidly to survive his present journey.

This appropriately meditative opening is followed without transition by a description of fortifications being constructed at Kakegawa: "The circumference of the outer castle is six or seven hundred ken;[5] the moat has been dredged; and an earthen embankment erected. It is roughly like the main castle." Sōchō made so many detailed notes about fortifications he observed that some scholars have suggested that he may have been a spy who obtained military information, taking advantage of the ease with which *renga* masters could travel around the country.

Sōchō had not only had considerable experience in warfare, but had even served as the negotiator of the terms of truce when soldiers of his lord, Imagawa Ujichika, were besieged in a castle. In *Account of Utsunoyama*, Sōchō recalled, "Troops of our province had been garrisoned in a castle called Katsuyama in the province of Kai. The *kokujin*[6] with whom we had been holding discussions had a change of heart, and communication with those inside the castle was cut off." Sōchō, by command of Ujichika, entered into fresh negotiations with the besiegers. "For fifty days I used my old wiles on friend and foe, mingling truth and falsehood, and on the 2nd day of the 3rd month, two or three thousand men left the castle without a single casualty."[7]

By cleverly mixing lies and truth, Sōchō succeeded in saving the lives of several thousand men. He explained his actions at the time in terms of his having been unable to refuse a command from his lord, but in certain other respects he was far from being a model vassal. While on the journey recorded in *Sōchō's Notebook* he learned, in the 6th month of 1526, of the death of Imagawa Ujichika. It was his duty to return to Suruga, but when he set out on this journey and took leave of Ujichika, he had predicted that, because of his advanced age, it was unlikely they would again meet. He reasoned therefore that there was no need to rush back to Suruga; but we can detect behind his arguments his determination to die either at the Daitoku-ji in Kyōto, where Ikkyū had been the abbot, or at the Shūon-an, where Ikkyū himself had died.[8]

Sōchō's devotion to Ikkyū's memory was revealed on numerous occasions. He generously contributed money for the rebuilding of temples that were associated with Ikkyū, and in 1525 sold his prize possession, the set of *The Tale of Genji* that he had devotedly read for years, to raise funds for this purpose. He also commissioned an artist to paint the portrait of Ikkyū holding a broadsword that later hung in the Shūon-an. Sōchō mentioned in his notebook that, after he had bowed before the portrait and offered incense,

Suruga yori	Not a day but that
isoganu hi naku	I've hurried from Suruga;
Yamashiro no	At Takigi in
Takigi wo oi no	Yamashiro, the burden
ni wo zo karomuru[9]	At last slips from my shoulders.

It is surprising that Sōchō should have venerated Ikkyū, a man with whom he was associated for only two or three years, even more than Sōgi, his teacher for forty years, or Imagawa Ujichika, whose family had protected him for sixty years. No doubt he felt some special spiritual bond linking Ikkyū and himself. Professor Haga Kōshirō attributed Ikkyū's appeal to the "recovery of human qualities that had been kept at a distance by artificial forms and regulations." Haga also found in Ikkyū "something signifying a revolt against medieval ways, anticipating the birth of the human being of recent times."[10]

Sōchō invariably paid his respects to Sōgi on the anniversaries of his death, but there was something impersonal in these tributes, even when he composed so affecting a verse as:

asagao ya	Morning glories!
hana to iu hana no	The dream of every flower
hana no yume	That is a flower.

Perhaps Sōchō had lived so long in Sōgi's proximity that he remembered Sōgi's failings no less clearly than his poetic genius; or he may have sensed that, although *renga* was for himself no more than a means of earning a living, it was for Sōgi a religion.

Sōchō had shared with Ikkyū not only his dislike of conventional behavior but his love of different arts that flourished at the time—*shakuhachi* music, the tea ceremony, and Nō. His frank admission that he had had two children by a washerwoman was in the vein of Ikkyū's avowals of amorous exploits. There was also a coarse, sometimes salacious side to Sōchō's humor. He attributed this tendency to his weariness of life, though we may not believe it: "For the past eighty-three years, I have thought morning and night of my last hours, and especially of late this has become an obsession. . . ."

negawaku wa	I only hope and pray
naki na wa tataji	I won't get a false reputation:
ware shinaba	If I should die
yaso amari wo	I'm sure the gods won't realize
kami mo shiraji yo[11]	I was over eighty years old!

This *waka* suggests that Sōchō's conduct, even when he was in his eighties, was so wayward that rumors were likely to spread. An even earthier example of his *waka* bears the introductory remark, "At the beginning of the 9th month I went some four or five *chō*[12] from here. On the way back I fell off my horse, and was half paralyzed. I could not use my right hand."

ika ni sen	What am I to do?
mono kakisusabu	Without the hand I use to write
te wa okite	For my amusement,
hashi toru koto to	How can I hold my chopsticks
shiri noguu koto[13]	Or wipe my behind?

Sōchō spent the last days of 1523 at the Shūon-an with two or three cronies, including Yamazaki Sōkan, who is often described as the originator of *haikai no renga* (the comic style of *renga*). Under the benign gaze of Ikkyū's portrait they sat around eating *dengaku*[14] and composing comic linked verse. The verses all have double meanings, one conventional and the other humorous, sometimes to the point of indecency. Similar sessions must have occurred innumerable times. When *renga* masters visited castles in different parts of the country, they were expected not only to give instruction in the lofty variety of *renga* espoused by Sōgi but to participate afterward in a session of comic *renga*, during which poetic composition was promoted by consuming large quantities of saké. Few examples of comic *renga* have been preserved apart from the examples given in *Sōchō's Notebook*, but this is probably no great loss, considering that they were intended to be nothing more ambitious than after-dinner entertainment. The development of *haikai* poetry can nevertheless be traced from Sōchō and Sōkan to the masters of the Tokugawa period.

Sōchō's Notebook is by no means devoted solely to amusing anecdotes. There are many descriptions of warfare, some recounted with narrative skill and with compassion for the defeated. The style throughout is resolutely prosaic in the manner of a real diary, rather than in the literary manner typical of earlier poets. Sōchō does not seem to have had any particular readers in mind as he wrote, and that may be why he so seldom indicates why a man of his age felt impelled to travel around a country that was torn by warfare. Perhaps the simplest explanation is that Sōchō never lost his interest in people and landscapes. He evinced to the end a joy in living, despite his constant insistence that he longed for death.

A Pilgrimage to Yoshino

Sanjōnishi Kin'eda (1487–1563), then aged sixty-six, decided in 1553 to make an arduous journey at the insistence of a friend, the *renga* master Satomura Jōha (1524?–1602), who persuaded Kin'eda that he ought to see the cherry blossoms at Yoshino. At the beginning of the diary *Yoshino Mōde no Ki* (*A Pilgrimage to Yoshino*) Kin'eda had this to say about his companion: "He is deeply committed to the art of 'the way to Tsukuba.'[1] Recently he has been living in the capital, and he has been a constant visitor, day and night. He is also well acquainted with byways in the province of Yamato, and he urged me to see the blossoms at Yoshino."[2] Jōha, a native of Yamato, was indeed an excellent guide for such a journey.

The two men traveled first to Nara, where they visited the Kasuga Shrine, the Great Buddha, the Yakushi-ji, and various other tourist attractions. They had planned to reach Yoshino at the beginning of the 3rd month but, learning that the cherry blossoms had not yet opened, they headed instead for Mount Kōya. The ascent had to be made on foot, a difficult climb for a man of sixty-six, but Kin'eda seems to have enjoyed his exertions. Two days later they left for Yoshino, where the cherry blossoms were even more magnificent than they had anticipated.

This summary of *A Pilgrimage to Yoshino* may suggest that it was a conventional travel diary, no doubt graced with the poetry composed along the way. However, the unspoken fact that a nobleman, the son of Sanjōnishi Sanetaka, the outstanding scholar-aristocrat of his day, was associating freely with the son of a temple servant made this journey exceptional. Perhaps Kin'eda thought of Jōha as merely a guide, but his remarks show no trace of condescension.

The diary is saved from being a routine account of a visit to a famous place by Kin'eda's exceptional eye for details. Indeed, when reading *A Pilgrimage to Yoshino* one becomes aware of how much had always been omitted from earlier diaries of the period. For example, the entry for the 25th day of the 2nd month includes this passage: "We arrived at the Futai-ji.[3] There is a painting of Narihira in his own hand. We were told that it is normally not displayed, but an acquaintance named Sōji who comes from this region spoke to them on our behalf, and we got to see it. The face is handsome, with regular features. It was like looking at a real person."[4] How often in the course of history have travelers arrived at a temple, church, or other famous building and asked to see the art there, only to be informed by the custodian that it is not open and that they should come again! Of course, as the custodian well knows, there is not much chance that the visitors will ever be able to return to this remote place, but that is no concern of his. Fortunately, Kin'eda had an acquaintance in the vicinity, and this "connection" enabled him to see Narihira's portrait. The occurrence must have been typical in the Muromachi period, but nobody except Kin'eda ever described it.

That night the travelers found lodgings nearby. Other diarists would have contented themselves with saying that the room at the inn was wretched or that it was surprisingly pleasant, but Kin'eda was more precise and therefore more interesting: "The owner of the inn where we stayed is a person of quality, and he has recently remodeled the second floor. Fresh green blinds have been hung all around, and when one looks out one can see Mount Ikoma, close enough to touch."[5]

The authors of earlier Muromachi travel diaries were like the *waki* (secondary actor) in a Nō play who notices unusual sights and asks appropriate questions about them, but has no personality of his own. Nobody in a play ever asks the *waki* questions about himself, and all we are ever likely to learn about him is that he is an itinerant priest. Kin'eda in some ways was also an "itinerant priest," but his perceptions were individual, and when he asked questions it was not of an anonymous villager or "person of the place" but of a little girl or some other person who, for a moment at least, lives before our eyes.

The specific details in the descriptions contained in *A Pilgrimage to Yoshino* impart a reality seldom encountered in other diaries of the period. I cannot recall having read elsewhere a passage like the following: "Yesterday brush fires could be seen here and there in the mountains. Today also a great tree burned, and flames leapt up from inside the broken-off trunk. To the right were mountains, to the left a deep valley. We passed under trees that were burning at our feet."[6]

Kin'eda described his arrival at the Hase Temple in equally vivid language: "The appearance of the place was exactly as it is described in *The Tale of Genji*. As I stood for a while under the blossoms, I really felt as if I were gazing at waves of the sea."

kogiyose yo	Row a bit closer
hana no shiranami	Over white waves of blossom
ama obune	The fisherman's boat:
Hatsuse no yama no	An evening breeze of the spring
haru no yūkaze[7]	At Hatsuse Mountain.

The poetic conceit of imagining that the white flowers he sees are waves of the sea is successful because of Kin'eda's unmistakable delight in being at the temple. The passage continues: "I approached the altar of the central divinity. Just at this time two women were singing songs, apparently by way of offering to the Buddha. They addressed me, 'You who dwell in the flowery capital, vouchsafe to compose a poem for us.' I replied, 'I do indeed come from the flowery capital, but I am much too perturbed to compose,' and I kept my mouth all the more firmly shut."[8] When Kin'eda spoke of keeping his mouth shut he meant, of course, that he would not compose a poem despite the women's request. This touch of humor is welcome, because humor seldom appears in diaries of the time.

On the 29th, at Tōnomine, "Hearing an owl hooting nearby, I supposed that it must still be the depths of the night, but when I got up and went outside, the sky was brightening with the dawn, a light quite unlike any other. Everything looked sharp and clear, and I thought that the mountain about which Su Tung-p'o wrote that 'one could count every tree' must have been like this. And the sky was even clearer."[9] Mention of an owl, rather than some more poetic bird, is surprising in the diary of a *waka* poet, and Kin'eda's joy as he watched the dawning sky is fresh, not a hackneyed expression.

When Kin'eda and Jōha finally reached Yoshino, they were enchanted by the sight. Some trees had already bloomed, and their petals were scattered; others were now in full glory; and still others had only buds. Kin'eda wrote, "When we climbed up as far as the Aizen Pagoda, the treetops nearby had yet to bloom, so we went back down to the trees that were in full flower and drank saké there. As the saké began to take effect, the blossoms grew more and more colorful. I had previously thought that I would compose some kind of poem to celebrate the occasion, but it seemed as if that would instead dispel the mood, and I quite lost the ability to write a poem."[10]

There is something indefinably modern about Kin'eda. His diary, unlike those kept by other travelers of the age, is not simply a collection of reflections stirred by the sight of *uta-makura*, the places mentioned in earlier poetry, but has an appealingly personal quality. It is dangerous, however, to use the word "modern" when writing about people of the past, for sooner or later one is likely to discover distinctly unmodern traits in them. For example, Kin'eda described how he hurried to the Hōryū-ji in order to be present when the relic of the Buddha (*shari*) was displayed: "The time for the display of the holy relic of the Buddha had been set. I hurried my horse ahead, afraid I might be late, but I arrived just as passages from the sermon on the relic were being read. I was delighted to hear this, and when the reading was over the relic was displayed. They said that old people and persons with disorders should come into the inner sanctum, so I went and paid my respects before the sacred treasures. Among the various holy objects on display, I was most impressed by the Bommyō-kyō [Net of Brahma Sutra], which used the Buddha's skin for the title slip and his blood to write the title words. I thought this was incomparable."[11] A sutra with Buddha's skin used for the title slip and his blood used for ink is definitely not in the modern taste. I wonder, on the other hand, why Kin'eda had not one word to say about the marvels of Buddhist art at the Hōryū-ji. Probably for him they were not works of art but sacred relics, not to be discussed in terms of artistic beauty.

Although there is a medieval quality to the piety in *A Pilgrimage to Yoshino*, it has freshness, too, and one hears the author's voice distinctly. It is tempting to conjecture that a new age was about to begin, but probably it is safer to ascribe the individuality to Kin'eda rather than to his time.

Journey to See Fuji

Satomura Jōha (1524–1602), thanks to his inborn talent and the opportune deaths of his rivals, attained recognition in 1563 as the outstanding *renga* poet of the day. In that year his last important rival died, leaving Jōha indisputably at the top. This was not an empty honor. Military leaders in all parts of the country were eager to attract the very best poets and artists to their domains, hoping to acquire the trappings of culture, and when they visited the capital they turned to professional *renga* masters for guidance so that they would not disgrace themselves if invited to attend *renga* gatherings at the court. Such men no doubt paid Jōha liberally, pleased to be taught by so highly esteemed a poet. They probably also paid him for introductions to the nobility, eager to meet men whose families could be traced back many hundreds of years. The nobles were not displeased when Jōha introduced country barons; they had fallen on hard times and gratefully received gifts from even the most boorish general. The Emperor himself was not above accepting presents, showing his appreciation by bestowing examples of his calligraphy on the donors. Jōha felt no hesitation over serving as a pander to the nobles, who were glad to sell the aura of their names to rustics infatuated with the old culture.

The year 1567 was marked by desperate fighting. The entire

country was torn by warfare, and in the capital there was no central authority. This was the year Jōha chose to realize his long-standing dream of viewing Mount Fuji. He states at the opening of *Fujimi no Michi no Ki* (*Journey to See Fuji*): "In the spring of this year, the 10th of Eiroku, the thought came to me with insistent force that I should go and see Fuji, as I had long desired, and from that day I began to keep this record."[1]

The diary does not really become engrossing until Jōha reached various sites associated with Sōchō in the area of Utsunoyama, but even earlier there are some interesting passages. For example, on the 27th of the 4th month Jōha visited Yatsuhashi (Eight Bridges), famed for its irises ever since it was described in *The Tales of Ise*. Many earlier travelers had recorded in their diaries their disappointment over not finding any trace of the eight bridges or of the irises, but Jōha seems to have been unprepared for the desolate appearance of the scene, and he wrote a letter to the governor bewailing the extinction of the irises. The complaints of so distinguished a visitor could not be ignored: the governor sent a messenger with a cask of saké for Jōha and a letter stating that he had given orders to local property owners to plant irises; however, he went on, travelers from all over the country had the bad habit of pulling up the irises by the roots for souvenirs, and that was why there were no longer any irises.[2] Jōha commented, "I could imagine that this was actually the case, considering that it can be seen that even the pillars of the bridges have been chipped away by tourists." I am reminded of the Moss Temple in Kyōto, from which souvenir hunters have mercilessly ripped up the moss, but the souvenir hunters of the past must have been even more pernicious if they actually chipped away the pillars holding up the eight bridges!

Jōha's sight of Utsunoyama inspired him to write the first artistic prose in the diary. "The path we were about to enter overlooked a valley to the right, and rose up toward the peak. Ivy and maples grew in great abundance, and as we walked under the trees our sleeves were dampened by the last of the gloomy spring rain. We arrived at the village feeling forlorn."[3] Soon afterward he reached Saiokuken, Sōchō's hermitage. He wrote, "When I looked around the hermitage, I noticed an old plaque inscribed 'Saioku' in the hand of the priest Ikkyū. A portrait of Sōchō was also hanging there. He had forbidden anyone to paint his portrait while he was still alive, but said that if a portrait was made after his death it should show him wearing light-green robes with a black cloak on top." The portrait, according to Jōha, exactly filled these specifications.[4] In the garden Sōchō's broken gravestone was covered by a thick incrustation of moss, the accumulation of the twenty-six years since his death. Jōha was informed that the place had been burned during the fighting the year before.

Jōha lingered several weeks in the area around Utsunoyama. He visited the Pine Grove of Miho and inspected the pine where the angel's feather cloak had been hung.[5] On the 8th day of the 5th month he met an old friend of Sōchō: "I have an acquaintance who lives near the Seiken Temple, the lay priest Okitsu Bokuun. He related that long ago he was loved by Sōchō and said that he still carried with him the love letters he had received. His story made me feel as if the fragrance of the sleeves of his ink-dyed robes had penetrated me."[6] Jōha made no comment about this disclosure. Probably he took such relations as a matter of course. In any case, he was so pleased to have met Bokuun that he decided to stage a *renga* session that night in honor of their meeting.

Journey to See Fuji continues with Jōha's accounts of the poetry composed at parties where saké flowed. Only an occasional entry indicates that the country was then plunged in civil warfare. On the 24th day of the 7th month, for example, Jōha mentioned that there was to have been a *renga* session at a certain castle but, because it was the day before the local forces went out to do battle, there was a great drinking party instead, for which all manner of rare delicacies had been assembled.[7] Jōha says not another word about the impending battle, but remarks that the people in the castle town were enthusiastic about *renga*.

Jōha's inadequacy as a chronicler of life in wartime is nowhere more apparent than in his description of the burning of Nagashima in Owari by the troops of Oda Nobunaga. "Some time after midnight I happened to look to the west, and I saw that the castle at Nagashima had been taken and many fires set. It was as bright as day, so I got up."

tabi makura	A traveler's pillow—
yumeji tanomu ni	I had set forth on a path of dreams
aki no yo no	But now I shall spend
tsuki ni akasan	This night of autumn moonlight
matsukaze no sato[8]	In a village of pine winds.

Who would guess the circumstances that inspired this conventionally pretty *waka*? It is an example of how indifferent some poets remained to the brutal realities of the world in an age of conflict. Although Jōha closely associated with the men who burned cities, he was oblivious to everything unrelated to his own advancement.

Toward the close of the diary Jōha expressed his happiness that he and his servants had returned safely to the capital after the journey; he says that they were "drunk with joy."[9] The diary concludes with some conventional expressions of the uncertainty of life. Other men really experienced such uncertainty, but Jōha revealed in his diary that he was resolved to control his own fate, and, to a degree surprising in an age of rapidly changing authority, he succeeded magnificently.

The self-portrait that emerges from Jōha's diary is not endearing, nor is our judgment of the man likely to be improved by what is written about him in other sources. He early realized the importance of generous patrons, and he did not shun anyone who seemed likely to advance his career. Jōha served by turns Oda Nobunaga; Nobunaga's enemy and assassin, Akechi Mitsuhide; Toyotomi Hideyoshi, who killed Mitsuhide; and Hideyoshi's nephew Toyotomi Hidetsugi, who was ordered to commit suicide by his uncle. Jōha had the genius of always being able to ingratiate himself with a new master. Despite his opportunism and other failings, however, Jōha was undoubtedly the best *renga* poet of his time. Perhaps opportunism was necessary in order for him to survive long enough to master his craft in an age of warfare and treachery.

The Diary of Gen'yo

One of Satomura Jōha's rare errors of judgment consisted in forming a close relationship with Toyotomi Hidetsugi, often called by the nickname "the murderous Chancellor" because of his extreme brutality.[1] When Hidetsugi fell from Hideyoshi's favor in 1595, Jōha, because of his connections with the disgraced man, was banished to Miidera, the temple overlooking Lake Biwa. Jōha's stipend of one hundred *koku*[2] was terminated, and his house and property were confiscated.

An account of Jōha in exile is found in the diary kept by Gen'yo, a priest who accompanied the nobleman Konoe Nobutada back to Kyōto from his place of exile in Kagoshima. Nobutada had been exiled by Hideyoshi in 1594 because of his overeagerness to join the expedition that Hideyoshi had mounted against Korea. (Hideyoshi did not approve of high-ranking nobles serving in the military forces.) In 1596 Hideyoshi relented and permitted Nobutada to return to the capital. *The Diary of Gen'yo* describes the journey, including his impressions of sights along the way, such as Shiramine in Shikoku, where the Emperor Sutoku had been exiled. Gen'yo also spent considerable time sightseeing after he reached Kyōto. It is agreeable for a contemporary reader to note that almost every building he mentions still stands, though almost nothing in Kyōto antedates the disastrous warfare of the late fifteenth century.

On the 13th day of the 10th month of 1596 Gen'yo went with Hosokawa Yūsai to visit Jōha at the Miidera. He recorded in his diary, "The priests' quarters at the Miidera are all in a state of extreme dilapidation. Jōha's dwelling is beside an old temple. We spent the whole day in quiet conversation. When it grew dark we left. There were many things to make us lonely, with the bell of the Miidera lingering faintly in the air."[3]

Gen'yo continued to correspond with Jōha while in the capital, sometimes sending him *renga* for his comments. In the 11th month of the same year he and Yūsai composed a *ryōgin*, a linked-verse sequence by two men, and Gen'yo sent it to Jōha. He later reported with satisfaction, "I received a letter of praise from old man Jōha."

Gen'yo visited Jōha again in the 2nd month of 1597, shortly before his return to Kyūshū. He wrote in his diary, "On the 19th I arrived in Ōtsu. That night I spent with Jōha, and we talked about many things. . . . When I was about to leave Jōha's lodgings, he presented me with a fan and other gifts, and he accompanied me a considerable distance."[4] Gen'yo was touched by this attention from a celebrated poet, and Jōha for his part was no doubt pleased that he had not been forgotten even though he was in exile. Jōha was pardoned in the autumn of 1597 and returned to the capital. Soon he was again taking an active part in *renga* sessions and had regained his old supremacy. In 1598 he accompanied Hideyoshi on an excursion to Daigo to admire the cherry blossoms. Clearly, Jōha had been forgiven.

The interest of Gen'yo's diary is not confined to his mentions of Jōha. His account of his pleasures while in Kyōto is intriguing for the contemporary reader because these pleasures—the tea ceremony, Nō, Go, and so on—are still enjoyed today. One feels that an unbroken tradition links his day and ours, and that the links between his day and the medieval past were gradually being broken. Although the transmission of knowledge had been largely secret during earlier times, Gen'yo mentions attending lectures on *The Tales of Ise* given by Yūsai, and of receiving instruction on the correct pronunciation of words in the Chinese preface to the *Kokinshū*.[5]

The differences between the late sixteenth century, when Gen'yo wrote his diary, and our time are also interesting. On the 26th day of the 11th month of 1596 he attended a performance of Nō at the Nanzen-ji, the Zen temple in the Higashiyama section of Kyōto, during which the fourth son of Yūsai appeared in nine different plays, evidence that the plays were performed much more quickly than at present.[6]

The diary of Gen'yo, like those written in Chinese about the same time, is of interest chiefly because of what it tells about life at the time, rather than because of what it reveals of the author. That is probably why Gen'yo and his diary are today almost completely forgotten.

Chōshōshi's Journey to Kyūshū

The most literary of the diaries that describe Hideyoshi's campaigns in Korea in 1592 and 1597 was undoubtedly Kinoshita Chōshōshi's *Kyūshū no Michi no Ki* (*Account of a Journey to Kyūshū*). It opens with a succinct account of the background: "The Great Minister of State having resolved to conquer China, it was decided that he would proceed to Tsukushi[1] toward the end of the Tenshō era,[2] and the warriors of the Land of the Rising Sun[3] without exception attended on him. He himself set out from the capital about the 5th day of the 1st month. . . ."[4]

Chōshōshi's travels took him along the northern coast of the Inland Sea as far as Shimonoseki, and from there across the straits to Kyūshū. At no point does he mention military preparations or convey any excitement concerning the approaching expedition to Korea. Instead, he gives poetic descriptions of places (especially *uta-makura*) he passed on his journey. As often in such accounts, he frequently asked people about landmarks that had disappeared or about old acquaintances who had died. However, he did not spend all his time brooding over the past. At Kashima, where he was respectfully welcomed, he suddenly felt like playing *kemari*, a courtly form of football. He wrote, "I so strongly insisted on playing *kemari* that they seemed resigned to it, and brought me the proper clothes and the rest. I enjoyed myself kicking around the ball until it grew dark. The men and women of the vicinity all gathered around to watch. Apparently, such exercise is a curiosity in the provinces."[5] This is a rare instance of a diarist who is addicted to sports, and the comment on the rustics who had never seen so elegant a sport as *kemari* before is typical of the humor found in Chōshōshi's poetry.

Chōshōshi seems to have taken up the study of *waka* merely as a diversion from his career as a soldier. He came from a minor samurai family that rose to great importance thanks to two fortunate marriages. His aunt became Hideyoshi's wife, and his daughter married the fifth son of Tokugawa Ieyasu. In 1587, when he was only seventeen years old, Chōshōshi was appointed lord of the Castle of Tatsuno, and in 1592, when the Korean expedition was organized, although he was still very much a junior commander, he accompanied Hideyoshi to Kyūshū. By this time he was already an accomplished *waka* poet, as his diary reveals in passages like the following, which describes his own experiences in terms closely derived from those of Narihira in *The Tales of Ise*:

"The moon had climbed in pure radiance to the edge of the mountains, and was so bright that I felt sure people in my old village would also be gazing on it in the same way. With such thoughts in mind, I went back. The path I had traveled, straight as a jeweled spear, did not extend any great distance; evidently I had not come very far. Thinking I should go inside, I entered the little temple on the corner across from the post-station and stood on the broken board floor until late at night. I murmured to myself, 'Is that not the moon? And is not the spring the spring of long ago?' When it grew light, I sent a letter to my old home. I wrote in these terms to a dear friend":

omoiki ya	Did I ever dream
onaji kono yo ni	That, although you and I still
arinagara	Are in this same world,
mata kaerikonu	Our separation might be
wakare sen to wa[6]	Without a later return?

The poem and the poetic allusions make it clear that this diary is the work not of a soldier but of a poet. Chōshōshi, expressing neither joy nor fear at the thought of impending battles, adopted the melancholy tones of Narihira to describe his own feelings: "The rain, appropriately for the spring, poured down. The day was at length growing dark, but I was not near any human habitation. I put in my boat at a little island off the shore, and managed somehow to spend the night there. I felt unutterably forlorn. I now knew from personal experience the sadness of sleeping on a boat. I did not even try to doze. My face was streaked with tears of awareness of the season when—most inopportunely—drops of rain, leaking through the rush matting overhead, fell on my sleeves."[7]

An affecting passage describes how Chōshōshi went ashore one moonlit night on a deserted strand. Seeing a fisherman's lights, he decided to look for a place to spend the night: "The house had no solid pillars, but was supported by oars, rudders, and suchlike things on all sides, over which was thrown a single layer of coarse matting. I lay down on the sand, my ears touching a corner of a rock. If I had been born in that station of life, what would have become of me? I suppose that, if I thought of it as home, the place would not be so depressing. At length the clear moon rose, and its light falling on the vast expanse of sand sparkled like scattered jewels."[8]

One does not expect this kind of writing from a soldier on his way to the front, but Chōshōshi was obviously no ordinary soldier. Later in life, torn by conflicting loyalties to the Toyotomi and Tokugawa families, he abandoned his military duties altogether and went to live in Kyōto, where he spent the remainder of his life in retirement, as a poet.

Korean War Diaries

The diaries of literary intent by men who participated in the Japanese invasion of Korea in 1592 seldom convey any impression of the warfare involved, but various nonliterary diaries describe the warfare in detail.

The battle diary *Kōrai Nikki* (*The Korea Diary*), kept by one Tajiri Akitane, is typical of the nonliterary diaries. Tajiri stated at the outset why he had bothered to keep a diary: he was so bored that he wrote the diary by way of distraction. This avowal may surprise readers who supposed that constant fighting would keep anyone from becoming bored, but it accords with my own experience: short periods of frightening activity are generally interspersed with long periods of boredom. Perhaps wars have always been fought that way.

Tajiri was anxious to describe exactly what had occurred, and he gave no thought to niceties of style. The entries in his diary are devoid of personal emotion or literary charm, even when, one would suppose, the events should have heightened the expression. For example, this is what he wrote on the 17th day of the 4th month, when the Japanese fleet first entered the Bay of Pusan: "From the hour of the Bird[1] we saw the Korean mountains, and shortly after the hour of the Boar[2] we rowed into the entrance to Pusan Bay. However, being unfamiliar with the geography, we ran into difficulties, not knowing which way to proceed. At this point a small boat rowed up, and after an exchange of words we learned exactly the lay of the harbor."[3] Considering that this was the first Japanese venture into Korea since the fall of their stronghold of Mimana over a thousand years before, a note of excitement would not have been out of place, but Tajiri's tone does not vary, even when he describes the hundreds of Koreans who were killed by the Japanese, or the many other Koreans who were taken prisoner and forced to work for the Japanese.

Tajiri's narration of the naval battle fought on the 28th day of the 5th month is somewhat more exciting. According to his account, some thirty small Japanese vessels successfully took on "several hundred barbarian ships."[4] Mention of this victory is followed by Tajiri's summary of the legendary Empress Jingū's victory over Silla, aided by the Japanese gods. It is not surprising that Tajiri celebrated the Japanese victories, but he was less squeamish than modern diarists would be when relating the brutal details: "Young soldiers went off some three *ri*, destroyed a big temple, and took provisions."[5] Another diarist was even more explicit in describing the assault on the same temple: "The temple gates were big. [Nabeshima] Naoshige and [Katō] Kiyomasa broke through the main gate, drove the priests out, and took rice, millet, gold, and silver."[6]

Even more chilling are the accounts found in various diaries of how the Japanese cut off the noses of the Korean dead to build a *hanazuka* (nose mound) in Kyōto: "Our doughty soldiers attacked their castles and occupied their land. They also killed countless Koreans. The heads of officers and men should have been cut off and sent home as trophies, but the distance across the sea is so great that we decided instead to cut off the noses, and offer them for the Great Minister of State [Hideyoshi] to inspect."[7]

Modern warfare is so much more terrible than even the worst deeds described in these diaries that we cannot fully comprehend its horror, but cutting off the noses, not only of soldiers but also of women and children, and wantonly burning defenseless cities are horrific even by modern standards. Closer to our own day, accounts of the beheading of Chinese prisoners, as described in Hino Ashihei's novel *Earth and Soldiers*, or of captured American aviators, as described in the diaries I read during the war, make the blood run cold; in contrast, the announcement of an air raid in some distant place, though it involves many more casualties, including innocent people, tends to become an abstraction.

Perhaps some of the Japanese soldiers who took part in the invasion of Korea enjoyed the fighting so much that they nostalgically related their deeds to their children, but for countless Japanese, as well as Koreans, the warfare inspired only terror. It is easy to understand their relief when the Battle of Sekigahara at last brought peace to the country and marked the beginning of a new age.

Diaries of the Early Tokugawa Period

I have read and described many of the diaries written in Japanese, from *The Tosa Diary* of the early tenth century to the various diaries of the late sixteenth century, as well as a few diaries written in Chinese that possess special importance; but so many diaries survive from the Tokugawa period (1600–1867) that it is impossible to read, let alone discuss, them all. I have had no choice but to make a selection, treating only diaries of literary interest that reveal something significant about their authors or their times.

The first literary diaries that are truly diaries (as opposed to the mixture of diary and autobiography typical of earlier times) date from the Tokugawa period. The diaries of previous ages were often written months or even years after the fact. Their accuracy is therefore open to doubt, but their literary value was probably enhanced by their having been filtered through time and the memories of the authors. In contrast, many diaries of the Tokugawa period were kept daily, with descriptions of the weather, visitors, minor illnesses, trivial occurrences, and so on.

When I was writing about diaries of this period, my attention was also distracted by the existence of autobiographies. Some earlier diaries (such as *The Gossamer Years* or *The Confessions of Lady Nijō*) are largely autobiographical, relating events in the authors' lives that took place many years before, but the authors pretended to be writing daily. In the Tokugawa period people wrote memoirs similar to those being written today, without any pretense that these were day-to-day chronicles. Matsunaga Teitoku's avowed purpose in writing *A Record of Favors Received* was to inform his readers of kindnesses with which he had been favored during his lifetime. His autobiography nevertheless contains the same kinds of insights into the personalities of the author and the people with whom he associated as the diaries of an earlier day, and I have therefore not hesitated to cross over the boundary line between diary and autobiography in this instance.

Many diaries of the Tokugawa period are in the tradition of the great diaries of the past. Those by Bashō, which include the best-known of all Japanese diaries, share much with the diaries of the nun Abutsu and the priest Sōgi, two writers he especially admired. There was also a conspicuous revival of diaries written by women; not a single diary kept by a woman survives from the preceding three hundred years.

The special interest of these diaries is that they describe the period that represents for most Japanese the source of authentic Japanese tradition. The architecture, attire, and cuisine that are now considered traditionally Japanese all date from the Tokugawa period. It is the period of most Japanese historical films, evidence that this is where Japanese fantasies about the past are located. Yet it is tantalizingly close: in 1953 I heard Tokutomi Sohō give a lecture in which he described his remembrances of men in armor fighting with swords. The literature of this period is nevertheless not so immediately accessible. We sympathize with the unhappy heroes and heroines of Chikamatsu's plays, but they clearly do not belong to our world. The characters in Saikaku's novels are even more remote. But in the diaries we find people who are as close to us as our own grandparents.

A Record of Favors Received

Matsunaga Teitoku's *Taionki* (*A Record of Favors Received*) does not belong to any easily identifiable literary genre. Although it contains autobiographical episodes, they are presented too unsystematically for the work to be called an autobiography; the most memorable sections, describing Teitoku's childhood, occur at the very end. Ostensibly, it is a record of the author's indebtedness to his teachers of poetry, especially Kujō Tanemichi, Hosokawa Yūsai, and Satomura Jōha. Teitoku expressed boundless admiration for all three men, though they belonged to quite different classes—a court noble, a daimyo, and a plebeian monk—and he related anecdotes about each, but *A Record of Favors Received* is not a series of biographies. Nor can it be considered as an example of *zuihitsu*, because the materials are organized and are generally restricted to Teitoku's experiences as a poet. Nor is it a diary, though it contains the kinds of materials encountered in earlier diaries. It seems nevertheless appropriate to consider it as a record of the time, one that is notable as the testimony of a man who lived through the last days of the age of warfare into the beginning of the Tokugawa peace.

One problem faced by students of literature of the Tokugawa period is the sincerity of the public professions of worship for the Tokugawa family. For example, Bashō's haiku—

ara tōto	How magnificent!
aoba wakaba ni	On the green leaves, the young leaves,
hi no hikari	The light of the sun.

—was composed at Nikkō and undoubtedly was a metaphor used to evoke the glory of the Tokugawa shoguns, whose mausoleums were there. In reading this haiku, a modern reader like myself finds it more agreeable to ignore the possible metaphorical content and accept it instead as a statement of Bashō's delight over the scenery; and if obliged to recognize that Bashō had the glory of the shoguns in mind, I tend to interpret this fact as no more than a conventional expression of respect. It is hard to imagine that Bashō could have admired a line of despots. But perhaps, regardless of what a modern reader may feel, Bashō was sincere.

In the case of Matsunaga Teitoku, his admiration for the Tokugawa family can hardly be doubted: "The debt we owe this family is higher than the mountains, deeper than the sea. Their blessings have not been conferred on one person alone, making it harder to perceive their magnitude, a fact that in itself proves its immensity. If one gives a lantern to a stranger traveling in the dark of night, one can easily imagine his joy; he is likely to consider it the kindness of a lifetime. But although the sun comes up each morning to illuminate the world, nobody joins his hands in prayer to express his gratitude."[1]

Teitoku lamented that many people took for granted the benefits that each person received from the Tokugawa family (as they took for granted the morning sun each day), but he could not forget the past. "During the many military disturbances that took place after I was born, gates in the towns were strengthened and ditches were dug at the crossroads. Sometimes new barriers were erected on the roads or barricades were thrown up, and even ordinary coming and going became difficult. This made it all the harder to discover what was happening in nearby or distant provinces; all one heard day and night were terrifying rumors. We hid our possessions and searched for somewhere to escape to."[2] Anyone who has lived through the kind of chaotic situation that Teitoku described will be able to understand why he felt so grateful to the Tokugawa family for having restored order.

It was not only the general disorder of the times that lingered in Teitoku's memory. In 1573, when he was two years old, fighting broke out in Kyōto between the followers of Oda Nobunaga and those of the Shogun, Ashikaga Yoshiaki. The inhabitants fled the capital, seeking refuge in the countryside. Teitoku's father and mother, taking their four children, headed north. Teitoku recalled: "The route we took was indescribable. The worst point was when we came to a mountain torrent where waves boiled ferociously over the rocks. Wading across was out of the question, and there was only a narrow log bridge. My father, taking one small child under his right arm, and leading my sister (who was only five) with his left hand, slowly moved sideways across the log. My mother stood on the near shore, one baby on her back and the other in her arms, watching him. I remember her telling me how, when my father reached the middle of the bridge, his face looked paler than the waters below. When I recall this now, I can imagine what my parents were going through, and it fills me with grief."[3]

Teitoku was too young to remember the experience, but it seems nevertheless to have colored his entire life. It accounts not only for his devotion to the Tokugawa family, who had brought the country peace, but for his conspicuously timid and conservative disposition.

It is ironic that Teitoku, remembered today as the man who first brought dignity to *haikai* poetry by providing it with principles of composition of the kind previously reserved for *waka* and *renga*, should have felt so acutely embarrassed to be associated with this kind of poetry that he at first refused when his disciples asked permission to publish a collection of his *haikai*. He finally gave grudging consent to the compilation of an anthology, but refused to allow his name to be included. The postscript to the collection spoke merely of "a certain old gentleman" to whom the text had been shown.

Behind this reluctance to allow his name to be connected with the most dynamic movement in Japanese poetry of the time was Teitoku's unbending conservatism, the product of his early experiences and of his education. When Teitoku was still a boy, his father, recognizing his precocious gifts as a poet, sent him to study *waka* with the court poet Kujō Tanemichi (1507–94), revered as a repository of authentic traditions. Tanemichi also seems to have been impressed by the boy prodigy. He instructed Teitoku in *waka* composition, and transmitted to the eleven-year-old the secret traditions of *The Tale of Genji*. These secrets consisted mainly of unusual pronunciations for the names of the chapters and similar recondite tidbits of scholarship, but Teitoku was deeply impressed by his teacher. He wrote in *A Record of Favors Received*, "When I went to study under him, he was already eighty years old, but he was not in the least senile."[4]

Tanemichi guided Teitoku in composing *waka* of the Nijō school. By this time the inspiration for such poetry had been so diluted by repetition of familiar themes that there was virtually nothing new to be said. Teitoku's *waka* are boring; worse, they are in so much the same manner throughout that it is almost impossible to detect any stylistic changes during the sixty years he composed them.

Teitoku was grateful to Tanemichi and also to Hosokawa Yūsai, his other teacher of *waka*, and never doubted that they knew everything of consequence concerning the art of the *waka*. On one occasion Yūsai criticized a *waka* by Teitoku that mentioned "the *hototogisu* at the Sano Crossing." In the first place, Yūsai said, "One does not compose poems about famous places in other provinces when one is at a poetry gathering in the capital."[5] Moreover, there were no precedents for combining the Sano Crossing and the *hototogisu* (a kind of cuckoo) in one *waka*. Teitoku, far from becoming impatient with such fussy traditionalism, thought it was precisely in order to receive this sort of guidance that one had a teacher: "Such matters fall under the heading of old traditions, and they are prized by poets of *waka*. Their meanings cannot be understood without a teacher. And even if someone should happen to learn them, there is no proof of their authenticity unless he has heard them from his teacher's mouth. The fact that I am writing them down now is to serve as evidence for future generations."[6]

Teitoku proudly claimed that the traditions of *waka* had been transmitted unbroken from Fujiwara Teika to Hosokawa Yūsai "from mouth to mouth, as water from one vessel to another."[7] Teitoku believed that oral traditions passed, as a special favor, from teacher to disciple were more important than the discussions of poetry found in books, and that there were many secret traditions concerning language. But even in his day some poets rebelled against the authority of secret traditions. Teitoku contrasted their attitudes with his own: "Up until the time when I was a young man, beginners in poetry of every kind considered that it was shameful to look into manuals of poetry without first hearing their teachers' explanations. Young people today, on the contrary, consider it shameful to learn from other people."[8]

Teitoku was aware, however, of a basic contradiction in his orthodoxy. He revered Teika as the supreme authority on *waka*, but Teika had written, "In *waka* composition there are no teachers; the only teachers are the old poems."[9] This opinion was unacceptable to Teitoku, who agreed instead with Tanemichi, who had once told him, "When one is learning to compose *waka*, there is no need to consult books of poetry. There have been far too many books of poetic theory. . . . When one is a beginner, the best thing is to compose poetry day and night and to accept guidance from a teacher."[10]

Teitoku's reliance on secret traditions seems to brand him as having been even more conservative than Teika, but there was another, more innovative side to his attitudes as a poet. Teitoku's teachers of *waka* had both urged him strongly to give up *renga*. He related, "Once I asked His Excellency [Tanemichi] the best way for me to learn to compose *waka*. He replied, 'The first thing you should do is to give up *renga*. It belongs to the same art of poetry, but it is a hindrance to the beginner in *waka*.' "[11] Yūsai also commanded him, "If you intend to compose *waka*, the first thing you should do is give up *renga*."[12] Teitoku, though he revered his teachers, ignored this advice, presumably because he was aware, like Sōgi before him, that recognition as a *waka* poet depended not only on talent but on birth. Although Teitoku's grandfather had been the daimyo of Takatsuki, his father had been raised as a priest and later became a professional *renga* poet. The father, aware that *renga* offered a talented boy of relatively humble birth better chances of advancement than *waka*, had sent him to study with Jōha, even though he and Jōha were enemies.

Teitoku would have given anything to be inducted into the mysteries of the *Kokin Denju* (*Transmission of the* Kokinshū), but Yūsai went no further than to show Teitoku the covers of the secret books. Without knowledge of the *Kokin Denju,* Teitoku could not hope to be recognized as an important *waka* poet, but he expressed no complaints. He apparently considered that it was his fate, as a baseborn person, to pursue the path of *renga* rather than *waka*. Tanemichi once criticized Jōha, saying that he was "clever at *renga* but has never attained an understanding of the old poetry." Teitoku's reaction (though he was still a boy) was that Tanemichi's criticism was entirely just. There was no trace of the rebel in him.[13]

Teitoku nevertheless could not help being carried along by the spirit of the times. In 1603 he made an important friend, a man twelve years younger than himself, Hayashi Razan (1538–1657). Razan, who had been studying the texts of Confucianism for several years, decided to offer public lectures on their interpretation, for the benefit of friends, mainly young Confucian scholars and doctors. They in turn asked Teitoku to lecture on *Tsurezuregusa* (*Essays in Idleness*). He was reluctant to take the unprecedented step of lecturing publicly on teachings that he had heard privately, but in the end he yielded to their persuasion. Teitoku lectured both on *Essays in Idleness* and on *Hyakunin Isshu* (*One Hundred Poets, a Poem Each*), marking the great importance of both works in popular education. When his teacher of Japanese classics, Nakanoin Michikatsu (1558–1610), heard about this, he was furious that he had, unsolicited, "spewed forth to ordinary commoners important secret traditions." Teitoku felt deeply ashamed of himself. He wrote about Michikatsu, "If he had been a baseborn person like myself, he would have called me to him and struck me, but being of the upper class, he did not reveal his feelings even in his expression. I felt thoroughly ashamed."[14] Despite his embarrassment, however, the course of Teitoku's future activity as a bringer of "enlightenment" had been established.

In 1619, perhaps under the influence of Razan, who in 1618 had founded the school that would grow into the Shōheikō, Teitoku opened a school in Kyōto where children, ranging in age from four to eleven and mainly from the samurai class, studied calligraphy and *sodoku*, the reading in unison of the Confucian classics. Itō Jinsai, Kinoshita Jun'an, and other important scholars of the period attended this school, the first of its kind in Kyōto.

In the meantime, Teitoku had acquired a reputation as a poet of *kyōka* (comic *waka*) and of the *haikai* style of *renga*. He, however, thought of such compositions as being no more than impromptu witticisms and unworthy to be recorded. Only after his disciples had published a selection of his poems in this vein in a book that attracted favorable attention did Teitoku reconsider his negative attitude. Quite against his will, he had been enthroned as the leading figure of the new *haikai* poetry. In the end he came to defend *haikai* as a poetic form with distinct aims and rules, and he bolstered its authority by revealing how many great men of the past had composed *haikai* poetry.

Teitoku's own poetry is not of much interest today, but he occupies an important place in the history of *haikai* poetry. *A Record of Favors Received* enables us to see how an archconservative became the leading spirit of the newest variety of Japanese poetry.

A Journey of 1616

The name Hayashi Razan (1583–1657) today evokes associations with the most orthodox form of Neo-Confucianism practiced during the Tokugawa period. Shōheikō, the school he founded as the private academy of his family, became a bastion of Confucian learning, and generation after generation of the Hayashi family maintained the Chu Hsi school of Confucianism as the philosophical basis of shogunate rule. Razan, while still a young man, was called before Tokugawa Ieyasu, and from 1607 became his intellectual adviser. Razan assisted Ieyasu, a military man, in becoming a man of peace by persuading him of the necessity of establishing an enduring social order based on Confucian ethical ideals.

Even scholars who recognize the central importance of Neo-Confucianism as the moral backbone of Japanese society are seldom tempted to browse in Razan's writings, because of the aura of dullness that hangs over them. It is hard to think of him with affection, or even to imagine what he was like when he was young and Neo-Confucianism was still unfamiliar and controversial. Matsunaga Teitoku's *A Record of Favors Received*, however, presents a rather different portrait of Razan. Compared with Teitoku, Razan was a youthful enthusiast for popular education, as he demonstrated by offering public lectures on the Chu Hsi texts of Confucianism. Although the Shōheikō Academy would soon develop into a stronghold of orthodoxy, it was originally intended to change the content of Japanese education by making a daring break with Buddhist traditions. Instead of teaching young men to live apart from this world as monks, it taught them how to live in society, emphasizing rationalism and human loyalties.

Razan's diary, *Heishin Kikō* (*A Journey of 1616*), was written when he was thirty-three years old. It describes, in a much more genial manner than his philosophical writings, how he traveled from Edo to Kyōto. His patron, Tokugawa Ieyasu, had died earlier that year, and the diary therefore contains occasional expressions of grief. Razan recalled at Nakaizumi (near Hamamatsu) that Ieyasu used to go hunting there every year because game was so abundant, and Razan always accompanied him.[1] Again, at Minaguchi he recalled, "On the 4th day of the 8th month last year, the Great Minister [Ieyasu] left his palace at Nijō [in Kyōto], and arrived here the following day. From that day it rained without letup, and he therefore remained here for three days. I waited on him until late each night. During this time he commanded me to read the opening section of the *Analects*.[2] I knelt before him and opened the book. When I came to the passage, 'You should, to the best of your ability, devote your entire strength; you should, to the best of your ability, offer yourself completely,'[3] he himself joined in the reading, and said that attention should be given to the words 'to the best of your ability.' He said, 'Loyalty and filial piety are not carelessly attained. Which is more important, to devote one's entire strength to one's parents or to offer one's life to one's lord?' When His Lordship asked my opinion, I answered by citing the example of Chao Pao.[4] Unable to forget this even now, I wring my tear-soaked sleeves."[5]

Such recollections of discussions of the *Analects* of Confucius are not, however, typical of the diary, which consists mainly of brief descriptions of places passed on his journey along the Tōkaidō. Razan naturally visited the *uta-makura* that travelers always visited, but his viewpoint was distinctive. At Miho, for example, the pine on which the celestial being had draped her cloak of feathers was pointed out to him. Earlier visitors were content to relate the legend, or else they sadly contrasted the present appearance of the pine grove with the accounts in old books, but

Razan noted, "People asked me in which text the legend first appeared. It must be the poem by the priest Nōin that contains the lines"

Udohama ni	On the beach of Udo,
ama no hagoromo	The heavenly cloak of feathers
mukashi kite . . .[6]	She wore long ago . . .

Razan, not satisfied with transmitting the legend, insisted on revealing *when* it originated.

A Journey of 1616 was perhaps the first travel diary to mention the souvenirs sold to travelers at the different stages along the Tōkaidō. At Shōno, for example, he mentioned, "In the private houses of this place they stuff parched rice into little 'bales,' which they set out at every door. The 'bales' are about fist-size; there are also some that look like hammers. They wrap them in the shape of hourglasses and tie them at the ends. Travelers buy them and take them home as souvenirs."[7] The Tōkaidō had already assumed the role it would play throughout the Tokugawa period, with "famous products" and literary associations for each of the fifty-three stages. *A Journey of 1616* is also the ancestor of the many works of fiction that would describe travel between Edo and Kyōto.

Even when Razan described places that were familiar from the accounts in many earlier diaries, a freshness in his point of view may strike readers as being "modern." At Ikeda, in the province of Tōtōmi, famous because it is the scene of the Nō play *Yuya*, he wrote: "In the past it was a place where samurai on their way to and from the capital and frivolous youths would tie their horses to the gate and buy the smiles of courtesans for a thousand pieces of gold. In what way was it inferior even to the ford at Eguchi?[8] Everybody knows that Yuya, who was summoned by the Yashima minister,[9] was a girl from this post-station of Ikeda. Now the scant traces of the station are on the eastern side of the Tenryū River, and the few inhabitants watch over the river-crossing."[10]

Razan was more skeptical than his predecessors concerning the various legends he was told. When he visited the Atsuta Shrine he reported, "Popular legend has it that it is because Atsuta is known as Hōrai[11] that people worship Yang Kuei-fei here. That is also why, in *Song of Japan* by Sung Ta-shih, it mentions a shrine to

Lady Yang in this province. Not only are there shrine buildings but also male and female mediums who communicate with the dead. There is much that is stupid and dubious in popular legends."[12]

A Journey of 1616 contains many poems by Razan, both *waka* and poems in classical Chinese. In one passage, written after he visited Mount Hiei, he analyzed a poem in Chinese he had composed years before, then added, "I must have been twenty-seven or -eight when I composed this poem. For years I have had no respite from my official duties, and I have not composed any poetry. The men of old were afraid of letting three days go by without composing a poem for fear their tongues would stiffen, but it is much worse in my case—the dust has piled on my brush and inkstone, and now that years have gone by, how could the thorns in my mouth turn into poetry? Nevertheless, hoping that perhaps the scenery might come to my assistance, I have managed to produce a few poems composed along the way."[13] Composing poetry on the journey probably helped Razan to appreciate the scenery, even if his poetic talent had become rusty.

It may even be that the diary was intended mainly to serve as the pretext for composing the poetry. One scholar suggested, "As travel along the Tōkaidō became more frequent, it led to a strong demand for this kind of guidebook, and it was probably in response to this demand that the work was created."[14] *A Journey of 1616*, it is true, is informative about the places Razan passed, but not consistently enough to be of practical use to someone planning a trip along the Tōkaidō. Moreover, it seems hardly likely that the Confucian adviser of the Shogun would have written a travel diary mainly to satisfy the increased public demand for guidebooks. Perhaps Razan, familiar with earlier diaries that described travels along the Tōkaidō, wanted to indicate how a gentleman—as opposed to a professional *renga* poet—made such a journey. A mixture of poetry in Chinese and Japanese, together with informed, sometimes skeptical comments about stories he heard at various places, made for a diary appropriate for a scholar. Razan was aware that he belonged to a new generation, and he felt a responsibility to bring Confucian enlightment to this generation and others to come. *A Journey of 1616* provided a model of how an educated man might enjoy the pleasures of travel.

Diaries of Seventeenth-Century Courtiers

The diaries of the early Tokugawa period, regardless of the authors, provide unmistakable evidence of how quickly the establishment of the new regime affected writers. This had not always been true in the past. Even after the collapse of the Taira power and the establishment of a new capital at Kamakura, most literary diaries were still written by court ladies in the old capital of Kyōto; and when the Kamakura shogunate in turn was overthrown, this did not mark an end to literary diaries written by itinerant priests. But the changes at the beginning of the seventeenth century had a more dramatic effect on the writing of diaries. Attention shifted from the past to the present, and even familiar *uta-makura* inspired unconventional, contemporary sentiments.

The mainstream of diaries during the Tokugawa period would flow in a new direction, but the literary traditions of the past were not forgotten. Some diaries, especially those written by nobles, only occasionally revealed that the authors were living in a new age. *Sasamakura* (*Pillow of Bamboo Grass*), for example, describes the journey of a certain nobleman from Kyōto to Edo in 1620. The diary has been attributed to Nakanoin Michikatsu (1556–1610), the nobleman-poet who was so annoyed when he learned that his pupil Matsunaga Teitoku had lectured publicly on the secrets of *Tsurezuregusa*. The style is worthy of Michikatsu, but he died ten years before the events described in the diary, making it hard to accept the traditional attribution.

Whoever wrote *Pillow of Bamboo Grass*, it is studded with beautiful passages that are at once traditional in mood and new in expression, as the following passage may suggest: "From Ejiri I set out for Seiken-ji. The scenery here is so lovely that no painter could do it justice. In the foreground the azure sea stretches endlessly, taking its color from the sky; beyond, blue peaks rise in layers, surrounding fishing villages. The cluster of trees around the temples on the cliffs have an ancient look, and the sound of the wind is fresh in one's ears. The waves that come in at Miho Point are worthy of being compared to those at Sue no Matsuyama. Following along the beach from here, I let my eyes range far into the distance. One or two little fishing boats were faintly visible at breaks in the far-off mist, but as, imperceptibly, I came closer, their numbers seemed to multiply."[1]

One might have expected that the author, a Kyōto nobleman, would have unfavorably contrasted the brash new city of Edo with the capital, but in fact it stirred him to express extremes of enthusiasm: "I arrived early in Edo. Its way of life now is surely superior to [China at the time of] Kao-tsu of Han or T'ai-tsung of T'ang. And one need hardly mention the days of the Minamoto and the Taira."[2] The day after his arrival he had an audience with the Shogun, Hidetada. The experience overwhelmed him; he wrote, "He displayed awesome magnanimity." His feeling of the "awesome" nature of the Shogun's kindness in granting an audience was a far cry from the disdain that in former days aristocrats often displayed toward the warrior class.

Even greater reverence for the Shogun was displayed by the courtier Karasumaru Mitsuhiro (1579–1638). His diary, *Nikkō-zan Kikō* (*A Journey to Mount Nikkō*) is the account, written in 1617, of how he accompanied the remains of Tokugawa Ieyasu when they were transferred from Mount Kunō, in the province of Suruga, to the newly built mausoleum at Nikkō. Mitsuhiro had studied *waka* composition with Hosokawa Yūsai, and had been granted the privilege of being inducted into the mysteries of the *Kokin Denju*, but he had been banished in 1609 because of his involvement with a married court lady. He was pardoned soon after the accession of the Emperor Gomizunoo in 1611 and restored to his position at court. He later rose to high office. His fame as a writer, and especially as a calligrapher, has lasted to this day.

In the diary Mitsuhiro described how reverently the funeral cortège was greeted along the route to Nikkō: "In this manner the portable shrine [*mikoshi*] arrived in Mishima. The people following in the procession, just as yesterday, must have gathered from all sixty and more provinces, each eager to be first in line. There was no one who did not offer his respects to the shrine by removing his hat and touching his hand to his forehead."[3] Mitsuhiro's praise for Ieyasu ran to hyperbole: he declared, among other superlatives, that Ieyasu was none other than an incarnation of Yakushi, the Healing Buddha.

Not all aristocrats were happy under the new regime. Its moral severity irritated some aristocrats who were accustomed to laxer ways. Nakanoin Michimura (1588–1653), the son of Michikatsu, noted in his diary, *Kantō Kaidōki* (*Journey Along the Seacoast Road in the Kantō*), when he arrived at Mishima, that beyond this place was the province where his sister had been exiled some years earlier and where she was still living.[4] Presumably she had offended the new regime by some lapse of morals. Michimura's annoyance with the shogunate was exacerbated by his work as a liaison man between the imperial court and Edo. When he failed to report to the shogunate the sudden abdication of the Emperor Gomizunoo in 1629, he was reprimanded, but it is said that he declared, "I am a subject of the Emperor. I am not a subject of Kantō." When the Shogun Iemitsu asked to be inducted into the mysteries of the *Kokin Denju*, Michimura refused, saying that this secret knowledge of the nobles could not be passed on to military persons.[5]

The aristocrats were of fading importance in the new culture. They still dominated *waka* composition, largely because of their monopoly over the *Kokin Denju*, but, as the most intelligent of them realized, they would have to adapt themselves to a changed world. Regardless of the degree of success with which courtiers adapted to the new order, however, their diaries ceased to be of literary importance.

Travels Round the East

The anonymous diary *Azuma Meguri* (*Travels Round the East*) opens intriguingly: "I am someone who in the past spent years of his life quite unremarkably in the neighborhood of the village of Shinobu in Ōshū.[1] Frustrated over not being able to make a living there, I became a traveler, not at all by choice." This is the first account of a journey that was inspired not by piety or by a yearning to see places mentioned in poetry but by the need to make a living. The author decided to travel to Edo because he had a better chance of finding suitable employment there than in his native place, remote Ōshū.

When he finally reached Edo, after a journey that he described in the usual clichés of travel literature, with a pun on almost every place name, he looked for somewhere to live. "I rented a room in the area of the well-known Great Buddha Teahouse, which stands on the dividing line between Shiba and Shinagawa, and spent days and months there, but there was absolutely nobody to whom a hapless visitor like myself could turn. Day and night I passed quietly and all alone, most disconsolately, my hopes fragile as a spider's thread. I resented all the time wasted in this way ever since leaving my native place, but the past does not return and the future is unknown, so my predicament only made me feel increasingly helpless."[2] The situation would be true of many Japanese in the twentieth century: a young man arrives in Tokyo, where he knows nobody and is desperately lonely, but he is ashamed to go back to the country a failure. The author summed up his feelings in a poem:

aware ge ni	Alas, I truly
uki toki tsururu	Wish I had a friend with me
tomo mo gana	When I feel depressed;
hito no nasake wa	People's kindness lasts only
yo ni arishi hodo[3]	As long as one is thriving.

One day, unable to bear his loneliness, he left his lodgings and wandered into the great temple Zōjō-ji. He had no intention of praying; he simply had nowhere else to go. The passage recalls a Sunday morning in London, when the traveler, in desperation, will attend church, the only place that is open. While in the Zōjō-ji the author observed "before the holy altar many elderly priests sitting in a row, ringing bells and reciting the sutras without pause from early evening until late at night." Carried away by the solemn splendor, he lingered in the temple, forgetting to go home.[4] He reflected on the evanescence of all things and briefly even considered becoming a priest; but he realized that he was still much too involved with worldly desires to take this great step.

He left the temple and went to a nearby Shintō shrine, where he watched the *miko* (shrine maidens) dance. The sight provided him with a splendid opportunity to relate the history of *kagura* dances. This done, he had exhausted the interest of the place, and wandered off again. The city was full of people, but the bustle only made his loneliness more acute. Enticed into a teahouse, he confessed to the proprietor: "I'm ashamed to tell you, but I am a country bumpkin by birth, and I come from a poor family. I had such trouble making a living that I crossed the mountains and came all the way here, far from home. Like the wild geese of Koshiji, whose cries have given out,[5] I have exhausted my funds and have not even the money to pay for tea. Take pity, and don't charge me anything!"[6] The shop owner, feeling sorry for the young man, treated him to two free cups of tea. The author asked why he was given two cups, and was told (by means of an untranslatable pun[7]) that they would assure him of prosperity in the future. Here begins another of the interminable digressions of which the author is so fond.

The reader at this point is likely to want to take the author and shake him, saying: "Stop telling us about the origins of tea-drinking, the history of all the famous bridges of Japan, or the sound of the bell of the Miidera, and tell us about yourself, without any allusions to classical poetry or plays on words. Did you finally get a job? What did you do? Who were your friends? Were you often depressed even after you got accustomed to Edo? Did you fall in love?" etc. It is true that the author describes a visit to the Yoshiwara licensed quarter, but his account serves mainly as a pretext for relating the history of prostitution in Japan. Toward the end of the diary he discusses with a loquacious boatman various current fashions in Edo. All this is not without interest, but it is the kind of information one gets abundantly in less personal writings of the period, and what we want is what a novelist might provide or what the daughter of Takasue, the nun Abutsu, and Lady Nijō in fact did provide, the portrait of a human being drawn from within. But that is precisely the quality we are least likely to find in the diary literature of the Tokugawa period.

A Journey in the Year 1667

Ikeda Tsunamasa (1638–1714), the author of *Hinotohitsuji Ryokōki* (*A Journey in the Year 1667*), was the son of Ikeda Mitsusada, the illustrious daimyo of the Okayama clan. Although Tsunamasa was not so distinguished as his father, who was renowned both as an enlightened ruler and as a scholar among daimyos, his diary is evidence that he was an exceptionally perceptive man. The diary chronicles a journey from Edo to Okayama in 1667. The prose is pleasingly direct, and the poems seem to reflect the author's actual feelings when he composed them; they are not simply repetitions of familiar sentiments aroused by familiar sights. If the diary fails ultimately to achieve high literary distinction, this may be because Tsunamasa had no thought of creating a work of literature.

Indeed, the diary contains some passages that strongly suggest Tsunamasa was writing only for himself. Here are two: "After passing through the suburbs, we entered Nagoya. This being Mitsuyoshi's castle town, we went by secretly."[1] "Captain Mitsumichi is staying at Sekigahara, and that is why we went by secretly."[2] Judging from the names, Mitsuyoshi and Mitsumichi were probably members of Tsunamasa's family, but he was evidently anxious to avoid them. This is the kind of entry not normally found in diaries intended for the eyes of other people; all the same, it is hard to imagine that Tsunamasa wrote the diary without at least the subconscious hope that someone else would read it.

This apparent ambivalence may account for the unusual mixture in this diary of traditional and wholly personal materials. Tsunamasa reported, with no touch of irony, that he asked about the whereabouts of "the pine on which the celestial maiden hung her robe" (otherwise known as the Pine of the Feather Cloak, *hagoromo no matsu*). He was informed that "it has now withered, and only traces of it remain. Deciding I would go there and have a look while the sun was still high, I set out in a southerly direction from the shrine and walked about six hundred yards. There was a tiny wayside shrine amid the sand dunes on the shore, and even that was in ruins."[3] The word "even" (*sae*) exactly conjures up the desolation of the spot.

When he reached Yatsuhashi, Tsunamasa did *not* inspect the site of the Eight Bridges and report, in the time-honored manner of countless travelers, that the irises had all disappeared; he merely gave the site a glance from the distance and passed on. From there he followed the coast to Atsuta. He noticed on the way, "Many people could be seen weeding in the rice fields. The heat was unbearable, and there was not even any shade from the burning sun. I thought, as I watched them toiling without respite, their bodies drenched with sweat, that they made a heartbreaking sight."[4] The sight of people working in the fields must have been familiar to every traveler, but nobody else thought it was worth mentioning. For modern readers, this brief description of the women sweating as they toiled gives the diary reality and a literary quality that no allusion to a conventional *uta-makura*, such as the irises at Yatsuhashi, could possibly have conveyed.

Like many other Japanese travelers, Tsunamasa was fascinated by place names, but his willingness to tell the truth about such names, even if the truth was disillusioning, keeps his account from being merely a grab bag of old lore. When, for example, he reached a place called the Village of Hagihara (Clover Fields), he asked someone if it had acquired this name because there used to be a great deal of *hagi* clover growing there, but the man replied, "No, it's just a name."[5] This is the first diary I have read in which a place name was reported to be without special significance. Again, at a particularly forlorn hamlet on the border between Mino and Owari provinces, he asked its name and was told it was Nemonogatari (Talking in One's Sleep). Tsunamasa wrote, "I thought what an absurd place I had come to, and laughed my way through the village."[6]

Tsunamasa's down-to-earth nature is evident in his description of an unannounced visit to a friend. Tsunamasa reasoned that if the friend were informed in advance of the visit he would be frantic with preparations to receive an honored guest. "He would fly around the house, sweeping the dust, beating the tatami, and finally getting things in order, at his wits' ends to cope with the sudden preparations." The friend was spared this trial by Tsunamasa's decision to appear without warning. It is true that the friend murmured the obligatory "It distresses and overwhelms me that you should have deigned to visit such a wretched house," but Tsunamasa nonchalantly replied, "I know, but I didn't expect to come here, either." In his diary Tsunamasa noted that he was delighted that he could detect no sign that the place had been specifically cleaned for him, and this made the house more interesting. "A thick tatami had been spread in the *kaminoma*, and he had been lying there ever since noon, enjoying the cool and waiting for the sun to go down. I was quite enchanted by the appearance of the house and garden, surprised to find such a thing as *this* in such a place as *that*."[7]

An unusual feature of Tsunamasa's diary is his habit of referring to eminent people by their names, rather than by their titles or by some circumlocution. For example, as he was approaching the capital he passed a sight familiar to him from history: "Pines grow thickly now on Mount Azuchi, where Oda Nobunaga once lived."[8] Later he referred to Toyotomi Hideyoshi without any honorific after his name. But even more surprising are his references to Tokugawa Ieyasu. After passing the place called Mikatagahara he remarked, "Long ago Lord Ieyasu from Hamamatsu fought here with Takeda from Kōfu. At that time there was nothing here except grass, but now pine saplings grow so thickly that one cannot see the fields."[9] The battle between Tokugawa Ieyasu and Takeda Shingen in 1572, to which Tsunamasa alluded, resulted in a disastrous defeat for Ieyasu, who barely escaped with his life. Respect for the Tokugawa family, the rulers of Japan, would probably have inhibited other diarists from referring to this battle, memories of which were certainly unwelcome.

Perhaps the most notable passage in the diary describes Tsunamasa's experience when he stopped for lunch at a place called Mitsukabi. He was intrigued by the appearance of the innkeeper, sure that there must be distinguished ancestors in the man's background. Tsunamasa invited him into his presence, and asked him to tell about himself, not concealing anything. The diary relates: "I thought that hearing his story might distract me from the hardships of the journey, so, stretched out on a thick tatami, I listened to his tale, and I must say I was astonished. He had an ancestor named Nakamura Genzaemon. When Lord Ieyasu held the castle at Hamamatsu, his mistress was a lady-in-waiting named Matsuko. He required her to attend him personally, and eventually her changed condition became noticeable. About this time Ieyasu's consort, Lady Tsukiyama, an extremely jealous woman, placed a curse on Matsuko. Lord Ieyasu, much upset, pondered the situation, at a loss what to do. Finally he ordered one of his retainers, the Genzaemon I have mentioned, to escort her to his dwelling and to look after her. The man accepted the responsibility devotedly, and took her with him to his home, a remote place some two *ri* from Hamamatsu. Lady Tsukiyama was an evil-hearted woman, and she pronounced maledictions of every sort, but Genzaemon, with no thought to his own safety, looked after the lady. Soon afterward she gave birth to a baby boy. There was no doubting the resemblance to Ieyasu; they were as alike as the pupil of one eye to the other, and since there was also a mark on the placenta,[10] Genzaemon reported this to Ieyasu, at which he was commanded to continue to look after the baby in an appropriate manner, since this must be kept from Lady Tsukiyama. In this way time passed, and the boy grew with the months and the years. Eventually Toyotomi Hideyoshi learned what had happened, and soon afterward adopted the boy. Later he gave him the title of governor of Mikawa. It is because of this background that even today, whenever the lords of Echigo, Echizen, or Izumo pass by in either direction, they faithfully pay their respects."[11]

Presumably it was Tsunamasa's high rank that emboldened him to refer to Nobunaga, Hideyoshi, and Ieyasu in such familiar terms. The reader senses also that for Tsunamasa these people now belonged to history, and could be described without special deference. He used the words *sono kami* (long ago) when referring to events of seventy years earlier, implying that it was permissible now to discuss such ancient matters objectively, but other writers of the period never lost their awe for Ieyasu or thought of him merely as a historical figure. When Bashō arrived at Nikkō in 1689 on his journey to the north, he referred to the authority still possessed by the Incarnation of Buddha of the Tōshōgū (Ieyasu) in these terms: "Now his holy light shines through the firmament, his blessings overflow to all eight corners of the realm, and the peaceful dwellings of the four classes are tranquil." His attitude was undoubtedly more typical than Tsunamasa's.

Tsunamasa related the story of Ieyasu's illegitimate son without adding any comment. He was also able to describe Lady Tsukiyama as being "evil-hearted" and to mention her attempts to use black magic, presumably because Ieyasu had discovered she was secretly communicating with the Takeda forces and personally killed her in 1579. There was no need to be polite about such a person, but surely if Tsunamasa expected his diary to be read by others he would have been somewhat more cautious in his expression. Perhaps he originally meant to write down no more than notes on a journey, but his inborn literary gifts led him into writing something far more interesting.

Bashō's Diaries

The five travel diaries by Matsuo Bashō (1644–1694) represent the climax in works of this genre, which originated almost eight hundred years earlier in Ki no Tsurayuki's *The Tosa Diary*. Bashō was keenly aware of the traditions of this kind of diary, and scholars have pointed out how much he borrowed from such works as *A Journey East of the Barrier*, but he imparted a new dimension to the genre, that of the professional writer. Earlier diarists had of course taken pains with their texts, and they undoubtedly hoped that their diaries would be read not only by the circle of their acquaintances but by people of future times. There was, however, a limit to the number of people who could read a single manuscript, and copying manuscripts was costly. Bashō lived at a time when the printing of books had become usual, and a thousand or more copies of a work could easily be produced from the same woodblocks. He also knew that his own disciples, their disciples, and many other people were eager to read whatever he wrote. This knowledge undoubtedly slowed the process of writing. Diarists whose ambition was solely to record their experiences during a journey could write as they went along or as soon as the journey was completed. It would not matter in that case if there were ineptly phrased passages or hackneyed poems in the completed work: the purpose was not to please discriminating readers but merely to preserve, while the memories were still fresh, the diarist's impressions of his travels.

Bashō always thought of possible readers, and he was reluctant to allow a diary to be published until he was satisfied that it was in final form. That, no doubt, is why none of his diaries was printed during his lifetime, and why several versions exist of each, representing different stages in his polishing of the manuscripts. The diaries were of great importance to Bashō, but not equally so. The second and fourth, describing his travels to Kashima and Sarashina respectively, though written with care and later revised, are short and relatively uncomplicated.

The first, third, and fifth diaries open with allusions to Chinese texts, a sure sign of literary intent, and contain passages that go far beyond the facts of the journey to reveal Bashō's most deeply felt convictions on the nature of literature.

The diaries do not tell us everything about Bashō. They reveal so little about his emotional life that it had long been customary to refer to him as *haisei*, "the saint of the haiku," a man whose involvement with his art kept him free of worldly passions. But although we may revere a saint, it is difficult to feel comfortable with anyone who seems so far removed from the emotions that trouble most men. That is why, when one scholar of Bashō discovered in a work written by a disciple of a disciple of Bashō's the statement that Bashō had a mistress, he exclaimed, "How good of you, dear Bashō, to have had a mistress!"[1] It is easier to think of Bashō as a man with human weaknesses than as the austere saint of haiku, but if Bashō in fact had a mistress, he does not mention it in his diaries.

The diaries also reveal extremely little about his finances. By the time he wrote *Oku no Hosomichi* (*The Narrow Road of Oku*) he was a celebrated haiku poet, and people along the way were delighted to have him stay with them; all the same, Bashō must have paid Hotoke Gozaemon and other innkeepers, as well as the people who helped in various ways, such as serving as his guides, or lending him horses. Money was an indelicate subject, avoided by those of refined tastes, but Bashō had to consider it when planning his journeys.

Other such instances of blanks in the information provided by the diaries could be cited. They would only prove what we know from the start, that they were written as works of literature and not simply as travel accounts. Bashō never stated why he wrote his diaries or which readers he had in mind, yet, whether he realized it or not, he was writing for all time and for everyone.

Exposed in the Fields

Nozarashi Kikō, literally "exposed-in-the-fields travel account,"[1] derives its name from the haiku that appears soon after the opening of the diary:

nozarashi wo	Exposed in the fields—
kokoro ni kaze no	At the thought, how the wind
shimu mi kana	Bites into my flesh!

Bashō wondered whether he might not die on his journey, leaving his whitened bones exposed in the fields. The haiku reflects his awareness of how many travelers of the past had died on the road. Certainly the journey ahead would be taxing, and Bashō's health was poor, but by this time travel along the main roads of Japan had become relatively easy and comfortable. Bashō nevertheless threw himself into the role of the poet-wayfarer. This was not a pose; it was part of his conscious effort to savor to the full the essence of travel, which meant not a pleasant room at an inn but uncertainty, fatigue, and sometimes danger.

The *Exposed in the Fields* journey may have been occasioned by word Bashō received that his mother had died in the 6th month of 1683 at Iga Ueno, his native town. But why did he not leave

Edo until the 8th month of 1684? Even if he could not arrive in time for the funeral, it is strange that he did not attempt to reach Iga Ueno for the first anniversary. It seems likely that Bashō's main reason for making the journey was his feeling that the time had come for creating a new style of haiku poetry. Perhaps he thought that a journey might help him to achieve this, and his mother's death may have fixed the destination of the journey. The fact that 1684 was the first year of the calendar cycle of sixty years, observed in Japan as well as China, may have confirmed its appropriateness as a time to make changes.

Bashō's reluctance to leave Edo is suggested by the second haiku of the diary:

aki totose	Autumn makes ten years;
kaette Edo wo	Now I really mean Edo
sasu kokyō	When I talk of "home."

Bashō had actually lived twelve, not ten, years in Edo, and probably his expression was modeled on the lines by the Chinese poet Chia Tao (779–843):

Ten frosts have passed since I
Took up traveler's lodgings in Ping-chou. . . .
Now when I look at Ping-chou from afar
I think, "There is my home."[2]

The first event of the journey occurred at the Fuji River: "As we walked along the Fuji River we noticed an abandoned child, perhaps three years old, weeping pitifully. I wondered if its parents, buffeted by the swift currents of the river and unable to withstand the rough waves of the floating world, had abandoned it here, thinking its life would last only as long as the dew. Would the tender clover blossoms scatter tonight in the autumn wind beneath the leaves, or would they wither tomorrow? With these thoughts I took some food from my sleeve and threw it at the child as we passed."

saru wo kiku hito	Men have grieved to hear monkeys—
sutego ni aki no	What of a child forsaken
kaze ika ni	In the autumn wind?

It was commonplace for Chinese poets to express their griefs when they heard the pitiful cries of monkeys. Bashō implies that such grief is nothing when compared with the feelings aroused by the sight of a child abandoned by its parents. Modern readers concur in this sentiment, but it is difficult to understand why Bashō merely threw some food at the child. Why could he not have lifted it in his arms and carried it to a place where someone would care for it?

Scholars have answered this question variously. Some point out that the sight of an abandoned child was far more common in Bashō's day than it is now. Others suggest that Bashō's consecration to his art compelled him to forsake normal obligations. Still others claim that the episode was a bit of fiction inserted by Bashō in his narration in order to underline the theme of the diary, death on a journey. But, however the incident is explained, it erects a momentary barrier between Bashō and ourselves. Though we know him well, we have suddenly been confronted with an unacceptable attitude with respect to the death of a child.

In the autumn of 1945, soon after the war ended, I was in the city of Tsinan in Shantung Province. As I walked to lunch with a Chinese army officer, I noticed a boy of about twelve lying by the roadside. I thought this was strange but said nothing. After lunch we passed the same spot. The boy was still lying there, his face now covered with flies. "He's dead!" I cried out in horror. "Yes," said the officer with indifference. Perhaps I, too, might have become as accustomed to children "exposed in the fields" if I had seen such sights as often as that officer.

The fact that we are shocked by Bashō's attitude proves that we do not think of him as a stranger, a man who lived three centuries ago, but as someone near to our hearts, with whom we desire total rapport.

The closest Bashō came in his diaries to revealing his personal life is the passage in *Exposed in the Fields* that describes his meeting with his elder brother for the first time since their mother's death: "At the beginning of the 9th month I returned to my old home. The day lilies in the northern hall had been withered by the frost, and there was no trace of them now. Everything had changed from the past. My brother's hair was white at the temples and his brow was wrinkled. 'We are still alive,' he said. 'Pay your respects to Mother's white hairs! This is Urashima's magic box—your eyebrows are also touched with gray.' For a while I wept."

te ni toraba kien	Taken in my hand it would melt,
namida zo atsuki	My tears are so hot—
aki no shimo	This autumnal frost.

This passage is extremely moving, even though it is conspicuously literary, and not a straightforward description of the scene or of the emotions Bashō experienced. The phrase "the day lilies in the northern hall," like much else in this diary, is derived from Chinese literature. Notes in modern editions inform the readers that it was customary for the mother of a family to live in the northern wing of a house, and that elderly ladies often planted day lilies (*kensō*) in their gardens. Were there really day lilies outside the room where Bashō's mother had lived? Or was the mention of "withered by the frost" only figurative? Why could Bashō not have expressed his grief more openly? Such questions do not originate with modern readers. Long before, in China, Po Chü-i, rejecting the involved expression of elegant poetry, had preferred to write simply enough so that even illiterate old women could understand his poetry; but few Chinese poets followed his practice. Tu Fu, whom Bashō admired most among the Chinese poets, is difficult, and if one fails to recognize the associations of the words as well as their meanings, one cannot fully appreciate his poems. In Bashō's case, too, such a phrase as "the day lilies in the northern hall" was not a pedantic affectation but an extremely concise way of linking Bashō's grief with the grief expressed under similar circumstances by generations of poets in China.

The haiku at the conclusion of the passage presents another kind of problem. If one were to read the haiku alone, without the prose that precedes it, I think it unlikely that the full meaning could be understood. Herein lies the special importance of Bashō's travel diaries: the prose and the poetry are both essential. It is not merely that the prose explains the circumstances of the poem, in the manner of the prefaces found in collections of *waka*. The haiku expresses Bashō's grief more compellingly than the prose, but the prose sets the scene, describing the sorrow of the brothers over their mother's death, their aging, and the difficulty they experience in trying to speak to each other. The comment made by the brother, "We are still alive" (*inochi arite*), brings to mind the similar phrase used by the poet Saigyō, *inochi narikeri*, conveying his surprise that he had lived so long. Probably the brother did not actually say these words, but Bashō "translated" the words of ordinary speech, inadequate in the face of tragedy, into the language of poetry.

Needless to say, this passage was not written by Bashō in his diary the same night, before going to bed. Such writing demands the full powers of a creative artist, and he surely rewrote the words many times. He seems not to have been satisfied even with the final version; he did not publish the diary during his lifetime.

Commentators have pointed out that the fusion of prose and poetry is less successful in *Exposed in the Fields* than in the later diaries, notably *The Narrow Road of Oku*. This is true, but Bashō was evidently more concerned at this time with his poetry than with his prose. The quality of the haiku in the diary is exceptionally high, as a few samples may suggest:

umi kurete	The sea darkens—
kamo no koe	The cries of the wild ducks
honoka ni shiroshi	Are faintly white.
yamaji kite	Walking a mountain road
nani yara yukashi	Something or other drew me:
sumiregusa	The wild violets.

Perhaps the lack of unity in this diary can be accounted for in terms of Bashō's disparate motives for making the journey. The shadow of death accounts for the somber tone of the opening of the work, but Bashō's journey was inspired also by his desire to enrich his poetry with new experiences. After reaching Ōgaki he wrote, "When I set out from Musashi Plain it was with the thought that my bones might lie exposed in a field."

shinu mo senu	I haven't died, after all,
tabine no hate yo	And this is where my travels led—
aki no kure	The end of autumn.

From this point on the diary becomes markedly more cheerful, and Bashō's work as a poet figures more prominently than themes of a personal nature. Poetry becomes the object of travel and the subject of his diary.

A Pilgrimage to Kashima

The journey recorded in *Exposed in the Fields* was an important stage in Bashō's development both as a haiku poet and as a prose writer. The sights along the way inspired him to compose a dozen of his best haiku, and he had added an important work to the body of Japanese travel diaries. On the return journey, when he stopped at Nagoya, he and his disciples composed together five *kasen* (sequences of thirty-six linked verses) of *haikai no renga*, which would be collected in the book *Fuyu no Hi* (*A Winter's Day*), the first of the seven collections of linked verse closely associated with Bashō's name. In addition, he renewed old acquaintances in Ueno and extended his circle of disciples to parts of the country (notably Kyōto) where he previously had not had one disciple. The last verse of this diary is in a far more cheerful mood than the first one:

natsugoromo	My summer clothing—
imada shirami wo	I still have not quite finished
toritsukusazu[1]	Picking out the lice.

Although Bashō alludes to the hardships of travel, epitomized by the lice he had picked up at some wayside inn, the tone is humorous rather than despondent.

Bashō returned to Edo at the end of the 4th month of 1685. His next journey did not take place for over two years. In the 8th month of 1687 he went to admire the moon at the Kashima Shrine, and described this journey in a brief prose account that is followed by seventeen haiku composed by Bashō and his companions along the way. Bashō apparently decided on the spur of the moment to see the harvest moon at Kashima, much in the manner of the *waki* in a Nō play who travels to a distant place merely to enjoy the scenery for which it is renowned at a particular time of year. Unlike *Exposed in the Fields*, *Kashima Mōde* (*A Pilgrimage to Kashima*) is almost free of allusions to Chinese literature. The sentences are simple, and the atmosphere throughout is unambiguously cheerful.

Probably the most interesting passage is Bashō's description of himself: "The other person was neither a priest nor of the laity but something like a bat, a cross between a bird and a rat."[2] Bashō, like other poets and philosophers of his day, shaved his head and wore black robes in the manner of a Buddhist priest. Indeed, he so much resembled a priest that he was refused admittance to the Inner Shrine at Ise, the holiest place of the Shintō religion.

Bashō never took Buddhist orders, but he had studied Zen with the monk Butchō. On the night of the 15th, the full moon, it rained, much to Bashō's disappointment, but he was consoled when he learned that Butchō was in retreat at a nearby Buddhist temple. Bashō at once called on his teacher. Being in the presence of this holy man refreshed Bashō's spirit and he recalled the words by Tu Fu: "It stirs one to deep thoughts."[3] Bashō spent the night at Butchō's hermitage. "Before dawn the next morning," he related, "the sky had cleared somewhat. The master wakened the other people and they all got up. The haunting combination of the moonlight and the sound of the rain moved me so profoundly I could find no words to describe my emotions."[4] As often in Bashō's case, a deeply moving experience seemed to prevent him from composing poetry. His most famous haiku on Mount Fuji tells of *not* seeing Fuji because of the mist and rain. At Matsushima, the most celebrated scenery he visited on his trip to the north, he left the task of composing a haiku to his companion Sora.

A Pilgrimage to Kashima concludes on a facetious note. Bashō, who had been disappointed not to see the moon or to compose a haiku at Kashima, found a spiritual companion in Sei Shōnagon, who, in her *Pillow Book*, related how she had failed to compose a poem on the *hototogisu* after having gone out into the countryside for the specific purpose of hearing one.[5]

A Pilgrimage to Kashima is a minor work but, like everything else that Bashō wrote, helps to throw light on the first figure of Japanese literature who speaks to us with the intimate voice of a friend.

Manuscript in My Knapsack

A little more than two months after returning from Kashima, Bashō set out on a much more ambitious journey, on the 25th day of the 10th month of 1687. The night before his departure Bashō was fêted and presented with various gifts intended to make his travels more agreeable. He wrote: "Old friends, acquaintances both intimate and casual, as well as disciples, visited and revealed their affection with their gifts of poems or essays of their composition or with money for my straw sandals.[1] I had no need to worry myself with 'gathering provisions three months in advance.' "[2] The haiku he composed at the farewell party contrasts strongly with the whitened bones he imagined when he was about to leave on his *Exposed in the Fields* journey:

tabibito to	Traveler—from now on
wa ga na yobaren	That's the name I shall be called:
hatsushigure[3]	The first wintry rain.

The journey was happy, and the diary reflects Bashō's good spirits. He was welcomed everywhere by disciples, old and new, as he traveled in the areas of Ise, Nagoya, Iga Ueno, Yoshino, Nara, and Suma. The diary, usually called *Oi no Kobumi* (*Manuscript in My Knapsack*), was probably written three or four years after Bashō returned to Edo, but it was not published until 1709, nearly twenty-three years after he completed the journey.

Manuscript in My Knapsack opens with a well-known passage: "There is a creature, called for the nonce Fūrabō—Gauze in the Wind—who lives within a frame of a hundred bones and nine apertures. The name no doubt refers to the ease with which gauze is torn by the wind."[4] Mention of "a hundred bones and nine apertures"—in other words, the human body—is a rather ponderous reference to the Chinese philosopher Chuang Tzu, whose writings possessed a special appeal for Bashō at this time. Bashō coined the nickname Fūrabō in keeping with his conception of the poet as a person who is easily torn, not only by the wind but by his encounters with the world. He took the name Bashō for a similar reason: the *bashō*, a kind of plantain that bears no fruit, was prized both in China and in Japan for the ease with which its fronds were torn by the wind, serving as a metaphor for the poet or scholar in its sensitivity.

Manuscript in My Knapsack continues, "He has long enjoyed 'wild verse,' and in the end he has made it his lifetime occupation." "Wild verse" or "crazy verse" was a pejorative way of referring to haiku, which Bashō modestly employed here. His interest in haiku poetry originated when he was a boy. At that time he could hardly have expected that this pastime would develop into a livelihood. Indeed, as he relates immediately afterward, he at one time tried to cure himself of the bad habit of writing haiku, though at other times he took pride in his compositions. "The conflict has raged within me, and because of it I have not enjoyed peace of mind. For a time I hoped to make a successful career for myself, but I was prevented by my poetry. For a time I thought I would study Buddhism and dispel my ignorance, but this hope was also shattered by my poetry. In the end, incapable and talentless as I am, I have tied myself to this one line of work."[5]

We know from other writings that after Bashō arrived in Edo he for a time sought advancement as an official, and he also studied Zen Buddhism with Butchō, but in the end he discovered that he could not renounce his art. This autobiographical material, though of the highest interest, is rather out of place in the account of a journey. What follows is even more absorbing but equally out of place: "There is one thing that Saigyō's *waka*, Sōgi's *renga*, Sesshū's paintings, and Rikyū's tea ceremony have in common, and in every other art it is the same: to follow nature and to have the four seasons as one's friends. Everything one sees should be a flower. Every thought one has should be as the moon. When the form of one's expression is not a flower, one is no different from a savage. When one's spirit is not a flower, one is of the same species as the birds and beasts. I say, leave behind the savages, remove yourself from the birds and beasts, follow nature, and return to nature."

This passage, one of the most remarkable in Japanese literature, is notable especially for the correspondences Bashō found among seemingly unrelated arts, and for his astute choices, as the masters of these arts, of the very men whom we would choose today. Bashō did not explicitly state that the thread that linked the other arts also ran through haiku poetry, but surely this is implied. Perhaps he even meant to suggest that Fūrabō ranked with Saigyō, Sōgi, and the other masters. Bashō was a modest man, but he had great confidence in his art, and he clearly believed that he himself followed his prescription of following nature and returning to nature.

Bashō followed this unconventional opening to the diary with an equally unconventional section in which he discussed the traditions of the travel diary. He insisted that unless the sights witnessed by the traveler were truly unusual he should not describe them.[6] As for his own travel diary, he dismissed it as being no more than "the mutterings of a man in his sleep."[7] Of course, Bashō did not expect that people would take him literally. He was attempting in *Manuscript in My Knapsack* to blend poetry and prose in a work of unquestionable artistic merit. The unfinished quality of some sections of the work has led scholars to conjecture that Bashō abandoned the manuscript without ever completing intended revisions. The haiku have also been criticized; few of the relatively large number count among Bashō's superior verses. However, if read with somewhat less rigorous standards, *Manuscript in My Knapsack* is an unusually appealing work, a sunny contrast to the dark tone prevalent in some of Bashō's diaries.

Bashō's companion during much of the journey was his disciple Tsuboi Tokoku (d. 1690), a young man who had been sent into exile for having speculated on rice he did not actually own. Bashō made a special trip to Irago Point, where Tokoku was living incognito. Irago Point was known in poetry as a place where hawks crossed land on their way to and from the north, and Bashō was therefore delighted to arrive in time to see a hawk, as his haiku suggests:

taka hitotsu	A solitary hawk—
mitsukete ureshi	How happy I was to find it
Iragosaki[8]	At Irago Point.

The sight of a hawk at the exactly appropriate place naturally pleased Bashō, but his haiku surely also referred to the undisciplined young hawk Tokoku. Of all his many disciples, Bashō was fondest of Tokoku. In *The Saga Diary* he related that he had dreamed about Tokoku: "In dreams I cried out something about Tokoku, and I awoke in tears. . . . For me to have dreamed about him must surely be a case of what they call a 'dream of longing.' He was so devoted to me that he traveled all the way to my home town of Iga Ueno to be with me. At night we shared one bed, and we got up and lay down at the same time. He helped me, sharing the hardships of my journey, and for a hundred days accompanied me like my shadow. Sometimes he was playful, sometimes sad—his solicitude impressed itself deep in my heart. I must have had such a dream because I cannot forget him. When I woke I once again wrung the tears from my sleeves."[9]

Perhaps the worshipful admiration of his other disciples had come to tire Bashō, and he found it enjoyable to be with a young man who was sometimes playful. In *Manuscript in My Knapsack* Bashō related that Tokoku had joined him at Ise. "Thinking that he would enjoy sharing the moving experiences of travel, and also that he would become my 'boy' and help me along the way, he bestowed upon himself the boyish name of Mangikumaru. It really is a typical name for a boy, and I found it very amusing. When we were at last on the point of setting out, I scribbled these words inside our hats by way of a joke: 'Two men, without homes on heaven or earth, traveling together.' "[10]

The mysterious affinities that make friends of people who may seem incompatible in age and tastes, and the equally mysterious lack of affinities that keep people who seem destined to be close friends from ever becoming more than acquaintances, cannot be logically explained. All one can say is that they exist. A rice speculator like Tokoku should have been antipathetic to an unworldly person like Bashō, but it was because of Tokoku that Bashō would remember this journey in his dreams years later. Perhaps the very happiness of the journey was the reason the haiku fell below Bashō's highest standards. Like many other poets, he created best when moved by grief, either personal or induced by the human condition.

Of course, even during the happiest periods of his life sad thoughts sometimes crossed his mind. During his *Manuscript in My Knapsack* journey at Suma he remembered tragic scenes from *The Tale of the Heike*, and after spending the night at nearby Akashi he composed one of his most famous haiku:

takotsubo ya	Octopus in a trap—
hakanaki yume wo	Its dreams are fleeting under
natsu no tsuki	The summer moon.

This haiku, alluding to the brevity of the life of the octopus, destined to be lifted from the sea and killed once the short summer night ends, surely also refers to human beings, equally unaware of how soon death will claim them. The haiku is followed by reminiscences of the section of *The Tale of Genji* describing Genji's exile at Suma: " 'Autumn at such a place.' Yes, the essence of this bay is surely to be appreciated most of all in autumn. The sadness, the loneliness, are indescribable. I thought that if it were autumn I might be able to express something of my feelings in a poem, but perhaps this indicates only my unawareness of the inadequacy of my poetic talent."[11] Other memories of *The Tale of Genji* and *The Tale of the Heike* lend a melancholy note to the concluding paragraphs of the diary.

After the journey ended, Tokoku returned to his place of exile.

Bashō went alone to Gifu, where he composed a haiku that, although it refers to the cormorant boats on the Nagara River, seems to epitomize his recent journey:

omoshirōte	Delightful, and yet
yagate kanashi	Presently how saddening,
ubune kana[12]	The cormorant boats.

Journey to Sarashina

In the middle of the 8th month of 1688 Bashō decided to travel to Sarashina in order to see the moon at a place that had been celebrated for its moon-viewing ever since the days of the poets of the *Kokinshū.* I cannot recall any European poet who traveled anywhere for the express purpose of seeing the moon there. The European poets frequently complained about the inconstant moon that changed its appearance from night to night, contrasting the "journeying moon and the stars that still sojourn." Wordsworth imagined the moon's delight on looking "round her when the heavens are bare," and Blake believed that

The moon, like a flower
In heaven's high bower,
With silent delight
Sits and smiles on the night.

Japanese poets never personified the moon in this manner, but they had much to say about the moon of the capital or the moon seen at other places commemorated in poetry.

No Japanese was more eloquent about the moon than the priest Kenkō. "Looking at the moon is always diverting, no matter what the circumstances,"[1] he declared. In an even more memorable passage he wrote, "The moon that appears close to dawn after we have long waited for it moves us more profoundly than the full moon shining cloudless over a thousand leagues. And how incomparably lovely is the moon, almost greenish in its light, when seen through the tops of the cedars deep in the mountains, or when it hides for a moment behind clustering clouds during a sudden shower!"[2] But, like Sei Shōnagon in her *Pillow Book*, he found the winter moon depressing, and was convinced that the autumn moon was beautiful beyond comparison. "Any man who supposes that the moon is always the same, regardless of the season, and is therefore unable to detect the difference in autumn, must be exceedingly insensitive."[3]

In view of this tradition of admiring the moon, it was not surprising that Bashō traveled all the way to Sarashina to see the moon, even after his disappointment at Kashima. *Journey to Sarashina*, like *A Pilgrimage to Kashima*, is a short diary consisting of one passage in prose followed by a number of haiku, none of first-rate quality.

The chief interest of the work is the background, the legend of Mount Obasute, where an old woman was abandoned to die. The story is told as early as the tenth-century *Tales of Yamato*. A man who had lost his parents while still a boy was raised by an aunt who loved him as if he were her own son. When the man married, however, his wife constantly complained about the old woman and urged him to take the aunt into the mountains and leave her there. The man, at length, very reluctantly agreed. Carrying his aunt on his back, he brought her to a remote spot where he left her, but when he got back home he felt ashamed of his action. As he gazed at the moon, wonderfully bright as it rose over the crest of the mountain, he composed the *waka*:

wa ga kokoro	My heart is not to be
nagusamekanetsu	Consoled as I gaze upon
Sarashina ya	The moon that shines
Obasuteyama ni	On Mount Obasute
teru tsuki wo mite	In Sarashina district.[4]

He went back to the aunt and carried her home, but from that time the mountain was called *obasuteyama*, "mountain where the old woman was abandoned," and it was often said that the gloom which still enveloped the place was so oppressive nobody could be cheerful there.

The theme of the woman who is abandoned on a mountainside probably reflected actual practices in the past, when unproductive members of society were left to die because there was not enough food for them. When Bashō saw the moon over Mount Obasute he composed the haiku:

omokage ya	I can see how she looked—
oba hitori naku	The old woman, weeping alone,
tsuki no tomo[5]	The moon her companion.

But, even given the special associations of the moon at Sarashina, it is hard to imagine that a man in frail health would take such a long journey, solely for the pleasure of viewing the moon at a place—at least in my recollections of Mount Obasute—that is by no means extraordinary. Such was the power of literature and of the moon.

Journey to Sarashina is of interest for another reason. It presents a unique picture of Bashō in the act of creating poetry. Some people suppose that a genius like Bashō could effortlessly dash off a haiku masterpiece whenever he felt inspiration. He did indeed write many impromptu verses, but few of them embody the artistry that was his goal. In *Journey to Sarashina* he related how, as he lay in his room at an inn, attempting to beat into shape the poetic materials he had gathered during the day, groaning and knocking his head in the effort, a priest, imagining that Bashō was suffering a fit of depression, tried to comfort him with stories about the miracles of Amida Buddha, thereby blocking Bashō's flow of inspiration. If the priest had not been so solicitous, perhaps the haiku in *Journey to Sarashina* would have been better!

The Narrow Road of Oku

Oku no Hosomichi (*The Narrow Road of Oku*) is the supreme example of the Japanese travel diary. It differs conspicuously, in both content and tone, from the celebrated diaries written at the Heian court, as the most casual reading will reveal. Bashō, unlike the court ladies, said little about himself, his emotional problems, or even why he had felt impelled to write a diary, and the events described are usually set in plebeian contexts. He gave only a cursory explanation at the outset of his reasons for embarking on such a long journey:

"Many of the men of old died on their travels, and I, too, for years past have been stirred by the sight of a solitary cloud drifting with the wind to ceaseless thoughts of roaming. Last year I spent wandering along the seacoast. In autumn I returned to my cottage on the river and swept away the cobwebs. Gradually the year drew to a close. When spring came and there was mist in the air, I thought of crossing the Barrier of Shirakawa into Oku. Everything about me was bewitched by the travel gods, and my thoughts were no longer mine to control. The spirits of the road beckoned, and I could do no work at all."[1]

Bashō was so possessed by the "spirits of the road" that he made only minimal preparations for the journey. Soon, he tells us, "the moon at Matsushima began to occupy my thoughts." He no doubt was also anticipating with pleasure the many *uta-makura*—sights traditionally mentioned in poetry—along the way. When he said goodbye to the friends who had accompanied him on the boat as far as Senju (where they all disembarked), he composed the first haiku of the journey:

yuku haru ya	The passing of spring—
tori naki uo no	The birds weep and in the eyes
me wa namida	Of fish there are tears.

This haiku, with its blend of sadness over the passing of spring and humor in the mention of tears in the eyes of fish, has been acclaimed as a masterpiece. It sets the tone perfectly for the work that follows, a union of poetry and prose that is rare in the entire world's literature.

Only after he had left behind his friends (with the exception of Sora, his companion on the road) did Bashō mention in greater detail the motivation for his journey. The explanation is poetic rather than logical: "This year, 1689, the thought came to me of going on a walking trip to the distant province of Oku. It did not matter if I should have the misfortune to grow gray on my travels, for I wanted to see places I had heard much about but never visited. It seemed to me that I should be fortunate if I managed to come home alive, but, leaving it to the future to decide this uncertainty, I pursued my journey to a town called Sōka, which we reached with some difficulty on the day of our departure."[2] Despite the seemingly casual nature of his reasons for undertaking so arduous a journey, its unique importance to Bashō can be inferred from the beauty of both the poetry and the prose, which he polished for five years after his return.

Some scholars have ascribed Bashō's decision to make his journey of 1689 to a desire to observe, by visiting sites associated with Saigyō, the five hundredth anniversary (by Japanese calculation) of the poet's death. References to Saigyō are scattered throughout *The Narrow Road of Oku*. It may be that Bashō saw himself, like Saigyō in Nō plays such as *Eguchi* or *Saigyō-zakura*, as the *waki*, a priest who visits places known from the poetry of the past, encountering the spirits of the dead associated with the place, asking their stories, and finally praying for their repose.

Bashō's main purpose seems to have been to renew his art by direct contact with sites that had inspired the poets of the past. He was sure that standing before a river or a mountain that had been described in many old poems would enable him to absorb the spirit of the place and in this way enrich his poetry. He had absolutely no desire to be the first person ever to set foot atop a mountain peak or to notice some sight that earlier poets had ignored. On the contrary, no matter how spectacular a landscape might be, unless it had attracted the attention of his predecessors, the lack of poetic overtones deprived it of charm for Bashō. When, for example, he traveled along a stretch of the Sea of Japan coast that had inspired no important poems, he did not mention the scenery.

Bashō's desire to treat familiar subjects was in the tradition of *honkadori*, or allusive variations on earlier poems. *Waka* poets customarily restricted themselves to the themes of their predecessors and often even borrowed the words, determined to remain faithful to their traditions; the contribution of the new poet was his particular sensibility, apparent in even the most familiar subjects and language. The evaluation of a new *waka* on the falling of the cherry blossoms was rather like our appreciation of a Kabuki actor's interpretation of a famous role, or a pianist's performance of a well-known sonata by Beethoven. We do not wish to be startled by a totally unconventional approach, but hope to be struck now and then by changes in emphasis that prove a fresh intelligence is at work, or, ideally, by shadings of interpretation that persuade us that we have never before fully understood the role or the sonata.

The Narrow Road of Oku is a grand summation of aspects of the existing travel literature of Japan and a bold exploration of new possibilities within the medium. Bashō took such familiar elements of the old diaries as combining poetry and poetic prose, narrating both experiences on the journey and reflections in solitude, and referring to places passed that were famous from old poetry. These customary elements acquired fresh significance because Bashō organized what had previously been mainly random impressions into a coherent whole, imparting a sense of form that heightened the traditional pleasure of reading diaries.

The travel diaries of Bashō's predecessors move us, even when lacking in form, thanks to their moments of poignance and compelling truth. We learn to tolerate and even to enjoy the dull passages if they tell us something about the authors or about the life led by people of their time. In *The Narrow Road of Oku*, however, such indulgence is unnecessary. It is true that not all of the work is at the dazzling level of the parts that everyone remembers, but there is no reason to suppose that Bashō was incapable of writing a diary of unflagging beauty. He was presumably guided by a sense of form that deliberately provided "breathing spaces" between passages of the greatest intensity. He could have evolved this technique intuitively, as did the European poets who were aware of the fatiguing effect of an unbroken series of verses of lapidary perfection, or Mozart, who included passages of recitative between his melodic arias. More likely, however, Bashō was influenced by the principles of *renga* (linked-verse) composition. The *renga* masters insisted on the importance of combining verses of strong design (*mon*) with others of plainer effect (*ji*) in order to provide variety and a smoothness of transition between successive strong verses. Professor Konishi Jin'ichi demonstrated that the *waka* in the *Shin Kokinshū* were arranged according to similar principles and that the collection therefore did not consist solely of masterpieces of the period but contained a fair number of second-rate poems deliberately included in the interests of the collection as a whole.[3]

Bashō included some relatively ordinary descriptions of places he visited in between his celebrated accounts of Matsushima and Kisakata. Of course, even such "relatively ordinary" sections included the memorable descriptions of the Ryūshaku-ji and of the Mogami River, each graced with superb haiku; but we are made aware, from the manner in which he opened his account of Kisakata, that this was the next great place he visited: "After having seen so many splendid views of both land and sea, my heart was stirred by the thought of Kisakata. . . . As the sun was sinking in the sky, a breeze from the sea stirred up the sand, and a misty rain started to fall. We groped ahead in the darkness. I felt sure that, if Kisakata were exquisite in the rain, it would prove to be no less wonderful when it cleared."

Bashō may also have obeyed the rule of *renga* composition that a verse devoted to love must be included in every extended sequence. A passage toward the end of his account of the journey describes two prostitutes who stayed at the same inn with Bashō. He overhears the touching messages they send back to their families in Niigata and relates how, the next morning, the women ask to follow behind him. Bashō refuses, epitomizing the experience with the haiku:

hitotsu ya ni	Under the same roof
yūjo mo netari	Prostitutes, too, were sleeping—
hagi to tsuki	Clover and the moon.

By accident, he and the prostitutes had slept under the same roof, but their worlds were as remote as the moon in the sky and the bush clover (*hagi*) it shines on. Bashō added, "I recited the poem to Sora and he wrote it down." But neither in Sora's own diary describing the journey nor in any other document is there mention of such an occurrence, and this has given rise to the suspicion that the story of the prostitutes is fictitious, an invention of Bashō's included to provide a distinctive note in *The Narrow Road of Oku*, probably under the influence of the practice of the *renga* masters. Of course, it is also possible that Sora, moved by a sense of decorum, decided to omit mention of an event that suggested that even the unworldly, saintly Bashō was familiar with women of a low profession.

Bashō's inventions and departures from the facts of his journey enhanced the lasting truth of *The Narrow Road of Oku*. He wrote in essence a work of fiction that was related only impressionistically to the journey. The notes he kept along the way and the first versions of the various haiku he composed during his travels were surely closer to the facts than the finished work, but Bashō seems to have found the facts insufficiently artistic.

A rough parallel to *The Narrow Road of Oku* and Sora's account of the journey can be found in the diaries kept by the Vicomte de Chateaubriand and his servant Julien during an 1807 journey to Greece, Jerusalem, Egypt, and finally Spain, whence they returned to France. The sections on Spain are interesting especially because they suggest what inspired Chateaubriand to write his historical romance *Les aventures du dernier Abencérage*, a work that combines prose and poetry in a manner reminiscent of the Japanese travel diary. Chateaubriand's diary depicted his travels as a leisurely excursion during which he stopped frequently to admire picturesque sights on the way, especially the great mosque (now a church) in Córdoba and the gardens of the Alhambra in Granada. Julien's uncompromisingly prosaic diary, citing exact dates, reveals that Chateaubriand was in a desperate hurry all the time. When they reached the great mosque at Córdoba, they stopped only long enough to give their horses water. At Granada they paused hardly one day, though Chateaubriand wrote as if his visit to the Alhambra had produced so powerful an impression he could hardly tear himself away. A modern scholar has calculated that while in Spain Chateaubriand averaged eighty kilometers a day. He did not enter a single house, talk to a single Spaniard, observe any aspect of contemporary life, or ask about the history of the places passed. He rose at dawn each morning to waken Julien and to demand if the horses were ready to leave.

By comparison, *The Narrow Road of Oku*, even when judged against the literal truths noted in Sora's diary, was a model of fidelity to the facts of the journey, but Bashō's purpose was essentially the same as Chateaubriand's: to create a work of permanent literary value which, though occasioned by the events of a journey, was by no means confined to them. Chateaubriand wished his readers to believe that he was an idle traveler, a gentleman of romantic impulses who went wherever his fancy dictated, with no practical purpose in mind, and who had discovered his own melancholy image in the ruins of the past. Bashō certainly did not picture himself so romantically, but he, too, brooded over the past, and he never forgot that he was a poet.

The Narrow Road of Oku would have us believe that Bashō got completely lost on his way from Sendai to Hiraizumi: "The countryside was deserted, and the road no better than a trail that hunters or woodsmen might follow." The ensuing description of the town of Ishinomaki makes clear his distaste for the place:

"Hundreds of merchant ships were gathered in the bay. In the town the houses fought for space, and smoke rose continuously from the salt kilns. I thought to myself, 'I never intended to come anywhere like this. . . .' "[4] The ever-truthful Sora reported in his diary that they went to Ishinomaki by invitation and stayed at a merchant's house, but Bashō evidently did not wish readers to think that he had voluntarily chosen to spend time in an industrial city instead of a lonely village. He altered some facts and telescoped others in order to present a self-portrait that accorded with the image of the poet-travelers of the past. He must have felt that it was incongruous for a humble poet to be hospitably received by merchants in a town where "smoke rose continuously from the salt kilns."

Bashō also changed the facts of his brief stay in Ishinomaki in another way. He mentioned that from the harbor "we could see Kinka Mountain, 'where bloom the golden flowers.' "[5] As a matter of fact, Kinka Mountain cannot be seen from the harbor of Ishinomaki, but Bashō was eager to associate his experience with the *waka* by Ōtomo no Yakamochi in the *Man'yōshū* that mentions the "golden flowers," another example of his adherence to artistic rather than literal truth.

So many passages in *The Narrow Road of Oku* are of beauty that it is hard to choose favorites. No one who has read the work can forget the celebrated opening, or Bashō's descriptions of Matsushima and Kisakata, but even single sentences not only linger in the mind but with time swell to the proportions of full-length episodes. Dante also had this ability: with a few lines he could create unforgettable people (like Paolo and Francesca) who would become central figures in the novels and plays of others.

The magic of Bashō's language is hard to define, but one can sense it in such a passage as "*Sandai no eiyō issui no uchi ni shite, daimon no ato wa ichiri konata ni ari. Hidehira ga ato wa den'ya ni narite, Kinkeizan nomi katachi wo nokosu*" ("The three generations of glory vanished in the space of a dream. The ruins of the Great Gate are two miles this side of the castle; the place where once Hidehira's mansion stood has turned to fields, and only the Golden Cockerel Mountain retains its appearance").[6] The translation does not do justice to the concision of the original, or to the language, a flawless combination of words of purely Japanese origin with words derived from Chinese, creating a texture incomparably richer than that of earlier diaries. The concision of the diary as a whole is particularly remarkable. I recall as a high point Bashō's account of the dangerous section of coastline known as Oyashirazu Koshirazu, where travelers are so intent on saving their own lives they "forget their parents, forget their children," but the description is hardly one line long.

Perhaps the section of *The Narrow Road of Oku* that moves me most is Bashō's reflections after seeing the "pot-shaped stone" at the ruins of Taga Castle. The inscription on this monument is not of much interest, relating only the circumstances of building and repairing the castle, but Bashō was deeply affected when he realized that here, before his eyes, was a relic that dated back indisputably to the middle of the eighth century. On his journey Bashō had in fact seen many sights that were even older—rivers, mountains, and trees. Not long afterward he would visit the castle of the "three generations of glory" of the Fujiwara family of Hiraizumi, where he would murmur to himself the famous lines of Tu Fu:

> The country has fallen but its rivers and mountains remain;
> When spring comes to the city its grass turns green again.

On that occasion, Bashō recalled, "I sat weeping, unaware of the passage of time." He then composed what was perhaps his finest haiku:

natsukusa ya	The summer grasses—
tsuwamonodomo ga	For many brave warriors
yume no ato	The aftermath of dreams.

At Taga Castle, however, Bashō was moved not by what had totally disappeared or had been metamorphosed into summer grasses but by what still remained. He wrote: "Many are the names that have been preserved for us in poetry from ancient times, but mountains crumble and rivers disappear, new roads replace the old, stones are buried and vanish in the earth, trees grow old and give way to saplings. Time passes and the world changes. The remains of the past are shrouded in uncertainty. And yet, here, before my eyes, was a monument that none would deny had lasted a thousand years. I felt as if I were looking into the minds of the men of old. 'This,' I thought, 'is one of the pleasures of travel and living to be old.' I forgot the weariness of the journey and was moved to tears of joy."[7]

With these words Bashō denied the eternity of rivers and mountains and even questioned the continuity implied in eternally regenerated trees. Only one thing survives forever: the written word. The pot-shaped monument can still be seen today, though Taga Castle has disappeared and the scenery around the site has been totally altered. In the same way, *The Narrow Road of Oku* will exist as long as there are people who can read Japanese, even if each place it describes is totally transformed. Senju, the first leg of Bashō's journey, is now a bustling commercial district, and Sōka, where he spent his first night on the road, contains a mammoth housing development. But the truth of *The Narrow Road of Oku* will survive such changes, as it has already survived the changes to the landscape at Kisakata. As the result of an earthquake in 1804, the lagoon at Kisakata became solid land, and the many islands that reminded Bashō of Matsushima are now no more than hillocks in the rice fields. But travelers to Kisakata today are likely to see the landscape not as it actually is but as Bashō described it. There is no longer any water, but Mount Chōkai still casts its reflections as in Bashō's day.

The months and the days are the travelers of the ages, but only because men have noticed this eternal but meaningless astronomical fact and given it significance with the beauty of their words. What more glorious tribute to the art of letters exists than this diary written so many months and years ago?

The Saga Diary

Saga Nikki (*The Saga Diary*) is more like a true diary than any other work by Bashō. The entries are all dated, and Bashō seems not to have revised the work in later years. It is of less literary interest than his earlier diaries, but what it lacks in literary quality is compensated for by the unique glimpses it provides into Bashō's ordinary daily life. The diary covers the few weeks in 1691 that Bashō spent at Rakushisha (The Hut of the Fallen Persimmons), the country house of his disciple Mukai Kyorai in Saga, to the northwest of Kyōto.

The diary opens with the matter-of-fact statement, "On the 18th day of the 4th month of the 4th year of Genroku [1691] I traveled to Saga and arrived at Kyorai's Rakushisha."[1] His host evidently expected that Bashō would spend more than a few days at Rakushisha; he had the *shōji* repapered and the garden weeded in honor of the visit. Bashō named the books he had brought with him: *Hakushi Shū* (*The Collected Works of Po Chü-i*), *Honchō Ichinin Isshu* (*One Chinese Poem Each by Japanese Poets*), *Yotsugi Monogatari* (*The Tale of the Succession*), *Genji Monogatari* (*The Tale of Genji*), *Tosa Nikki* (*The Tosa Diary*), and *Shōyō Shū* (*A Collection of Pine Needles*).[2] This was a surprising choice of books for a haiku poet to take to the country: it contained none of the standard collections of *waka* or *renga*, not even the works of the poets whom Bashō most admired. Perhaps he was hoping to use his vacation to "catch up" on books he had long meant to read.

Bashō's stay at Rakushisha was not, however, solely a vacation. At night, when he was unable to sleep because he had napped during the day, he took out and polished the rough drafts of manuscripts he had written while staying during the previous year at Genjūan (The Hut of Dwelling in Unreality). Bashō did not specify which works he went over at this time, but perhaps they included *The Narrow Road of Oku.*

A steady stream of visitors from Kyōto and elsewhere came to see Bashō at Rakushisha. He apparently enjoyed this company, though he also liked being alone. On the 22nd day of the 4th month, a rainy day, he wrote, "Today I had no visitors, and in my loneliness I amused myself by scribbling down various things." This seems to suggest that he missed having company and possibly was bored, but his "scribblings" describe instead the pleasures of solitude: "The person in mourning is a slave to sorrow. The person who indulges in liquor is a slave to pleasure. The fact that the Holy Man Saigyō wrote 'How dreary life would be without loneliness' indicates that *his* master must have been solitude."[3]

Bashō, continuing in this vein, declared that "there is nothing so enjoyable as living alone. The retired gentleman Chōshōshi[4] said, 'If a visitor gets half a day of someone's leisure, it means that his host has lost half a day of leisure.' Sodō[5] always repeats this saying with admiration. I too once composed the lines:

uki ware wo	I beg you, cuckoo,
sabishigarase yo	Now that I am so depressed,
kankodori	Make me lonely, too.

I wrote these lines when I was staying alone in a certain temple, to express my feelings."

Bashō must often have suffered from "people fatigue." That was probably why he had chosen in 1690 to live alone at Genjūan, south of Lake Biwa, or why in 1693 he would bar the gate of his house in Edo and refuse to admit visitors. It is gratifying for a teacher to be surrounded by worshipful disciples, but it is also exhausting. One can visualize Bashō's disciples copying down his every word and expressing profound admiration for even his most casual remark. What a relief it must have been to be alone!

Bashō was not, however, a misanthrope. Clearly he was happy when Kyorai, Bonchō,[6] and others visited him at Rakushisha or when he received letters from Edo informing him of what had happened during his absence. Besides, the composition of the *haikai* style of *renga* (several examples of which are given in *The Saga Diary*) required the participation of several people. That, presumably, was one reason why Bashō had chosen to live in Edo rather than in some mountain retreat. The contradictory desires to be alone and to be with other people were shared by Bashō with many other poets.

Bashō never lost his interest in people. His descriptions of the people he met during his journeys, no less than his evocations of nature, make his diaries memorable. One of his last haiku, written during his final illness, expressed his yearning for human company:

aki fukaki	Autumn has deepened
tonari wa nani wo	I wonder what my neighbor
suru hito zo	Does for a living.

As the year grew closer to its end, Bashō felt the loneliness of life. He wondered what the man in the next room—perhaps he had heard sounds that indicated the presence of somebody—did for a living, what kind of man he was. Bashō shared the normal human impulse to seek companionship, but he knew in his heart that it was the destiny of the poet to be lonely, as another of his last poems suggests:

kono michi ya	Along this road
yuku hito nashi ni	There are no travelers—
aki no kure	Nightfall in autumn.

Diaries of the Later Tokugawa Period

Journey to the Northwest

In the early spring of the 2nd year of Genroku (1689), the same year in which Bashō made his journey along the Narrow Road of Oku, the distinguished Confucian philosopher Kaibara Ekiken (1630–1714) decided to tour the provinces of Tango, Wakasa, and Ōmi. He was sixty years old by Japanese reckoning, a venerable age at the time, and the journey would be in part over difficult roads, but he expressed none of the gloomy forebodings about the likelihood of returning home alive that are so commonly found in earlier diaries.

He stated at the outset of the work his purpose in traveling and his reason for keeping a diary: "When we see places famed for their scenery and regions of surpassing poetic beauty, are we to take pleasure in them only for the brief moments we are actually there? If at times, even after some years have passed, we recall the appearances of the different places, we feel the same as when the sights were actually before our eyes, a mixture of wonder and nostalgia. It was in order not to forget what I had seen, even in my old age, that I decided to set down on paper with my clumsy brush the sights in the different regions where I traveled this year. I intended to make these memories last for the rest of my life. It also occurred to me that if I wrote down a few of my observations for the perusal of other people of the same inclinations as myself it might be of some use to them, especially if they were thinking of setting forth on travels to famous places and there were still many with which they were unfamiliar."[1]

Ekiken enjoyed travel. Later in the same year he would go to Kishū and Yamato, and in other travel diaries he recorded journeys from Sekigahara, in Mino, to Tsuruga, in Echizen, and along the Tōkaidō from Kyōto to Edo and back. On the whole, these diaries possess slight literary interest, though they are worth reading for what Ekiken tells us about the places he visited or (though he does not describe them often) his reactions to what he saw and heard. Naturally, there is none of the despair that marked the medieval travel diaries. Some sites that Ekiken visited, though famous from references in the literature of the past, were now in ruins, but this did not move him to melancholy reflections, only to a recognition of how much time had passed. He was resolutely prosaic and rational. These are admirable qualities, but they deprive his diaries of the pleasures we expect of diary literature. *Seihoku Kikō* (*Journey to the Northwest*) is the earliest Japanese diary I have read that contains not a single poem by the author.

Ekiken's attitude with respect to the various romantic stories he heard along the way was always down-to-earth. He managed always to find rational explanations even for supernatural phenomena. When, for example, he saw some foundation stones in the vicinity of Futasegawa and was informed that this was where the dwelling of the demon Shutendōji had stood, he rejected this bit of folklore and offered instead a more prosaic analysis of the legend: "Shutendōji was a bandit who lived long ago. He intimidated people by disguising himself as a demon [*yasha*], robbing people of their possessions and stealing their wives and children. In recent times similar cutthroats banded together in the area of Mount Ibuki and the province of Ōmi. They got themselves up like devils and harassed the people there, but I am told that they were cut down and killed by a brave man from Kaga named Ibe Hachirō."[2]

The contemporary reader is likely to welcome Ekiken's explanation, not because it is more interesting than the old legends about Shutendōji but because it suggests a critical mind at work. In a similar manner, when Ekiken visited Obama, in the province of

Wakasa, and was told that as a result of eating the flesh of a mermaid a certain woman had lived eight hundred years, his comment (easier for us to accept than the prodigy) was, "Eight hundred years is hard to believe!"[3]

Readers who take up Ekiken's diaries in the hopes of enjoying literary pleasure are bound to be disappointed, but Ekiken himself is an appealing man, and the influence of his diaries was considerable. The voluminous diaries of Sugae Masumi (1754–1829), which described travels about a century after Ekiken's, are in his tradition, and his influence can be detected even in the diaries of Motoori Norinaga and Ōta Nampo, men of a totally dissimilar outlook from his own. The scientific accumulation of information about all parts of Japan began with the travel diaries of Kaibara Ekiken.

Perhaps the most affecting section of *Journey to the Northwest* is Ekiken's account of two villages in Ōmi that were buried by the great earthquake of 1662. He recalled: "Years ago, when I was living in Kyōto, a man from one of those villages came to Kyōto and I heard his story. The day of the great earthquake, he had gone in the morning into the mountains to cut firewood. Frightened by the great earthquake, he returned to his village, only to discover that a mountain had crumbled and the whole village was buried in the ground. His parents, brothers and sisters, and other relatives had all been buried alive and perished. He alone had escaped death, as he related in tears."[4]

These words made me recall my visit to the ruins of Saint-Pierre on the island of Martinique. Lafcadio Hearn lived in this city prior to going to Japan, and he wrote lovingly of its unique charm. But in 1902 the nearby volcano, Mount Pelée, erupted and rained death on the city, killing some thirty thousand people. Only one person survived, a criminal in a dungeon deep underneath the local prison. What must it be like to be a sole survivor?

One cannot help wishing that Ekiken had a little more poetic spirit. He says absolutely nothing about his reactions to the sad story he heard from the survivor of the earthquake. Perhaps natural reticence kept him from expressing sympathy. If so, it is understandable, but still disappointing. Ekiken was certainly not unfamiliar with poetic literature. When he visited Jakkō-in, the convent north of Kyōto, he remembered Kenreimon'in, the former Empress who had ended her days in this lonely retreat: "Kenreimon'in's tomb is situated on high ground, a little above the living quarters of the convent. It is a small grave. In the old days there used to be a little pond before the main hall, and there were cherry trees known as 'the cherries at the water's edge,' but now there is neither a pond nor cherry trees."[5] At Ono he recalled, "Narihira composed poetry at this place, as we know from *The Tales of Ise*. Again, in the *Ukifune* chapter of *The Tale of Genji*, the description of the place where Ukifune lived makes it clear that it, too, was Ono."[6] But that was all Ekiken had to say about a place rich in literary associations: his poetic imagination did not extend beyond this point.

The postscript to *Journey to the Northwest* provides another kind of "human touch." Ekiken wrote, "I, Ekiken Kaibara Atsunobu,[7] wrote this in the 2nd month of Genroku 2 [1689]. It is now the 8th year of the Hōei era [1711] and I am already eighty-two years old.[8] Again and again I have recalled this journey. Now that I have grown so old, it makes me nostalgic to think back on the different places I saw long ago."[9] The prediction he made at the outset of his diary proved to be true: twenty-two years afterward his recollections of the journey, no doubt kept alive by the descriptions in his diary, still made him feel nostalgic.

Ekiken's later diaries, such as *Nan'yū Kikō* (*Journey to the South*), are in much the same vein as *Journey to the Northwest*, and far less poetic than even the diaries kept by warriors during the age of warfare. Ekiken was not insensitive to beauty; if he had not enjoyed looking at scenery, he would not have bothered to travel to so many places. But even when most impressed by landscapes, he never forgot his vocation as a Confucian rationalist.

His inquiries into the nature of things led him to investigate the waves at Wakanoura, a bay often mentioned in poetry: "According to popular belief, there are male waves [*onami*] but no female waves [*menami*] in this bay. That is why they speak of male-only waves [*kataonami*]. This theory is false. By 'male waves' is meant big waves. By 'female waves' is meant small waves. I have never believed in this theory. I wondered how it was possible there should exist in heaven or earth such a deviation from eternal principles.

After I got back home I discussed the matter with others, and then, in order to clear up the delusion, I spent some time at this bay, and I observed it carefully and at length. It was apparent that the waves did not in the least correspond to vulgar belief. The bay was just like any other: 'male' waves and 'female' waves reared up together again and again. When it says in old poems that when the tide comes in there are 'male-only' waves, it does not mean what people popularly believe, but that when the tide comes in it swallows up the beach."[10] How like Ekiken to make a special trip to Wakanoura just to verify that (as at every other beach) there were not only male but female waves! But he also seems to have appreciated the scenery: "The beauty of the scene, exceeding what I had heard about it, dazzled me."[11] That is about as far as Ekiken went in expressing enthusiasm for a view.

It is ironic that, in the same year that Bashō wrote the masterpiece among poetic diaries, Ekiken's remained so resolutely prosaic. The diaries of these two men would become models for the two kinds of diaries most characteristic of the latter half of the Tokugawa period.

Some Diaries by Women

Kaibara Ekiken was more concerned than any other Japanese Confucian scholar with the education of women. *Onna Daigaku* (*The Great Learning for Women*), the best-known work on the education of women written during the Tokugawa period, has often been attributed to Ekiken, though more probably it was compiled by someone else from opinions expressed in various of Ekiken's writings on the kind of education he deemed appropriate for women. These views are likely to seem extremely old-fashioned to modern readers, and they have been denounced as being a starting point for the subjection of women, but, read against the background of the education women of previous centuries had generally received, his prescriptions are in some respects unusually enlightened. The following passage from *Wazoku Dōjikun* (*Precepts for Children of the Laity*, 1710) indicates the kind of education for girls that Ekiken favored: "From the age of seven they should be made to learn the *kana* and also Chinese characters.[1] They should be made to read old poetry that is free of improper thoughts, and should learn the elegant arts. As in the case of boys, they should first be made to read and memorize a great many individual phrases and short selections. Afterward they should be taught filial piety, obedience, chastity, and bravery by having them read the opening chapter of *The Classic of Filial Piety*, the first section of the *Analects, The Precepts for Women* by Ts'ao Ta-chia, and other works."[2]

Up to this point Ekiken's precepts were in advance of their time; most Japanese would have considered it unnecessary and possibly dangerous to teach girls to read the Chinese classics. But Ekiken's views on education for women were not uniformly enlightened. He followed the statements quoted above with: "From the age of ten they should not be allowed out of doors but should remain in the women's quarters and should be taught embroidery and spinning. They should not under any circumstances be permitted to hear anything improper. *Kouta*, *jōruri*, the samisen, and suchlike entertainments favor an erotic vocal delivery, and harm the mind."[3] Ekiken urged parents to exercise great care in choosing the fiction to be read by their daughters. He warned them that, although the language of *The Tales of Ise* and *The Tale of Genji* is elegant, it is not advisable to show these books to girls too soon, because they describe immoral behavior.[4] Such advice would no doubt have been as welcome in Victorian England as in Tokugawa Japan.

Although Ekiken was naturally familiar with the works of the great women writers of the Heian period, he was not in favor of women's devoting themselves to literature. Harmony and obedience, rather than the literary skill of Murasaki Shikibu or of the daughter of Takasue, were the qualities he most admired in women. Presumably it was because of the feminine virtues displayed in the diaries of Inoue Tsūjo (1660–1738) that he recommended them to a Kyōto publisher, even though Tsūjo had not obeyed his rule that women should not leave their quarters after the age of ten.

Tsūjo was known, even as a child, for her unusual intelligence. Her father, an official at the castle in Marugame, in Sanuki Province, himself instructed her in the Japanese and Chinese classics, then sent her to Kyōto to study with the Confucian philosopher Hayashi Shunsai (1618–80). She demonstrated special ability at composing both *waka* and poetry in Chinese, and before she was twenty wrote two didactic works on the proper behavior for women. Her reputation within the clan was so high that she was summoned to Edo when she was twenty-two, to become a lady-in-waiting to the mother of the local daimyo, who was then in residence in Edo. Tsūjo's journey from Marugame to Edo is described in *Tōkai Kikō* (*Journey Along the East Coast*), the first surviving diary by a woman (as far as I know) since *Account of the Takemuki Palace*, written some 350 years earlier.

The style of *Journey Along the East Coast* is an old-fashioned *wabun* (pure Japanese prose), and the diary is sprinkled with *waka* in the manner of earlier diaries, but there are also many allusions to Chinese literature and even some poems in Chinese of her own composition. The opening sentence typifies the style: "*Ama no yawaragu hajime no toshi, shimo wo fumite, kataki kōri ni itaru korooi nareba, toshi furu Marugame wo fune yosoishite, Azuma no kata ni omomuku.*"[5] It is impossible to produce the same effect in a translation, but the general meaning is something like: "In the first year calmed by heaven, about the time when one treads on frost and the frost turns to hard ice, a ship put in at Marugame, where I have long lived, and headed then in the direction of the East." The "year calmed by heaven" was Tsūjo's elegant manner of referring to the era name Tenna, and she was in this way indicating that she left Marugame in the first year of Tenna, or 1681. The next words (about the frost and ice) are an allusion to a passage in the *I Ching* (*Book of Changes*), but she is also indirectly stating that she left Marugame in the 11th lunar month, known as *shimotsuki*, or "frost month." The phrase "where I have long lived" (*toshi furu*) was probably used as an epithet for the place name Marugame (literally, Round Tortoise), longevity having been an attribute of tortoises.

Despite this ponderous beginning and the disagreeable display of erudition, the personality of the diarist soon begins to reveal itself, bit by bit, and we are likely to end up thinking that, even if Tsūjo was overly indoctrinated by Ekiken's theories of education for women, she was an exceptionally interesting woman.

Tsūjo's journey from Marugame to Edo began with a trip by boat across the Inland Sea. She noted, "We put out to sea amid rough waves and wind, and drifted from shore so quickly that soon my old home was far away," and then alluded in rapid succession to Kakinomoto no Hitomaro, Tu Fu, and Sugawara no Michizane, a suitably learned group of poets. After the ship reached the other side of the Inland Sea, she traveled overland by palanquin. At first nothing much worth mentioning in a diary occurred, but Tsūjo, like all educated people of the time, was eager to see *utamakura*, places celebrated in poetry, and this gave the journey special interest. She discovered, just as every other traveler between Kyōto and the East had discovered for five hundred years, that not much was left of the Eight Bridges dear to Narihira, and the irises had long since withered.

Until Tsūjo and her party reach the barrier at Arai, hardly anything distinguishes this diary from the travel accounts of many predecessors, but no earlier woman diarist ever mentioned being stopped at a barrier because her papers were not in order. Efficient Tokugawa officials had replaced the lax, venal guards of the past, and Tsūjo's documents were thoroughly scrutinized. Here is her account of what happened: "When I showed the people at the barrier the document with the official seal I had been given in Naniwa [Osaka], where it should have said 'young woman with open sleeves' for some unknown reason it said merely 'woman.' In the wording of the official document it also said only 'woman,' so they refused permission to pass the barrier. I had to go back to the inn fruitlessly. It can be imagined how unhappy and frustrated I felt, and how annoyed I was with myself, wondering how I had failed to notice such a thing."[6] The difference between *wakiaketaru otome* (a girl whose sleeves were open) and *onna* (a woman whose sleeves were sewn together) seemed so crucial to the guards at the barrier that they refused to allow the unmarried Tsūjo, whose sleeves were open, to pass. There was nothing to do but send a messenger back to Naniwa for new credentials. Tsūjo nervously wondered if the messenger would reach Naniwa and, even if he did, if he would bring back the necessary papers. If not, she would have to return to Marugame, having traveled all the way to Arai to no avail. As she lay awake at the inn, weeping and listening to a fierce rain, "everything seemed indescribably depressing."[7] Late at night she heard the sounds of passing travelers and their horses, and she wrote, "How I envied them! Women are always faced with many obstacles, regardless of the situation, and now so many disagreeable things had crowded together that I was at a loss to tell the difference between day and night."[8] But the messenger returned unexpectedly soon, and the new documents enabled Tsūjo to pass the barrier without difficulty.

Journey Along the East Coast concludes with a description of Tsūjo's crossing the Tenryū River. She had developed a bad cold, and her father, who was accompanying her, forbade her to write any more, lest the strain of keeping the diary further impair her health. She resumed her habit after she had reached Edo. The new diary, called *Edo Nikki* (*The Edo Diary*), is the longest but least interesting of her three diaries. This diary is in much the same style as those kept by many young women in Japan today. Unlike the diaries of the past, which were couched in literary language and often described events long after they actually occurred, *The Edo Diary* faithfully records what happened on each day, no matter how little interest it possessed. Tsūjo never fails to mention the weather, visitors, and so on. Only occasionally is there even the slightest suggestion of literary intent, as in an entry written in the 9th month of 1682: "It is raining. I feel somehow terribly depressed. Everything—the sound of the wind, the cries of the insects—seems to be one with my mental state. When I heard the voices of the wild geese, so loud as to be startling, I felt yearning for the people at home, and I feel envious of the old days, when they used to carry messages."[9] Tsūjo greatly missed her family, and the arrival of letters from Marugame was her chief joy while she lived in Edo.

Tsūjo's duties in Edo consisted mainly of serving as a companion to the elderly mother of the daimyo, preparing her medicine, attending to her correspondence, and so on. Tsūjo's poetry soon attracted attention in Edo. One official, after examining poetry in Chinese and Japanese that Tsūjo composed, told her, "It is most unusual for a woman to compose such things. You are destined to follow in the footsteps of Sei Shōnagon and Murasaki Shikibu."[10] Perhaps Tsūjo really had the literary talent to follow in the footsteps of the great Heian-period women writers, but the times were not propitious for women with literary inclinations. Tsūjo spent her days quietly, attending to Her Ladyship's needs, writing poetry, and reading Japanese fiction. One day was much like another. There was not much to recall the varied activities of the ladies of the Heian court. *The Edo Diary* is a dull book, but the dullness was the fault not of Tsūjo but of the circumstances in which she had been placed by her society.

The lady whom Tsūjo had been serving died in 1689, and Tsūjo decided therefore to return home to Marugame. Members of the lady's family, impressed by Tsūjo's accomplishments, begged her to remain in Edo. It was difficult to refuse them, but Tsūjo longed to be reunited with her aged parents. Perhaps, too (though she does not say so), she hoped to get married. She was now thirty by Japanese reckoning.

She describes how she was importuned to stay in Edo a little while longer. Finally, realizing that if she delayed any longer, she might never leave, Tsūjo paid her last respects at Her Ladyship's grave and informed everyone of her departure. Perhaps her determination to leave was so strong because she had never thought of Edo as being her home. Tsūjo's stay in Edo seemed in retrospect only a fleeting interval in her life: "Close to ten years have passed, but I feel as if I arrived only yesterday, or even today."[11] It must have been painful nevertheless to say goodbye to people with whom she had lived for so long.

Tsūjo was delighted that her younger brother, Masumoto, would be accompanying her on the journey back to Marugame, and for this favor (among many) she was grateful to the family she had served. On the morning of the 11th day of the 6th month of 1689, about two months after Bashō left Edo for the north, Tsūjo and her brother set out for Shikoku. She wrote: "Before it had become completely light, people came to inform us that it would soon be time to leave and we must hurry, but the men, high and low alike, brought out saké cups, saying that they must have a parting drink before they got on their horses. In their different ways they expressed their boundless regrets over leaving, making a speedy departure quite impossible. The loud neighing of the horses sounded rather cheerful, but I felt very sad all the same."[12]

Kika Nikki (*Returning-Home Diary*) is by far the most enjoyable of Tsūjo's diaries. Although she reveals few of her own emotions, and in this respect is certainly less appealing than the Heian lady diarists, she showed a compassion (of a kind that they seldom expressed) for people she noticed along the way: "All I could see of a man who was cutting grass was his hat. The farmers sing their rice-planting songs amusingly. It came home to me each time I saw these people, more vividly than ever before, what a truly difficult thing it is to make a living, and what a terrible thing it is to be guilty of living slothfully off others. Again, when I saw a man plowing a field at the edge of the mountain, his body black as ink, wipe the sweat, the oppressiveness of the heat was so evident as to make me realize the truth of Tseng Tzu's words when he used cultivating the land in summer heat as a metaphor for pain."[13] Tsūjo's Confucian training accounted not only for the references to Mencius and Tseng Tzu but to her concern for the human condition.

Before they left Edo, Masumoto was issued with identification papers to enable them to get through the troublesome barriers at Hakone and Imagire, but they were stopped all the same at the Barrier of Hakone. Tsūjo was ordered to go into the guardhouse to be searched. She reported: "When I went up to the place where the guards were, the people there called to an old woman. Masumoto said that they had ordered me and my women to be searched by the woman. I had no choice but to comply. She examined our faces carefully, pushing back the hair. This weird-looking woman was old but sturdy, very rough, and when she came up close and said something in her thick dialect, it was most unpleasant to have to obey her, but I was afraid of what she might do."[14] They were at length permitted to pass the barrier, much to Tsūjo's relief.

Although there were still such inconveniences in travel, Tsūjo was sure that it was much easier than in the past. "In recent times the roads have been much improved by our enlightened government, a great convenience for all travelers, for which they are bound to feel grateful."

There are some amusing episodes in the diary. For example, Tsūjo, to help pass the time, asked Masumoto to compose a poem in Chinese, but he begged off, saying that it was difficult to compose poetry on horseback. Instead, he sang the Nō play *Miidera*, much to the surprise of Tsūjo, who had no idea that her brother had studied the singing of Nō texts. Her accounts of the conversations she overheard of palanquin bearers and ferrymen provide particularly vivid touches, and there are also passages of unconventional description: "It was delightful to see how, when the boat was borne from shore by the waves, the houses on the bank seemed to move away from us. Houses of merchants and houses of ordinary people, forming a town, stretched on into the distance. As it grew dark, the lights from these houses, now visible, now hidden by pines, looked like stars. When we passed villages here and there, I was told their names."[15]

The journey on the whole was enjoyable, but Tsūjo was eager to be home, and her joy on seeing from the ship the white walls of the castle at Marugame is unfeigned. This is where her diary ends, leaving the reader to wish it had been a bit longer.

As education for women became more general, it was natural that women should have turned increasingly to literary composition. The tradition of women's composing *waka* poetry had never died out, but now it was given new life by women not only of the nobility, but of humbler status, even prostitutes. Some women, under the influence of their readings in the diary literature of the distant past, began to keep literary diaries, and these writings eventually caught the attention of scholars of Japanese literature.

In 1807 the scholar Shimizu Hamaomi (1776–1824) published the diary *Kōshi Michi no Ki* (*Account of a Journey of 1720*), written by a certain Takejo. Two other learned authorities on Japanese literature contributed prefaces to the diary, and all three men extolled the work in extravagant terms. Murata Harumi (1746–1811) wrote, "The fragrance of its flow of language is worthy of *Kagerō* and *Murasaki*; and, most remarkably, its charming expression is not inferior even to *Sarashina* or *Izayoi*."[16] Not only were these scholars pleased to have discovered, relatively close to their own time, a woman diarist who could be compared to the greatest diarists of the past, but they were delighted that she was by profession a *shirabyōshi* (the old-fashioned way of referring to a geisha) and not a bluestocking like Inoue Tsūjo. Shimizu Hamaomi's postscript to his edition of the diary listed various other women of the same profession who had gained fame by their literary gifts, including Higaki (a poet of the *Gosenshū*), Eguchi (who appears in several works concerning Saigyō), and Tora in *The Tale of the Soga Brothers*, but he conceded that the tradition of literary *shirabyōshi* seemed (until this diary was discovered) to have died out long before.

Almost nothing is known about Takejo except what she recorded in this diary. At one time various scholars were of the opinion that Takejo was the *jiki* (personal attendant) of Tokugawa Muneharu, the daimyo of Owari, and that he raised her to the rank of court lady. An imposing tomb in Nagoya was said to be hers. However, in 1939 a scholar expressed the view that the source of this information about Takejo's later days was probably a forgery by Shimizu Hamaomi, who was eager perhaps to inflate the importance of his discovery. He continued, "Takejo is said to have been originally a *shirabyōshi*. It is not clear whether this meant a prostitute or a geisha, but if she was so talented as to attract the attention of the Lord of Owari, she should have established something of a reputation before she left Edo."[17]

Hamaomi probably polished the text of the diary, adding suitable literary allusions to enhance its claim to rank with the diaries of the Heian court ladies, but it is clear that the work on the whole was written by a woman, and that this woman was a *shirabyōshi* and not a court lady. It is possible that Takejo's relations with Tokugawa Muneharu began at a time when he was serving in Edo, and that he later summoned her to his fief in Owari, but this is only a guess.

The special qualities of Takejo's diary stem from her life as a *shirabyōshi*, but the work opens atypically with a paraphrase of a statement in the Confucian classic *Li Chi* (*Book of Rites*): "It is said in an old text that women should not cross boundaries." This quotation was doubtless chosen by way of suggesting the difficulties women then experienced in passing through barriers (*sekisho*) along the main roads, but Takejo added, "However, this surely refers to persons of quality. A fisherman's daughter, with no one to depend on, lets herself drift with whatever water invites her, flowing to the west, wandering off to the east, her final destination uncertain, a piteous, depraved way of life."[18] Unlike ladies of fine families, a "fisherman's daughter" was obliged by her profession to drift from place to place, wherever men summoned her, and she was not considered to be important enough to be stopped at the various barriers. The expression "fisherman's daughter" was ultimately derived from a poem in the thirteenth-century anthology *Shin Kokinshū* but also recalls the passage in *The Narrow Road of Oku* where two prostitutes from Niigata, who refer to themselves as "fishermen's daughters," dictate a letter in which they quote the *Shin Kokinshū* poem. The words "*sasou mizu*" ("water that invites") were from the famous poem by Ono no Komachi:

wabinureba	So lonely am I
mi wo ukigusa ni	My body is a floating weed
ne wo taete	Severed at the root;
sasou mizu araba	Were there water to entice me
inan to zo omou	I would follow it, I think.[19]

Takejo relates how she was stopped at a barrier on her journey from Nagoya to Edo. At first she was frightened by the martial equipment she saw: "In the barrier house bows and quivers were imposingly displayed, enough to terrify even an innocent person like myself; my hands and legs were trembling."[20] She was also ashamed that her face was not properly made up and her hair was a mess from perspiration. But she was soon informed that prostitutes and others of their ilk were not bound by the rules that governed the conduct of human beings, and that she was therefore at liberty to pass through the barrier. She commented, "I didn't know whether to be pleased or sad."

Takejo reveals that she had not been happy in Nagoya, but when she left the city behind her, probably for the last time, she felt a pang of regret, as she revealed in this *waka*:

ukarishi mo	I was unhappy, yes
ima zo koishiki	But when I think of leaving,
Shikasuga ni	At Shikasuga,
sumikoshi sato wo	The province where I have lived,
idenu to omoeba[21]	What love it now arouses!

Shikasuga was a village on the border between Owari and Mikawa provinces; mention of leaving behind Shikasuga implied that she was leaving Owari, where she had been in the daimyo's service.

But whatever regrets Takejo felt did not last long; she was happy to be returning to the east, the part of the country from which she originally came. On the way she passed Yatsuhashi, the Eight Bridges celebrated in poetry, but she was unable to stop by to see (in the manner by now traditional for travelers in that region) whether or not the irises still bloomed.

The pace of the journey was leisurely. Every sight reminded her of some *waka* or poem in Chinese. She was disappointed that some places mentioned in the old poetry had lost their former appearance, but she was able to discover resemblances between herself and the poets of the past. For example, at Arae she recalled, "In China there was a man named Chia Tao who lived for a long time in the province of Ping-chou. Later, when he was on his way back to the capital and about to cross a river at the ford of Sang-hsien, he composed a Chinese poem that flashed into my head because it applied so well to my present state." She composed the following poem in Chinese, changing only a few of Chia Tao's words:

> Seven years I dwelt, a stranger, in Bishū,
> Yearning to return, I day and night remembered Tōyō.
> But when, unexpectedly, I again crossed the Arae waters
> I realized I actually thought of Bishū as home.[22]

The place names in the original poem by Chia Tao were changed: his Ping-chou became Bishū (another name for Owari), Hsien-yang became Tōyō (meaning Edo), and the Sang-hsien River became Arae. As previously related, Chia Tao's poem had served as the inspiration for Bashō's haiku:

aki totose	Autumn makes ten years;
kaette Edo wo	Now I actually mean Edo
sasu kokyō	When I talk of "home."

Perhaps Takejo's variation on Chia Tao's poem was a sincere expression of her longing to return to Edo (and her contradictory reluctance to leave Owari), but when she read it aloud aboard the boat crossing the river, everyone laughed at her clever parody of the original.

This was not the only time during the journey that Takejo's poetry made people laugh. In Hamamatsu she composed a *waka* that people found so amusing they all laughed aloud.[23] She was certainly not like the ladies of good family who normally kept diaries.

When Takejo passed Sayo no Nakayama, she remembered the description of the place given in *Journey Along the Seacoast Road*, and she composed this *waka*:

toshi wa mada	Although I am still
misoji ga hodo ni	Only thirty years of age,
yuku to ku to	Going and coming
yatabi koekeri	I have eight times crossed over
Sayo no Nakayama[24]	Sayo no Nakayama.

Assuming that Takejo was telling the truth about her age in this poem, we infer that she was then about thirty and that she had made the journey between Edo and Nagoya a total of eight times. She mentions also that at the age of fifteen she had traveled to Kyōto with a priest who was her uncle.[25] Probably the other journeys she made were at the behest of the Lord of Owari. If she was actually thirty when she made the journey described in this diary, it is all the more unlikely that she was the Takejo buried in Nagoya sixty-two years later.

The journey along the Tōkaidō is effectively described, though by this time there was not much left to be said about the sights along the way. The passage of the Ōi River was perhaps the memorable event of the journey: "Words cannot describe how frightened I was at the thought I might fall at any moment into the raging waters. We barely made it to the opposite shore. Just to recall the experience is enough to make my hands tremble as I write even now, later on, and I have omitted much of what I went through at that time."[26]

Takejo arrived home on the 5th day of the 3rd month. She had been traveling since the 20th day of the 2nd month. Naturally, she was overjoyed to be with her family again after seven years' absence. A younger sister who had been a mere child when Takejo last saw her was now fully grown, and Takejo at first did not recognize her.

This is where the diary ends, and there is no clue as to what happened to Takejo afterward. If the diary had not been discovered, she would have been as utterly forgotten as the other *shirabyōshi* of her time. But this short work has more than a hint of the charm that so captivated the Lord of Owari.

Travels of Gentlemen Emissaries

The tradition of keeping diaries in Chinese continued throughout the Tokugawa period. Confucian scholars were especially adept at writing classical Chinese, and it was natural for them to use this language for such informal works as travel diaries as well as for philosophical essays. One of the most interesting of such diaries is *Fūryū Shisha Ki* (*Travels of Gentlemen Emissaries*)[1] by Ogyū Sorai (1666–1728), the account of a journey from Edo to the province of Kai in 1706. Sorai was requested to make this journey by Yanagisawa Yoshiyasu (1658–1714), a favorite of the Shogun Tsunayoshi, who had been granted the fief of Kai two years earlier. Not only was Kai much more important than his previous domain but Yoshiyasu's ancestors had lived there. He was so pleased by this promotion that he immediately set about building a castle at Kōfu, the chief city in Kai, and a temple where his tomb was to be erected. He himself prepared an inscription for the tombstone that related the various achievements of his family. Yoshiyasu was afraid, however, that there might be mistakes in the geographical matter included in the inscription, and he therefore dispatched Ogyū Sorai and another Confucian scholar, Tanaka Seigo (1668–1742), to verify the facts.

Sorai and his friend Seigo traveled together from Edo to Kōfu and back, stopping frequently to admire the scenery and to compose poems in Chinese. *Travels of Gentlemen Emissaries* seems to have been written day to day, but Sorai undoubtedly polished the text later on. He also made a shortened version of the diary in a more literary Chinese style, but omitted the poems and the incidents that give the original diary its genial appeal.[2]

Sorai and Seigo left Edo on the 7th day of the 9th month. As emissaries of a powerful statesman, they traveled in palanquins and were accompanied by spear carriers, secretaries, and many servants. This was Sorai's first journey in many years, and he was intrigued by everything he saw and heard from the first day. He noted disapprovingly while in Fuchū, "Although I had traveled just a few dozen *ri*,[3] I already could observe that the pronunciation of the children was not good."[4] The same day, he visited the Rokusho Myōjin Shrine,[5] which he found in a most dilapidated state: "The stone torii had fallen over and broken into three or four pieces that lay on the ground. The ruined roof provided no protection against the wind and rain, and the statues of the guardian warriors[6] to the left and right of the gate were dismembered." He met the priest of the shrine, who looked like a peasant and was so deferential as to remind Sorai of a mendicant priest. He sourly commented, "He was unspeakably coarse."[7]

Once beyond the town of Hachiōji, the emissaries traveled through mountainous country. This was not Sorai's first experience of such terrain. In 1679 he had accompanied his father into exile in Kazusa (the modern Chiba Prefecture) when the father was banished by Tokugawa Tsunayoshi shortly before he became Shogun. But, Sorai wrote, "Although I was accustomed to extremely twisting roads in the mountains, I could not help saying, 'I have never seen such extraordinary scenery.' "[8] Seigo, even less accustomed to such scenery, from time to time got down from his palanquin to admire the views.

From the height of one steep place, the two men looked down into a deep valley where they could see a few houses. The spot looked both beautiful and remote. "The green of the trees rising into the sky shone in reflected light, and the pure beauty aroused our envy. People all seemed only an inch tall. It was like looking at things inside a bowl."[9] Sorai felt sure that Taoist hermits must live in such an idyllic place, and the two men, leaving their palanquins, made their way down the steep path. What they saw in the valley came as a shock: "When we got there we found hovels. The misery was indescribable. I saw an old woman wearing clothes patched together from a hundred bits of rags. Her grandson, who must have been eight or nine, looked pallid, like a famished demon. It surprised me that they were capable of speech. Seigo, moved to pity, searched in his bag until he found some cakes, which he gave them to eat before we left."[10]

The experience seems to have shaken both men. For a moment the two gentlemanly emissaries were confronted with a harsh reality that threatened to disrupt the cheerful atmosphere pervading their journey, but Sorai was ready with allusions to various ancient Chinese texts that relieved them of the obligation to feel sorry for the wretched people they had met.

Sorai and Seigo made excellent companions, although they were temperamentally quite different. Sorai explained his relationship with Seigo in these terms: "From the time the two of us lived in the clan residence in Edo, we made good partners in refined pursuits. Shigenori [Sorai's personal name] is forty-one. Seigo is thirty-nine but he looks older. However, Shigenori is susceptible to illness and has often been confined to a sickbed; and when it comes to eating, he is far from being a match for Seigo. He is also extremely lazy by nature. . . . Seigo as a boy learned fencing; he is eloquent and musters righteous indignation effectively; he is quick in his reactions. For this reason Shigenori is sometimes criticized as a slothful priest,[11] but there is no way of excluding Seigo from the ranks of Confucian heroes."[12]

Sorai contrasts his laziness with Seigo's combination of scholar and warrior, but at one point in the diary we are told that Seigo, rejecting Sorai's suggestions that they take advantage of the fine weather to walk for a change, declared, "I am a man of letters [*bunjin*]. My muscles are slack, my flesh sags. I have already lost the habit of hurrying, and my legs can no longer carry me as they once did. The least effort and the noontime bell starts to sound."[13] Each man imagined that the other was far more energetic than himself.

Sorai recounted how whenever he and Seigo met they always joked together. *Travels of Gentlemen Emissaries* is dotted with mentions of the great laughs they shared. They also both enjoyed composing Chinese poetry. In the diary a quatrain composed by Sorai is usually followed by one by Seigo. On one occasion, when Sorai was unable to complete a quatrain after composing the first two lines, he asked Seigo to finish it, but Seigo was unable to rescue the poem.[14]

Among the amusing anecdotes Sorai related about Seigo was one concerning Seigo's habit of spending the night in Zen meditation and not getting to sleep until dawn. The night before they reached Kōfu, Seigo as usual practiced meditation. They set out at dawn. Seigo fell asleep while in his palanquin and did not realize that they had entered a city until he was awakened by the noise around him. "Suddenly his eyes opened. He exclaimed in surprise, 'I thought we were taking the road to Kōfu. Why did we turn back on the way and return to Edo?' His secretary said with a smile, 'Is Your Excellency talking in his sleep? We're in Kōfu!' At this Seigo woke up and rebuked the man, 'I was practicing the words of a hymn of praise.[15] What do you mean by saying I was talking in my sleep?' "[16] Sorai teased Seigo about this answer, and everyone shared in the laugh.

When they finally reached the temple where the monument to Yanagisawa Yoshiyasu's ancestors was to be erected, Sorai brought out the tombstone inscription composed by Yoshiyasu and read it aloud. Even as he read, everyone was amazed that there was not the slightest mistake with respect to the topography, the sites of scenic places in the region, and so on. Yoshiyasu, though a thousand *ri* away (a gross exaggeration of the distance), had envisaged the landscape of Kai so exactly that nothing required correction. Sorai accordingly expressed in his diary his belief that there had been no need to make the journey. Seigo disagreed; he was sure that their personal experiences were of value in substantiating the truth of the inscription composed by their master. Sorai was not convinced, but (after giving a laugh) he composed this poem:

The gentlemanly emissaries, delighting in quiet pleasures,
Have aimlessly wandered over a space of a thousand *ri*.
This journey has taught them the greatness of their lord's favor;
Sated with famous mountains, they return without profit.[17]

Sorai used the word *kun'on*, meaning "the favor of one's lord," but he actually seems to be referring not to Yoshiyasu's "favor" but to his remarkable knowledge of geography. The "return without profit" refers to the futility of making a journey to verify the accuracy of Yoshiyasu's incomparable knowledge of local geography.

The journey may not have served any useful purpose, but it provided Sorai and Seigo with three enjoyable weeks together. Readers today will find Sorai's diary a rare and enjoyable description of Confucian scholars in their lighter moments that tells us what *fūryū* meant to the gentlemen-scholars of the past.

The Frolic of the Butterfly

Bashō's style of haiku fell into disfavor after his death. His direct disciples split into contesting factions, and when they died the situation deteriorated even further. Not until some thirty-five years after Bashō's death was there a revival of the worship of Bashō that had been normal during his lifetime. By 1743, the fiftieth anniversary of his death, the revival was in full swing. Haiku poets traveled to the north of Japan, following Bashō's course on his *Narrow Road of Oku* journey, and monuments were erected at places mentioned in his diary. From this time on, Bashō's reputation would not be shaken.

Of course, Bashō was not forgotten even during the period when his writings were neglected. His direct disciples did not all accept Bashō's advocacy of *karumi* (lightness) as a guiding principle of the haiku, but they were otherwise faithful to his memory. Soon after his death, some disciples traveled to sites associated with his writings. For example, in 1700, seven years after Bashō died, Hattori Ransetsu (1654–1707), a senior disciple, traveled to Irago Point, the Great Shrine of Ise, and then to the Gichū-ji, a Buddhist temple in Zeze, where he paid his respects before Bashō's grave. In the diary describing his travels, Ransetsu wrote, "By the tomb of my master at the Gichū-ji, *bashō*[1] plants grow abundantly, but their leaves are broken, and moss, which has seen the dews and frosts[2] of seven years, has covered the stone."[3]

Ransetsu was unquestionably moved as he stood before Bashō's grave, but the description of this experience is disappointingly brief. Moreover, the remainder of the diary is devoted mainly to a cheerful account of the Gion Festival and other celebrations he witnessed in Kyōto; his enjoyment was apparently untinged by recollections of the lonely grave.

The most intriguing work occasioned by the revival of Bashō's reputation is probably *Chō no Asobi* (*The Frolic of the Butterfly*), the diary of Yamazaki Hokka (1700–c.1750), who was also known as Jidaraku Sensei (Master Sloppy). Hokka is not often mentioned in histories of haiku poetry, and he does not figure prominently even in stories about eccentrics of the period, but he was a most unusual man. Ōta Nampo (1749–1823) related in an essay the best-known incident of Hokka's life: "On the last day of the 4th year of Gembun [1739], Hokka, then in his fortieth year, in a frivolous moment ordered a coffin. He got into the coffin and, escorted by friends who shared his sense of humor, he was borne to the Yōfuku-ji in Yanaka,[4] where a funeral service was performed. Just as the resident priest began to chant the prayer that precedes touching fire to the coffin, Hokka broke open the coffin and jumped out. His friends, who had followed the cortège to the temple, had brought along food and drink. They enjoyed themselves singing and dancing, to the astonishment of everyone."[5] The gravestone erected for the mock funeral still stands.

In 1738, the year before the mock funeral, Hokka followed Bashō's footsteps to Matsushima. He described the journey in *The Frolic of the Butterfly*. The title of the diary was derived from the famous "butterfly dream" of Chuang Tzu, but refers specifically to the haiku composed by Hokka in his dream about Kisakata:

Kisakata ya	Kisakata—
ware chōchō no	A place where I frolicked
asobidoko[6]	When I was a butterfly.

The diary, also known as *The Sequel Narrow Road of Oku*, opens with a paraphrase of Bashō's celebrated text: " 'The spirits of wanderlust took possession of things and bewitched me out of my senses, and when I was beckoned by the gods of the road, nothing I took in my hands stayed put. I patched up the holes in my breeches and changed the cord of my bamboo hat. Then no sooner had I had moxa burned on my shins[7] than the moon of Matsushima began to occupy my thoughts.' The above is what the old master wrote, and he was telling the truth. The spirits of wanderlust took possession of me, too, and when the gods of the road vouchsafed to beckon, Matsushima began to occupy my thoughts for days and even years. Eventually I secured permission to leave, and in this year, the 3rd of Gembun, on the 22nd of the 3rd moon, I slung a pack onto my back, tied the strings of my straw sandals, and set off toward the Barrier of Shirakawa, intending to cross it."[8]

Hokka decided to travel alone, although friends urged him to take a servant along in case of an emergency. He was sure that the journey would not be too difficult, especially since he was not in any hurry. Besides, if a servant carried his baggage and all he had to do was to stroll along empty-handed, it would not be in the most refined traditions of travel. The country was at peace, after all, and there was no need to worry. But, just to be on the safe side, he put a sword in his pack.[9]

Although Hokka followed more or less the same course as Bashō in traveling from Edo to Matsushima, his account of the journey creates a quite different impression. Unlike the abstemious Bashō, Hokka enjoyed drinking saké wherever he went. (The epitaph on the monument erected for his mock funeral states, "He enjoyed the flesh of birds, beasts, fish, and turtles, and he knew the taste of saké better than a Chinese. When he got drunk he would sleep, and when he sobered up, he would lie down. He spent his days in idleness without a thought on his mind.") At the first stop on the journey, a place called Ōsawa, in the post-station of Koshigaya, Hokka sent for saké but found it depressing to drink alone. He invited the innkeeper and his wife to join him. The innkeeper, an amateur haiku poet, composed the verse:

misakana ya	What nice food you serve—
hajimete nagara	Although it's for the first time,
shitashimono	I like these boiled greens.

Hokka, impressed, wrote, "He used the right number of syllables and included a *kireji*,[10] but there is no seasonal word. I was impressed particularly by his pun on *hitashimono* [greens boiled with soy] and *shitashimono* [an intimate], in that way saying that, although we met for the first time, he already felt intimate. Such skill must have come from practice at composing *maekuzuke*.[11] Truly, a remarkable innkeeper!"[12]

The innkkeeper guided Hokka to various places of interest in the vicinity, including a huge willow. Hokka was informed that Benkei[13] had planted a toothpick that had taken root and grown into this willow. Hokka commented, "There are many traditions of this kind in every province, but most of them have not a shred of evidence behind them. I couldn't believe this one for a moment."[14] Hokka was less ready than Bashō to accept the truth of local legends.

Not long afterward Hokka saw a horse-driver, dozing on his horse, fall into a river. The man was unhurt but furious. He beat the horse and then let forth a string of curses. The sight inspired Hokka to make this comment on the political situation: "There are many examples in the world to recall this horse-driver. Governors of provinces or the heads of large families leave worldly business to other people while they themselves doze on horses, or enjoy themselves in sightseeing, only to have their horses stumble."[15]

Hokka visited Muro no Yashima. He alluded to Bashō's account of the place in *The Narrow Road of Oku*, then composed a most unconventional haiku about the smoke for which the place was famous:

hito kuyuri	People emit smoke:
Muro no Yashima no	At Muro no Yashima
tabako kana[16]	See the tobacco!

Hokka's fondness for tobacco is attested by many references in the diary.

Hokka arrived in Nikkō exactly fifty years to the day after Bashō. He reflected, "That Buddha Gozaemon he wrote about is dead, and the master has also departed this life and left behind only his reputation, but the spring is still the same spring,[17] and today, sleeping here on my journey, I shall see the last of the spring."[18] The next day, the 1st of the 4th month, marked the beginning of summer and was the day on which people traditionally changed to summer clothes. Bashō had written on this day fifty years earlier the haiku:

hitotsu nuide	I remove one layer
sena ni oikeri	And carry it on my back:
koromogae	The day to change clothes.

Hokka, in a similar mood, wrote:

momohiki wo	I have discarded
kyahan ni shitari	My breeches for leggings:
koromogae	The day to change clothes.

When Hokka was about to leave Nikkō for Nasunohara, he was warned that the road might be dangerous. In the past there had been many highwaymen, and even now it was advisable to travel in broad daylight. Hokka was resolved to proceed according to plans: "I tucked up the hems of my kimono, securely fastened my straw sandals, braced the hanging part of my sleeves, and, taking my sword from my pack, fastened it to my side. Fortifying myself in this heroic manner lightened the load on my back. I removed my rain hat and, parting my whiskers to right and left, threw angry glances and brandished a stick. The look on my face seemed to say that I was ready to cope with anything suspicious. I set forth onto Nasu Plain glaring in all directions. My appearance was hardly appropriate for a poet. However, only the fool fails to equip himself properly when faced with danger."[19]

It is amusing to think of Hokka planning to frighten bandits by his appearance, but (as the above indicates) he was well aware of the incongruity of a haiku poet's getting himself up to look like a demon-queller. However, he felt sure that, even if he had the heart of a lamb, as long as he looked like a tiger or a wolf, bandits would hesitate before attacking. Hokka never had the occasion during this journey to test whether or not his ferocious appearance actually scared off bandits.

When Hokka reached the Barrier of Shirakawa, he at first could not compose a single haiku. He had an ingenious explanation for his trouble in thinking of a poem: Shirakawa stood at the border between the provinces of Shimotsuke and Michinoku, and each province was protected by its own god of *waka*. For this reason, "I wondered what I should say at the Barrier of Shirakawa that would be compatible with the will of both gods and also suitable to this famous place. I was unexpectedly awe-stricken and, bowing deeply in reverence, was about to pass the barrier without saying a word when a *hototogisu* [a kind of cuckoo] sang." He thereupon composed the haiku:

wa ga oshi wo	Is it making fun
warau ka seki no	Of my muteness? The cuckoo
hototogisu[20]	At the barrier.

In Sukagawa, Hokka was shown mementos of Bashō, who had stopped there on his journey to the north. At Asaka, remembering that Bashō had asked people to show him the plant called *katsumi*, Hokka asked people the same, but nobody could help him. After inspecting marshes in the vicinity, he spent the night at a place called Motomiya. The master of the inn, a boy of fourteen or fifteen with a youthful widowed mother, was away that night. Just when Hokka and the other guest at the inn, a blind mendicant priest, were preparing to go to bed, a villager appeared and insisted on spending the night at the inn so that the widow would not be lonely. She replied that she was grateful for his thoughtfulness but that there was no danger of becoming lonely with two guests at the inn. Besides, people might gossip if they learned he had spent the night under the same roof as a young widow. He insisted, despite her protests, and lay down beside the other two guests.

That night Hokka was awakened by the sound of a baby crying. He supposed that the baby might have been bitten by some insect and called to the widow, but there was no reply. Instead he heard sounds that suggested people wrestling. He eventually discovered that the villager, enamored of the widow, had intended to take advantage of the absence of her son to have his will with her. When the woman resisted, attempting to preserve her chastity, he tried to take her by force "in what was perhaps the manner of the eastern savages."[21] The woman, determined not to give in, pushed the villager away as best she could. In the meantime, her baby, deprived of its mother's breast, crawled off into the dark and began to wail. Those were the sounds Hokka had heard. When it grew light, the villager slunk away.

Hokka continued along the route Bashō had taken. When he passed the place where Bashō had composed the haiku:

fūryū no	The beginning of
hajime ya Oku no	Artistic taste—an Oku
taue uta	Rice-field planting song.

Hokka composed a haiku in what he called the "parrot style":

fūryū no	The pillar of
hashira ya Oku no	Artistic taste—an Oku
taue uta	Rice-field planting song.

Hokka admired the twin-trunked pine at Takekuma and was particularly moved by the stone monument at Taga Castle, which had inspired some of the finest writing in *The Narrow Road of Oku*. He composed this haiku:

senzai no	Still the same after
mukashi mo onaji	A thousand years have elapsed—
hototogisu[22]	The mountain cuckoo.

Shiogama was even more wonderful than Hokka had expected, and he was overjoyed when he finally reached Matsushima, which he described in detail. The next high point of the journey, as in *The Narrow Road of Oku*, was Kisakata. Hokka described how he found a deserted-looking retreat near the Kammanju-ji.[23] There were no signs of life, so he decided to search the temple for someone, to ask for a light for his tobacco and, if possible, for some tea. The temple grounds, to his surprise, proved to have a splendid garden, full of flowers and birds. There was also a *bashō* plant, and near it a cottage overgrown with ivy and other creepers. When Hokka went up to the cottage and opened the door, he saw there a priest, some fifty years old, who asked who Hokka was and on what business he had come. After getting a light for his tobacco and drinking a cup of tea, Hokka launched into an account of his career, mentioning the various samurai households where he had served. He also related that he had given up his samurai status because of poor health and a lack of interest in his official duties. Since then he had lived as he pleased. Asked about his bizarre appearance, he replied, "I haven't shaved my forehead because I have trouble using a razor. I let my beard grow for the fun of it. I have dyed my teeth black because they are decayed."

The priest in turn identified himself: he was none other than Bashō. He asked Hokka about his studies of haiku and confirmed that Hokka, who had studied under a pupil of Bashō's disciple Kyorai, was in the authentic tradition of Bashō. At this point Hokka woke up and discovered that he was still at Matsushima. All that he had experienced at Kisakata was a dream. He reasoned that, if he actually went to Kisakata after having had such a dream, he would surely be disappointed, so he decided to return to Edo instead. His return journey was recounted in his usual carefree manner.

Hokka has been all but forgotten, but his diary is one of the most enjoyable written in the tradition of Bashō. He was an eccentric and lived during a golden age of Japanese eccentrics, but his voice was individual.

Diary of the Nagasaki Border Guard

By the middle of the Tokugawa period there was a steady increase in the numbers of people profiting by the safety of the roads to travel, and the places they went were more varied than in the past. Nagasaki, the only corner of Japan where foreigners (a handful of Dutch merchants and a few thousand Chinese) were permitted to reside, became a destination both for officials who traveled there on state business and for scholars, physicians, artists, and others who hoped to learn something from the foreigners. Surviving accounts by those who made the journey prove that, despite the official policy of *sakoku* (closure of the country), Japanese interest in the outside world was mounting.

The study of the West, known as *rangaku* (Dutch learning), originated in the middle of the eighteenth century. Even before then, some government officials stationed in Nagasaki had been capable interpreters of Dutch, but these men contributed little to the Japanese knowledge of Europe. Most Japanese at the time, if they thought about the Dutch at all, dismissed them as being *kōmō* (red-hairs), a designation that owed more to the association of the Europeans with the red-haired demons in Buddhist painting than it did to the actual color of the Dutchmen's hair.

One early visitor to Nagasaki, Hirazawa Kyokuzan (1733–91), journeyed to Nagasaki in 1774 as a member of a daimyo's entourage. He learned about a mysterious ship that had called at a port in Awa (on the island of Shikoku) three years earlier. The captain of the ship, grateful for the provisions he had received from the Japanese, warned them that a Russian attack was imminent.[1] This warning would be pondered by many Japanese writers over the next thirty years, some of whom attempted for patriotic reasons to verify its truth by visiting Nagasaki.

However, it was not easy for a Japanese, even once he reached Nagasaki, to obtain permission to visit Deshima, the small, artificial island where the Dutch were confined. Shiba Kōkan declared in his diary that a visit to Deshima was a rare privilege for natives of the city, who seldom got so much as a glimpse of a foreigner. Even daimyos could not visit Deshima whenever they chose: "I was informed that the daimyos from the western provinces and the region of Nagasaki are allowed to visit this island only once in a lifetime and at no other time."[2]

Another early visitor to Deshima was Nagakubo Sekisui (1717–1801), an official from Mito who traveled to Nagasaki in 1767 in order to receive some castaways, originally from his province, who had been shipwrecked two years earlier in Annam, and who had been brought to Nagasaki aboard a Chinese ship. His diary, *Nagasaki Kōeki Nikki* (*Diary of the Nagasaki Border Guard*), opens with an account of his departure from Mito in the 9th month, and concludes with his return home in the 12th month. Sekisui, because he was traveling on official business, was accompanied by a large retinue, twenty-one men in all.

He was a cultivated man, and along the way he took notes on literary and historical sites. At a temple in Odawara, for example, he noted: "The *renga* poet Sōgi died at this temple in the Bunki era [1502]. I was told that they kept his valedictory verse and other poems at this temple. Going a little bit farther on, one reaches the Soga Hall. It was there that the haiku poet Bashō composed a *hokku* on violets,[3] and some lover of his poetry has had this haiku carved into a stone that stands by the road."[4] But Sekisui was far from accepting every legend at face value. When informed that an old bell at the Miidera had been fetched from the Palace of the Dragon King under the waves, he declared, "It's enough to make one split one's side with laughter."[5]

The diary contains a number of poems in Chinese by the author (as we would expect in the diary of a Confucian scholar). When, for example, he passed Sayo no Nakayama, famous because of a *waka* by Saigyō,[6] Sekisui wrote this poem:

Long ago I made a pleasure trip to the capital;
The cottage where I lived was at Kaitō.
Could I have possibly dreamed that, with white hair,
I should cross through these mountains again?[7]

Sekisui and his retinue reached Nagasaki on the 12th day of the 10th month. His first impression of this exotic city was provided by the surroundings: "In this region pigs and goats are allowed to pasture alongside the roads, and I saw them wandering here and there. When I asked about them, I was informed that these animals were bred in large numbers as food for the Chinese in Nagasaki."[8]

The main attraction of Nagasaki for Sekisui was not the Dutch but the Chinese. The day afer his arrival he sent a poem in Chinese, together with his calling card, to a local official. He had been told that among the Chinese who were then staying at the guest pavilion there were some literary men. He was eager to meet them and to exchange poetry, and he asked the official to arrange a meeting.

The ceremony of acceptance of the castaways (from the Chinese who had rescued them) took place the same day. "All the officials, including ourselves, changed to formal dress, and we were led by a guide to the magistrate's residence. When the examination of the four castaways was completed, we returned to our lodgings along with the ship's crew."[9] Sekisui wrote not a word about the castaways, either because he was reluctant to discuss official business in a private diary or because he was essentially uninterested in shipwrecked fishermen.

On the 14th Sekisui visited the quarters of the Dutch on Deshima. He wrote: "The island has been built out into the bay, and is surrounded on all sides by an extremely steep stone wall. One enters or leaves the island by the one stone bridge. By the side of the gate there is a guardhouse. At the entrance is a flagpole that is like a *sekkan*.[10] The buildings are two stories high. I saw some

Dutchmen peering out from the windows on the second story. Their eyes glitter and their eyebrows are a rusty color; they look extremely peculiar. I could also see some women standing by them. I was told that they were local prostitutes. The members of my party all entered through the kitchen and climbed upstairs. The Dutchmen came out to meet and guide us. Their skins are extremely white. They shave their heads and wear black wigs. Their clothes are like our *momohiki*.[11] They cover their arms and legs and close the ends with buttons. Their jackets have no sleeves but are joined together in front with buttons. The lower part of their garments is divided, resembling the costumes our acrobats wear."[12]

Sekisui was obviously not impressed by the Dutchmen, but the decoration of the room of the factory director was more to his taste. He was intrigued by a thermometer, but noted, "It was all in barbarian writing, so I could not read it." The framed pictures on the wall also produced a favorable impression: "The decorations all around were extremely beautiful. There were many kinds of pictures, including landscapes and portraits. The brushwork was done with such precision one could not easily distinguish the paintings from the real things."[13] Like most other visitors to Deshima, Sekisui was curious about Dutch liquor: "There was a table in the middle of the room on which pewter flasks were lined up. I was told they were all famous liquors."[14]

Sekisui's interpreter addressed a Dutchman who "made a deep obeisance and, this done, sat on his chair once again." This gesture of deference was surely humiliating to the Dutchmen, but they realized that unless they complied they would have to leave Japan. Some years later the factory director Hendrik Doeff was ordered to make a bow to an official in the presence of a visiting Russian. The Russian recalled that the Dutchman was required to incline his body until it formed nearly a right angle, and was forced to remain in this position with his arms extended until the official at length gave him permission to stand in his natural posture.[15] But Doeff later defended himself, saying he did no more than conform to the customs and etiquette of the Japanese. He wrote, "One cannot expect that a nation to which one comes in order to seek the friendship of the same should conform to the customs of the visitors."[16]

Sekisui had harsh comments to make on the manner in which the Dutch had expanded their empire to Java and elsewhere: "The Red-Hairs, being basically scoundrels and pirates, capture weak countries and make their populations into new Red-Hairs. This is why we cannot be lax. Whenever a Red-Hair ship enters or leaves port, the daimyo on duty at the time immediately musters his forces, and guards the vicinity with two or three thousand troops."[17] Sekisui understandably believed that it was necessary to keep the Dutch in a state of subservience, lest they attempt to make the Japanese into new Red-Hairs.

Sekisui also visited the Chinese settlement and described the Chinese he saw there. Unlike the Dutchmen, "they are not contemptible. Their faces look exactly like those of Japanese."[18] But, not having received permission to associate with the Chinese, he was denied the pleasure of "brush conversation."[19] "All I did was bow and leave. I couldn't have regretted it more."

Diary of Kōkan's Trip to the West

The most interesting of the visitors to Deshima was Shiba Kōkan (1747?–1818), a painter, philosopher, and great eccentric. His journey to Nagasaki in 1788 is described in *Kōkan Saiyū Nikki* (*Diary of Kōkan's Trip to the West*), a work marked by the author's unique personality and by the frankness with which he related his experiences. Reading Kōkan's diary, we may feel the shock of suddenly being brought face to face with a three-dimensional figure after the many two-dimensional diarists of the preceding couple of centuries. It is tempting (but probably incorrect) to surmise that the techniques of European painting, which Kōkan studied and employed, had enabled him to portray himself in the round, as a creature with the complexity and even contradictions of a real human being, rather than as a mere figure in the landscape of a handscroll depicting a journey. Not since the thirteenth century's *The Confessions of Lady Nijō* had any diarist presented himself so candidly.

Many passages in the diary demonstrate Kōkan's individuality, but the following is perhaps the most startling. On the 3rd day of the 2nd month of 1789, while on his return journey from Nagasaki to Edo, Kōkan was invited to a deer hunt in the province of Bitchū. He related: "A deer showed itself by the pond, only to escape into the mountains on the other side. Guns rained bullets on the deer until one finally struck him and he emerged into a bamboo thicket. I ran up and tore off one of the deer's ears. I sucked the deer's lifeblood, to the consternation of everyone. I did this because I had heard that a deer's living blood is an excellent medicine for promoting long life." Later he heard others in the party say, "That's Kōkan from Edo. He tore off a deer's ear and drank the blood—that's the kind of frightening man he is."[1]

Kōkan's action may horrify the reader, but he will not forget it or the author. Moreover, although Kōkan made no comment about the people who gossiped about him, he clearly felt superior to them and their conventional ways. I cannot recall a similar passage in any work written before the twentieth century. Kōkan's action was barbarous, but it may strike us as also being curiously modern in its unpredictability. It is impossible to imagine earlier diarists of the Tokugawa period behaving in so unusual a manner.

Kōkan emerges from the pages of his diary as a complete extrovert. Wherever he went he displayed his copperplate etchings and his camera obscura (*nozokimegane*), and, as he often reported, people were inevitably struck dumb with admiration, unable to believe that such wonderful inventions could have been made in Japan. Kōkan was sure that every Japanese with an education knew about him: "No matter where I go, few people are unfamiliar with my name."[2] He reported that, when he showed a certain man an oil painting he had executed on glass (*biidoro*), the man paid him the deference due a god.[3] Kōkan's readiness to talk about himself, when more modest men would have remained silent, extended to his sex life. He described without embarrassment the nights he spent at brothels, and gave not only the names of the prostitutes with whom he slept but the price.

A memorable section of the diary is devoted to a description of a whale hunt. When, on the return journey, Kōkan reached the island of Ikitsukishima, he showed such interest in the stories he heard about whaling that the whalers urged him to go to sea with them. He demurred, but early one morning "they came around to hurry me. 'Let's go!' they said, so I poured cold water on my rice and gulped down a bowl, and went immediately afterward on board. I don't know which was faster, my getting aboard or their plying of the oars. In any case, the whole thing went by as quick as an arrow."

Not until evening was a whale sighted. Kōkan recorded: "I had eaten nothing since morning but one bowl of rice. I was tossed about by the waves, and seasickness made me feel terrible. However, the boat all but flew under the furious beat of the oars toward Oshima. The men called as they rowed, '*Ariya, ariya, ariya, ariya*.'[4] I felt surprisingly unwell, and lay down amid the ropes attached to the harpoons. After we had run some four *ri*, I lifted my head just in time to see a whale leap out of the water, blow salt water, then return to the depths of the ocean. Seven or eight boats surrounded it. The owner, Matanosuke, shouted, 'We've caught a whale!' This made me feel a lot better. While I watched, I could see the handles and ropes of the harpoons as the boats were rowed a bare two or three *ken* away from the whale, all but riding on the whale's back. The whale took seventeen harpoons. This meant that it was dragging seventeen boats. Gradually the whale weakened, and it stopped spouting sea water and spouted only air instead."[5]

One does not often encounter such exciting passages in diaries, probably because few diarists have possessed Kōkan's adventurous disposition. Kōkan never stated why he kept a diary, but undoubtedly he intended to publish it. The first version of his diary account of his journey to Nagasaki, called *Saiyū Ryodan* (*Chats on a Journey to the West*), was published in 1790, a year after his return to Edo, and was reprinted several times, sometimes with a changed title and illustrations. The final version, *Diary of Kōkan's Trip to the West*, was not published until 1815. At the conclusion of this work Kōkan explained, "Some years ago I illustrated and published in five volumes *Chats on a Journey to the West*. At present I have retired and am of no use to the world. I have recorded here the travels of twenty-eight years ago, basing myself on what I set down daily at the time."[6] Twenty-eight years (by Japanese calculation) after he made the journey, it still ranked as so important an event in his life that he rewrote the account once again, making it even fuller and more detailed.

At the outset of the diary Kōkan declared, "I have made up my mind to go now to Nagasaki and to tour other provinces, resolved not to return before three years have elapsed."[7] He gave no explanation as to why he had decided to go to Nagasaki. At various places along the way, acquaintances tried to dissuade him from making so long a journey, but he was absolutely adamant. Scholars have often suggested that Kōkan's purpose was to study Dutch painting. Perhaps so, but Kōkan made no mention in his diary of inquiring about Dutch painting, either of the Dutchmen he met on Deshima or of the Japanese painters in Nagasaki who practiced the Dutch style. He mentioned having met the painter Araki Tamenoshin (known as Gen'yū, 1732–99), but all he said about this man was, "He serves as an appraiser of pictures, and for that reason paints a little himself. Completely inept."[8]

Indeed, Kōkan never suggests that he had anything to learn from another person. He had boundless confidence in his abilities. Again and again he noted in his diary how impressed people were with his paintings. At Yamada (near Ise), to his great surprise, he met a man who had never heard of him. He described the experience:

" 'I am a person called Shiba Kōkan from Edo. Have you never heard my name?' The man answered, 'That's right. I've never heard your name before.' At this point I took out the various paintings I had brought with me and showed them to him. Among them were some painted in the Dutch style. There was one in which a man's frizzy whiskers seemed to be alive. Seeing them, his attitude changed abruptly. He said, 'Go first to the Inner Shrine,[9] and tonight I'll have the pleasure of putting you up. Please stay as long as you wish.' I therefore paid my respects at the shrine, and on the way back stopped at his place. He had a feast ready, quite a change from his previous attitude, and he urged me to try his saké and the things to eat with the drinks. That night I planned to stay there, but he asked me for a Dutch-style picture. Dutch pictures, unlike the crude sketches he wanted, are painted with wax oil and cannot be executed in a couple of hours. So I made my escape, telling him that I would like to take a look at the brothel across the street. I went there and was soon surrounded by thirteen or fourteen prostitutes."[10]

Kōkan illustrated the diary with sketches made on the spot. The first version of the diary had line drawings, but in *Diary of a Trip to the West* he used shading and other Western techniques. These pictures show landscapes, a child eating the remains of Kōkan's lunch, gravestones, fishermen at Ikitsukishima, and so on. Kōkan also mentioned having drawn the portrait of Yoshio Kōsaku (1724–1800), the chief interpreter at Deshima: "I dashed off a portrait in ink of Kōsaku seated and dressed in *hakama* and *haori*,[11] with a Dutch book in his hand, and with trumpet-playing angels above."[12] This portrait has been preserved. The name "Yoshiho

Koosak" appears near the top of the picture, and immediately below the name are two cavorting cupids, one blowing a trumpet and the other holding a plaque inscribed with Shiba Kōkan's name in roman letters. The portrait is hardly a combination of the best in traditional Japanese and Dutch techniques of painting, but it testifies to the boldness of Kōkan's imagination.

The high point of Kōkan's visit to Nagasaki was his visit to the Dutch factory[13] on the island of Deshima. He encountered more than the usual difficulties in obtaining permission to make the visit, because the local officials supposed he might be a spy (*ommitsu*) of the Senior Councilor (*rōjū*), Matsudaira Sadanobu. He dressed himself as a merchant from Edo, and in this guise finally secured the needed permission. Before being allowed on the island, however, he was carefully searched. It was forbidden to bring anything to the island, no doubt for fear of smuggling.

Kōkan had met the Dutch surgeon Stoessel the year before at the inn in Edo where the Dutch stayed during their visits to the Shogun's capital, and had promised to meet him again in Nagasaki. Kōkan related: "That was why he got up as soon as he saw me and led me to a deserted cowshed. On the way he talked about something or other, but I couldn't understand anything. The only word I could catch was *tekenen* [drawings]. He meant by this that he wanted my drawings of the castle in Edo and the various *mitsuke* [approaches to the Shogun's palace]. After that he said, '*Mijnheer kom kamer, kom kamer.*' This I understood perfectly. *Mijnheer* means 'you.' *Kamer* is a room. *Kom*, *kom* means 'come, come.' So I followed him and went up to the second floor, still wearing my muddy shoes. Dirty tatami were spread on the floor. Everybody was standing, and no one sat down."[14]

Kōkan unhesitantly followed the Dutchman upstairs. His ease with the foreigners impressed the other Japanese. "When they saw me chatting with the Dutchman, they were really astonished."[15] Kōkan was offered some liquor, which he drank. "It was some sort of drink like *doburoku* [unrefined saké]. It tasted sour, and I said *sushi*, *sushi*, to which he replied *kusuri*, *kusuri*,[16] and pointed at an egg. *Kusuri* is a Japanese word." The Dutchman had evidently picked up a smattering of Japanese.

Kōkan went next to the interpreters' room. Yoshio Kōsaku and the others escorted him to the room of the factory director. Kōkan was surprised by the director's servant: "This black man was not from Holland but from the island of Java, a Dutch overseas base in the region of India, or he may have been a native of the African continent. He was born in a tropical country called Mōtāpa."[17] The director's room was about twenty mats in size. Kōkan noted the framed pictures on the walls, the row of chairs, and the silver spittoons next to each chair. As for the room itself, "They had spread over the tatami a woven material, rather like a felt carpet, with a floral pattern, and they hung from the ceiling a chandelier made of glass. Hidden behind a crimson curtain was a place looking like a study. The windows are all of glass." The director, a long pipe in his hand, came forward to meet Kōkan. He said with satisfaction, "Splendid room, isn't it?" Kōkan sarcastically commented, "He probably said this because they think it is extremely unrefined of the Japanese not to decorate their rooms in this way. I replied that I was dazzled by the splendor."[18]

At this point two black servants came in bearing silver trays on which were placed glasses and decanters ornamented with gold designs. The liquor served was *anyswijn* (anise wine), which, according to Kōkan, was a variety of alcohol made with fennel. Kōkan wrote, "It is strong liquor, so I gave it back to the person who had offered it to me."

Kōkan had also met the captain (the factory director) in Edo, and would meet him once more, during his return journey to Edo from Nagasaki. Nothing extraordinary occurred during Kōkan's visit to Deshima, but his ability to get along familiarly with Dutchmen undoubtedly confirmed his high opinion of himself. That night, after leaving Deshima but still in its spirit, he ate raw beef. "It tastes rather like wild duck," he commented.

One finds equally diverting insights into Kōkan's personality in his essays. Arthur Waley, writing in 1927 about one collection, said, "Shiba Kōkan was the first person in Japan to feel that to be Far Eastern meant, in the world sense, to be provincial; to realize that his own country lay and had lain for centuries far aside from the main stream of human culture and discovery."[19] One may not agree with this judgment, but Kōkan's writings are bound to strike any reader as unprecedented, the faithful reflection of an extraordinary man.

Journal of a New Era

The fame of Ōta Nampo (1749–1823) is as a comic writer, though he received the education in the Confucian classics appropriate for a member of the samurai class and was so precocious a scholar that he published a study of Ming poetry at the age of seventeen. His education, however, did not at first help him to earn a living, and he therefore followed his natural bent and took to composing and publishing comic poetry in Chinese, comic *waka*, and eventually comic books not much different from today's. Because he belonged to the lowest rank of samurai, he seemed to have virtually no chance of ever advancing in governmental service; but after the death of the corrupt Tanuma Okitsugu in 1786, his successor as the head of the government, Matsudaira Sadanobu, initiated a program of reform and offered official positions to talented samurai, even those of humble rank. Nampo responded to this opportunity and became an official. Although he had already won a reputation as a comic writer, he took his official duties seriously and was steadily promoted. In 1801, the first year of the Kyōwa era, he was commanded to proceed to the copper exchange in Osaka. His diary records this first important journey of his life; the title refers to the change in era name.[1]

Nampo prepared himself for the journey by reading everything available concerning the Tōkaidō, ranging from *The Sarashina*

Diary to the latest book on famous sights. He dutifully stopped at well-known places and listened to the explanations offered, but he was generally skeptical; and sometimes he even refused to look at dubious relics.[2]

As he traveled, Nampo made it his practice to copy down the inscriptions on every stone monument or ornamental plaque he noticed. Perhaps that is one reason I feel so close to the author as I read his *Journal of a New Era.* Such monuments and plaques still survive. Within a one-minute walk of my apartment house in Tokyo there are monuments dating from the eighteenth century which Nampo might have seen had he been traveling in the opposite direction. Sometimes, however, he had trouble deciphering the inscriptions. At the Sōun-ji, the Zen temple in Hakone built by the Hōjō family, he informs us: "When I got down from my palanquin and went inside the temple grounds, the Kyōto cherry trees were blooming profusely. I tried to make out the inscription on the bell tower, but the words were so defaced that I could barely read the characters for '2nd year of Gentoku' [1330]. I took out the waxed ink[3] I keep in my wallet and made a rubbing."[4] I can visualize Nampo making a rubbing of the inscription, then searching for the tombs of the five generations of Hōjō regents. "Moss had spread over the gravestones, but the writing could be read clearly. They must have been erected in later times. When I thought of the power of the Hōjōs, once a fair match for the over seventy castles of the Ch'i,[5] I could not stop the tears from flowing."[6]

On the whole, however, Nampo's impressions of his journey were cheerful. Although he traveled on official business, he did not hesitate to mention mundane occurrences. When he stopped for a while at a place called Hata because his palanquin bearers were tired and his escorts were not feeling well, "From the row of wine shops women came swarming out, and their cries, urging us to rest at one place or enter another place, sounded like the chirping of a hundred, or even a thousand birds."[7]

Nampo revealed himself in the pages of his diary as a staunch adherent of the Tokugawa family. When he passed Shizuoka, the place from which the Tokugawas had originated, he wrote, "When I heard that the castle at Sumpu[8] during the Keichō era[9] was the seat of the god whose name I mention with reverence, I felt somehow afraid and bent low in my palanquin as we passed."[10] Later, in the province of Mikawa, he visited the temple Hōzō-ji, where he saw a pine that was known as "the pine where the copybook was hung" because "our divine lord as a child practiced penmanship at this temple and hung his copybook on this pine to dry."[11] But such expressions of awe are not what make Nampo's diary so appealing. It is because of the closeness we feel to a traveler who describes a Japan that still survives vestigially.

Nampo strikes the reader as being "modern" because he was more interested in what he actually saw than in the traditional, poetic associations of the various sites. He journeyed over a route that was familiar from the accounts of many earlier travelers, but he relied on his own eyes and never became an anonymous wanderer. To the end he remained Ōta Nampo, and he scattered bits of autobiographical information here and there in his diary, such as his references to his granddaughter: "Today is the 3rd of the 3rd month,[12] and I am sure that people at home are gathering around my granddaughter and exchanging cups of peach wine. Since it also happens to be my birthday, I gave my attendants silver coins to celebrate."[13] After reaching Kyōto, he wrote, "When I looked up at the height of the Yasaka Pagoda, I recalled how the great Jōzō tried out his spiritual powers. In this area people sell clay dolls in their houses. Thinking it might amuse my granddaughter at home, I bought one and put it in the fold of my cloak."[14] I had never before heard about the priest Jōzō, who, by dint of prayers, righted the leaning Yasaka Pagoda, but I well know the street behind the pagoda Nampo visited, and the shops there still sell clay dolls.

Nampo's references to what he ate during his journey are more specific than those in earlier diaries. At Arai, for example, "I heard that the eels were good, and when I stopped at a certain drinking place and ate some, the flavor was indeed excellent."[15] At Kameyama he was tempted by the tofu: "The market below the castle is hardly bustling. It is a provincial place where they hang square signs from the eaves saying 'Boiled Tofu,' 'Fried Tofu,' or just plain 'Tofu' or 'Devil's Tongue,' etc."[16]

The city-bred Nampo naturally found Kameyama provincial,

and it was with relief that he arrived in Kyōto. Outside the city he changed clothes, as a mark of respect for the capital: "When we reached a place called Keage Springs, there was to the left a clean-looking teahouse. I went in and changed from my travel gear to a short-sleeved crested robe and a linen *kamishimo*.[17] Then I returned to my palanquin and sat formally inside. As we went along, I looked to my right, and there was Sanjō Street."[18] That night, after changing back to his travel garb, he went sightseeing in the city. He stopped at one shop "and I ate the famous tofu *dengaku*[19] and drank saké. The noise of the women cutting the tofu was deafening. Next to us, behind bamboo blinds, many people were disporting themselves. They called a woman and had her cut tofu for them. She came quickly, carrying a chopping board. The sound of the chopping resembled that of rhythmical cutting of the Seven Herbs."[20]

My pleasure in reading Nampo's account of his visit to Kyōto is heightened by the knowledge that almost every building he mentioned still stands. It is possible to follow his footsteps from temple to temple, and to admire the same votive pictures and plaques he described. In that sense, too, he may seem modern.

Nampo left Fushimi by boat for Osaka, where he was to spend a year. He reflected: "As I lay in my cabin this evening on the Fushimi boat, I recalled all the sad and happy things that had occurred during the fifty-three stages of the journey from Azuma, 'where birds sing,' to Ōtsu, 'where horses return when it gets dark,'[21] as I climbed over steep mountains and crossed over broad expanses of sea. Since this year I also turned fifty-three, I had written in my New Year's poem:

> My path through the world is like traveling the Tōkaidō;
> There are fifty-three inns, one for each stage of life.

I realize now that I must have had a premonition I would take this journey, and the premonition took form in words. I turned and tossed in bed any number of times, neither awake nor asleep, and before I knew it, we seem to have gone the thirteen *ri* down the river."[22]

Journal of a New Era probably consisted originally merely of notes taken by Nampo along the way. In Osaka he was busy with official duties, but "in my moments of leisure I dashed off my recollections of the journey I took, as they came back to me."[23] Nampo, instead of including within the diary itself the poems he had composed on the way, gathered them in an appendix. Perhaps he considered that comic poetry was beneath the dignity of an official, but these examples prove he had not lost his touch as a *kyōka* (comic-*waka*) poet. The diary concludes, "I have written down only personal matters, omitting everything of a public nature. My style is clumsy, my inspiration halting, and the contents are tedious. I ask my descendants, if—heaven willing—I have any, not to show the work to strangers."[24] Fortunately, his descendants disregarded the injunction and preserved for us this enjoyable example of a travel diary.

Bakin's Diaries

When reading the diaries of such writers as Shiba Kōkan or Ōta Nampo, we are often struck by perceptions or opinions that seem surprisingly "modern." It gives us pleasure to discover traits in them that we ourselves share, though they lived in a world quite different from our own. But such traits do not constitute the whole person. We know almost nothing, for example, about Kōkan's relations with members of his family, his friendships, or, for that matter, what discontent he may have felt with his society. When we read the diaries of Takizawa Bakin (1767–1848), on the other hand, almost nothing is kept from us. We learn not only his life within his family, his work as a writer, and his daily round of activities but (indirectly, at least) his feelings about contemporary society. He is the first Japanese whom we know in such detail, and his are the first truly modern diaries.

Bakin's surviving diaries were first printed only in 1973, in four volumes. The unique copies of other diaries were destroyed during the Great Earthquake of 1923, when the library of Tokyo University burned. We know of these destroyed manuscripts only the excerpts made in 1911 by several scholars. The volume published at that time is easier to read than the unedited diaries, because it presents significant passages classified under such headings as "his blindness," "his reverence for the gods," and "his friendships." Reading these excerpts is the best introduction to the four-volume collection of diaries.

A special feature of Bakin's diaries that sets them apart from earlier diaries kept in Japanese is that they were kept day to day, rather than written months or even years after the events described. The diaries written in Chinese by statesmen of the past were kept in the same manner, but they rarely discussed the private matters that abound in Bakin's diaries. Writing so detailed a diary each day must have cost Bakin considerable effort, but he never neglected the diary, even after his health deteriorated. In 1836 he wrote, "Of late I have been so busy I have not had a moment to spare. I always write this diary in the morning, but today I had pressing business, things to write and so on, and I wrote the diary after dark by lamplight."[1]

He persisted in keeping the diary even after his eyesight began to fail, though he then had to confine himself to recording only essentials. He wrote in 1840: "My eyesight has deteriorated so much that I can no longer distinguish fine print. This makes writing extremely inconvenient, so this year I will abbreviate my diary and record only visitors, work performed, and important matters that absolutely cannot be omitted. However, there are still blank pages left in this diary, and I will continue keeping the diary as long as there is paper left."[2]

The importance of the diary to Bakin was not primarily literary. Like the courtiers of the past who scrupulously kept diaries in Chinese in order to record precedents and other court matters that they deemed vital, Bakin relied on his diary as an authentic record of what happened in his life each day. By consulting the diary he could tell, for example, what he had promised other people or what they had promised him. But our reasons for reading his diaries are of course different. Although they are only occasionally of literary appeal, they describe faithfully the daily round of activities of the leading man of letters of his age. The diaries cover, for example, the period when Bakin was writing his most celebrated novel, *Hakkenden* (*The Biographies of Eight "Dogs"*), and make it possible for us to follow his efforts to produce a masterpiece. For example, on the 5th day of the 2nd month of 1832 he wrote, "I have written a preface of two and a half pages for the eighth volume of *Hakkenden*. However, on thinking it over, I found that some places still seem inappropriate, and I have decided therefore not to use these pages. I will rewrite the preface tomorrow. Tonight I did not get to bed until past ten." The next day he noted, "I finished writing the preface to the eighth volume of *Hakkenden*, but there is still much to correct. I spent the whole day mulling it over, but did not manage to get through it."[3]

The problems Bakin encountered when writing *Hakkenden* were not confined to his own text. He worried also about the illustrations, and later complained that the versions made for the Kabuki and Jōruri stages were unsatisfactory. Nowhere else in premodern Japan does one find so complete a picture of an author at work.

Bakin's diary is memorable also for what it tells us concerning his relations with his wife, son, and daughter-in-law. He seems never to have loved his wife, Ohyaku, and though she bore him four children she made life miserable for him with her hysterical outbursts. One especially dramatic entry in the diary relates an event of 1838:

"Tonight Ohyaku once again poured out her grievances on me, and said she was going to take Buddhist vows and suchlike things. I quietly remonstrated with her, saying that the turmoil that has afflicted our household during the past seven years was, in the final analysis, entirely my own fault, and she had no reason to feel bitter toward anyone else. When a man and wife are over seventy years old, how many years more do they have left to live? I patiently urged her not to wear herself out mentally with anger that served no useful purpose, but to recognize that everything was the result of my shortcomings. But she was by no means satisfied with this. She vented a little more of her wrath before she finally stopped. It is difficult even for a sage to train women and worthless people.[4] How much truer this is for an ordinary man like myself. It's really shaming."[5]

Ohyaku's hysteria was aggravated by various physical ailments, and more than once she created scenes that made it impossible for Bakin to work: "The disorder in the house was such that today I had to discontinue my writing, and I gave up trying to dispose of other affairs. It is all because of my lack of virtue, and I feel resentment toward no other person. I am the only one at fault. This is terrible. It calls for the greatest caution."[6] Bakin not only endured Ohyaku's bouts of hysteria but even blamed himself for the unhappy atmosphere in his household.

Ohyaku died in 1841. The part of Bakin's diary that describes her death has been lost, but we can infer his reactions from a letter written at the time, which contains this poem of mourning:

mare ni mitsu	Days when she still lived
mare ni towarete	And I saw her but rarely,
arishi hi wo	And rarely was addressed,
ima koso oshime	I recall now with regret—
tsui no wakareji	The last parting of the ways.

Bakin's relations with his son Sōhaku constitute another important section of his diaries. Bakin was determined that Sōhaku restore the Takizawa family to its rightful status as samurai. Bakin himself as a young man had left service with the Matsudaira family and become a *rōnin*, but he had never reconciled himself to being a mere townsman. He could not regain his samurai status; instead, he pinned his hopes on Sōhaku. He saw to it that Sōhaku received training as a physician, and his efforts to establish Sōhaku's credentials as a samurai seemed to have been crowned with success when Matsumae Akihiro, the former daimyo of Ezo (Hokkaidō), appointed Sōhaku as physician to his clan, thereby conferring samurai status. Akihiro was restored to his fief in 1821, but Sōhaku refused to accompany him to Ezo. In the following year Sōhaku fell ill, and this illness persisted until his death in 1835.

Bakin at first seems to have been crushed by this misfortune, but somehow he roused himself and began to write again the continuation of *Hakkenden*. He was now troubled by failing eyesight. The first ominous signs of what would develop into near blindness occurred in 1834, as he recorded in his diary: "My right eye has not been normal since this morning, and it gives me some pain. I cannot see at all with the right eye. I described my condition to Sōhaku, and I have been bathing my eye with a solution all day." A month later he wrote, "I have been writing small characters at night by lamplight. That must be why my left eye also gives me a little pain and sometimes it blinks. I have decided that henceforth I will not write at night. I must rest my eyes."[7] Increasingly gloomy entries trace the deterioration of his sight. He all but despaired of ever completing *Hakkenden*. In the 5th month of 1840 he wrote, "Today my eyes are in terrible shape. I have to grope in order to write." But in the depths of despair he discovered that succor was at hand. Just a month after writing about the terrible condition of his eyes, he stated in his diary: "My old eyes have of late been more and more clouded over. I am unable to write a manuscript in small characters, so this afternoon I composed a text in my head and told Omichi how to write it. It was two and a half pages, to the end of the second chapter, and I bound it in with what had come before. It was dictation, pure and simple."[8] Omichi, the widow of Sōhaku, became Bakin's amanuensis during his years of near blindness, and was also his greatest comfort.

Sōhaku had not been a good husband to Omichi. The pressure from his father to restore the fortunes of the Takizawa family exhausted him spiritually and contributed to his illness; this in turn occasioned the terrible tantrums he directed at Omichi and the servants. As his illness grew worse, he feared (quite understandably) that after his death Omichi would leave a household where she had experienced only unhappiness. He wrote for her benefit a last testament in which he stated that he would not hold it against her if she decided to remarry, but he urged her to remain in his house a while longer, to look after his aged parents and their own small children. Omichi accepted this responsibility, and after Sōhaku's death made herself indispensable to Bakin, preparing the medicines he needed and serving as his scribe. As early as 1837 Bakin wrote, "Ever since we moved here, in the 11th month of last year, Omichi has been particularly diligent. She really has not a moment of her own. We could not do without her."[9]

Bakin was indeed fortunate to have had so willing and devoted a scribe, but it was by no means easy for him to dictate his compositions to a woman whose education had not prepared her for such a task. Occasionally, impatient because she had not recognized the Chinese character in a book she was reading aloud to him, he would terminate a session. Fortunately, Omichi was intelligent, and learned so quickly that she was eventually able even to sign his name convincingly.[10] Without Omichi's assistance *Hakkenden* could not have been completed.

Bakin's diaries contain innumerable references not only to his family but to such friends as the painters Katsushika Hokusai, Tani Bunchō, and Watanabe Kazan, and to such authors as Ryūtei Tanehiko. Perhaps the most affecting entry concerning his friends is one dated the 23rd day of the 1st month of 1842:

"It has been reliably reported that Watanabe Noboru, also

known as Kazan, the *yōnin*[11] of Miyake, the governor of Bingo,[12] who had been under house arrest, committed suicide at Tawara in Mikawa during the middle of the 12th month of last year.[13] Yamakawa Hakushu[14] first heard this as a rumor. He characterized it as the resolution of a loyal subject. A most pitiable event . . . Kazan had his parents, his wife, his daughter. What an unhappy fate for all of them!"[15]

This was about as close to expressing a political opinion as the cautious Bakin ever came. He was terrified lest he share the fate of other writers and artists who were arrested during the Tempō Reforms.[16] He reported in his diary entry for the 6th day of the 4th month of 1842: "It is reported that Ichikawa Ebizō[17] is much given to extravagance in his daily life. He is being kept in manacles pending an investigation. Making note of this serves no useful purpose, but I have let my brush scribble it down, to aid my memory." In the 6th month of the same year Bakin reported in his diary that new decrees had been proclaimed by the government regulating the publication of books and woodblock prints. On the 15th of that month he wrote: "I hear that seven publishers, the artist [Utagawa] Kuniyoshi, and three woodblock cutters have been fined five *kanmon*[18] each. The author [Tamenaga] Shunsui was sentenced to fifty days in manacles; the blocks of his books were planed down or broken; and the bound books, after being broken apart, have been consigned to the fire."[19] In the 8th month Bakin noted that the celebrated author Ryūtei Tanehiko had died in prison.[20]

The above excerpts from Bakin's diaries are preserved in the extracts made by the novelist and theater critic Aeba Kōson (1855–1922). It is unfortunate that Aeba did not copy more of the diaries before they were destroyed in the Great Earthquake. Some diary entries, like those that describe the Tempō Reforms, are noteworthy because of their contents; others are expressed so beautifully that the Meiji-period scholar Yoda Gakkai (1833–1909) declared, "The wonder of the style of Kyokutei [Bakin] is exhibited to the highest degree in these diaries."[21] The reader will find much to interest him in the individual entries, though the accounts of trivial occurrences at times are tedious; but most of all the reader is likely to be attracted by the detailed portraits the diaries as a whole present of a great writer and his world.

The Diary of Iseki Takako

The diary of Iseki Takako (1785–1845) was unknown until it was discovered in 1972. Six years later an annotated text of the diary in three volumes was published, but attracted little attention. It is nevertheless a diary of exceptional interest, worthy to stand alongside Bakin's as a document of the late Tokugawa period and superior to his in literary interest. A typical diary entry begins with the mention of some event, then develops into one or more essays on related topics. This format has tempted enthusiasts into referring to Takako as the "Sei Shōnagon of the Edo period." Her diary has none of Sei Shōnagon's flashing wit, but the vivid expression of her views on the world and the unusual range of topics treated entitle Takako to a place in the company of major diary writers.

Takako kept her diary from 1840 to 1845, between her fifty-sixth and sixtieth years. She died three weeks after writing the last entry. These diaries were written so late in Takako's life that there is naturally none of the romantic interest found in the diaries of the Heian court ladies. There is, in fact, surprisingly little autobiographical material, but as an evocation of life during the Tempō era it is superb.

Takako was the daughter of one *hatamoto*[1] and the wife of another. Her husband was a widower nineteen years older than herself, but she seems to have experienced no difficulty in thinking of his son and grandson as her own. Her birth and the positions of her husband's son and grandson in the Shogun's palace enabled her to move in high circles, and this made it possible for her to be better informed about the Shogun's court than an outsider, and for her diary to be at times more accurate than the official records.

She gave her reasons for keeping a diary in these terms: "What I am now writing, with my inadequate intelligence and clumsy brush, is not intended to be broadcasted to the world. I am writing this in order to let the young people of my family and their children in future generations know a little of how our family lives today and what our world is like. No doubt these scraps of paper will become the haunt of bookworms or be dragged off by mice for their nests, but even if that happens, it will make a wonderful diversion."[2]

This passage is typical of Takako's manner. She wrote in the pseudo-Heian style called *gabun* (elegant language), perhaps because of her devotion to *kokugaku* (national learning);[3] her preference, evident throughout the diary, was always for what was "purely Japanese." The use of *gabun*, rather than the epistolary style favored by Bakin or the mixed style of other diarists of the period, was normal for an educated woman, but Takako clearly also had literary intent when she wrote her diary, despite her claim that she was writing only for her descendants. Some entries, such as the long and highly dramatic account of a failed lovers' suicide, unmistakably reveal her literary gifts. But this literary aspect does not contradict the stated purpose of the diary. Takako believed that, although people do not change fundamentally, customs do change from generation to generation, and it is through literature that we understand the past:

"When we look at the romances of long ago, they seem to have been inspired by a desire to portray, exactly as they were, in an interesting and amusing manner, the customs of the past and the circumstances in which people lived. However, the world has greatly changed, and even though human emotions are not all that altered, innumerable things differ from what they were in the past, from the laws of the land to the daily life of the people, and in most respects the differences are surely more numerous. If someone today planning to write an essay or a story merely imitates the elegance of the past, and does not describe the splendid world we live in now, this will surely be both unsatisfying and regrettable."[4]

As this passage demonstrates, Takako was by no means a blind worshipper of the past. She insisted on the importance of the present as well, and warned people not to overrate things solely because they were old: "It is human nature to revere the things and writings of the past. That is why people crave old things, though not all the writings and poetry of long ago are masterpieces. Even extremely dirty-looking and ugly things are prized as treasures, providing they are over five hundred years old."[5]

Such down-to-earth reasoning is characteristic of Takako, but, for all her rejection of a mindless veneration of the past, she seems to have been unable to take the daring step of expressing herself in the language of her own day.

Contrasting the ways of past and present, Takako noted that hair styles, even of women of the better class, were now modeled on those worn by entertainers, actresses, and prostitutes. She continued, "Change, according to the occasion, is the way of the world, not only in how the hair is dressed but in the sewing of clothes, the shapes of dyed stuffs, and in fabric patterns."[6] In the past well-born ladies had dyed and sewn even formal kimonos, but today such work was left to professionals.

In such matters Takako seems to have preferred the old ways, but in more crucial respects she thought the present was superior. She could not tolerate old superstitions, and took pride in the fact that she had never been influenced by them: "In the past everybody, whether of the upper or lower classes, was terribly afraid of such things as 'forbidden directions' and 'taboos,'[7] and took every precaution not to offend, but nowadays nobody even talks about such things. In general, beliefs of that nature were from the outset devised by human minds, and even if it is convincingly argued that there is textual authority, the words and the beliefs themselves were the work of human beings of the past, and in most cases were probably devised by yin-yang diviners[8] and suchlike dubious priests."[9]

Takako was merciless in her contempt for superstition. She asked rhetorically what possible harm could befall one if one disregarded beliefs invented by deluded people. Some persons still believed in superstitions, but it brought them no benefits. "These things have lingered on from the past, but they are of absolutely no use."[10] She herself had never suffered because she had refused to believe in superstitions: "From my childhood days I have paid not the least attention to any of the taboos, but nothing unusual has happened to me; in fact, I have been fortunate enough to live longer than the people who observed them."[11] Ki no Tsurayuki in *The Tosa Diary* mentioned that he had not trimmed his nails on a certain day because it was inauspicious, but she had never worried about such things, and nothing untoward had ever occurred.

Takako was suspicious of priests of all kinds. She was particularly critical of *inori no shi*, priests who prayed on behalf of other people: "They all do it to make a living. At first they act as if they don't want any reward, lulling any suspicions, but in the end there is not one who does not take presents."[12] Takako also distrusted stories of miracles. She described, for example, the wife of Maki, the daimyo of Shima, who found a small golden image of Kannon in her garden. It was clearly not of Japanese workmanship, and it seemed to have been buried in the ground for a long time. Everyone was overjoyed by this miraculous discovery, and the image was at once enshrined. But, Takako continued, "I hear that the wife took sick and passed away this spring. The empty belief that Buddha comes to welcome people to the Pure Land, or whatever it is called, seems to have come unexpectedly true, but what a pitiable and detestable thing to have happened!"[13]

She disliked Taoism no less than Buddhism, strangely equating Taoism with Christianity: "These 'immortals' try to prolong their lives, but they also want to impress people with their weird tricks and in this way drag them into their religion. They are much like those people who practice the ways of Yaso [Jesus], a religion strictly forbidden in this country."[14]

It might have been expected that Takako, as a woman of the samurai class, would have believed in Confucianism, but she in fact wrote about it unfavorably, mainly because she associated it with China, a foreign country. Here is how she characterized the Confucianist's attitudes with respect to Japanese traditions: "It is the rule for Confucianists to speak with respect about the beginning of heaven and earth and the other miraculous legends of the age of the gods, but in private they go to extremes of mockery and slander, and think they can infer everything from the Five Elements of yin and yang or the principle of the will of heaven."[15]

The only religion she could believe in was Shintō. She wrote that it was more important for Japanese to know the traditions of their own country than to acquire foreign learning: "People who are born in this holy land of the gods should preserve the traditions of the ancient age of our country. They should not seek to display their cleverness, but should accept as unknowable the miraculous and wonderous things of heaven and earth which human intelligence cannot fathom, and excel instead in large-heartedness of spirit."[16]

Takako apparently began her study of *kokugaku* after the death of her husband in 1826. She did not take formal lessons from a particular teacher, but read the works of such eighteenth-century scholars of *kokugaku* as Kamo no Mabuchi and Motoori Norinaga, as well as the *Kojiki* and other basic texts of Shintō. She wrote with admiration of Norinaga that he, above all other scholars of the recent past, deserved credit for having clarified ancient matters and demonstrated that Japan was superior to all other countries.[17]

Her nationalism probably unconsciously reflected an awareness that Japan was in a state of crisis, threatened both with internal dissension and invasion from abroad. She approved of the stringent Tempō Reforms, intended to curb extravagance, and expressed satisfaction that the Kabuki actor Ichikawa Ebizō had been forbidden to come within ten *ri* of the city. "He was punished because he went to extraordinary limits of extravagance in his house, garden, and so on, in the furnishings of his house, and in his clothes. Besides, the costumes he wore in performances were not temporary things but real armor and helmets of surpassing manufacture."[18]

She described with horror the revolt in 1837 of Ōshio Heihachirō (1793–1837), whom she called "a terrible bandit," and was glad that he and all who had joined with him in rebelling against the authority of the shogunate had perished. She even composed a comic poem (*kyōka*) revolving around the name Ōshio, which means literally "Big Salt" or "Big Tide":

misago iru	The people of Naniwa[19]
iso uchikoeshi	Have had a most bitter[20] time
ōshio ni	Because of the big tide
karaki me mitsuru	That has swept over the beach
Naniwabito kana[21]	Where the ospreys dwell.

It was natural for Takako, whose family served the shogunate, to approve of its sumptuary laws or to be indignant when anyone threatened its authority. Her dislike for *rangaku* (Dutch studies) stemmed from the fear that Japanese who studied European science might betray their country. She was especially outraged that Takahashi Kageyasu (1785–1829), the official astronomer and magistrate-librarian,[22] had passed on to the German physician Philipp Franz von Siebold (who was then stationed on Deshima) the survey charts of Japan made by Inō Tadataka (1745–1818), in exchange for a set of Dutch books of exploration. She declared: "It was revealed that he had turned over to the foreigner not any ordinary maps of our great country but copies he himself had made of the official charts. He died while under investigation for this crime, but since he was no commonplace criminal, they say his body was pickled in salt so that the investigation could continue."[23]

It is hard to imagine that a woman of Takako's breeding should have been pleased that a man—even an enemy—had died under torture, and had then been pickled in salt, but her patriotism ran to extremes. Nor did she have any sympathy for Watanabe Kazan when she learned of his arrest, blaming it on his Dutch learning: "He became infatuated with these studies and exchanged letters with others in strange writing. There was a report that these people had formed a faction and that they must be up to some mischief, and they were all officially investigated, but they seem not to have been guilty of any great crime."[24]

Takako was willing to admit that the Dutch (and, by extension, other Europeans) had made scientific discoveries, but she doubted their ultimate importance. The Red-Hairs, as the Dutch were called, had decided the earth was round. Perhaps it was, but the only way really to know the earth was to leave it and observe it from a distance, in much the same way that, in order to see a house properly, one must go outside and examine it from afar. Takako's resistance to science may seem unenlightened, but there was one chink in her defense against foreign learning: medicine. Japan at the time was afflicted with smallpox. Almost no one, not even in the Shogun's palace, escaped the disease. Takako related the experience of her grandchild: "One year Chikakata's son Jirō, who was about four at the time, caught the sickness and died. He was the first. Later Tarō also got sick. His was not a mild case, and for the longest time we were desperately afraid, wondering what we could do to save him. He barely managed to pull through, but the two girls still have not had it, and we are filled with apprehension."[25]

When Takako heard that the Dutch had introduced in Nagasaki a "water treatment,"[26] said to cure all manner of diseases, she expressed no doubts about the propriety of Japanese use of foreign medicine.[27]

Takako's political opinions are especially striking because it was unusual for a woman of that time to express any, but they do not typify the diary as a whole. It is filled with an incredible variety of subjects, each related to some event of a particular day and treated with the perceptivity of a remarkable woman.

The Uraga Diary

Nine years after Iseki Takako penned the last entry in her diary, her fear of foreign enemies assumed concrete form when an American fleet appeared off Uraga. This first step in the "opening of Japan," the most important event of modern Japanese history, has been chronicled in the diaries of several men who actually saw the American and, somewhat later to arrive, Russian fleets. Apart from this historical interest, the diaries also describe, often in a touching manner, the initial contacts of the authors with Western people. The discovery that these foreigners, for all their strangeness, were human beings like themselves is one that persons of both East and West have made again and again in the years since then.

Sakuma Shōzan (1811–64), an adviser of the Matsushiro clan, which was charged with coastal defenses, learned of the arrival of foreigners on the morning of the 4th day of the 6th month of 1853, and this was where he began his diary. He reached Uraga the same night. The next day he recorded in *Uraga Nikki* (*The Uraga Diary*): "This morning I climbed a hill from which I could see the foreign ships lying at anchor. I went to the same place in the evening for another look. The ships could be seen very clearly with the sun shining on them, even places that had not been visible in the morning. At the time they were playing music aboard the ships. The tempi and the rhythms were more or less the same as the drums used during Dutch military drills."[1] It is ironic that the long-dreaded arrival of the foreigners should have been accompanied by a brass band.

The next day one of Commodore Perry's steamships headed north. The Japanese feared it might enter Edo Bay and be joined there by the rest of the fleet. If this happened, the whole city would probably be thrown into a state of panic. Shōzan rushed from Uraga to Ōsawa, where he borrowed a sailboat in which he tried to follow the American steamship, but it soon left him behind. It proceeded as far as Hommoku (in present-day Yokohama), where two small boats were lowered and took soundings, then headed back to Uraga, much to Shōzan's relief.

The presence of the foreign fleet caused immense concern. Shōzan composed a memorial to the shogunate in the name of the daimyo of Shinano, whom he served, in which he urged that troops of the Matsushiro clan be stationed at places where they could make maximum use of the cannons they possessed for defending the coast. Before an answer could be received, the four vessels of the American fleet entered Edo Bay. It seemed likely that they would penetrate to the heart of Edo. Shōzan frantically drilled the inexperienced defense troops. The short *Uraga Diary* concluded on the 13th with the statement, "Practiced handling cannons all day. In the evening a dispatch came reporting the foreigners were leaving their anchorage. We all felt somewhat relieved."[2]

The next year the Americans, with the consent of the shogunate, landed at Yokohama to offer gifts from President Fillmore. Shōzan recorded what took place in *Yokohama Jinchū Nikki* (*The Diary of the Yokohama Camp*). On the 15th day of the 2nd month boats from the foreign ships brought the presents ashore. Shōzan confessed in his diary his curiosity to see what they were: "I went there and cajoled the yeoman[3] into letting me get a private look at the items that the foreigners are offering to the Shogun."[4]

The gifts included three small boats made of copper sheeting. Shōzan was impressed: "This newly invented boat is capsize-proof, no matter how foul the weather may be."[5] There were also miniature trains and agricultural implements with which Shōzan was already familiar from the Dutch encyclopedia he had read.

Two days later one of the foreigners produced a daguerreotype camera[6] and took a picture of Shōzan's horse. This was the first time anyone in Japan had seen a camera, but Shōzan knew about them from Dutch books he had read. He asked the foreigner (through an interpreter) if his camera used iodine or chromium.[7] The American, astonished and delighted that Shōzan knew these words, beckoned to him and allowed Shōzan to examine the camera. Finally, he took Shōzan's picture.[8]

The next day some young Japanese soldiers, annoyed at the lack of discipline among the Americans, which they took as a sign of disrespect, prepared to attack them, but Shōzan, afraid that this would upset the shogunate's arrangements, assembled the soldiers and dissuaded them from any such rash action. He was aware that attacking a handful of foreigners in Yokohama would not solve the problems facing Japan. Soon afterward he was arrested for having encouraged Yoshida Shōin to go abroad on an American ship, and narrowly escaped being sentenced to death. But, despite such setbacks, the course of opening the country he had chosen was moving steadily closer to realization.

The Nagasaki Diary

Kawaji Toshiakira (1801–68) was appointed commissioner of finance (*kanjō bugyō*) in 1852, and was at the same time named officer in charge of coastal defense. This was a critical moment to be assigned these duties: when the American fleet appeared off Uraga in the following year, Toshiakira had to decide how to counter the threat. He in fact recommended to Tokugawa Nariaki (1800–60), the adviser to the senior councilor (*rōjū*), that no drastic action should be taken: the Japanese should calmly wait for the foreigners to go away. This advice so pleased Nariaki that he chose Toshiakira, a newcomer to higher shogunate politics, to go to Nagasaki in the 10th month of 1854 and negotiate with the Russian envoy, Vice Admiral E. V. Putiatin. A year later Toshiakira met the Russians again, this time in Shimoda, where he concluded a treaty of friendship.

Toshiakira's diary of the journey to Nagasaki is by no means the cut-and-dried composition we might expect of an official on a state mission. Following the traditions of the diarists of the past, Toshiakira composed *waka* at various places, sometimes in the lighthearted mood of this one, the first of the journey:

wa ga kuni no	I don't know about
Chishima no hate wa	The ends of the Kurile Islands,

e zo shiranu	A part of our country,
sari tote yoso ni	But all the same, let's not allow
kimi wa torasu na[1]	Another country to rule them.

The diary entries are likely to surprise readers today for another reason: they are the first Japanese diaries to include the daily temperature, given in Fahrenheit. Even more surprising is the personal element, unexpected in a diary kept by a shogunate official, as in this message addressed to his sons and grandsons: "I want you to pay strict attention to what I am about to write. This year, from the 6th to the 7th months, I suffered on the coast through the indescribable heat. Then, from the 11th to the 12th months, I made a journey in the dead of winter, when the cold was equally indescribable. But because I think of the summer as training for the heat, and the winter as training for the cold, traveling in a palanquin, whether in heat or in cold, is no worse for me than a ceremonial entry into a town.[2] If you, having a father or grandfather who disciplines himself in this manner, do not discipline yourselves sufficiently, but hope to be sent in adoption to some good family, or to enjoy an income of five hundred *koku* without stirring from your beds, and you do not bear this in mind, you will surely be punished, and you never in your lifetimes will rise above other people. My sons and grandsons, I'm not interested in any display from you of filial piety. I want you instead to perform your duties to the court and become masters of the literary and martial arts."[3]

These injunctions show Toshiakira in an uncharacteristically severe mood, but even here, in the mention of his refusal to accept filial piety from his sons and grandsons, a little of his unconventionality is suggested.

Along the way to Nagasaki he frequently noted the beauty of the landscapes. These were not *uta-makura*, known chiefly from mentions in poetry, but places that genuinely moved him. On occasion, too, a note of irritation breaks the familiar pattern of the poetic journey: "Today I spent all day in a palanquin; indescribably boring."[4] He went sightseeing in Himeji, inspected kilns for Bizen pottery in Okayama, and observed with dismay that, in the province of Bitchū, "manners suddenly get worse; maids at the inns look like prostitutes; lodgings at the post-stations are extremely poor; and there are many houses in ruins."[5] He expressed astonishment that the province of Aki, despite the richness of its soil, should look so impoverished.[6] When, a month after leaving Edo, he at last reached Miyaichi, in the province of Suō, at the thought that he still had a considerable distance to go before he arrived in Nagasaki he wrote, "This journey has worn us all out."[7]

From Shimonoseki (where he smelled coal for the first time in his life) he crossed to Kyūshū and headed for Nagasaki, which he reached on the 8th day of the 12th month. On the following day he recorded in his diary, "The Japanese translation of another letter from the Russian barbarians has arrived. Now that things have turned out just as I have long expected, my worries for the nation could not be greater. I have no worries about myself; my desire all along has been to offer up my life."[8] Toshiakira did not discuss the contents of the Russian letter, but it proposed an agreement on two issues, the border between Japan and Russia in the north of Japan, and the establishment of trade relations. Probably he felt it was improper to mention official matters in a private diary.

Even before the negotiations began, Toshiakira was faced with such specific problems as whether it would be proper for the Russians to sit on chairs[9] and the Japanese on tatami during the discussions. In the manner of a conscientious Confucian official, he searched for precedents for his decision, going back as far as the record in the *Engi Shiki* (*Procedures of the Engi Era*), compiled in the early tenth century, where it is recorded how the tribal people called the Hayato were received. He also recalled that, when Arai Hakuseki (1657–1725), a Confucian scholar and an adviser to the shogunate, met officials from the Ryūkyū Islands, they had all sat on chairs and stools.[10] However, when the meeting between the Japanese and the Russians actually took place, the Russians brought their own chairs and the Japanese sat on unusually high tatami platforms,[11] the first of many compromises.

On the 11th day of the 12th month, three days after his arrival in Nagasaki, Toshiakira was invited with the other Japanese officials aboard a Russian warship. At first he refused: "I sent word that I would not be able to visit their ship because it involved the national polity of Japan."[12] Eventually, however, he changed his mind, and agreed to visit the Russian ship on the 17th. In the meantime, on the 14th, the Japanese entertained the Russians on shore. Toshiakira seems to have been especially impressed by the hat worn by the Russian envoy: "He wore on his head a hat shaped like a small, tapered tub. It was decorated with gold and had white fur on top. When he went through a door, he removed the hat and carried it in his hand. He kept it in his hand throughout. He wore a sword. This man looks like Nagai, the daimyo of Noto. He has brown hair, which he has let grow about three inches. His beard is the same. They say he is thirty-one, but he looks like sixty."[13]

Toshiakira continued to refer to the Russians as *rojū*—"Russian barbarians"—but he obviously did not consider Putiatin to be a barbarian in the usual sense of the word, as he indirectly indicated by saying that the Russian looked like a daimyo. He was misinformed about Putiatin's age (he was actually fifty-one), but then, as now, Japanese had trouble guessing the ages of foreigners.

After the Russians landed, they were led to a Japanese-style room. It was just the time for a meal, and the Japanese produced a banquet of "three soups and seven vegetables" as well as saké. Unfortunately, the Russians did not know how to use chopsticks, and it was necessary to send hastily for spoons from the Dutch factory on Deshima. Conversation through interpreters (Russian to Dutch to Japanese and vice versa) must have been painful, but Toshiakira was pleased to note that the Russians praised the Japanese food. The meal ended at four in the afternoon, but the Russians were not in a hurry to leave. One young Russian officer, who had apparently picked up a little Japanese, said in the Nagasaki dialect, "*Nagasaki onna, yoka yoka*" ("Nagasaki women, good good").[14] The merrymaking continued into the night. Toshiakira reported that the Russians had been heard imitating the cries of the street fish-vendors and shouting "*aba aba.*" He concluded his description by saying, "However, Japanese were with them all the time. One cannot take chances."[15]

Toshiakira was approached the next day by Matsudaira, the daimyo of Mino, who offered to slash his way aboard the Russian ships with nineteen retainers who were resolved to "die gallantly." They planned to take a small boat, on which they had loaded gunpowder, to the Russian escort ship, transfer the gunpowder to the escort, light it, and then ram the flagship, blowing up both vessels and in this way ridding Japan of the foreign menace. After the daimyo of Mino had taken his leave, Toshiakira assembled his colleagues and addressed them in these terms: "What the daimyo of Mino proposes makes good sense. Attacking and burning the Russian barbarian ships would free us at once from a number of enemies, and for this we should be deeply grateful. However, by doing this we would be creating for the court a new enemy, a big country, and this would not be appropriate. That is why, in the end, I have decided that no one should die."[16]

On the 17th, Toshiakira, along with Tsutsui (the daimyo of Hizen) and various others, went aboard the Russian frigate, where they were welcomed with great ceremony. When the formalities had ended, they were shown "something like a curtain dyed with the ship's emblems[17] of Japan and Russia intertwined as an indication of how fond they were of Japan." Toshiakira commented sarcastically, "It's the same trick that the prostitutes in Edo use to deceive samurai from the country."[18]

Despite the sarcasm, Toshiakira was impressed by the reception in the envoy's cabin. He enjoyed the French wine: "It is made from the juice of grapes. Even if one consumes a great deal, one becomes only slightly drunk, and one sobers very quickly." He made no mention of problems with the unfamiliar food or with using the tableware. He even understood the use of napkins: "Each person is given something like a *furoshiki*.[19] This is placed on the lap against occasions when food is spilled. (Used to wipe the hands and the mouth. Probably also used to wipe the nose.)"[20]

The Japanese, though initially most wary, soon felt quite at home. "I was really astonished at how good they were at entertaining people," commented Toshiakira. He then added parenthetically, "I have been told that foreigners weep with joy if one speaks about one's wife, so I told them that my wife is either the most beautiful or second-most-beautiful woman in Edo."[21] He mentioned how much he missed her, and the Russians, as expected, were delighted. Toshiakira's elderly colleague the daimyo of Hizen joined the conversation to predict that he would still have another child, despite his age. To this the Russians responded with a proverb: "Few babies are born when the father is in his fifties, none at all in his sixties, and even fewer in his seventies, but he becomes young again in his eighties and will have many babies." The overjoyed daimyo of Hizen replied, "I hope things go according to the proverb!"

Toshiakira's conclusion was, "Even though we don't understand each other's language, if you spend thirty days together you can make out the meaning in general. There is not the least difference in human feelings [*ninjō*]. And as for their faces, most of them have big noses and are too pale, but they are all fine-looking men, and if this were Edo some of them would cut quite a figure."[22]

The Shimoda Diary

Before Kawaji Toshiakira left Nagasaki, he was given many presents by the Russians, including a woman's parasol. He attributed this gift to his boastful claim that his wife was one of the most beautiful women in Edo. In his diary he added with wry humor, "Everybody in Nagasaki knows what a beautiful woman Osato is!"[1]

Toshiakira's confidence in his ability to size up men was now extended to include the Russians. He wrote about Putiatin, the envoy, "This is a man of the first importance. There is something extraordinary about the look in his eyes. Indeed, an exceptional man." About Putiatin's secretary, Ivan Alexandrovich Goncharov (1812–91), who was later to gain fame as the author of the novel *Oblomov*,[2] he wrote, "He always sits by the envoy's side and often interposes his own comments. He looks as if he might be a staff officer."[3] Toshiakira could not have foreseen that Goncharov would a few years later publish *The Voyage of the Frigate Pallada*, in which he made fun of the appearance of the Japanese and expressed scorn for their military capabilities.

Toshiakira paid a final visit to Putiatin's ship after accepting three letters that he was to deliver to the shogunate. There were further exchanges of presents, and he had one more look at the interior of the ship. He noticed in particular the portrait of the father of the thirteen-year-old cabin boy who had played the zither (*kin*) for him: "The painting looks as if it's alive. Although he is a foreigner, his love for his son is depicted very movingly. In general, the people of this country all have such feelings."[4] His discovery of universal human sentiments that transcended nationality was quite unlike the usual attitudes of shogunate officials.

When Toshiakira was about to take leave of Putiatin, the latter, detaining him a while, gave him a special present, a miniature train that ran by burning alcohol. He predicted, "We'll meet again in Sakhalin!" However, the two men met next not in Sakhalin but in Shimoda, in the 10th month of 1854. *Shimoda Nikki* (*The Shimoda Diary*), which describes their meetings, contains many noteworthy pages, such as the passage where the Russians ask permission to take Toshiakira's photograph. He relates:

"The Russian barbarians approached me with a request to take my picture. I declined several times, but they would not listen to me, so I tried to evade them in a way that surprised myself, by saying that I have always been ugly, and now that I was old as well, I look like a monster. I asked, 'If it is said that this is what a Japanese man looks like, how do you suppose handsome Japanese men would feel? Besides, I don't want to be laughed at by your Russian beauties.' They replied, 'Among Russian women, the silly ones discuss the merits and demerits of men; the clever ones discuss the merits and demerits of government service. And it is stupid to discuss whether a man is handsome or ugly. There is nothing for you to worry about.' I had known all along that I was an ugly man, but I hadn't realized I was quite *that* ugly. Putiatin, who is a clever man, also seemed rather nonplussed by the turn of phrasing."[5]

In the midst of long, exhausting negotiations, a tidal wave struck Shimoda following a great earthquake. Many people were swept out to sea. The Russian fleet was battered and lost all but the flagship, but the Russians managed nevertheless to save the lives of three Japanese. Toshiakira wrote, "The Russians saved people who were on the point of dying, treated them with every care, even to massaging them. The people who were saved bowed with tears of gratitude."[6] Toshiakira up to this point had almost always referred to the Russians as *rojū*, "Russian barbarians," but from this point on he called them *rojin*, "Russian people." Their kindness had proved that they were human beings.

Kawaji Toshiakira makes an exceptionally attractive figure. His humor and his willingness to abandon his prejudices and recognize that foreigners were human beings and not devils undoubtedly helped him to conclude an advantageous pact with the Russians at Shimoda. His diary does not enter into details of the treaty, but he noted Putiatin's words: "He said, 'I intend to do nothing that will be bad for Japan. You should not have the slightest worry about Sakhalin.' He expressed his thanks in many words. It was rather as if a famished tiger or wolf, encountering a man, drooped its tail and asked for something to eat. Nevertheless, as a human being, standing between heaven and earth, he, too, must at times feel grateful."[7]

Toshiakira was later dispatched to Kyōto to supervise the rebuilding of the imperial palace, which had burned, and he wrote two diaries there. Still later he fell afoul of Ii Naosuke (1815–60), the Great Elder, during the Ansei Purge, and after being deprived of his office was confined to his house. In 1863 he was released and appointed commissioner of foreign affairs (*gaikoku bugyō*), but his health had deteriorated and he soon resigned. On the 15th day of the 3rd month of the 1st year of the reign of the Emperor Meiji, learning that the gates of Edo Castle had been opened to the imperial troops, he committed *seppuku*. Four days before his death he changed his literary name (*gō*) to Gamminsai, meaning something like Studio of the Obstinate Subject, perhaps to indicate his stubborn refusal to follow the new regime, but the understanding he had gained of the West was surely in advance of his time.

Conclusion

In the course of writing *Travelers of a Hundred Ages* I have considered Japanese diaries beginning with Ennin's of 847 and ending with Kawaji Toshiakira's of 1854, a period of a little over a thousand years. Some diaries are only a few pages in length, others run to volumes. The Heian-period diaries, especially those by the court ladies, have often been printed with elaborate commentaries, but many diaries of the Muromachi and Tokugawa periods are available only in collections compiled a hundred years ago and have never been given the benefit of a commentary or even a carefully edited text. Needless to say, the literary value of these diaries varies greatly, ranging from such masterpieces as *The Gossamer Years* and *The Narrow Road of Oku* down to various travel accounts that are of interest only because of a single episode or even a few lines. But I think I have found in all of these diaries, whether short or long, what I was looking for—images of the Japanese in their own words, conveyed in the most personal of literary forms.

An unbroken series of diaries extends from Ennin to Toshiakira and, of course, even to our own day. As far as I am aware, there is no other literature in the world of which this is true. Even amid the warfare of the Middle Ages the diarists continued to write, hoping (perhaps unconsciously) to preserve something from the destruction raging around them. Their hopes were fulfilled, sometimes in ways that they could not have foreseen. Could Sōchō have dreamed as he scribbled his notebook that the comic *renga* he recorded there would be the only examples to survive from the period? And it would have surprised Gen'yo to learn that his diary would provide useful evidence concerning the speed at which Nō plays were performed in his day.

But I did not turn to the diaries for such information. It was for the pleasure of discovering people, in some ways similar to people I know now, in the writings of the past. The best diaries are those that reveal most about their authors, just as the least satisfying are those that merely repeat the traditions of the *utamakura* learned from the poetry and diaries of their predecessors. It is obvious that the Japanese, of both past and present, have taken particular pleasure in seeing with their own eyes sights known from their readings, or eating the "famous products" of a particular place, also as recorded in literature. Some critics have even suggested that the Japanese have never looked at landscapes except across their preconceptions. This is an exaggeration, but it is easy to assent to such a theory when one reads the long series of diaries describing travels along the Tōkaidō, each relating the author's impressions on visiting the same spots as his predecessors. A repetition of experiences, whether participation in the festivals or observances performed on the same day each year or visits to places made famous by people of the past, is indeed typical of Japan, but this is not the only characteristic of the diaries. The intensely personal nature of the Heian-period diaries, or of *Journey Along the Seacoast Road*, *Fitful Slumbers*, and *The Confessions of Lady Nijō*, is not encountered again until the nineteenth century, but the individuality of the writers keeps surfacing again and again in the diaries of even the most traditional writers. It has been in the hopes of finding such passages, where the author reveals himself before our eyes, that I have read diaries, even those that were not as a whole of literary interest, and I have not often been disappointed in my search.

The diary writers are eternal travelers of the ages, whose words reach out to us over the centuries and make them our intimates.

Glossary

aware Pathos or a similarly touching quality, but sometimes used to mean "sensitivity."

biwa A stringed musical instrument somewhat resembling the mandolin in appearance. Sometimes translated as "lute."

chōka A "long poem." The best examples are found in the eighth-century collection *Man'yōshū.*

Cloistered Emperor An emperor who, after having abdicated, takes vows as a Buddhist priest.

-dera At the end of a proper noun signifies a Buddhist temple.

engo A "related word." Refers to the practice of maintaining a unity of imagery by choosing among synonyms one that has a meaning related to the theme. "The airlines launched a crash program" contains an example of an *engo* in English.

gembuku The coming-of-age ceremony formerly undergone by Japanese boys.

hagi A plant whose botanical name is bicolor lespedeza. It has lavender or white blossoms that open in autumn. Sometimes translated as "bush clover."

hokku The opening verse of a linked-verse sequence. It developed into what is now called the haiku, an independent verse in seventeen syllables arranged in three lines.

hototogisu A bird, the *Cuculus poliocephalus*. Sometimes translated as "cuckoo," sometimes also translated as "nightingale."

-ji At the end of a proper name usually signifies a Buddhist temple.

kagura Ritual dances still performed at Shintō shrines.

kakekotoba A "pivot word" that changes in meaning depending on the following word. "What do I see weed on the shore" is a (poor) English attempt at a *kakekotoba*.

kambun Prose written in classical Chinese.

kana The Japanese syllabary, containing such elements as *ka*, *ki*, *ku*, *ke*, *ko*.

kemari The ritual football, still practiced at certain shrines. The point is to kick the ball in such a way that it will be easy for the next man to kick it, rather than to compete.

ken A measurement of about six feet.

Kokin Denju The secret traditions of reading the ninth-century collection of *waka* poetry, *Kokinshū*. The transmission of these secrets was a closely guarded privilege.

kokugaku "National learning," the study of the Japanese classics, often with nationalist intent.

kotobagaki A prose introduction to a poem of varying length, giving the circumstances of composition.

makurakotoba A fixed epithet, generally placed before a noun; "ox-eyed Hera" and "fleet-footed Achilles" are two Western examples of *makurakotoba*.

monogatari A tale; the word means literally "a telling of things."

mono no aware "The pity of things"—the touching or tragic nature of human life. Sometimes used to mean "a sensitivity to things."

nikki The usual word for "diary." It covered a far broader range of nonfictional writings than the English word.

renga "Linked verse," a form of poetry usually composed by two or more poets. "Links" in seventeen and fourteen syllables alternate.

Retired Emperor An emperor who has abdicated but not taken Buddhist vows.

ri A measurement of distance, approximately 2.5 miles.

rōnin A samurai who no longer serves a master, whether because of his own fault or because the master has lost his authority.

shakuhachi A musical instrument made of bamboo with five holes that are covered by the player's fingers to produce different notes. It is played rather like the recorder.

Shakyamuni The historical Buddha, also known as Gautama Buddha.

Shintō The native Japanese religion, essentially this-worldly, and usually practiced in conjunction with Buddhism.

shirabyōshi A female entertainer (generally a dancer) of the twelfth century and later who usually dressed in white (*shira*). Sometimes used to designate geishas or prostitutes of much later times.

shōji A sliding door consisting of a wooden frame over which white paper has been stretched.

shū A collection, generally of poetry.

uta-awase A poem competition. Two or more poets were asked to compose *waka* on a given theme.

uta-makura A poem topic, usually a place that has been mentioned in poetry.

uta monogatari A "poem-tale." Poem-tales originated as explanations of the circumstances of composition of *waka*. When a number of *waka* by the same poet were explained in this way (as in the case of *The Tales of Ise*), it created the impression of a single work.

wabun Prose written in Japanese, as opposed to *kambun*.

waka The classic Japanese verse form, consisting of thirty-one syllables arranged in five lines, of five, seven, five, seven, and seven syllables.

waki The secondary actor in a Nō play, often a priest, who initiates the action by asking questions of some person he encounters.

yūgen A quality that may be translated as "mysterious depths." It is generally associated with the Nō plays.

zuihitsu The term means literally "following the brush," and was used to describe collections of miscellaneous essays of varying lengths, not arranged in any particular order.

Notes

Heian Diaries

The Record of a Pilgrimage to China in Search of the Buddhist Law

1. Edwin O. Reischauer, trans., *Ennin's Travels in T'ang China*, p. 37.
2. Ibid.
3. Ibid., p. 199. See also Edwin O. Reischauer, *Ennin's Diary: The Record of a Pilgrimage to China in Search of the Law*, p. 232. The entry is dated the 17th day of the 5th moon of 840.
4. Reischauer, *Ennin's Travels*, p. 200. Reischauer, *Ennin's Diary*, p. 233.
5. Reischauer, *Ennin's Travels*, p. 117. Reischauer, *Ennin's Diary*, p. 196, entry for 25th day of 3rd moon, 840.

The Tosa Diary

1. Hagitani Boku, *Tosa Nikki Zenchūshaku*, p. 223.
2. Ibid., p. 293.
3. Ibid., pp. 486–90.
4. Ibid., pp. 481–84. See also Hagitani Boku, "Kaisetsu" (Introduction) to *Shintei Tosa Nikki*, pp. 24–29.
5. Hagitani, *Tosa*, p. 399.

The Gossamer Years

1. Kimura Masanori and Imuta Tsunehisa, eds., *Kagerō Nikki*, p. 207.
2. Her skill as a poet is mentioned in *Ōkagami*, the late-Heian historical tale. See the translation by Helen Craig McCullough, *Ōkagami: The Great Mirror*, pp. 166–67. Other evidence is given by Kimura and Imuta, *Kagerō*, pp. 96–99. Her status as one of the three most beautiful women is found in the genealogical table of her family given in *Sompi Bummyaku*, a work compiled by Tōin Kinsada (1340–99).
3. Edward Seidensticker, trans., *The Gossamer Years*, p. 71. Kimura and Imuta, *Kagerō*, p. 203.
4. Seidensticker, *Gossamer*, p. 48. Kimura and Imuta, *Kagerō*, p. 156.
5. Seidensticker, *Gossamer*, p. 61. Kimura and Imuta, *Kagerō*, p. 184.
6. Seidensticker, *Gossamer*, p. 53. Kimura and Imuta, *Kagerō*, p. 168.
7. Kimura and Imuta, *Kagerō*, p. 202. See also Seidensticker, *Gossamer*, p. 69. *Niki* here is an alternate spelling of the more normal *nikki*.
8. Seidensticker, *Gossamer*, p. 95. Kimura and Imuta, *Kagerō*, pp. 250–51.
9. Seidensticker, *Gossamer*, p. 44. Kimura and Imuta, *Kagerō*, pp. 149–50.
10. Seidensticker, *Gossamer*, p. 88. Kimura and Imuta, *Kagerō*, p. 237.
11. See Kimura and Imuta, *Kagerō*, p. 394.
12. This and the following excerpt are in Seidensticker, *Gossamer*, pp. 46–47. See also Kimura and Imuta, *Kagerō*, pp. 153–55.

The Master of the Hut

1. Two priests called Zōki appear in the literary history of the tenth century, and there has been considerable confusion as to which of them wrote this diary. It seems generally agreed now that it was the second of the two, a man who was still active during the reign of the Emperor Ichijō (986–1011), and that the section of the diary describing his journey to Yoshino was probably written during the last decade of the tenth century. See Masubuchi Katsuichi, *Ionushi: Hombun Oyobi Sakuin*, pp. 107–11. Oka Kazuo, on whom Masubuchi depended for much of his argumentation, suggested a date of 951–52 for the diary. See Oka Kazuo, *Genji Monogatari no Kisoteki Kenkyū*, p. 244.
2. Masubuchi Katsuichi, *Ionushi*, p. 1. *Kikō-hen*, in Gunsho Ruijū series, p. 348.
3. Masubuchi, *Ionushi*, p. 1. *Kikō-hen*, p. 348.
4. Ibid.

5. Kawabata Yasunari, *Kawabata Yasunari Zenshū*, vol. XXIII, p. 47. This passage appears in *Tōkaidō*, written in 1943. Quoted in my *Dawn to the West*, vol. I, p. 822.
6. Masubuchi, *Ionushi*, p. 2. *Kikō-hen*, p. 349.

The Izumi Shikibu Diary

1. Edwin O. Cranston, *The Izumi Shikibu Diary*, pp. 8–9, gives a translation of the passage from *Eiga Monogatari* describing Prince Tametaka's infatuation.
2. See Cranston, *Izumi*, p. 13. His source is *Midō Kampaku Ki*; see also his note 69 on p. 202.
3. Cranston, *Izumi*, p. 175. Text in Nomura Seiichi, *Izumi Shikibu Nikki*, p. 65.
4. Cranston, *Izumi*, p. 136. Nomura, *Izumi*, p. 18.
5. Cranston, *Izumi*, p. 140. Nomura, *Izumi*, p. 22.
6. Cranston, *Izumi*, p. 142. Nomura, *Izumi*, p. 25.
7. Cranston, *Izumi*, p. 150. Nomura, *Izumi*, p. 35.
8. Cranston, *Izumi*, p. 163. Nomura, *Izumi*, p. 51.
9. Edward Seidensticker, trans., *The Tale of Genji*, p. 3.
10. See Helen Craig McCullough, trans., *Ōkagami: The Great Mirror*, pp. 165–66, for the account.
11. Cranston, *Izumi*, p. 191. Nomura, *Izumi*, p. 85.

The Murasaki Shikibu Diary

1. Translation in Richard Bowring, *Murasaki Shikibu: Her Diary and Poetic Memoirs*, p. 137. For text, see Yamamoto Ritatsu, *Murasaki Shikibu Nikki*, p. 96. *The Chronicles of Japan* is (in the diary) *Nihongi*, more commonly known as *Nihon Shoki*, but here seems to refer to all six of the early histories of Japan written in Chinese.
2. Yamamoto, *Murasaki*, p. 90.
3. See Bowring, *Murasaki*, pp. 22–24.
4. Ibid., p. 53. Yamamoto, *Murasaki*, p. 20.
5. Bowring, *Murasaki*, p. 43. Yamamoto, *Murasaki*, p. 11.
6. Bowring, *Murasaki*, p. 153. Yamamoto, *Murasaki*, pp. 109–10.
7. Bowring, *Murasaki*, p. 91. Yamamoto, *Murasaki*, p. 52. Fujiwara no Kintō apparently asked for "*Waka Murasaki*," the title of chapter 5 of *Genji Monogatari*; but Hagitani Boku preferred the reading *waga Murasaki*, or "our Murasaki." See Bowring, p. 90.
8. Bowring, *Murasaki*, p. 91. Yamamoto, *Murasaki*, pp. 52–53.
9. Bowring, *Murasaki*, p. 119. Yamamoto, *Murasaki*, p. 76.
10. Bowring, *Murasaki*, p. 131. Yamamoto, *Murasaki*, pp. 88–89.

11. Bowring, *Murasaki*, p. 135. Yamamoto, *Murasaki*, p. 94.
12. Bowring, *Murasaki*, p. 93. Yamamoto, *Murasaki*, pp. 54–55. Bowring notes (p. 92) that *onsōshizukuri* indicates that the texts were bound into booklets, rather than made into scrolls.
13. Bowring, *Murasaki*, p. 92, suggests that this passage provides evidence that copying texts in this manner was how the work reached its audience.
14. Ibid., p. 95. Yamamoto, *Murasaki*, p. 57.
15. Bowring, *Murasaki*, p. 143. Yamamoto, *Murasaki*, pp. 102–3.

The Sarashina Diary

1. The translation of this diary by Ivan Morris is entitled *As I Crossed a Bridge of Dreams*, but I have used here a more literal translation of the title.
2. Ivan Morris, *As I Crossed a Bridge of Dreams*, p. 41. Text in Sekine Yoshiko, *Sarashina Nikki*, vol. I, p. 13.
3. Sekine, *Sarashina*, vol. I, p. 87. In Japanese her words are: *"Monogatari motomete mise yo mise yo."*
4. Morris, *As I Crossed*, p. 55. Sekine, *Sarashina*, vol. I, pp. 105.
5. Morris, *As I Crossed*, pp. 55–57. Sekine, *Sarashina*, vol. I, pp. 105–6.
6. Morris, *As I Crossed*, p. 55. Sekine, *Sarashina*, vol. I, p. 105.
7. Morris, *As I Crossed*, pp. 78–80. Sekine, *Sarashina*, vol. I, p. 204.
8. Morris, *As I Crossed*, p. 80. Sekine, *Sarashina*, vol. I, pp. 204, 208.
9. Morris, *As I Crossed*, pp. 71–72. Sekine, *Sarashina*, vol. I, p. 174.
10. Morris, *As I Crossed*, p. 72. Sekine, *Sarashina*, vol. I, p. 175.
11. Morris, *As I Crossed*, p. 74. Sekine, *Sarashina*, vol. I, p. 190.
12. Morris, *As I Crossed*, p. 78. Sekine, *Sarashina*, vol. I, p. 199.
13. Sekine, *Sarashina*, vol. II, p. 13.
14. Morris, *As I Crossed*, p. 84. Sekine, *Sarashina*, vol. II, p. 13.
15. Morris, *As I Crossed*, p. 84. Sekine, *Sarashina*, vol. II, p. 14.
16. Morris, *As I Crossed*, p. 87. Sekine, *Sarashina*, vol. II, p. 35.
17. Morris, *As I Crossed*, p. 91. Sekine, *Sarashina*, vol. II, p. 50.
18. Morris, *As I Crossed*, p. 91. Sekine, *Sarashina*, vol. II, p. 50.
19. Morris, *As I Crossed*, p. 95. Sekine, *Sarashina*, vol. II, p. 59.
20. Sekine, *Sarashina*, vol. II, p. 65. See also Morris, *As I Crossed*, p. 95.
21. Ibid.
22. Sekine, *Sarashina*, vol. II, pp. 100–101. See also Morris, *As I Crossed*, p. 107.
23. Morris, *As I Crossed*, p. 98. Sekine, *Sarashina*, vol. II, p. 74.
24. Morris, *As I Crossed*, p. 119. Sekine, *Sarashina*, vol. II, p. 135.

The Tale of the Tōnomine Captain

1. Tamai Kōsuke, *Tōnomine Shōshō Monogatari*, p. 50. The last line of Takamitsu's poem, *"tsuyu mo wasureji,"* means "I will not forget you in the least," but (using another meaning of *tsuyu*) it also means "I will not forget the dew," referring to the image in his wife's poem.
2. Ibid., pp. 51–52.
3. Ibid., p. 62.
4. Ibid., p. 65.
5. Ibid., p. 73.
6. Ibid., p. 85.
7. Ibid., p. 96.
8. Ibid., p. 106.

The Collection of the Mother of Jōjin, the Ajari

1. *Ajari* (*acārya* in Sanskrit) meant "teacher," and was a rank bestowed on priests who were ritualists skilled in mystic practices and who led in prayers for good harvests and for the welfare of the country.
2. She was actually eighty-four by Japanese or eighty-three by Western reckoning, but she was probably rounding off the figure for poetic effect.
3. Hirabayashi Fumio, *Jōjin Ajari Haha no Shū no Kisoteki Kenkyū*, pp. 53, 99. See also Miyazaki Shōhei, *Jōjin Ajari Haha no Shū*, p. 13.
4. Some scholars think he was the younger. See Hirabayashi, *Jōjin*, p. 56. The writer invariably referred to her sons by their titles, and gave no indication of which was the elder.
5. Hirabayashi, *Jōjin*, p. 65. Miyazaki, *Jōjin*, pp. 73–74.
6. Hirabayashi, *Jōjin*, p. 65. Miyazaki, *Jōjin*, p. 73.
7. Hirabayashi, *Jōjin*, p. 64. Miyazaki, *Jōjin*, p. 74.
8. Hirabayashi, *Jōjin*, p. 66. Miyazaki, *Jōjin*, p. 75.
9. Hirabayashi, *Jōjin*, p. 64. Miyazaki, *Jōjin*, p. 74.
10. Hirabayashi, *Jōjin*, pp. 66–67, 118. Miyazaki, *Jōjin*, p. 75.
11. This is poem 67 of the work, Hirabayashi, *Jōjin*, p. 67. Miyazaki, *Jōjin*, p. 76.
12. Hirabayashi, *Jōjin*, p. 69. Miyazaki, *Jōjin*, p. 90.
13. Hirabayashi, *Jōjin*, p. 70. Miyazaki, *Jōjin*, p. 90.
14. Hirabayashi, *Jōjin*, p. 71. Miyazaki, *Jōjin*, p. 100.
15. Hirabayashi, *Jōjin*, p. 74. Miyazaki, *Jōjin*, p. 112.
16. Hirabayashi, *Jōjin*, p. 81. Miyazaki, *Jōjin*, p. 152.
17. The duet toward the end of *Il trovatore* would seem to be an ex-

ception, but Manrico is actually not Azucena's son.

18. Hirabayashi, *Jōjin*, p. 92. Miyazaki, *Jōjin*, p. 209.
19. Hirabayashi, *Jōjin*, p. 94. Miyazaki, *Jōjin*, pp. 216–17.
20. Hirabayashi (*Jōjin*, p. 96) suggests that the place to which the mother expects to be led by the moon is Ryōjusen, or Eagle Mountain, mentioned in her previous poem. Eagle Mountain is where Shakyamuni Buddha taught the Lotus and many other sutras. The implication, however, is that she will be guided to paradise.

The Sanuki no Suke Diary

1. The American edition of the English translation by Jennifer Brewster is called *The Emperor Horikawa Diary*. The original Australian edition (in English) is called *Sanuki no Suke Nikki*.
2. Nagako took the name Sanuki from the office of her father, the governor of Sanuki. Her own title, *suke*, was an abbreviated form of *naishi no suke*, or Second-in-Charge of the Mirror Room, a position of the Junior Fourth Rank.
3. Fujiwara no Munetada, *Chūyūki*, vol. II, p. 144.
4. Translated under this title by Delmer M. Brown and Ichirō Ishida. An earlier, partial translation by J. Rahder bore a more literal translation of the title: *Miscellany of the Personal Views of an Ignorant Fool.*
5. See Brown and Ishida, *Future and Past*, pp. 83–84. The appearance of Raigō's ghost at Horikawa's deathbed was reported by Nagako herself. See Morimoto Motoko, *Sanuki no Suke Nikki*, p. 51; also, Brewster, *Horikawa Diary*, p. 67.
6. Quoted by Tamai Kōsuke in *Sanuki no Suke Nikki*, p. 9. The source of the quotation is *Chūyūki*, vol. II, p. 223, where other details are given. The doctrine of *mappō*, or the Latter Days of the Buddhist Law, a period when it would become impossible to observe the commandments of Buddhism, would gain great prominence later in the twelfth century.
7. Translation by Brewster, *Horikawa Diary*, p. 100. Original text in Tamai, *Sanuki*, p. 178; also Morimoto, *Sanuki*, pp. 165–66.
8. Brewster, *Horikawa Diary*, p. 60. Tamai, *Sanuki*, p. 118; also Morimoto, *Sanuki*, p. 28.
9. Brewster, *Horikawa Diary*, pp. 60–61. Tamai, *Sanuki*, p. 119; also Morimoto, *Sanuki*, p. 28.
10. Brewster, *Horikawa Diary*, p. 62. Tamai, *Sanuki*, p. 121; also Morimoto, *Sanuki*, p. 35.
11. Brewster, *Horikawa Diary*, p. 72. Tamai, *Sanuki*, p. 137; also Morimoto, *Sanuki*, p. 71.

12. Brewster, *Horikawa Diary*, p. 82. Tamai, *Sanuki*, p. 150; also Morimoto, *Sanuki*, p. 101.
13. Brewster, *Horikawa Diary*, pp. 87–88. Tamai, *Sanuki*, p. 159; also Morimoto, *Sanuki*, p. 118.
14. Brewster, *Horikawa Diary*, p. 88. Tamai, *Sanuki*, p. 160; also Morimoto, *Sanuki*, p. 124.
15. Brewster, *Horikawa Diary*, p. 103. Tamai, *Sanuki*, p. 181; also Morimoto, *Sanuki*, p. 174.
16. Brewster, *Horikawa Diary*, p. 112. Tamai, *Sanuki*, pp. 194–95; also Morimoto, *Sanuki*, p. 209.
17. Quoted in Brewster, *Horikawa Diary*, p. 22.
18. Tamai, *Sanuki*, p. 197; also Morimoto, *Sanuki*, p. 215.

Chūyūki

1. *Chūyū* was an abbreviation for *Naka*mikado *U*daijin, or Nakamikado Minister of the Right, read in Sino-Japanese pronunciation. *Ki* means "record."
2. Toda Yoshimi, *Chūyūki: Yakudō suru Insei Jidai no Gunzō*, p. 276. Original text in Fujiwara no Munetada, *Chūyūki*, vol. V, p. 235.
3. Toda, *Chūyūki*, p. 278.
4. Ibid., p. 285.
5. Ibid.
6. Ibid., p. 59.
7. Munetada, *Chūyūki*, vol. III, pp. 230–31. Tamai Kōsuke, in *Sanuki no Suke Nikki*, pp. 75–76 gives a *yomikudashi* version of the *Chūyūki* text. Brewster, in *Horikawa Diary*, p. 18, gives a translation of the biographical passage.
8. Toda, *Chūyūki*, p. 296.
9. Ibid., p. 297.

Poetry Collections and Poem Tales

1. Richard Bowring, *Murasaki Shikibu: Her Diary and Poetic Memoirs*, p. 239.
2. Shimizu Akira, *Shijōnomiya no Shimotsuke Shū*, pp. 2–10.
3. *Kingyoku* means "gold and jade"; this was a private collection of poems he particularly admired, compiled by Fujiwara no Kintō (966–1041).
4. Text in Shimizu, *Shijōnomiya*, pp. 287–92. I have omitted another exchange of poems in the same section. There is a pun on *soru* meaning "to shave one's head and enter the Buddhist clergy," and *soru* meaning "to avoid," used of the falcon fleeing captivity. Shimotsuke

suggests in her poem that her beloved books keep her attached to this world like bait that might prevent a falcon from flying away.

The Poetic Memoirs of Lady Daibu

1. I have followed the translation of the title given by Phillip Tudor Harries in his book *The Poetic Memoirs of Lady Daibu*. He explains the full title in these terms: Kenreimon'in was the name Empress Tokuko received on becoming a retired empress, and it serves to define Lady Daibu as one who was in her service. *Ukyō no daibu* means Superintendent of the Right-hand Half of the Capital, and some scholars have suggested that her father held this title, though there is no record of his having done so. One of the two other men who actually held the title about the time when she served at court might have been her sponsor, occasioning the name, but this is only conjecture. *Shū* means "collection," and although the work contains many more descriptive passages than the usual poetic collection, it was probably considered to be primarily a collection of poetry, rather than a diary. See Harries, pp. 14–16.
2. Harries, *Lady Daibu*, p. 191. Original text in Itoga Kimie, *Kenreimon'in Ukyō no Daibu no Shū*, p. 98.
3. Harries, *Lady Daibu*, p. 207. Itoga, *Kenreimon'in*, p. 111.
4. Harries, *Lady Daibu*, p. 207. Itoga, *Kenreimon'in*, p. 111.
5. Harries, *Lady Daibu*, p. 77. Itoga, *Kenreimon'in*, p. 9.
6. Harries, *Lady Daibu*, pp. 76–77. Itoga, *Kenreimon'in*, p. 9.
7. Harries, *Lady Daibu*, p. 79. Itoga, *Kenreimon'in*, pp. 9–10.
8. Harries, *Lady Daibu*, p. 89. Itoga, *Kenreimon'in*, p. 18.
9. Harries, *Lady Daibu*, p. 111. Itoga, *Kenreimon'in*, p. 33.
10. Harries, *Lady Daibu*, p. 113. Itoga, *Kenreimon'in*, p. 34.
11. Harries, *Lady Daibu*, p. 115. Itoga, *Kenreimon'in*, p. 36.
12. Harries, *Lady Daibu*, p. 119. Itoga, *Kenreimon'in*, p. 40.
13. Harries, *Lady Daibu*, p. 141. Itoga, *Kenreimon'in*, p. 57.
14. Taira no Kanemori died in 990. See Harries, *Lady Daibu*, p. 140; Itoga, *Kenreimon'in*, p. 57.
15. Harries, *Lady Daibu*, p. 153. Itoga, *Kenreimon'in*, p. 68.
16. Harries, *Lady Daibu*, p. 165. Itoga, *Kenreimon'in*, p. 78.
17. Harries, *Lady Daibu*, p. 187. Itoga, *Kenreimon'in*, p. 95.
18. Harries, *Lady Daibu*, p. 189. Itoga, *Kenreimon'in*, pp. 96–97.
19. Harries, *Lady Daibu*, p. 191. Itoga, *Kenreimon'in*, p. 98.
20. Harries, *Lady Daibu*, pp. 191–93. Itoga, *Kenreimon'in*, p. 99.
21. Harries, *Lady Daibu*, p. 197. Itoga, *Kenreimon'in*, p. 103.
22. Harries, *Lady Daibu*, pp. 181–83. Itoga, *Kenreimon'in*, p. 91.
23. Harries, *Lady Daibu*, pp. 197–99. Itoga, *Kenreimon'in*, p. 104.

24. Harries, *Lady Daibu*, p. 199. Itoga, *Kenreimon'in*, p. 105.
25. Harries, *Lady Daibu*, p. 213. Itoga, *Kenreimon'in*, p. 116.
26. Harries, *Lady Daibu*, pp. 261–63. Itoga, *Kenreimon'in*, p. 151.
27. Harries, *Lady Daibu*, p. 283. Itoga, *Kenreimon'in*, p. 167.
28. Harries, *Lady Daibu*, pp. 227–29. Itoga, *Kenreimon'in*, p. 127.

Diaries of the Kawakura Period

Chronicle of the Bright Moon

1. Imagawa Fumio, *Kundoku Meigetsuki*, vol. I, p. 19.
2. Daibu (usually known as Impumon'in no Daibu) was the daughter of Shunzei, and thus a sister of Teika's. She was a distinguished poet of both *waka* and *renga*.
3. Identified as Fujiwara no Kin'hira by Imagawa Fumio in *Meigetsuki Shō*, p. 18.
4. Identified as the daughter of Kamo no Arinori by Imagawa, ibid.
5. Entry for the 4th year of the Bunji era, 29th day of the 9th month. Ibid., pp. 18–19.
6. Fujiwara no Suetsune, the leader of the rival Rokujō school of *waka* poetry.
7. Imagawa, *Kundoku Meigetsuki*, vol. I, p. 209.
8. Ibid., p. 210.
9. Ibid., p. 212.
10. Ibid., p. 214.
11. Ibid., p. 215.
12. Ibid., vol. II, p. 297. Kengozen was Teika's elder sister.
13. Hisamatsu Sen'ichi and Nishio Minoru, *Karon Shū, Nōgakuron Shū*, pp. 149, 268–69.
14. *Gotoba-in Gokuden* (1239), ibid., p. 149.
15. Ibid.
16. The incident is reported in the form of a *kotobagaki* in Teika's private collection of poetry, *Shūi Gusō*. It is also quoted in many books on Teika, such as Kubota Jun, *Fujiwara Teika*, p. 212.
17. For "ignorant monarchs" Teika used the names of two Chinese emperors of the Latter Han, Huan and Ling, both of whom were known for their foolishness. The "Sage Kings" were Yao and Shun, the legendary rulers of ancient China.
18. Imagawa, *Kundoku Meigetsuki*, vol. V, p. 184.
19. Ibid.
20. Ibid., p. 186.
21. Ibid., p. 192.
22. Ibid., pp. 252–53.

The Diary of Minamoto Ienaga

1. Ishida Yoshisada and Satsukawa Shūji, *Minamoto Ienaga Nikki Zenchūshaku*, p. 211.
2. Ibid., p. 217.
3. Ibid., p. 215.
4. Ibid., pp. 101–2.
5. Ibid., pp. 63–64.
6. Ibid., p. 34.
7. Ibid., p. 36.
8. Ibid., p. 5.
9. Ibid., p. 23.
10. Ibid., pp. 24–25.
11. Reference is made to Fujiwara no Nariie, son of Shunzei and elder brother of Teika. He had been promoted to the Third Rank only a month before the birthday celebration. Ishida and Satsukawa, *Minamoto Ienaga*, p. 133.
12. Ibid., p. 132.
13. Ibid., pp. 110–11.

The Visit of the Emperor Takakura to Itsukushima

1. Mizukawa Yoshio, *Minamoto no Michichika Nikki Zenshū*, p. 236.
2. Ibid., p. 268.
3. Ibid., p. 280.
4. Ibid.
5. Ibid., p. 324.
6. Ibid., p. 367.
7. Ibid., p. 382. Moxa (*mogusa* in Japanese), an herb, is burned at various places on the body, cauterizing the skin. The treatment is still widespread.
8. H. E. Plutschow, *Tabi suru Nihonjin*, p. 253. This book, though written by a European, is in Japanese. I have made the translation of this excerpt.
9. That is, the ship on which the Emperor rode.
10. Mizukawa, *Minamoto*, p. 306. See also the translation in Herbert Plutschow and Hideichi Fukuda, *Four Japanese Diaries*, p. 35.
11. Mizukawa, *Minamoto*, p. 314.

The Ascension to Heaven of the Late Emperor Takakura

1. Mizukawa Yoshio, *Minamoto no Michichika Nikki Zenshū*, p. 409. After the death of Shakyamuni Buddha it was long believed that the

Buddhist Law prevailed only in the north. The west was the direction of the Buddhist paradise.

2. Ibid., p. 594.
3. Ibid., p. 562.
4. Reference is being made to the *waka* by Ariwara no Narihira: "Is that not the moon? And is the spring not the spring of old? Yet only this body of mine still seems the same body." The poem is number 747 in the *Kokinshū*, and its circumstances are given in section 4 of *The Tales of Ise.*
5. Mizukawa, *Minamoto*, p. 587.
6. Ibid., p. 607.

Journey Along the Seacoast Road

1. Text in Noro Masashi, *Kaidōki Shinchū*, p. 78.
2. The text (Noro, *Kaidōki*, p. 11) gives "*gekai no sojūon tenchō no chikugashū.*" Sojūon was one of the four gardens of Sakra. When Sakra, the Lord of the Devas, wished to go forth and do battle, the garden would of itself produce the armor he needed. Yen-chou (in modern Kansu Province) was the site of an ancient Chinese fort.
3. Ibid., p. 11.
4. Ibid., p. 208.
5. Ibid., p. 209.
6. Ibid., p. 23.
7. Ibid., p. 134.
8. Ibid., p. 244.
9. Ibid., pp. 52–53.
10. Ibid., p. 126.
11. Ibid., p. 112.
12. Ibid., p. 141.
13. Ibid., p. 96.
14. Ibid.
15. Ibid., p. 97.
16. Ibid., p. 156.

The Diary of the Priest Shunjō

1. Tonomura Nobuko, *Utsunomiya Asanari Nikki Zenshaku*, pp. 291–93. The poem has several plays on words that communicate Shunjō's full intent. For example, *ware mo arashi* is a virtual homonym of *ware mo araji*, meaning "I shall probably not be there," and *ha wa* is used for *haha*, meaning "mother." The same harsh wind that

has deprived the children of their mother now threatens to take their father away, too; Shunjō is therefore asking the gods to protect them.

2. Ibid.
3. Ibid., p. 97. This poem was included in the imperial anthology *Shoku Gosenshū*, compiled in 1251 by Fujiwara Tameie.
4. Tonomura, *Utsunomiya*, pp. 117–18. The quotation is from the Lotus Sutra.
5. Tonomura, *Utsunomiya*, pp. 133–34. There is a play on words in the last line: *yadosazu* means both "to reflect (an image)" and "to put up for the night." The place name Ikeda consists of *ike*, meaning "pond," and *ta*, meaning "wet rice field." Probably these meanings were intended to be taken into account.
6. Ibid., pp. 179–86.
7. A mountain in Shinano where, according to a well-known legend, an old woman was left to die.
8. An allusion to the poem (number 1103 in *Gosenshū*) by Fujiwara no Kanesuke (877–933) saying that a parent's love for his children will make his heart wander in the paths of delusion.
9. Tonomura, *Utsunomiya*, pp. 198–201. The text offers problems of interpretation: the word *onnagodomo*, which I have translated as "children," taking it to refer to Shunjō's daughter and son, may be *onna, kodomo*, referring to a woman previously mentioned and to the children. I have followed Tonomura, *Utsunomiya*, p. 199. The words *sama wo kaete*, which I have translated as "shave our heads," means literally "change our appearance," meaning to put on Buddhist robes.
10. Ibid., p. 198.

A Journey East of the Barrier

1. Kasamatsu Yoshio, *Tōkan Kikō Shinshaku*, p. 3.
2. Ibid., pp. 5–6.
3. Ibid., p. 15. *Sazanami ya* was the *makurakotoba* for Ōtsu. Shiga is roughly the area of modern Shiga Prefecture, and Ōtsu is the main city. The capital was at Ōtsu before a permanent capital was established in Nara in the eighth century.
4. Ibid., p. 26.
5. Ibid., p. 39. The quotation is part of poem 55 in the *Kokinshū*: "Is seeing them enough? One wants to tell others about them, the cherry blossoms. Each visitor breaks off a spray for the sake of those who have not seen them."
6. Kasamatsu, *Tōkan*, p. 69.

Fitful Slumbers

1. Tsugita Kasumi, *Utatane Zenchūshaku*, pp. 13–15.
2. Ibid., p. 40.
3. Ibid., p. 45. Tsugita analyzes (on p. 46) the plays on words and *engo* (related words) in this poem that amplify the meaning. The verb *nageku* contains *nage*, the stem of the verb meaning "to throw," and suggesting she is throwing herself into the river. The word *ato* in the last line refers to her spirit after she is dead, having drowned in the river.
4. Ibid., p. 52.
5. Ibid., p. 55.
6. Ibid., p. 63.
7. Ibid., p. 69.
8. Ibid., p. 73.
9. Ibid., p. 83.
10. Ibid., p. 93.
11. Ibid., p. 121.

The Diary of the Waning Moon

1. Motoyama Motoko, *Izayoi Nikki, Yoru no Tsuru*, p. 96.
2. Ibid., p. 15.
3. She is modestly making light of the priceless treasure of pages of poetry and works of poetic criticism she was given by her husband.
4. Motoyama, *Izayoi*, pp. 20–21.
5. A reference to the well-known poem by Fujiwara no Kanesuke in the collection *Gosenshū*, "Though a parent's heart is not in darkness, it will wander astray for love of its child." The poem was often quoted as an example of how a parent's love for his child will deprive him of his ability to make rational judgments.
6. An oblique reference to the scrupulously fair courts in Kamakura. "Tortoise mirror" (*kikan*) was used to mean a model for people, from the use of tortoise shells in ancient Chinese divination.
7. Motoyama, *Izayoi*, p. 24.
8. Ibid., p. 44.

The Diary of Asukai Masaari

1. Tsukamoto Yasuhiko, *Jojō no Dentō*, p. 12.
2. The text is worm-eaten at this spot, and is therefore not certain. I have followed the emendation made by Mizukawa Yoshio in *Asukai Masaari Nikki Zenshaku*, p. 43. Masaari says that the authors were

all women, but of course *The Tosa Diary* was written by a man; perhaps he took at face value the author's statement that a woman had written the diary.

3. Mizukawa, *Asukai*, pp. 43–48.
4. Ibid., pp. 44–49.
5. There is some confusion among commentators as to whether the hair is growing down in a semicircle that includes part of the forehead and the nose, or if the semicircle is the only place where the hair does not grow. I have followed Mizukawa, *Asukai*, p. 174, in the latter interpretation.
6. Ibid., p. 171.
7. Ibid., p. 146.
8. Ibid., pp. 146–48.
9. Ibid., p. 61.
10. Ibid., pp. 61–65. Some of the language of this passage is ambiguous; when in doubt, I have followed Mizukawa.

The Diary of Lady Ben

1. The title *naishi* designated a female palace attendant who waited on the Emperor. I shall henceforth refer to the two ladies in question as Lady Ben and Lady Nakatsukasa.
2. Tamai Kōsuke, *Nakatsukasa no Naishi Nikki Shinchū*, p. i.
3. Ikeda Kikan, *Kyūtei Joryū Nikki Bungaku*, p. 277.
4. Tamai Kōsuke, *Ben no Naishi Nikki Shinchū*, p. 24.
5. Ibid., pp. 157–160.
6. Ibid., p. 79.
7. Ibid., pp. 211–12.
8. Ibid., pp. 230–32.

The Diary of Lady Nakatsukasa

1. Tamai Kōsuke, *Nakatsukasa no Naishi Nikki Shinchū*, p. 8. The Shakyamuni Buddha at a temple in Saga (or Sagano), to the northwest of Kyōto, was described in many other literary works of the time. The jewel referred to, here called *nyoihōju*, could bring the possessor anything he desired.
2. Yoshida Kenkō, *Tsurezuregusa*, section 7. The translation given here is my own, and is found in *Essays in Idleness*, p. 7.
3. Tamai, *Nakatsukasa*, p. 13.
4. Ibid., p. 39. The Kitayama-dono was a residence of the Saionji family in the northern hills (*kitayama*) of Kyōto, on the site of the future Kinkakuji.

5. Gofukakusa (reigned 1242–59) was the Retired Emperor (*jōkō*) until his death in 1304.
6. The chief officer of the crown prince's household. This particular *daibu* was Saionji Sanekane (1249–1322). Sanekane figures prominently in *The Confessions of Lady Nijō* as Akebono, one of Nijō's lovers.
7. Tamai, *Nakatsukasa*, p. 39.
8. Ibid., p. 78.
9. Ibid., p. 119.
10. Ibid., p. 98. For *kagura*, see Glossary.
11. She is contrasting the crudity of the people now surrounding her with the exquisite refinement of the Kitayama Mansion, as she described above.
12. Tamai, *Nakatsukasa*, p. 54.
13. This poem is number 114 in *Shin Kokinshū.*

The Confessions of Lady Nijō

1. The title means literally *An Unsolicited Story*, but I have used the title given by Karen Brazell to her translation of the diary.
2. Karen Brazell, *The Confessions of Lady Nijō*, p. 1. Tomikura Tokujirō, *Towazugatari*, p. 205.
3. See Helen McCullough, trans., *The Tales of Ise*, p. 77. In this section of the work the mother of a certain girl sends a poem to the girl's suitor encouraging him with the words:

Miyoshino no	The wild goose that shelters
tanomu no kari mo	On Miyoshino's fields
hitaburu ni	Cries that it looks
kimi ga kata ni zo	In your direction
yoru to naku naru	And in no other.

4. Brazell, *Confessions*, p. 3. Tomikura, *Towazugatari*, p. 206.
5. Brazell, *Confessions*, p. 4. Tomikura, *Towazugatari*, p. 207.
6. Brazell, *Confessions*, p. 8. Tomikura, *Towazugatari*, p. 210.
7. Fukuda Hideichi, *Towazugatari*, p. 20. Brazell, *Confessions*, p. 8.
8. Brazell, *Confessions*, p. 9. Tomikura, *Towazugatari*, p. 210.
9. Edward Seidensticker, trans., *The Tale of Genji*, vol. I., p. 180.
10. Brazell, *Confessions*, p. 10. Tomikura, *Towazugatari*, p. 211.
11. Brazell, *Confessions*, p. 25. Tomikura, *Towazugatari*, p. 221.
12. Brazell, *Confessions*, p. 30. Tomikura, *Towazugatari*, p. 225.
13. Brazell, *Confessions*, p. 34. Tomikura, *Towazugatari*, p. 227.

14. He figures prominently (under his real name) in *The Diary of Lady Nakatsukasa*.
15. Cf. Brazell, *Confessions*, p. 46; Tomikura, *Towazugatari*, p. 235. Reference is made to the anonymous poem 647 in the *Kokinshū*, "Our meeting in the dark last night is less certain than the vividness of a dream."
16. Brazell, *Confessions*, p. 46. Tomikura, *Towazugatari*, p. 235.
17. Brazell, *Confessions*, p. 116. Tomikura, *Towazugatari*, p. 281.
18. Brazell, *Confessions*, p. 118. Tomikura, *Towazugatari*, p. 282.
19. Brazell, *Confessions*, p. 120. Tomikura, *Towazugatari*, p. 284.
20. Brazell, *Confessions*, p. 75. Tomikura, *Towazugatari*, p. 269.
21. Brazell, *Confessions*, p. 75. Tomikura, *Towazugatari*, p. 255.
22. Brazell, *Confessions*, p. 80. Tomikura, *Towazugatari*, p. 258.
23. Brazell, *Confessions*, p. 81. Tomikura, *Towazugatari*, p. 259.
24. Brazell, *Confessions*, p. 89. Tomikura, *Towazugatari*, pp. 264–65.
25. Brazell, *Confessions*, p. 90. Tomikura, *Towazugatari*, p. 265.
26. Brazell, *Confessions*, p. 122. Tomikura, *Towazugatari*, p. 286.
27. Brazell, *Confessions*, p. 124. Tomikura, *Towazugatari*, p. 287.
28. Brazell, *Confessions*, p. 143. Tomikura, *Towazugatari*, p. 299.
29. Brazell, *Confessions*, p. 252. Tomikura, *Towazugatari*, p. 378.
30. Brazell, *Confessions*, p. 41. Tomikura, *Towazugatari*, p. 231.
31. Brazell, *Confessions*, p. 241. Tomikura, *Towazugatari*, p. 371.

Account of the Takemuki Palace

1. I have not found an authenticated reading for the name. Rather than call the woman Meishi, the coward's way out, I have used the most obvious (though uncommon) pronunciation.
2. Mizukawa Yoshio, *Takemuki ga Ki Zenshaku*, pp. 3–4. The crown prince was the future Emperor Kōgon.
3. Ibid., pp. 7–8.
4. Hino Suketomo (1290–1332) figures in sections 152–54 of *Tsurezuregusa*. In section 153 Kenkō related how Suketomo had seen the poet Kyōgoku Tamekane being arrested and led off by soldiers. He exclaimed, "How I envy him! What a marvelous last remembrance to have of this life!" He did not foresee that he would die in a similar manner. See my translation, *Essays in Idleness*, p. 136.
5. Saionji Kinmune (1310–35) was Acting Major Counselor at the time (1331), despite his youth. He was put to death four years later for plotting to overthrow the Emperor Godaigo, who had in the meantime regained power. See H. Paul Varley, *Imperial Restoration in Medieval Japan*, pp. 90–91.
6. Mizukawa, *Takemuki*, p. 24.
7. Ibid.

8. Actually, a *shaku*, or tablet on which Confucian officials were supposed to write admonitions and other court matters. It came to be used by rulers, too, as a symbol of their office.
9. Mizukawa, *Takemuki*, p. 55.
10. Ibid., p. 102.
11. Ibid., p. 104.
12. Ibid., p. 110.
13. Ibid., p. 119.
14. Ibid., p. 125.
15. Ibid.
16. Ibid., p. 135.
17. Ibid., p. 140.
18. Meaning that she is pregnant.
19. Yamashita Hiroaki, *Taiheiki*, vol. II, p. 278.
20. Ibid., p. 280.

Diaries of the Muromachi Period

Account of a Pilgrimage to the Great Shrine of Ise

1. For a concise discussion of the relations between Buddhism and Shintō at this time, see W. T. de Bary, Ryusaku Tsunoda, and Donald Keene, *Sources of Japanese Tradition*, pp. 268–71.
2. Katō Genchi, *Kenkyū Hyōshaku: Saka-ō Daijingū Sankeiki*, p. 2. See also A. L. Sadler, trans., *Saka's Diary of a Pilgrim to Ise*, p. 27.
3. Jūbutsu gave these poems in *Man'yō-gana*, the archaic writing system used for the eighth-century anthology *Man'yoshū*.
4. Katō, *Kenkyū*, p. 3. Sadler, *Saka's Diary*, p. 30.
5. A quotation from Narihira's celebrated poem:

   kimi ya koshi
   ware wa yukiken
   omōezu
   yume ka utsutsu ka
   nete ka samete ka.

   The poem has been translated by Helen McCullough (*The Tales of Ise*, p. 48), as:

   Did you, I wonder, come here,
   Or might I have gone there?
   I scarcely know. . . .

Was it dream or reality—
Did I sleep or wake?

6. Katō, *Kenkyū*, p. 4. Sadler, *Saka's Diary*, p. 31.
7. The season of Jūbutsu's visit to Ise is winter.
8. Katō, *Kenkyū*, p. 5. Sadler, *Saka's Diary*, p. 33.
9. The Great Shrine at Ise was by tradition rebuilt every twenty years. An exact copy was built alongside the old shrine buildings, which were then removed. This practice was reinstated, and is now observed regularly except when most unusual circumstances (such as the defeat in 1945) have compelled a delay.
10. Katō, *Kenkyū*, p. 15. Sadler, *Saka's Diary*, p. 54.
11. Katō, *Kenkyū*, p. 18. Sadler, *Saka's Diary*, p. 60. Mild Light (*wakō*) and Beneficial Things (*rimotsu*) are both Buddhist terms; the former refers to the practice of the Buddha of tempering the strength of the light he shines to the degree of capacity of the recipient, the latter to the benefits that the Buddha brings to all sentient creatures.
12. The vow made by Amida Buddha to save all beings who called his name.
13. Katō, *Kenkyū*, p. 19. Sadler, *Saka's Diary*, p. 61.
14. Katō, *Kenkyū*, p. 21. Sadler, *Saka's Diary*, p. 66.
15. V. Pritchard, *English Medieval Grafitti*, p. 182. The church is Ashwell, Hertfordshire. The original grafitto is in Latin, the quoted passage being "*superest plebs pessima testis.*" The study of this particular inscription was made by Bruce Dickins.

Gifts from the Capital

1. The poem is number 351 in the *Man'yōshū*. This passage from Sōkyū's diary is found in *Zokuzoku Kikō Bunshū Shūsei*, p. 529.
2. *Zokuzoku*, p. 540.

Reciting Poetry to Myself at Ojima

1. *Zoku Kikōbun Shū*, p. 63.
2. Ibid., p. 64. The allusion to Tsurayuki's poem is followed by Yoshimoto's own poem. The characters used for *ukiyo* are those for the "floating world," but the homonym, meaning the "sad world," might be more appropriate. The verb *shiguru* should mean the "falling of the late-autumn rain," but here (since the leaves have not yet changed color), it is probably still only early autumn. In any case, the primary meaning was undoubtedly the poet's tears that wet his sleeve rather than any natural phenomenon.

3. *Zoku Kikōbun*, p. 66.
4. Ibid., p. 67.
5. I am thinking of such passages as, "He had never before been on such a journey, however short. All the sad, exotic things along the way were new to him. The Ōe station was in ruins, with only a grove of pines to show where it had stood." (Edward Seidensticker, trans., *The Tale of Genji*, vol. I, p. 230.)
6. *Zoku Kikōbun*, p. 67.
7. Ibid., p. 72.
8. Ibid., p. 73.
9. Ibid., p. 76.
10. Ibid.

Pilgrimage to Sumiyoshi

1. *Sumiyoshi Mōde*, in *Zoku Kikōbun Shū*, p. 73. I have translated *shūka* as "poetry of intricate expression," meaning *waka* poetry with *kakekotoba, engo*, and so on; but the same word can also mean simply "superior poetry." I have not chosen the latter meaning because I assume that *all* poets want to write superior poetry.
2. Ibid. "The Way of Shikishima" was a poetic name for the art of the *waka*. Shikishima itself was originally the name of a particular place, was then used for the Yamato region, and finally came to be another name for Japan.
3. See Donald Keene, *Dawn to the West*, vol. I, p. 822. The shoguns mentioned by Kawabata ruled in the late fifteenth and early sixteenth centuries.
4. *Taoyameburi* and *masuraoburi* are untranslatable terms referring to the delicacy of women and the manliness of men, complementary ideals.
5. Donald Keene, *Some Japanese Portraits*, p. 60.
6. *Zoku Kikōbun*, p. 71.
7. Ibid., p. 74.

The Visit to Itsukushima of the Lord of the Deer Park

1. Yoshimitsu's title was taken from the Deer Park in India, where five monks were converted to the Buddhist faith after hearing Gautama Buddha teach the four noble truths; this was taken to represent the beginning of Buddhism.
2. *Zokuzoku Kikōbun Shū*, p. 75.
3. Translation by Donald Keene in *Essays in Idleness*, p. 23.

4. Zeami, "Sandō," in Hisamatsu Sen'ichi and Nishio Minoru, eds., *Karon Shū, Nōgakuron Shū*, p. 480.
5. This presumably refers to the Dazaifu near the modern Fukuoka.

A Source of Consolation

1. *Zokuzoku Kikōbun Shū*, p. 112.
2. Ibid., pp. 112–13.
3. See Donald Keene, *Some Japanese Portraits*, pp. 44–45. Presumably, everyone was too diffident to sit in the *yokoza*, so the place of honor had remained empty until Shōtetsu arrived.
4. *Zokuzoku Kikōbun Shū*, p. 113.
5. Ibid. Of course, Shōtetsu meant by these elaborate phrases that Tametada had died early in the year.
6. Ibid., p. 114.
7. Ibid.
8. Ibid., p. 116.
9. Ibid.
10. The word *makurazōshi* (pillow book) came to mean a pornographic book in the Tokugawa period. Perhaps it is used with that meaning here.
11. *Zokuzoku Kikōbun*, p. 116.
12. That is, from the area around modern Tokyo to the Sea of Japan coast.
13. They were fifteen or sixteen years old, as we know from the style in which their hair was done, the *agemaki*, or "triple loop."
14. *Zokuzoku Kikōbun*, p. 121.
15. Ibid., p. 119.
16. Ibid., pp. 119–20.
17. See Keene, *Some Japanese Portraits*, p. 48. The original text is in *Shōtetsu Monogatari*.
18. There is a study of this aspect of the diary by Tanaka Shin'ichi called "Shōtetsu no Koi," published in *Kokugo to Kokubungaku*, September 1966.

Journey to Fuji

1. Poem is given in Shirai Chūkō, *Chūsei no Kikō Bungaku*, p. 6.
2. Asukai Masayo, *Fuji Kikō*, p. 86.
3. Ibid., p. 89.
4. At this time all of Japan, except for the area around the capital, was divided into seven circuits (*dō*), geographical areas whose names are still familiar: Tōkai, Tōsan, Hokuriku, San'in, San'yō, Nankai, and

Saikai. Here, "Seven Circuits" is used to mean all of Japan.

5. "The Eight Great Islands" (*ōyashima*) was another way of referring to Japan. The islands are said to have been Honshū, Shikoku, Kyūshū, Awaji, Iki, Tsushima, Oki, and Sado, but "eight" was probably no more than a large number when the term was first used.
6. *Zoku Kikōbun Shū*, p. 608.

Journey to Zenkō-ji

1. An epithet for the Buddha, meaning "Thus Come" but sometimes translated as "Bearer of Truth."
2. *Zenkō-ji Kikō*, in *Zokuzoku Kikōbun Shū*, p. 138.
3. Ibid., p. 135.
4. *Zokuzoku Kikōbun*, pp. 136–37.
5. The first sentence may suggest the mixture of styles: *"Banjaku senjin ni sobadachite, nozomu ni shinshō wo wasure, hatō banri ni kasanarite, rōchō kudaru koto kagirinashi."*

Account of Fujikawa

1. His name is also read "Kanera."
2. Tonomura Nobuko, *Ichijō Kaneyoshi Fujikawa no Ki Zenshaku*, p. 44.
3. The text of the poem is given in Tonomura, *Ichijō*, p. 43.
4. Ichijō Kaneyoshi, "Fude no Susabi," in Ijichi Tetsuo, *Rengaron Shū*, pp. 282–83.
5. Ibid., p. 283.
6. See Burton Watson, *The Complete Works of Chuang Tzu*, p. 49, for a translation.
7. Ibid., p. 284.
8. Tonomura, *Ichijō*, pp. 68–73.
9. Ibid., p. 51.
10. Ibid., p. 88; see also pp. 96, 102. Various puns are embedded in the poem: for example, *toshinami* means "number of years," but *nami* by itself means "waves," associated with the river. Tonomura discusses peculiar grammatical features of the poem on p. 96.
11. Ibid., p. 90.
12. Ibid., p. 204; see also pp. 205, 208.
13. Ibid., p. 118. The word I have translated as "giraffe," *kirin*, is a fabulous animal that does not resemble anything in the Western bestiary.
14. Ibid., p. 125.
15. Ibid., p. 126. Kaneyoshi gives the names of the *bugaku* dances per-

formed: Michinaga's elder son, then ten years old, danced *Ryōō*, and his younger son, aged nine, danced *Nasori*. *Bugaku* were performed to the accompaniment of the ancient *gagaku* music.

16. Ibid.
17. Ibid., p. 39.
18. Ibid., p. 232.
19. This is the interpretation ibid., p. 234.
20. Quoted ibid., p. 41.

Journey to Shirakawa

1. Text in Imoto Nōichi, *Sōgi*, p. 108; translation from Robert Brower and Earl Miner, *Japanese Court Poetry*, p. 331.
2. Imoto, Sōgi, p. 109. There is a *kakekotoba* on *omoinasu* ("to consider") and Nasu, the place-name.
3. From "Kyoriku Ribetsu no Kotoba," in Sugiura Shōichirō, *Bashō Bunshū*, p. 206.
4. Ibid., p. 91.
5. Kaneko Kinjirō, *Sōgi Tabi no Ki Shichū*, p. 92.
6. Ibid., p. 10.
7. Both were poets of the Heian period who composed well-known *waka* on the subject of the Barrier of Shirakawa.
8. Kaneko, *Sōgi*, p. 15. For another translation, see Steven D. Carter, "Sōgi in the East Country."

Journey Along the Tsukushi Road

1. The cedars (*sugi*) of the Kashii Shrine (in modern Fukuoka) and the pine forest of Iki (to the west of Fukuoka) were both celebrated places in northern Kyūshū.
2. Kaneko Kinjirō, *Sōgi Tabi no Ki Shichū*, p. 33. See also Imoto Nōichi, *Sōgi*, p. 152. There is an English translation of the diary by Eileen Kato in her "Pilgrimage to Dazaifu."
3. That is, the 9th month according to the lunar calendar.
4. Kato, "Pilgrimage," p. 343. Original text in Kaneko, *Sōgi*, p. 37. See also Imoto, *Sōgi*, pp. 154–55.
5. Kato, "Pilgrimage," p. 346. Kaneko, *Sōgi*, pp. 46–47. See also Imoto, *Sōgi*, p. 163.
6. Kato, "Pilgrimage," p. 347. Kaneko, *Sōgi*, p. 47.
7. Kaneko, *Sōgi*, p. 49, interprets the poem as referring specifically to the Taira warrior Noritsune. I have attempted to translate *azusa yumi* (the name of a kind of bow), which Kaneko dismissed as a meaningless *makurakotoba* (pillow word). It is used here before

shioai (the ebbing tide) as a substitute for the verb *hiku* (to draw, as a bow); but it also suggests, appropriately, a warrior.
8. See p. 181.
9. Kato, "Pilgrimage," p. 354. Kaneko, *Sōgi*, p. 67.
10. Sugiura Shōichirō, *Bashō Bunshū*, p. 81.
11. Kato, "Pilgrimage," p. 356. Kaneko, *Sōgi*, p. 75.
12. Kato, "Pilgrimage," pp. 359–60. Kaneko, *Sōgi*, pp. 81–82.
13. Kato, "Pilgrimage," p. 362. Kaneko, *Sōgi*, p. 88.
14. Kaneko, *Sōgi*, p. 92.

Account of Sōgi's Last Hours

1. A *hokku* was the opening verse of a linked-verse sequence. It later came to be composed as an independent form of verse which (since the end of the nineteenth century) has been known as haiku.
2. Kaneko Kinjirō, *Sōgi Tabi nō Ki Shichū*, pp. 103–5.
3. Ibid., p. 104.
4. Ibid., p. 109.
5. Ibid.
6. Ibid., pp. 109, 113–14.
7. Ibid., p. 110.
8. Ibid., p. 115.
9. Ibid., pp. 115–16. The Barrier of Seiken was situated just before one reached the famous temple Seiken-ji.

Account of Utsunoyama

1. A form of early theater whose name means literally "rice-field music." However, the name was sometimes used for Nō, especially after the two theatrical arts merged in the fifteenth century.
2. Sōchō, *Utsunoyama no Ki*, p. 403.
3. Ibid., p. 404. See also John Whitney Hall and Toyoda Takeshi, eds., *Japan in the Muromachi Age*, p. 261.
4. See Hall and Toyoda, *Japan*, p. 262.
5. Mount Kōya was the site of the great Shingon monastery founded by Kūkai at the end of the eighth century. Translation from Donald Keene, "The Comic Tradition in Renga," p. 261.
6. Ibid.
7. Ibid., p. 262.
8. Tsukushi is the poetic name for Kyūshū; Azuma (the East) designated the general area around modern Tōkyō.
9. Sōchō, *Utsunoyama*, p. 397.
10. Perhaps some relative of the Nō dramatist Miyamasu, about whom

little is known except that he was the author of a number of plays.
11. Sōchō, *Azumaji no Tsuto*, p. 773.
12. Ibid., p. 780.

Sōchō's Notebook

1. Shimazu Tadao, ed., *Sōchō Nikki*, p. 7, identifies the man in whose suite Sōchō traveled as Asakura Norikage (1474–1552), the *shugo* (provincial constable) of Echizen.
2. The name Kaeru is the homophone of the verb *kaeru*, "to return." The mountain was an *uta-makura* used when writing poetry about Echizen.
3. Utsunoyama was the place in the province of Suruga where Sōchō had built his hermitage; Sayo no Nakayama (Nakayama of the Night), in the same general area, was famous especially because of the celebrated *waka* by Saigyō.
4. Shimazu, *Sōchō*, p. 7.
5. A *ken* was about six feet.
6. Local samurai, not under the control of central authority.
7. *Utsunoyama no Ki*, pp. 400–401.
8. Shimazu, *Sōchō*, p. 135.
9. Ibid., p. 90.
10. Haga Kōshirō, *Kinsei Bunka no Keishiki to Dentō*, p. 30.
11. Shimazu, *Sōchō*, p. 145. See also John Whitney Hall and Toyoda Takeshi, *Japan in the Muromachi Age*, p. 274.
12. A *chō* was about one hundred yards.
13. Shimazu, *Sōchō*, p. 51. See also Hall and Toyoda, *Japan*, p. 274.
14. Tofu, sweetened with miso and grilled on a skewer.

A Pilgrimage to Yoshino

1. An elegant way of referring to the art of *renga*.
2. *Yoshino no Mōde no Ki*, p. 197.
3. A temple of the Shingon Ritsu sect, popularly known as the Ariwara-dera because of its connections with Ariwara no Narihira.
4. *Yoshino no Mōde no Ki*, p. 200.
5. Ibid.
6. Ibid., p. 206.
7. Ibid., p. 202.
8. Ibid., p. 203.
9. Ibid.
10. Ibid., p. 298.
11. Ibid., p. 211. The sutra, *Brahmajāla-sūtra* in Sanskrit, was translated

into Chinese by Kumarājiva in 406. It is the basis of Mahāyāna beliefs.

Journey to See Fuji

1. *Fujimi no Michi no Ki*, p. 217.
2. Ibid., p. 227.
3. Ibid., p. 229.
4. Ibid., p. 230.
5. Ibid. Reference is made to the Nō play *Hagoromo* in which a *tennin* (celestial being) leaves her cloak on a pine bough, where it is found by a fisherman who insists that she dance for him if she wishes him to return the robe.
6. Ibid., p. 232.
7. Ibid., p. 238.
8. Ibid., p. 242. See also Donald Keene, *Some Japanese Portraits*, p. 59.
9. *Fujimi*, p. 243.

The Diary of Gen'yo

1. The nickname *sesshō kampaku* had another (more common) meaning: *sesshō* meant "regent," and *kampaku*, "chancellor," the two titles having been used originally for a member of the Fujiwara family who governed as regent for an emperor who was still a minor, or else as chancellor for an emperor who had attained his majority.
2. A *koku* was about five bushels of rice; stipends were calculated in terms of the number of *koku* a person received in a year.
3. *Gen'yo Nikki*, p. 250.
4. Ibid., p. 254.
5. For the lectures on *Ise Monogatari* see ibid., p. 250; for the instruction in *Kokin Manajo no Seidaku Denju*, see p. 253.
6. *Ibid.*, p. 251. Judging from the number of plays, they must have been performed at about twice the speed they would today.

Chōshōshi's Journey to Kyūshū

1. The old (or poetic) name of Kyūshū.
2. The Tenshō era lasted from 1573 to 1592. Chōshōshi followed Hideyoshi to Nagoya, in the province of Hizen, in 1592.
3. Chōshōshi uses poetic language—*tsuwamono* for "soldiers" and *Hi no moto* for "Japan"—whose flavor I have attempted to suggest.
4. *Kyūshū no Michi no Ki*, p. 269.

5. Ibid., p. 271.
6. Ibid. The passage contains several references to the fourth episode of *The Tales of Ise*, notably the quotation of the first words of Narihira's poem: "*Tsuki ya aranu haru ya mukashi. . . .*" See above, p. 111.
7. Ibid., pp. 271–72.
8. Ibid., pp. 273–74.

Korean War Diaries

1. The two-hour period from 5:00 to 7:00 P.M.
2. The two-hour period from 9:00 to 11:00 P.M.
3. Kitajima Manji, *Chōsen Nichinichiki, Kōrai Nikki*, p. 375.
4. Ibid., p. 378.
5. Ibid., p. 379.
6. Ibid., p. 96.
7. Ibid., p. 308.

Diaries of the Early Tokugawa Period

A Record of Favors Received

1. Odaka Toshio, ed., *Taionki*, p. 89. This work is otherwise treated in my book *Landscapes and Portraits*, pp. 72–78.
2. Odaka, *Taionki*, p. 89.
3. Ibid., p. 93.
4. Ibid., p. 41.
5. Ibid., p. 55.
6. Ibid., p. 56.
7. Ibid., p. 32.
8. Ibid., p. 29.
9. Quoted ibid., p. 27.
10. Ibid., p. 46.
11. Ibid., p. 45.
12. Ibid., p. 46.
13. Ibid., p. 43.
14. Ibid., p. 60.

A Journey of 1616

1. *Heishin Kikō*, in *Nihon Kikōbun Shūsei*, vol. III, p. 295.
2. The opening chapter is known by the first two words spoken by Confucius, *gakuji* in Japanese pronunciation.

3. This is part of the seventh section of chapter 1 of the *Analects*. In context it means that one should devote one's entire strength to one's family and should be ready to offer one's life to one's sovereign.
4. Chao Pao killed his mother in order to maintain his loyalty to his lord, then committed suicide to atone for his lack of filial piety.
5. *Heishin Kikō*, p. 302.
6. Ibid., p. 289. Udo Beach (Udohama) is in the modern Shizuoka Prefecture, near the celebrated Pine Grove of Miho. The quoted poem appears in the anthology *Go Shūi Shū* (1086). Nōin lived in the late tenth and early eleventh centuries.
7. Ibid., p. 301.
8. Eguchi was also famous for its courtesans, and the encounter of the priest Saigyō and the best-known of the courtesans is the subject of the Nō play *Eguchi*.
9. Apparently a designation for Taira no Munemori, who figures in the Nō play *Yuya* as the lover of the courtesan Yuya.
10. *Heishin Kikō*, p. 295.
11. The name of a mythical island (P'êng-lai in Chinese) where, according to the celebrated poem *Song of Everlasting Sorrow* by Po Chü-i, Yang Kuei-fei's spirit went after her death.
12. *Heishin Kikō*, p. 299.
13. Ibid., p. 304.
14. *Gunsho Kaidai*, vol. XII, p. 154.

Diaries of Seventeenth-Century Courtiers

1. *Sasamakura*, p. 308.
2. Ibid., p. 310.
3. *Nikkō-zan Kikō*, p. 317.
4. *Kantō Kaidōki*, p. 312.
5. See article in *Nihon Koten Bungaku Daijiten*, vol. IV, p. 516. He meant by "Kantō" the Shogun, of course.

Travels Round the East

1. *Azuma Meguri*, p. 307. The village of Shinobu, in the northern province of Michinoku (also called Ōshū), was often mentioned in poetry. The author of the diary, however, says that he spent his time unpoetically (*kokoronaku*).
2. Ibid., p. 309.
3. Ibid., p. 310.
4. Ibid.
5. Koshiji usually refers to the provinces on the Sea of Japan coast—Echizen, Etchū, and Echigo—whose names include the character

koshi. The wild geese of Koshiji are mentioned in various works of classical literature, including *Heike Monogatari*, probably because migrating geese seemed to come from that direction. This passage, like most of the rest of the diary, is studded with allusions to classical literature—so many, in fact, as to suggest parody.

6. *Azuma Meguri*, p. 313.
7. The pun is on *nifuku* ("two cups," but also "two *fuku* [happiness]") and *fukufuku* ("flourishing").

A Journey in the Year 1667

1. *Hinotohitsuji Ryokōki*, in *Nihon Kikōbun Shūsei*, vol. IV, p. 336.
2. Ibid., p. 338.
3. Ibid., p. 332.
4. Ibid., p. 336.
5. Ibid., p. 337. *Hagi* is the bicolor lespedeza, sometimes called "bush clover" by translators.
6. Ibid., p. 339.
7. Ibid., pp. 340–41. The *kaminoma* was the room containing the place of honor of the house. It was where guests were received.
8. Ibid., p. 341.
9. Ibid., p. 334.
10. It was popularly believed that a mark (generally the father's crest) was found on the placenta of the newborn baby, indicating whether or not it was legitimate.
11. *Hinotohitsuji*, p. 334. One *ri* was about 2.5 miles.

Bashō's Diaries

1. The scholar was Nunami Keion (1877–1927). His remark is quoted by Asō Isoji in *Nihon Bungaku no Sōten*, vol. V, pp. 137–39.

Exposed in the Fields

1. See "Bashō's Journey of 1684," in my *Landscapes and Portraits*, pp. 94–108, for a complete translation of this diary.
2. See Imoto Nōichi et al., *Matsuo Bashō Shū*, pp. 73, 287.

A Pilgrimage to Kashima

1. Imoto Nōichi et al., *Matsuo Bashō Shū*, p. 299.
2. Ibid., p. 303.

3. Ibid., p. 305. Tu Fu wrote the words at the Feng-hsien Temple in Lung Men, referring to the early-morning bell at the temple.
4. Ibid., p. 306.
5. For a translation of this section of *Makura no Sōshi*, see Ivan Morris, trans., *The Pillow Book of Sei Shōnagon*, vol. I, pp. 104–9. The *hototogisu*, a bird resembling the cuckoo, was celebrated by poets for its melodious song from the time of the *Kokinshū*. It sings in the rainy season.

Manuscript in My Knapsack

1. "Money for my straw sandals" (*waraji no ryō*) was a poetic way of saying "money for travel expenses." *Waraji* were straw sandals laced above the ankles and worn when traveling, but normally not within the city where one lived.
2. The quotation is from Chuang Tzu: "A person who is going 100 *li* should make his preparations the night before; the person who is going 1000 *li* should gather provisions three months earlier."
3. Imoto Nōichi et al., *Matsuo Bashō Shū*, p. 313.
4. Ibid., p. 311.
5. Ibid.
6. See pp. 3–4, for a translation of the relevant passage.
7. Imoto, *Matsuo Bashō*, p. 314.
8. Ibid., p. 316. See also Donald Keene, *World Within Walls*, p. 96, for a comparison of the three haiku on the same theme composed by Bashō on this occasion.
9. Ibid., p. 398.
10. Ibid., p. 320. Japanese of Bashō's time (and much later) were known by various names during their lifetimes. A man's official name (the one he was given at birth) was considered to be too formal for a boy, and suitably boyish nicknames were used instead. It is still common for pilgrims who wear Japanese dress and who are traveling together to write inscriptions such as the one Bashō scribbled inside their bamboo hats.
11. Ibid., pp. 328–29.
12. Ibid., p. 458.

Journey to Sarashina

1. Donald Keene, trans., *Essays in Idleness*, p. 22. Episode 21 in *Tsurezuregusa*.
2. Keene, *Essays in Idleness*, p. 118. Episode 137 in *Tsurezuregusa*.
3. Keene, *Essays in Idleness*, p. 175. Episode 212 in *Tsurezuregusa*.

4. See Mildred Tahara, trans., *Tales of Yamato*, pp. 109–10.
5. Imoto Nōichi et al., *Matsuo Bashō Shū*, p. 336.

The Narrow Road of Oku

1. Imoto Nōichi et al., *Matsuo Bashō Shū*, p. 336.
2. Ibid., p. 343.
3. Quoted in Robert H. Brower, trans., *Fujiwara Teika's Hundred-Poem Sequence of the Shōji Era*, pp. 6–7.
4. Imoto, *Matsuo Bashō*, p. 363.
5. Ibid. The allusion is to the *waka* by Ōtomo no Yakamochi in the *Man'yōshū*, number 4097.
6. Imoto, *Matsuo Bashō*, p. 364. It is impossible to make a literal translation that would be easily intelligible in English, and I have had (unwillingly) to add some phrases. For example, "*Hidehira ga ato wa*" means literally "the remains of Hidehira," suggesting the subject is his mummy, which in fact exists, but Bashō was presumably referring to the ruins of Hidehira's castle.
7. Ibid., pp. 358–59.

The Saga Diary

1. Imoto Nōichi et al., *Matsuo Bashō Shū*, p. 389.
2. *Hakushi Shū* was more commonly called *Hakushi Monjū* (or sometimes merely *Monjū*), and had enjoyed great popularity among educated people in Japan since the Heian period. *Honchō Ichinin Isshu* was published in 1665 by Hayashi Gahō (the son of Hayashi Razan). It consists of one poem each by over three hundred poets of *kanshi* (poems in Chinese), ranging in time from the seventh-century Prince Ōtomo, to Tokugawa Yoshinao of the seventeenth century, but poems by the Buddhist monks of the Five Mountains (Gosan) were not included. The title *Yotsugi Monogatari* was given to both *Eiga Monogatari* and *Ōkagami*, two historical writings of the Heian period. *Shōyō Shū* is apparently a shortened version of the title *Shōyō Meisho Waka Shū*, a collection of *waka* describing famous places in Japan.
3. Imoto, *Matsuo Bashō*, pp. 392–93. The statements on mourning and drink were derived by Bashō from the writings of Chuang Tzu. The quotation from Saigyō occurs in a *waka* found in the collection *Sankashū*. The full poem is:

tou hito mo	In the mountain village,
omoitaetaru	Quite forgotten even by
yamazato no	Those who visited,

sabishisa nakuba	If there were no loneliness
sumiukaramashi	How dreary life would be!

4. Kinoshita Chōshōshi (1569–1649), a general with poetic aspirations, gave up his military office to live as a hermit in the Higashiyama district of Kyōto and devoted himself to *waka* poetry. An account of him may be found in my *Some Japanese Portraits*, pp. 79–96.
5. Yamaguchi Sodō (1642–1716) was one of Bashō's chief disciples.
6. Nozawa Bonchō (d. 1714), a physician who was a devoted disciple of Bashō's. He and his wife, the nun Ukō, were living in Kyōto at this time and visited Bashō several times at Rakushisha.

Diaries of the Later Tokugawa Period

Journey to the Northwest

1. Kaibara Ekiken, *Seihoku Kikō*, in *Nihon Kikōbun Shūsei*, p. 347.
2. Ibid., p. 354. The pronunciation of the name is uncertain.
3. Ibid., p. 360.
4. Ibid., p. 366. His *Account of a Journey to Kyūshū* is discussed on pp. 252–54.
5. Ibid., p. 368.
6. Ibid.
7. "Ekiken" was his *gō* (style), and "Atsunobu" was his personal name. The order of *gō* + surname + personal name is frequently found.
8. Ekiken, *Seihoku Kikō*, p. 369. Eighty-one by Western count. Ekiken says deferentially that he has added years [as meaninglessly] as a dog or horse (*kenba no yowai*).
9. Ibid.
10. Kaibara Ekiken, *Ekiken Zenshū*, vol. VII, p. 116. Ekiken's explanation of *kataonami* or, more properly, *kata wo nami* is generally accepted today. The term occurs in a *Man'yōshū* poem by Yamabe no Akahito, where it indeed has the meaning of high waves wiping out a beach. But the popular belief that there were only "male" waves at Wakanoura was long accepted.
11. Ibid.

Some Diaries by Women

1. Ekiken actually says "*otoko moji*", meaning "men's writing." This was an appellation often given to Chinese characters, as opposed to *kana*, which were known as "women's writing."
2. Kaibara Ekiken, *Ekiken Zenshū*, vol. III, p. 396.

3. Ibid. *Kouta* were short songs sung to samisen accompaniment; *jōruri* were the texts of puppet plays, also sung to samisen accompaniment.
4. Ibid., p. 397.
5. Inoue Tsūjo, *Tōkai Nikki*, in *Nikki Kikō Shū*, p. 245.
6. Ibid., pp. 257, 260.
7. Ibid., p. 260.
8. Ibid.
9. It was often stated in poetry (both Chinese and Japanese) that wild geese carried messages north or south on their twice-annual migrations.
10. Inoue, *Edo Nikki*, p. 302. The man who praised Tsūjo is identified as Sado Taishū-kō, presumably a Chinese-style title used by Tsūjo in referring to the governor of Sado.
11. Inoue Tsūjo, *Kika Nikki*, in *Nikki Kikō Shū*, p. 263.
12. Ibid., p. 269.
13. Ibid., pp. 270–71.
14. Ibid., pp. 274–75.
15. Ibid., p. 298.
16. *Nikki Kikō*, p. 314. The four works referred to are *Kagerō Nikki* (*The Gossamer Years*), *Murasaki Shikibu Nikki* (*The Diary of Lady Murasaki*), *Sarashina Nikki* (*The Sarashina Diary*), and *Izayoi Nikki* (*The Diary of the Waning Moon*).
17. Watanabe Tōsui, *Shirabyōshi Takejo*," in *Denki*, vol. VI, 8, p. 4.
18. *Nikki Kikō*, p. 317.
19. This is poem number 938 in the *Kokinshū*. Translation is from my *Anthology of Japanese Literature*, p. 79.
20. *Nikki Kikō*, p. 328.
21. Ibid., p. 318.
22. Ibid., p. 321. See p. 290 for Chia Tao's original poem.
23. Ibid., p. 322.
24. Ibid., p. 323.
25. Ibid.
26. Ibid., pp. 323–24.

Travels of Gentlemen Emissaries

1. *Fūryū* is a hard word to translate. When used as an adjective, it can be translated as "elegant," "refined," "tasteful," or "fashionable," depending on context, but none of these adjectives seems entirely appropriate for Sorai and Seigo. They were gentlemen of taste who enjoyed their travels in the manner of the *bunjin* of China. "Tasteful emissaries" sounds peculiar, and "emissaries of taste" suggests that they were bringing culture to the hinterland, certainly not their aim.

2. The shortened version, entitled *Kyōchū Kikō*, has been translated into English, with an extensive introduction and copious notes, by Olof G. Lidin in *Ogyū Sorai's Journey to Kai in 1706.*
3. One *ri* was about 2.5 miles, but Fuchū, now in the Tokyo Metropolitan District, is by no means that distant from the heart of Tokyo. Perhaps Sorai was thinking in terms of the Chinese *li*, which is about one-third of a mile. Or perhaps his *sūjūri* ("several tens of *ri*") is to be understood figuratively.
4. Kawamura Yoshimasa, ed., *Kyōchū Kikō, Fūryū Shisha Ki*, p. 118.
5. More frequently called Okunitama Shrine at Fuchū.
6. Sorai here refers to the large, menacing statues, usually called Niō, which stand behind wooden fences on either side of the main gate of a Shintō shrine.
7. Kawamura, *Kyōchū*, p. 118.
8. Ibid., p. 122.
9. Ibid., p. 126.
10. Ibid.
11. The text uses the word *shukuhansō*, meaning a priest who eats rice gruel in the morning and boiled rice for dinner, the implication being that he does little more than eat.
12. Kawamura, *Kyōchū*, pp. 342–43.
13. Ibid., p. 174. The phrase *goshō hibikan to hossu* seems to have a colloquial meaning, perhaps the creaking of his bones.
14. Ibid., p. 134.
15. The word *santan* or *sandan* designated a *ge*, or hymn of praise to the Buddha.
16. Kawamura, *Kyōchū*, p. 150.
17. Ibid., p. 180.

The Frolic of the Butterfly

1. For the *bashō*, see p. 299.
2. "Dews" is used for spring and "frosts" for autumn. Counting years by springs and autumns was common in China and Japan.
3. *Nihon Kikōbun Shūsei*, vol. IV, p. 424.
4. The text gives a fuller address: Yanaka Niibori-mura Fudasan Yōfuku-ji. The temple is not far from Nippori Station, and the imposing monument to Jidaraku Sensei may still be seen.
5. Imaizumi Teisuke, *Shin Hyakka Zeirin*, vol. III, pp. 727–28.
6. *Zokuzoku Kikō Bunshū*, p. 410.
7. For moxa treatment, see above, p. 408.
8. *Zokuzoku*, p. 391.
9. Ibid., p. 392.

10. A "cutting word" that serves to divide the two parts of a haiku; here it refers to *ya*.
11. A form of composing linked *haikai*-style verse that consists in adding a verse that precedes rather than follows the verse made by another person.
12. *Zokuzoku*, p. 393.
13. Legendary warrior-monk of the twelfth century. Also called Musashibō Benkei (d. 1189). His loyalty to Yoshitsune is celebrated, and he was known for his immense strength.
14. *Zokuzoku*, pp. 393–94.
15. Ibid., p. 395.
16. Ibid., p. 396.
17. An allusion to the famous poem by Ariwara no Narihira (*Kokinshū* number 747) already cited, p. 111.
18. *Zokuzoku*, pp. 396–97.
19. Ibid., p. 398.
20. Ibid., p. 400.
21. *Azuma ebisu* ("eastern savages") was a term that had been used by people in Kyōto to designate the unruly, crude warriors of the eastern provinces. At this time, however, it seems to have designated rustics of the eastern or northeastern provinces in general.
22. *Zokuzoku*, p. 407.
23. A temple associated with legends of the Empress Jingū, who was said to have possessed a pearl (*ju*) that enabled her to control the tides, whether low (*kan*) or high (*man*).

Diary of the Nagasaki Border Guard

1. This was the celebrated "Benyowsky's Warning." In 1771 Baron Moritz Aladar von Benyowsky, who had engineered a revolt among exiles in Kamchatka, seized control of a small vessel. When the ship called at Awa, a province on the island of Shikoku, he was given provisions, and in gratitude (or so he said) he informed the Japanese, through the Dutch on Deshima, of the Russian menace.
2. Shiba Kōkan, *Kōkan Saiyū Nikki*, p. 110.
3. Reference is probably being made to Bashō's haiku that begins "*yamaji kite*" (Sekisui used the older word *hokku*) quoted on p. 293. However, this poem was composed, according to a headnote, on the way to Ōtsu, whereas Sekisui was in the vicinity of Odawara, an entirely different place. There seems to have been some confusion of tradition.
4. *Zokuzoku Kikōbun Shū*, p. 478.
5. Ibid., p. 486.

6. The *waka* has been cited above, p. 236.
7. *Zokuzoku*, p. 482.
8. Ibid., p. 497.
9. Ibid.
10. A pole with a flame-shaped metal "jewel" at the top, erected before Buddhist temples. Sekisui is referring to the flagpole on Deshima, which during the Napoleonic invasion of Holland bore the only Dutch flag in the world. The base of the flagpole still exists. The Japanese at this time did not fly their flags from poles.
11. Closely fitting breeches worn mainly by laborers.
12. *Zokuzoku*, p. 498.
13. Ibid.
14. Ibid., p. 499.
15. See Donald Keene, *The Japanese Discovery of Europe*, p. 5.
16. Ibid.
17. *Zokuzoku*, p. 511.
18. Ibid., p. 502.
19. That is, communicating by writing messages in classical Chinese, intelligible to both Chinese and Japanese even if they could not understand each other's spoken words.

Diary of Kōkan's Trip to the West

1. Kuroda Genji and Yamaga Seinosuke, eds., *Kōkan Saiyū Nikki*, pp. 166–67.
2. Ibid., p. 169.
3. Ibid., p. 168.
4. *Ariya* is the burden of a work song; it has no meaning.
5. *Kōkan*, pp. 142–43.
6. Ibid., p. 191.
7. Ibid., p. 3.
8. Ibid., p. 103.
9. Naigū, one of the two important buildings at the Ise shrine, the other being the Gekū, or Outer Shrine.
10. *Kōkan*, p. 44.
11. The *hakama* is the lower garment in formal Japanese dress, *haori* the jacket worn with the same.
12. *Kōkan*, p. 122.
13. The word "factory" is used in the sense of a business establishment for commercial agents or factors in a foreign country.
14. *Kōkan*, p. 107.
15. Ibid., p. 110.
16. *Sushi* means "sour"; the Dutchman mishears the word, and thinks

Kōkan has said *kusuri*, meaning "medicine." It is not clear why he points at an egg.

17. *Kōkan*, p. 108. I have not identified Mōtāpa.
18. Ibid., p. 109.
19. Arthur Waley, *The Secret History of the Mongols*, p. 108.

Journal of a New Era

1. It was customary to change the era name (*nengō*) at least twice during the cycle of sixty years, in the first (*kōshi*) and fifty-eighth (*shin'yū*) years. The era name was also changed without reference to these years, in order to reflect auspicious occurrences or to ward off apprehended disaster, and it was generally changed at the beginning of a new reign.
2. *Kaigen Kikō*, p. 718.
3. *Rōzumi*, a mixture of wax and ink, was used for making rubbings.
4. *Kaigen Kikō*, p. 723.
5. Apparently a reference to the exceedingly prosperous Chinese dynasty founded in 379 B.C. It lasted about 150 years. I do not recognize the reference to the "over seventy castles."
6. *Kaigen Kikō*, p. 723.
7. Ibid., pp. 723–24.
8. Sumpu was the chief city of the province; now called Shizuoka.
9. The Keichō era, one of the most celebrated of Japanese history, lasted from 1596 to 1615.
10. *Kaigen Kikō*, pp. 730–31.
11. Ibid., p. 743.
12. This was the day of *momo no sekku*, or the Dolls' Festival. It is still celebrated by arranging on several tiers dolls that represented the Emperor, Empress, and other members of the court. When it was celebrated according to the lunar calendar (as here), peach blossoms would be in bloom.
13. *Kaigen Kikō*, p. 738.
14. Ibid., p. 766.
15. Ibid., p. 740.
16. Ibid., p. 751.
17. A formal garment worn by samurai during the Tokugawa period. It consists of an upper garment with projecting shoulder boards, worn over a formal kimono, and trousers of the same material.
18. *Kaigen Kikō*, p. 765.
19. *Dengaku* is tofu on a skewer that has been coated with miso and baked.
20. *Kaigen Kikō*, p. 766. Shortly after New Year's it was customary to

cut and serve the seven herbs of spring. The cutting was accompanied by a rhythmical chant.

21. The words in (single) quotation marks seem to be *uta-makura*, but I have not been able to trace them.
22. *Kaigen Kikō*, pp. 770–71.
23. Ibid., p. 776.
24. Ibid., p. 771.

Bakin's Diaries

1. Aeba Kōson, *Bakin Nikki Shō*, p. 8.
2. Ibid., p. 9.
3. Ibid., pp. 175–76.
4. A quotation from the *Analects* of Confucius that came to be used as a proverb in Japan. It was sometimes amplified to explain that if one is kind to women (*joshi*) and men of no virtue (*shōjin*) they become familiar, and if one treats them distantly they become resentful.
5. Aeba, *Bakin*, p. 63.
6. Ibid., p. 64.
7. Ibid., pp. 41–42.
8. Ibid., p. 53.
9. Ibid., pp. 68–69.
10. Ibid., p. 75.
11. An officer of a clan who ranked below *rōshin*. He was in charge of finances.
12. The Miyake family served as the daimyos of the small Tawara fief. It is not clear why Bakin referred to this Miyake as "*Bingo no kami dono*" ("His Excellency, the governor of Bingo").
13. Watanabe Kazan (1793–1841), a high-ranking official of the Tawara domain, was famed as a painter. He came under suspicion for advocating closer relations with European countries, and was arrested along with other scholars of Dutch learning in 1839. The death sentence was commuted to life imprisonment. The last two years of his life were spent mainly in reading and painting. He committed suicide for fear that his presence was harmful to the daimyo of the fief.
14. I have not been able to identify this man.
15. Aeba, *Bakin*, pp. 222–23.
16. The Tempō Reforms (*Tempō no kaikaku*) were undertaken by the Senior Councilor Mizuno Tadakuni in 1841–43. They had such laudable aims as the increase of food production and the elimination of corruption within the government, but in the effort to improve

the morals of the samurai class and the general public, certain books were banned, along with gambling and unlicensed prostitution. Sumptuary regulations were strictly enforced, and this militated against the production of elaborate works of art or brilliant Kabuki performances. The reforms were not successful enough to bolster the Tokugawa regime during its final years.

17. One of a line of celebrated Kabuki actors.
18. *Kanmon* or *kan* was the equivalent of a thousand copper coins. Four *kanmon* were the equivalent of one *ryō* in gold. The fine was a heavy one.
19. Aeba, *Bakin*, pp. 275–76.
20. Ibid., pp. 231–32.
21. Quoted ibid., p. 6.

The Diary of Iseki Takako

1. A *hatamoto* (bannerman) was a direct samurai retainer of the Tokugawa shogunate. Most were descendants of samurai who had helped Tokugawa Ieyasu to found the shogunate, and they occupied important positions within the government.
2. Fukasawa Akio, ed., *Iseki Takako Nikki*, vol. I, p. 48.
3. By *kokugaku* was meant the study of the Japanese classics, especially the *Kojiki* and *Man'yōshū*, as practiced by such eighteenth-century scholars as Motoori Norinaga. *Kokugaku* was often accompanied by nationalistic tendencies.
4. Fukasawa, *Iseki*, vol. I, p. 79.
5. Ibid., p. 48.
6. Ibid., p. 31.
7. *Katatagae* and *monoimi* were ways of avoiding harm from the gods by refraining from traveling in unlucky directions or partaking of certain foods. There are frequent mentions of these superstitions in the literature of the past, notably *The Tale of Genji*.
8. *Onyōji* in Japanese. These were diviners who predicted the future and "avoided calamity" in accordance with the Five Elements (wood, fire, earth, metal, and water) that, by an elaborate system of correspondences, constituted the planets, the directions, the seasons, and the signs of the zodiac. See Wm. Theodore de Bary, ed., *Sources of Japanese Tradition*, pp. 55–60.
9. Fukasawa, *Iseki*, vol. I, p. 45.
10. Ibid.
11. Ibid., p. 46.
12. Ibid., p. 69.
13. Ibid., p. 153.
14. Ibid., vol. III, p. 27.

15. Ibid., vol. I, p. 178.
16. Ibid., p. 139.
17. Ibid., vol. III, p. 337.
18. Ibid., vol. II, p. 361.
19. The old name for Ōsaka, still used poetically.
20. The word *karaki* means both "salty" and "bitter"; used here as a pun.
21. Fukasawa, *Iseki*, vol. I, p. 47.
22. These were two offices of the shogunate, both under the supervision of the *waka-toshiyori*. The *temmon-kata* was in charge of astronomy, calendar-making, surveying, geography, and European books; the *shomotsu bugyō* was in charge of the Koyōkan Bunko, the library of the shogunate. Both were important offices; Takahashi held them because of his outstanding ability.
23. Fukasawa, *Iseki*, vol. II, p. 65. For a brief account of the unhappy Takahashi Kageyasu, see my *The Japanese Discovery of Europe*, pp. 147–52. He was found guilty a year after the investigation began, and the head was struck from his pickled corpse.
24. Fukasawa, *Iseki*, vol. I, p. 139.
25. Ibid., p. 123.
26. She used the word *suikyū*, which is "water moxa cauterization"; probably she heard a garbled account of vaccination.
27. Fukasawa, *Iseki*, vol. I, p. 162.

The Uraga Diary

1. Satō Toratarō, *Shōzan Zenshū*, vol. I, p. 1123.
2. Ibid., vol. I, p. 1131.
3. This is a rough approximation of *yoriki*, a minor official who carried out administrative directives for the organization to which he was attached.
4. The text uses the word *kakurō*, another name for the *rōjū*, the second-highest-ranking officer of the shogunate. It is not clear why Shōzan thought the gifts were for him, rather than for the Shogun, but the American undoubtedly intended the gifts for the Shogun.
5. Satō, *Shōzan*, vol. I, p. 1136.
6. The text gives *tageurotaipen*.
7. The text gives *iojiumu* and *furomiumi*.
8. Satō, *Shōzan*, pp. 1135–36.

The Nagasaki Diary

1. Fujii Sadafumi and Kawata Sadao, eds., *Nagasaki Nikki, Shimoda Nikki*, p. 3. Toshiakira seems to mean by this poem that, although

he (or perhaps the Japanese in general) cannot learn about the remote islands at the end of the chain of Kurile Islands (known in Japan as Chishima), he does not want the Russians to rule them. There is a pun in the third line between *e zo*, which, with a negative, means "cannot," and Ezo, the name for both Hokkaido and the Kuriles.

2. *Shukuiri* was the ceremonial entrance into a town of the procession of a daimyo. Every effort was made to impress persons of the town with the importance and grandeur of the particular daimyo. Toshiakira seems to be suggesting that it was uncomfortable for the participants.
3. Fujii and Kawata, *Nagasaki*, pp. 9–10. The "court" mentioned at the end of this quotation is that of the Shogun, not the Emperor.
4. Ibid., p. 13.
5. Ibid., pp. 27–28.
6. Ibid., p. 30.
7. Ibid., p. 34.
8. Ibid., p. 46.
9. The Japanese normally did not use chairs, but *kyokuroku* of Chinese origin were used in Buddhist temples, especially those of the Zen sect.
10. The *gosshi* were low, backless seats used mainly at the court during ceremonies.
11. The *nijōdai* (translated as "tatami platforms") were used in Kabuki as the seats of high-ranking generals and nobles. These "platforms" were two *jō* (about two yards square) in size. The usual height was eight inches; presumably several were piled one on top of another to raise the Japanese to the height of the Russians' chairs.
12. Fujii and Kawata, *Nagasaki*, p. 50. Presumably he meant that he, like all Japanese subjects, was forbidden to go abroad, and he at first feared that the Russian ship was "abroad."
13. Ibid., p. 53. A well-known painting by a Japanese (in the Waseda University Theatre Museum) of Putiatin's predecessor, Rezanov, shows him wearing just such a hat.
14. Ibid., p. 54.
15. Ibid. "*Aba aba*" seems to be an equivalent (in the language of Japanese children of the time) to "bye-bye." But it may also be meaningless syllables, rather like the "hubba-hubba" used during World War II to express enthusiastic approval, especially of young women.
16. Ibid., p. 65.
17. *Funajirushi* were pennants and similar signs used to indicate the name, ownership, or sometimes the identity of a (distinguished) passenger. In this case perhaps the flags of both countries are meant. During the Tokugawa period the Rising Sun flag was used as a "ship's

emblem" (*hinomaru funajirushi*), but the Russians may have taken this for a national flag.

18. Fujii and Kawata, *Nagasaki*, p. 70. Toshiakira seems to be saying that this display of international friendship is no more than a trick of one country to persuade another country of affection it does not actually feel, like a prostitute who has a sash dyed with her crest and that of a customer intertwined. Toshiakira used the word *kinbanmono*, a samurai from a fief elsewhere who is on alternate attendance duty in Edo without his family.
19. A large piece of cloth, often beautifully dyed silk, used to wrap parcels, etc.
20. Fujii and Kawata, *Nagasaki*, pp. 71–72.
21. Ibid., p. 72.
22. Ibid.

The Shimoda Diary

1. Fujii Sadafumi and Kawata Sadao, eds., *Nagasaki Nikki, Shimoda Nikki*, p. 82.
2. *Oblomov* strongly influenced the Japanese novelist Futabatei Shimei, whose *Ukigumo* (1887–89) is often stated to have been the first modern Japanese novel.
3. Fujii and Kawata, *Nagasaki*, p. 93.
4. Ibid., p. 98.
5. Ibid., pp. 148–49.
6. Ibid., p. 153.
7. Ibid., p. 191.

Bibliography

Note: All Japanese books, except as otherwise noted, were published in Tokyo.

Aeba Kōson. *Bakin Nikki Shō*. Bunkaidō Shoten, 1911.

Asō Isoji. *Nihon Bungaku no Sōten*, vol. V. Meiji Shoin, 1969.

Azukai Masayo. *Fuji Kikō*, in *Zoku Kikōbun Shū*. Nihon Tosho Sentā, 1979.

Bowring, Richard. *Murasaki Shikibu: Her Diary and Poetic Memoirs*. Princeton: Princeton University Press, 1982.

Brazell, Karen, trans. *The Confessions of Lady Nijō*. Garden City, NY: Doubleday, 1973.

Brewster, Jennifer, trans. *The Emperor Horikawa Diary*. Honolulu: The University Press of Hawaii, 1977.

Brower, Robert H. *Fujiwara Teika's Hundred-Poem Sequence of the Shōji Era*. Tokyo: Sophia University, 1978.

Brower, Robert, and Earl Miner. *Japanese Court Poetry*. Stanford, Calif.: Stanford University Press, 1961.

Brown, Delmer M., and Ichirō Ishida. *The Future and the Past: A Translation and Study of the Gukanshō*. Berkeley: University of California Press, 1979.

Carter, Steven D. "Sōgi in the East Country: *Shirakawa Kikō*." *Monumenta Nipponica*, vol. 42, no. 2 (1987).

Coates, Harper Havelock, and Ryugaku Ishizuka. *Honen the Buddhist Saint*. Tokyo: Kodokaku, 1930.

Cranston, Edwin A., trans. *The Izumi Shikibu Diary*. Cambridge, Mass.: Harvard University Press, 1969.
de Bary, W. T., Ryusaku Tsunoda, and Donald Keene. *Sources of Japanese Tradition*. New York: Columbia University Press, 1958.
Fujii Sadafumi, and Kawata Sadao, eds. *Nagasaki Nikki, Shimoda Nikki*, in Tōyō Bunko series. Heibonsha, 1968.
Fujiwara no Munetada. *Chūyūki*, in Zōho Shiryō Taisei series, vol. XI. Kyōto: Rinsen Shoten, 1965.
Fujiwara Teika. *Gotoba-in Kumano Gokō Ki*, in Gunsho Ruijū, Kikōbun series. Zoku Gunsho Ruijū Kankōkai, 1959.
Fukasawa Akio, ed. *Iseki Takako Nikki*, 3 vols. Benseisha, 1978.
Fukuda Hideichi. *Towazugatari*, in Shinchō Nihon Koten Shūsei series. Shinchōsha, 1978.
Haga Kōshirō. *Kinsei Bunka no Keishiki to Dentō*. Kawade Shobō, 1948.
Hagitani Boku. *Shintei Tosa Nikki; Ki no Tsurayuki Zenshū*, in Nihon Koten Zensho series. Asahi Shimbun Sha, 1969.
———. *Tosa Nikki Zenchūshaku*, in Nihon Koten Hyōshaku Zenchūshaku Sōsho series. Kadokawa Shoten, 1967.
Hall, John Whitney, and Toyoda Takeshi, eds. *Japan in the Muromachi Age*. Berkeley: University of California Press, 1977.
Harries, Phillip Tudor, trans. *The Poetic Memoirs of Lady Daibu*. Stanford, Calif.: Stanford University Press, 1980.
Hino Ashihei. *Earth and Soldiers*, trans. Shidzue Ishimoto. New York: Rinehart, 1939.
Hirabayashi Fumio. *Jōjin Ajari Haha no Shū no Kisoteki Kenkyū*. Kasama Shoin, 1977.
Hisamatsu Sen'ichi, and Nishio Minoru. *Karon Shū, Nōgakuron Shū*, in Nihon Koten Bungaku Taikei series. Iwanami Shoten, 1961.
Horton, H. Mack. "Saiokuken Sōchō and the Linked-Verse Business." *The Transactions of the Asiatic Society of Japan*, 4th series, vol. I (1986), pp. 45–78.
Hotta Yoshie. *Teika Meigetsuki Shishō*, 2 vols. Shinchōsha, 1986–88.
Ijichi Tetsuo. *Rengaron Shū*, vol. I, in Iwanami Bunko series. Iwanami Shoten, 1953.
Ikeda Kikan. *Kyūtei Joryū Nikki Bungaku*. Shibundō, 1965.
Imagawa Fumio. *Kundoku Meigetsuki*, 6 vols. Kawade Shobō Shinsha, 1977.
———. *Meigetsuki Shō*. Kawade Shobō Shinsha, 1986.
Imaizumi Teisuke. *Shin Hyakka Zeirin*, vol. III, Yoshikawa Kōbunkan, 1931.
Imoto Nōichi. *Sōgi*. Kyōto: Tankōsha, 1974.
Imoto Nōichi et al. *Matsuo Bashō Shū*, in Nihon Koten Bungaku Zenshū series. Shōgakukan, 1972.

Inoue Tsūjo. *Tōkai Kikō* and *Kika Nikki*, in *Nikki Kikō Shū*, in Yūhōdō Bunko series, 1915.

———. *Edo Nikki*, in Joryū Bungaku Zenshū series, vol. I. Bungei Shoin, 1918.

Ishida yoshisada, and Satsukawa Shūji. *Minamoto Ienaga Nikki Zenchūshaku*. Yūseidō, 1968.

Itoga Kimie. *Kenreimon'in Ukyō no Daibu no Shū*, in Shinchō Nihon Koten Shūsei series. Shinchōsha, 1979.

Kaibara Ekiken. *Ekiken Zenshū*, 8 vols. Tokyo: Ekiken Zenshū Kankōbu, 1910–11.

———. *Seihoku Kikō*, in *Nihon Kikōbun Shūsei*, vol. 3. Nihon Tosho Sentā, 1979.

Kaneko Kinjirō. *Sōji Tabi no Ki Shichū*. Ōfūsha, 1970.

Kasamatsu Yoshio. *Tōkan Kikō Shinshaku*. Daidōkan Shoten, 1940.

Kato, Eileen. "Pilgrimage to Dazaifu," in *Monumenta Nipponica*, vol. XXXIV, no. 3 (Autumn 1979).

Katō Genchi. *Kenkyū Hyōshaku: Saka-ō Daijingū Sankeiki*. Fuzambō, 1939.

Kawabata Yasunari. *Kawabata Yasunari Zenshū*, 35 vols. Shinchōsha, 1980–83.

Kawamura Yoshimasa, ed. *Kyōchū Kikō, Fūryū Shisha Ki*. Yūsankaku, 1971.

Keene, Donald. "The Comic Tradition in Renga," in Hall and Toyoda, *Japan in the Muromachi Age*.

———. *Dawn to the West*. New York: Holt, Rinehart & Winston, 1984.

———. *The Japanese Discovery of Europe*. Stanford, Calif.: Stanford University Press, 1969.

———. *Landscapes and Portraits*. Tokyo: Kodansha International, 1971. Contains the essays "Bashō's Journey to Sarashina" and "Bashō's Journey of 1684" (trans.).

———. *World Within Walls*. New York: Holt, Rinehart & Winston, 1976.

Keene, Donald, ed. *Anthology of Japanese Literature: Earliest Era to Mid-Nineteenth Century*. New York: Grove Press, 1955.

Keene, Donald, trans. *Essays in Idleness*. New York: Columbia University Press, 1967.

Kimura Masanori, and Imuta Tsunehisa. *Kagerō Nikki*, in *Tosa Nikki, Kagerō Nikki*, in Nihon Koten Bungaku Zenshū series. Shōgakukan, 1973.

Kinoshita Chōshōshi. *Kyūshū no Michi no Ki*, in Gunsho Ruijū, Kikōbun series. Zoku Gunsho Ruijū Kansei Kai, 1928.

Kitajima Manji. *Chōsen Nichinichiki, Kōrai Nikki*. Soshiete, 1982.

Kubota Jun. *Fujiwara Teika*. Shūeisha, 1984.
Kuroda Genji, and Yamaga Seinosuke. *Kōkan Saiyū Nikki*. Sakamoto Shoten, 1927.
Lidin, Olof. *Ogyū Sorai's Journey to Kai in 1706*. London: Curzon Press, 1983.
Masubuchi Katsuichi. *Ionushi: Hombun Oyobi Sakuin*. Kasama Shoin, 1971.
Matsuura Rei, ed. *Sakuma Shōzan*, in Nihon no Shisō series. Chūō Kōron Sha, 1970.
McCullough, Helen Craig, trans. *Ōkagami: The Great Mirror*. Princeton: Princeton University Press, 1980.
———. *The Tales of Ise*. Stanford, Calif.: Stanford University Press, 1968.
Miner, Earl. *Japanese Poetic Diaries*. Berkeley: University of California Press, 1969.
Miyazaki Shōhei. *Jōjin Ajari Haha no Shū*, in Kōdansha Gakujutsu Bunko series. Kōdansha, 1979.
Mizukawa Yoshio. *Asukai Masaari Nikki Zenshaku*. Kazama Shobō, 1985.
———. *Minamoto no Michichika Nikki Zenshū*. Kasama Shoin, 1978.
———. *Takemuki ga Ki Zenshaku*. Kazama Shobō, 1972.
Morimoto Motoko. *Sanuki no Suke Nikki*, in Kōdansha Gakujutsu Bunko series. Kōdansha, 1977.
Morris, Ivan. *The World of the Shining Prince*. New York: Alfred A. Knopf, 1964.
Morris, Ivan, trans. *As I Crossed a Bridge of Dreams*. New York: Dial Press, 1971.
———. *The Pillow Book of Sei Shōnagon*. New York: Columbia University Press, 1967.
Motoyama Motoko. *Izayoi Nikki, Yoru no Tsuru*, in Kōdansha Gakujutsu Bunko series. Kōdansha, 1979.
Murayama Shūichi. *Meigetsuki*. Kōtō Shoin, 1947.
Nagakubo Sekisui. *Nagasaki Kōeki Nikki*, in *Zokuzoku Kikōbun Shū*. Nihon Tosho Sentā, 1979.
Nomura Seiichi. *Izumi Shikibu Nikki; Izumi Shikibu Shū*, in Shinchō Nihon Koten Shūsei series. Shinchōsha, 1981.
Noro Tadasu. *Kaidōki Shinchū*. Ikuei Shoin, 1935. (A reprint was issued in 1977 by Geirinsha.)
Odaka Toshio. *Matsunaga Teitoku no Kenkyū*. Shibundō, 1953.
———. *Matsunaga Teitoku no Kenkyū, Zokuhen*. Shibundō, 1956.
Odaka Toshio, ed. *Taionki, Oritaku Shiba no Ki, Rantō Kotohajime*, in Nihon Koten Bungaku Taikei series. Iwanami Shoten, 1964.
Oka Kazuo. *Genji Monogatari no Kisoteki Kenkyū*. Tōkyōdō, 1966.
Plutschow, H. E. *Tabi suru Nihonjin*. Musashino Shoin, 1983.

Plutschow, Herbert, and Hideichi Fukuda. *Four Japanese Travel Diaries of the Middle Ages.* Ithaca, NY: Cornell University East Asia Papers, 1981.

Pritchard, V. *English Medieval Grafitti.* Cambridge, England: Cambridge University Press, 1967.

Reischauer, Edwin O. *Ennin's Travels in T'ang China.* New York: Ronald Press, 1955.

Reischauer, Edwin O., trans. *Ennin's Diary: The Record of a Pilgrimage to China in Search of the Law.* New York: Ronald Press, 1955.

Reischauer, Edwin O., and Yamagiwa, Joseph K. *Translations from Early Japanese Literature.* Cambridge, Mass.: Harvard University Press, 1951. (Contains Reischauer's translation of *Izayoi Nikki*).

Sadler, A. L., trans. *Saka's Diary of a Pilgrim to Ise.* Tokyo: The Meiji Japan Society, 1940.

Sanjōnishi Kin'eda. *Yoshino no Mōde no Ki*, in *Nihon Kikōbun Shūsei*, vol. III. Nihon Tosho Sentā, 1979.

Satō Toratarō, ed. *Shōzan Zenshū.* Nagano: Shinano Kyōikukai, 1913.

Satomura Jōha. *Fujimi no Michi no Ki*, in *Nihon Kikō Bunshū Shū*, vol. III. Nihon Tosho Sentā, 1979.

Seidensticker, Edward, trans. *The Gossamer Years.* Tokyo: Charles E. Tuttle Co., 1964.

———. *The Tale of Genji*, 2 vols. New York: Alfred A. Knopf, 1976.

Sekine Yoshiko. *Sarashina Nikki*, in Kōdansha Gakujutsu Bunko series, 2 vols. Kōdansha, 1977.

Shiba Kōkan. *Kōkan Saiyū Nikki.* Sakamoto Shoten, 1927.

Shimazu Tadao, ed. *Sōchō Nikki*, in Iwanami Bunko series. Iwanami Shoten, 1975.

Shimizu Akira. *Shijōnomiya no Shimotsuke Shū Zenshaku.* Kasama Shoin, 1975.

Shioiri Yoshimichi, ed. *Nittō Guhō Junrei Gyoki*, in Tōyō Bunko series, 2 vols. Tokyo: Heibonsha, 1970.

Shirai Chūkō. *Chūsei no Kikō Bungaku.* Bunka Shobō Hakubunsha, 1976.

Shōtetsu. *Nagusamegusa*, in *Zokuzoku Kikōbun Shū*, vol. IV. Nihon Tosho Sentā, 1977.

Sōchō. *Azumaji no Tsuto*, in *Gunsho Ruijū*, *kan* 480. Zoku Gunsho Ruijū Kansei Kai, 1976.

———. *Utsunoyama no Ki*, in the same volume.

Sugiura Shōichirō, Miyamoto Saburō, and Ogino Kiyoshi. *Bashō Bunshū*, in Nihon Koten Bungaku Taikei series, 1959.

Tahara, Mildred, trans. *Tales of Yamato.* Honolulu: The University Press of Hawaii, 1980.

Tamai Kosuke. *Ben no Naishi Nikki Shinchū.* Taishūkan Shoten, 1966.

———. *Nakatsukasa no Naishi Nikki Shinchū.* Taishūdō Shoten, 1958.

———. *Nikki Bungaku no Kenkyū*. Hanawa Shobō, 1965.

———. *Sanuki no Suke Nikki*, in Nihon Koten Zensho series. Asahi Shimbun Sha, 1953.

———. *Tōnomine Shōshō Monogatari*. Hanawa Shobō, 1960.

Tanaka Shin'ichi. "Shōtetsu no Koi," in *Kokugo to Kokubungaku* (September 1966).

Teruoka Yasutaka. *Bakin Nikki*, 4 vols. Chūō Kōron Sha, 1973.

Toda Yoshimi. *Chūyūki: Yakudō suru Insei Jidai no Gunzō*. Soshiete, 1979.

Tomikura Tokujirō. *Towazugatari*. Chikuma Shobō, 1966.

Tonomura Nobuko. *Ichijō Kaneyoshi Fujikawa no Ki Zenshaku*. Kazama Shobō, 1983.

———. *Utsunomiya Asanari Nikki Zenshaku*. Kazama Shobō, 1977.

Tsugita Kasumi. *Utatane Zenchūshaku*, in Kōdansha Gakujutsu Bunko series. Kōdansha, 1978.

Tsuji Hikosaburō. *Fujiwara Teika Meigetsuki no Kenkyū*. Yoshikawa Kōbunkan, 1977.

Tsukamoto Yasuhiko. *Jojō no Dentō*. Shōbunsha, 1966.

Varley, H. Paul. *Imperial Restoration in Medieval Japan*. New York: Columbia University Press, 1971.

Waley, Arthur, trans. *The Secret History of the Mongols*. London: Allen and Unwin, 1963.

Watson, Burton, trans. *The Complete Works of Chuang Tzu*. New York: Columbia University Press, 1968.

Whitehouse, Wilfrid, and Eizo Yanagisawa, trans. *Lady Nijo's Own Story*. Tokyo: Charles E. Tuttle, 1974.

Yamamoto Ritatsu. *Murasaki Shikibu Nikki*, in Shinchō Nihon Koten Shūsei series. Shinchōsha, 1980.

Yamashita Hiroaki. *Taiheiki*, vol. II, in Shinchō Nihon Koten Shūsei series. Shinchōsha, 1980.

Yamazaki Hokka. *Chō no Asobi*, in *Zokuzoku Kikō Bunshū*, vol. IV of Nihon Kikōbun Shūsei series. Nihon Tosho Sentā, 1979.

Listings by Work

Azuma Meguri, in *Nihon Kikōbun Shūsei*, vol. III. Nihon Tosho Sentā, 1979.

Gen'yo Nikki, in *Gunsho Ruijū*, vol. II. Zoku Gunsho Ruijū Kansei Kai, 1976.

Gunsho Kaidai. Zoku Gunsho Ruijū Kansei Kai, 1979.

Heishin Kikō, in *Zoku Gunsho Ruijū*, vol. 18b. Zoku Gunsho Ruijū Kansei Kai, 1979. Also in Nihon Kikōbun Shūsei series. Nihon Tosho Sentā, 1979.

Kaigen Kikō, in *Zoku Kikōbun Shū*. Nihon Tosho Sentā, 1979.
Kikō-hen, in Gunsho Ruijū series. Zoku Gunsho Ruijū Kansei Kai, 1959.
Miyako no Tsuto, in *Zokuzoku Kikōbun Shūsei*. Nihon Tosho Sentā, 1979.
Nihon Kikōbun Shūsei, vols. III, IV. Nihon Tosho Sentā, 1979.
Nihon Koten Bungaku Daijiten, vol. IV. Iwanami Shoten, 1984.
Nikki Kikō Shū, in Yūhōdō Bunko, 1927.
Ojima no Kuchizusami, in *Zoku Kikōbun Shū*. Nihon Tosho Sentā, 1979.
Ōta Nampo Shū, in Yūhōdō Bunko series. Yūhōdō, 1928.
Rokuon'in-dono Itsukushima Mōde no Ki, in *Zokuzoku Kikōbun Shū*. Nihon Tosho Sentā, 1979.
Sumiyoshi Mōde, in *Zoku Kikōbun Shū*. Nihon Tosho Sentā, 1979.
Zenkōji Kikō, in *Zokuzoku Kikōbun Shū*. Nihon Tosho Sentā, 1977.
Zoku Kikōbun Shū. Nihon Tosho Sentā, 1977.

Index

NOTE: *Japanese names are listed according to predominant treatment in text. Thus, many writers will be found under their familiar literary names* (gō)*: Bashō, Chōshōshi, etc. Literary works will be found under their English titles.*

Index